PIMLICO

320

CHILDREN OF SILENCE

Michael Wood is the author of *Stendhal*, *America in the Movies*, *García Márquez: One Hundred Years of Solitude* and *The Magician's Doubts: Nabokov and the Risks of Fiction* (also available in Pimlico). He writes film and literary criticism for the *London Review of Books*, the *New York Times Book Review* and other publications. He studied Modern Languages at St John's College, Cambridge, where he was later a Fellow. He taught for a long time at Columbia University in New York and then at the University of Exeter. He is currently Professor of English at Princeton University. He is a Fellow of the Royal Society of Literature.

316

X

CHILDREN OF
SILENCE

Studies in Contemporary Fiction

Published by Pimlico 1998

2 4 6 8 10 9 7 5 3 1

Copyright © Michael Wood 1998

Michael Wood has asserted his right
under the Copyright, Designs and Patents Act 1988
to be identified as the author of this work

First published by Pimlico 1998
Pimlico
Random House, 20 Vauxhall Bridge Road,
London SW1V 2SA

Random House Australia (Pty) Limited
20 Alfred Street, Milsons Point, Sydney,
New South Wales 2061, Australia

Random House New Zealand Limited
18 Poland Road, Glenfield,
Auckland 10, New Zealand

Random House South Africa (Pty) Limited
Endulini, 5A Jubilee Road, Parktown 2193, South Africa

Random House UK Limited Reg. No. 954009

A CIP catalogue record for this book
is available from the British Library

ISBN 0-7126-7356-3

Papers used by Random House UK Limited are natural,
recyclable products made from wood grown in sustainable forests.
The manufacturing processes conform to the environmental
regulations of the country of origin

Printed and bound in Great Britain by
Mackays of Chatham PLC

For Paco
and the music of his music

Contents

Acknowledgments

Very early versions of some of these chapters were given as lectures at Birkbeck College, London, Harvard, and New York universities; or written as essays or reviews for the *London Review of Books*, the *New Republic*, and the *New York Review of Books*. My essay "Angela Carter" appeared in *British Writers: Supplement III*, George Stade, gen. ed., and Carol Howard, assoc. ed., pp. 79–93; copyright © Charles Scribner's sons; used by permission of Charles Scribner's Sons Reference Books, an imprint of Simon & Schuster Macmillan. I am very grateful for these invitations and instigations, and for the many helpful comments that came in their wake.

I give my warmest thanks to Jennifer Crewe, for her faith and patience and reminders; and to Jenny Uglow, for believing in this book too.

Children of Silence

Novel into Story

Contemporary fiction is full of invitations to thought, but a number of the invitations overlap, and certain themes recur in various contexts in this book. The persistence of the idea of paradise, for example, or of several different ideas of paradise, the feeling that however shabby the idea may have become, it can't quite be shaken off. The notion that silence is what literature longs for but can't reach, not only because its very condition is language but because a complicated fidelity to silence is one of literature's most attractive attainments. The sense that fiction is often a form of criticism, and that criticism can be fiction, not only full of stories but driven by stories, seeking fables rather than the explanation of fables. But the main movement of the book is the tracing of a crisis in the novel and the beginning of a liberation of the story.

I'm using *novel* and *story* in a sense close to Walter Benjamin's, although the resonances are quite different in contemporary fiction and criticism. The novel for Benjamin has to do with the withering of experience and the loneliness of print:

> What distinguishes the novel from the story . . . is its essential dependence on the book . . . . The birthplace of the novel is the solitary individual, who is no longer able to express himself by giving examples of his most important concerns, is himself uncounseled, and cannot counsel others . . . In the midst of life's fullness, and through the representation of this fullness, the novel gives evidence of the profound perplexity of the living.

Stories can be found in books too, but the form doesn't have its origins in print. Its birthplace is not the solitary individual but the person who lives in a community and has experiences he/she can pass on:

> In every case the storyteller is a man who has counsel for his readers. But if today "having counsel" is beginning to have an old-fashioned ring, this is because the communicability of experience is decreasing. In consequence we have no counsel either for ourselves or for others.

"Today" was 1936. We are all novelists and novel readers, was Benjamin's implication, scarcely able to hang on to the memory of story, to reconstruct through nostalgia what stories and experience and communities used to be. In the later today of Roland Barthes and Milan Kundera, in the 1970s ands 1980s, it is the novel we have lost or almost lost, and the solitary individual comes to inhabit what Calvino called the "paradise of reading," a site of chosen loneliness, of freedom and kindness, a model of democratic exemption from the hustle of totalitarian or merely busy politics. Novels may depict dark worlds but they leave the reader in the light. The novel is liberal and humane in this view; nondirective, ambiguous; dedicated to the complexity of human behavior and motive. This is the novel that Kundera still writes and even Beckett still wrote; that Barthes longs to write, and that Calvino's characters long to read. It is a sad but generous mode; it teaches us a lot about losing, reminding us, as Benjamin says in another context, that "courage, humor, cunning, and fortitude" are not the exclusive or even the usual virtues of history's winners. It's not that having counsel has an old-fashioned ring, it sounds like the invasion of the social worker.

But if our stories don't have counsel, we have plenty of stories. Calvino writes stories, even if his characters want to read novels. Story makes a triumphant return in García Márquez, Salman Rushdie, Toni Morrison, and Angela Carter, and a little earlier in Günter Grass. "I'm telling you stories. Trust me" is the refrain of Jeanette Winterson's *The Passion*, where "stories" means both tales and tall tales, the truth of lies. Edward Said argues eloquently for the importance of what he calls broken narratives, stories that include and resist the reasons for their breaking.

Stories come back, more often than not, *inside* novels—even take over novels, so that there is scarcely any novel left, in Benjamin's sense, in a text like *One Hundred Years of Solitude*. There is no evasion of print here—how could there be in a published work?—no return to a lost oral community. There is not even, very often, an imitation of such a return, although this does occur.

But there is a sense that the lonely novel, the work predicated on the isolation of the reader, had shut too many things down, particularly the multiple, invisible community that any reader has in the head. The story is less fussy than the novel in this view, more welcoming to variety, less keen to sift the plausible from the fantastic, memory from history. There is no particular politics here, nothing to correspond to the liberalism of the novel in this context. A story is not necessarily radical; can be liberal too; or even more conservative than the novel, because often more traditional, less wedded to the modernizing world.

Does a contemporary story communicate experience? What does it have instead of counsel? It has no naive faith in experience, since it usually accepts some version or other of Benjamin's argument that experience is withering or has withered—in its skeptical forms, it wonders if there ever was any experience to wither. But it believes in fragments of wisdom, the value of riddles, a broken but still perceptible connection at least to the dream of experience. Instead of counsel it has hints and hunches—which it will not give up. The contemporary story, in or out of novels, is like a memory of the secret evoked in Thomas Pynchon's *Gravity's Rainbow*:

> As some secrets were given to the Gypsies to preserve against centrifugal History, and some to the Kabbalists, the Templars, the Rosicrucians, so have this Secret of the Fearful Assembly, and others, found their ways inside the weatherless spaces of this or that Ethnic Joke.

The idea of the secret saved from history or littered about history's unlikely places is taken up by Umberto Eco as the very plot of *Foucault's Pendulum*, the comic and frightening point being, I take it, that fragments of the secret are everywhere, even if the secret itself is a joke. They are everywhere not because there definitely is a secret but because we can't believe there isn't. Contemporary stories are like this, ghostly refusals of reason, dedicated to the possible truths of irrational fear and hope, the precarious wisdom of gossip and legend.

The Dream of Eden

Paradise, silence, story. These names and notions not only kept coming back in the work I was reading, they began to form something like a figure for criticism itself—or for the criticism I was trying to do. Auden thought a critic had an obligation to declare his or her idea of Eden, because the pleasure of a work of art, at the moment of enjoyment, is our pleasure and not someone else's:

So long as a man writes poetry or fiction, his dream of Eden is his own business, but the moment he starts writing literary criticism, honesty demands that he describe it to his readers, so that they may be in the position to judge his judgements.

Or even just to look at the critic's assumptions. I'm inclined to believe that writers of any kind do in fact declare their dream of Eden, whether they set out to or not—at least in implication, and for those readers who care to find it. And I'm not sure that their dream of Eden is the first thing I want to know about a critic, or anyone else. I might want to know about their idea of affection, or their notion of cruelty. But then perhaps these things are already contained in the dream of Eden.

Auden pursued his game quite literally, that is, followed out the metaphor with entire, owlish seriousness. He wanted to know what Eden would look like and how it would be ruled, and grouped his questions under these headings: landscape, climate, ethnic origin of inhabitants, language, weights and measures, religion, size of capital, form of government, sources of natural power, economic activities, means of transport, architecture, domestic furniture and equipment, formal dress, sources of public information, public statues, public entertainments. The list itself is miniature autobiography, of course; and Auden was very funny on these topics (weights and measures: "Irregular and complicated. No decimal system"; formal dress: "The fashions of Paris in the 1830s and '40s"; public statues: "Confined to famous defunct chefs").

I started on a description of my idea of Eden, more as a form of textual hostage than out of any great urge to confess or parade. Landscape: mountains as in the rainier parts of Mexico or Vermont; trees; changes of color and light. Climate: warm in the daytime, cold enough for fires at night. Some really bad weather now and again, for virtue's sake. Language: a mixture of English and French, only with American gags. This is perhaps not what Auden means by language, but I'd like to have English adjectives in Eden (scruffy, raffish, tacky, snotty, stodgy, etc.) and a French idiom of precision for the emotions. And the American throwaway, as when a friend responded to my description of a mini-earthquake shaking the house at breakfast by saying "I've had breakfasts like that." Religion: I want to say none, but that is perhaps an argument, a stiff principle, rather than a feature of my dream of Eden. Lapsed catholicism, perhaps, or better, lapsed protestant dissent, the dissent going elsewhere; sternness experienced and then given up, exchanged for tolerance. But why would there be even the memory of dissent in Eden? Form of government: Socialist, like Clement Attlee's in Britain after the war, only more cheerful, a little keener on pleasure. Architecture: a few Roman ruins.

Otherwise a mixture of modernism and whatever the current avant-garde (if there is one) is up to. A dose of brutalism here and there. An old convent or monastery or two.

But I gave up, because I can't really want any of this. I want the world we have, the very world, as Wordsworth says, which is the world of all of us, and that I should like to see improved by human will, not rewritten by a dreamer or a God. Am I campaigning for the abolition of paradise? Well, I would if I thought we could bear its absence, or make some sort of future without the gleam it confers on our thought. But I'm not sure we can. It turns out then that "honesty demands," for me, not a description of a dream of Eden but a response to the very notion of such a dream—not quite Auden's suggestion but still within its range, I think.

When I began this book, I had another garden in mind, or another version of this ubiquitous, haunting, and haunted place. It is a garden in Mexico, and it provokes a drunken Geoffrey Firmin, in Malcolm Lowry's *Under the Volcano*, to a remarkably sinister variation on the theme of paradise. Firmin is talking to his American neighbor in a town that much resembles Cuernavaca:

> Do you know, Quincey, I've often wondered whether there isn't more in the old legend of the Garden of Eden, and so on, than meets the eye. What if Adam wasn't really banished from the place at all? That is, in the sense we used to understand it. . . . What if his punishment really consisted in his having to go on living there, alone, of course—suffering, unseen, cut off from God . . . Yes. . . . And of course the real reason for that punishment—his being forced to go on living in the garden, I mean, might well have been that the poor fellow, who knows, secretly loathed the place! Simply *hated* it, and had done so all along. And that the Old Man found this out.

Remaining in Eden is the ultimate form of banishment; in an Eden that is and always has been a loathed place, a version of Hell; Hell because it is Eden, because we are not up to it, because we can only spoil what Lowry earlier calls "the beauty of the Earthly Paradise." The Fall in this story would be a chance of happiness, but it cannot occur. Or rather it has already occurred, but only because Adam "simply hated" where he was: his only disobedience a distaste for his posting. It is significant that there is no Eve in Firmin's Eden, and that the vision, along with its grim and brilliant wit, contains much self-pity and self-absorption, all the paranoid pleasures of complacent loneliness. But we don't have to share Geoffrey Firmin's view to feel the scare and the force of his image, and I offer it as a kind of device or emblem, a heraldic summary of much that I can't collect into consecutive prose. We have never left Eden; our problem is not our place but how we feel about it; and criticism can usefully be seen as seeking to reimagine our relation to perfection.

Criticism and Silence

"Books," Marcel Proust says, "are the work of solitude and the *children of silence*. The children of silence should have no portion with the children of the word—thoughts that owe their being to the wish to say something, to a disapproval, or an opinion; that is, to a vague idea." "Should have no portion with" is *"ne doivent avoir rien de commun avec,"* literally "must have nothing in common with." The translation (by Sylvia Townsend Warner) responds appropriately to a certain confusion or anxiety in the thought, because it's not clear that having things in common, as distinct from sharing things, say, is a matter of choice. John Sturrock translates the phrase as "can have nothing in common with." What the confusion means is that the children of silence shouldn't have anything in common with the children of the word, but unfortunately they have. What they have in common is nearly everything: language itself. The children of silence are not themselves silent. Both sets of children talk; the difference lies in the imputed origin of their speech. The children of the word belong to the busy social and historical world of Sainte-Beuve, whose method Proust was attacking, and are measured by their capacity to "say something." The children of silence don't say anything, have no part in any social conversation. They are pure performances, works of art that have not only aspired to the condition of music but actually got there. Put this way, the idea is very familiar. It was almost everyone's idea of poetry, for example, until quite recently. A child of silence "makes nothing happen" (Auden); "should not mean/But be" (MacLeish). Prose fiction presents more of a difficulty, since it would seem to be made up, in Proust's case as much as anyone's, of complicated and unending conversations between the two sets of children and their attendant responses to the world. Many novels, we might argue, precisely pit a child of silence, the nondiscursive poem of a place or a sensibility or a society, against the captious, practical understanding of the word's many and successful children.

But I want to take the notion of silence one stage further, or rather to suggest that contemporary fiction, in its insistent dealings with silence, asks us to think further about the question. In my chapter on Kazuo Ishiguro I look closely at the idea of the unspeakable, but it inhabits the work of many other writers too, most obviously Beckett but also Barthes and Calvino. The children of silence, in this displaced sense, would be defecting children of the word, works that came to see silence as the very condition of speech. The most lurid but also the clearest modern instance of such a concern would be the temptation to silence on the subject of the Holocaust, or the atrocities of Hiroshima and Nagasaki. What could be more decorous than silence, what words will *not* give offence, seem too easily to encompass the uncompassable? The difficulty, which contemporary writers urge on us in all kinds of ways, is to see that silence, in extreme cases, is almost always preferable but can't be preferred. Or to put that the other way round, the endless inadequacy of words in extreme cases is no excuse for mere, passive, or self-congratulating silence. The children of silence, to repeat, can't leave all the talking to the other children. This is T. W. Adorno's objection to Ludwig Wittgenstein's famous invitation to the abandonment of words: "What we cannot speak about we must pass over in silence." Adorno saw in this "the gesture of reverent authoritarian authenticity," and went on, "If philosophy can be defined at all, it is an effort to express things one cannot speak about, to help express the nonidentical despite the fact that expressing it identifies it at the same time.'

Marjorie Perloff, quoting this passage and defending Wittgenstein, says the famous aphorism is "no more than the commonsense recognition that there are metaphysical and ethical aporias that no discussion, explication, rationale, or well-constructed argument can fully rationalize—even for oneself." But that is just what Adorno is claiming. Common sense encounters the ineffable and gives up the game, caves in to the unarguable impossibility of the impossible. For Adorno, this is not a place to stop but a place to start. His definition of philosophy is close to Beckett's definition of writing—"The expression that there is nothing to express . . . together with the obligation to express"—although Adorno would not say there was nothing to express. But then I don't think Wittgenstein was offering us a "commonsense recognition" of any kind; rather a picture of philosophical humility. What we have here are two versions of European asceticism. Wittgenstein's "must" is like Proust's: a dream of Eden. Failing to remain silent about things one cannot speak of is what philosophers (and many others) do for a living. Wittgenstein proposes an unattainable vow of muteness; Adorno thinks philosophy just *is* the breaking of any such vows. What the two have in common is a sense of the hubris and excess of speech on unspeakable subjects. That silence is or must be invaded does not diminish the sense of invasion.

The situation of criticism in relation to such problems looks very peculiar, doubly garrulous. The chatty child of the word seeks to say for the children of silence what they don't (want to) say for themselves, or don't want to *say* at all—this would be criticism's ordinary relation to the performances of art—and does this now in relation to work that has dedicated itself to a special intimacy with silence. This sounds pointless, if not offensive, but we could take it as an invitation to think again about what criticism might be.

Much criticism is explanation and information, of course, analysis and judgement. These are useful activities, and we don't have to be too daunted by the fact that they are the very things Proust wanted to keep the children of silence away from: saying something, disapproval, opinions, vague ideas. The children of the word have work to do. It is not a fault to want to say something, and ideas don't have to be vague. And it is a form of snobbery to think, as much romantic aesthetic theory does (not only Proust's but Jeanette Winterson's) that the children of the word are second-class citizens. Edmund Wilson loved to tell his public and his friends about books he had read and they hadn't, and many people, especially publishers and professors, are baffled by the idea that criticism could be anything *other* than explanation. But when I think of Henry James's definition of criticism as the mind reaching out for the reasons of its interest, I don't picture anyone reporting on books, or explaining anything. Or rather I see whatever reporting or explaining goes on as caught up in something else. I do see considerable amounts of analysis, but analysis won't tell us what a text means or how we are to feel, only how the text works and (maybe) why we feel what we already feel. Serious reading, Flaubert said to one of his correspondents, is not "reading books about solemn matters, but reading well-made, and above all well-written books, paying attention to the way things are done (*en se rendant compte des procédés*). Are we novelists or agriculturalists?" This may suggest rather too strict a concentration on technique, but paying attention to the way things are done could be seen as a prerequisite for thinking about almost any form of representation.

But what could the something else of criticism be? Could it only be a bad novel, impressionism, or faint-hearted autobiography? A first step toward an answer would be to get rid of the stark opposition between ignorance and expertise. The critical alternative to telling people about books they haven't read or don't know how to read is not necessarily talking to people who have read (several times) the same books as you have, and probably written on them. It is, I think, the attempt to start a conversation, not always literally picked up but always possible and sometimes actual if rather slow—especially when we are thinking of criticism in printed volumes—with people who have read some of the same books as you have, have read books like the ones you want to talk about, and have read lots of books you haven't read. They don't need explanations, and there isn't anything you could explain to them. When you reach out for the reasons of your interest, they will understand the interest, either because it is already theirs or because it could be, but they will be mainly taken by the reaching and the reasons. More precisely, they will be taken by the showing of the reaching and the reasons; like the showing of working in mathematics. This makes criticism "a metaphor for the act of reading," as Paul de Man called it, but also a performance, and it is here that I think of criticism as looking, as modern philosophy often does, for a story rather than an verdict or an explanatory pay-off. The story would not be just the retelling of the narrative of (say) a novel, nor just an account of the adventure of reading, although both of those activities might play a part. Nor would it just evoke the novel or recreate the reading. It would reframe and reexamine the ground and the preoccupation of a work, or of its context, or its world, and it would seek to offer this critical labor as an experience the reader could share, a road to be traveled rather than a destination to be named. We could think of "counsel" again, or whatever it is we hope we have in its place. "After all," Benjamin says, "counsel is less an answer to a question than a proposal concerning the continuation of a story which is just unfolding," and "knowing how to go on" is one of Wittgenstein's favorite models for understanding. Again, analysis is not excluded here, a criticism driven by stories is not itself all story, and anything that helps us to reach for the reasons of our interest is welcome. Criticism in this spirit would prolong the creative work without miming it or competing with it, and would become, for some of the time at least, a modest child of silence because in a strict sense it wouldn't be *saying* anything, and couldn't be satisfactorily summarized or paraphrased, only lived with for a while.

Time After Time

The poet Stéphane Mallarmé once wrote that anyone who claimed to be their own contemporary was ill-informed. The remark is not obscure by Mallarmé's dizzying standards, but it's pretty opaque all the same. Yet in its gnomic compactness, its air of knowing more than it says, it may help us to understand a little better a certain notion of the contemporary.

Contemporary fiction, I want suggest, is not just recent or current fiction, or fiction that comes later than the stuff we call modern. It is the fiction of our own time, the fiction that is the same age as we are. This is not often literally a matter of dates of birth, although the figures here are one way of beginning to draw the picture. Of the fourteen writers I consider at some length in this book, nine are older than I am; eight are still living. The dates of birth run from 1906 (Beckett) to 1959 (Winterson). My own birth date, 1936, is pretty close to halfway in between; it is also, although needless to say I didn't plan it that way, the "today" of Benjamin's essay on the storyteller.

But the fiction of our own time includes masses of material we can't have read, let alone thought of writing about. "Contemporary," if it is to make any constructive sense, must mean something like that which defines or focuses the time for us, which seems to make our age what it is, or to form a crucial part of the way that age understands itself. This is where Mallarmé's remark offers such a useful warning. Among its possible translations or paraphrases are: People who think they are up-to-date are out-of-date, or those who thinks they know their time don't know what time it is. Claiming to be your own contemporary loses you any credibility the claim might have had before you made it.

And of course it isn't the writers who are our real contemporaries, it is their work. The actual time on the clock is the time we met the books, the day and hour they came into our life and altered it, became part of who we are. The time includes the way we read the books too; the reason and the mood; the setting, the season of our habits or interests. I read fiction addictively, like a stolen pleasure, and also for information, the way I watch the evening news. I love the children of silence, but I spend hours upon hours with the children of the word. And because I've been doing this ever since I learned to read, whole worlds have built up inside my head and fiction must make up a large part of what I think I know. I don't believe this makes my knowledge merely fictional, but it certainly makes it indirect.

I also read a lot of fiction in order to review it, but I'm not sure the reviewer's relation to a book has to be different from that of the thief of pleasure. My feeling, possibly blinkered by what I don't want to think about, is that reviewing just allows you to get paid for stealing pleasure and, more important, provides a fantastic, virtually irresistible excuse for not doing other things. Reviewing, as I understand and try to practise it, involves providing readers with the strongest possible sense of what it feels like to read the work in question, and thereby with the means to begin to make their own judgement; and also speculating, within the space available, on where the work leads, what's at stake in its picture of the world, and why we should care about it. "What's the difference?" was a question de Man eloquently discussed, and "Who cares?" is another good question. It helps to know when it's rhetorical, and what it means if it is or it isn't.

My reading age then includes, to give a few random but freighted examples, an impatient waiting for Tolkien to finish his *Lord of the Rings*, and for Mervyn Peake to bring out the (disappointing) last volume of his *Gormenghast* novels; a deep infatuation with Lawrence Durrell, followed by a later inability to read him at all; the discovery of other contemporary English novelists (William Golding, Iris Murdoch, Anthony Powell) in Paris, a gesture perhaps toward the homesickness I was not acknowledging; an immersion in Faulkner (*Sartoris*), which took me out of circulation for a week and made me think I hadn't really known what fiction was until then. It includes finding Borges some time in the early 1960s, a figure who came to live, who still lives, among most of the pages I read or write, and who led me to many other writers, in Latin America and elsewhere. I read a lot of science fiction at one stage, but that has eased off a little. I have been reading thrillers for as long as I can remember and still do, at the slightest drop of a clue or a corpse.

Around the Borges time, I discovered Raymond Queneau's fabulous *Zazie dans le métro* and also decided to review *Pale Fire* for a Cambridge journal I was editing, starting an interminable relationship not exactly with Nabokov but with what he seemed to be doing with language and fiction. Not everyone likes wordplay, or has to like it; but I can't separate fiction from doing things with words, and it is in play that words find their simplest, most immediate form of liberty and life. Pretty soon after, thanks to invitations from imaginative, indeed inspired editors, my addiction and my reviewing activities merged as if they were made for each other, as if Mr. Hyde had made peace with Dr. Jekyll.

This book is not a survey, and I have not attempted the "coverage" of any area or moment, but I have tried to evoke what seem to me the most interesting possibilities of contemporary fiction, and I have tried to think about the notion of possibility itself, as one of fiction's constant analogues and preoccupations. This means that I have (often reluctantly) left out a number of very good novelists who don't happen to push the notion of possibility very far, and that Barthes and Calvino play a guiding role they wouldn't necessarily play in other books. It's not quite that Calvino *is* the writer Barthes dreamed of being, as I have sometimes thought; Barthes himself was that writer. It's that Calvino's fiction enacts and extends, converts into magical practice, the very questions that, in Barthes, seem most irreducibly critical and theoretical. Fiction becomes criticism and theory in the process; it changes the chances of fiction too.

Like everyone else I know, I live in and out of whatever time it is, more out than in, no doubt. But I can't escape the feeling that I share a world with the writers I have studied here, in a way I don't share a world with only slightly older writers such as Proust. This is strictly a temporal matter, I think, rather than spatial or social. I've met people who knew Proust, but they seemed like messengers from another age. I can't pretend to have any knowledge, except the knowledge that a willing imagination gives, of some of the terrible conditions evoked by Reinaldo Arenas, Toni Morrison, or Edward Said, but I'm not suggesting that sharing a world is a matter of closeness to writers or their subjects. It is a matter of shared historical markers, political and literary. To put it in brutal shorthand, this is a world later than the Great Depression; later, for most of us, than the Second World War and the Holocaust; it has in it Vietnam, the Cuban Revolution, the Civil Rights Movement, the death of Kennedy, and the new nations of various postcolonial settlements. Into it are born structuralism, post-structuralism, a revived feminism, a revamped psychoanalysis, the sudden conviction that we are all historicists, even as Marxism, our old ally in the argument for context, gets itself into trouble. This world takes modernism for granted, imagining it knows more about it than it does; it falls at last for the notion of postmodernism because it can't do without a name for what seems to be its mood.

This doesn't add up to a single world in any final form, of course; it is because there are so many worlds here that it's absurd to claim to be the contemporary of all of them. But there may be, I'm suggesting, a single time-world, what we might think of as an extended historical moment, which makes us contemporaries along at least one line of arrangement. This moment is not exactly just now, it's older than that. But not much older. It's what you can see when you look around from now, in all directions. What you can see without adjusting the viewfinder for a historical shift, another language.

This is a book about fiction rather than politics or history, but it is an aspect of being a contemporary that one takes the centrality of politics and history for granted even if one doesn't talk about them all the time. To be plain: I do not see politics and history as narrowly determining literature, but neither do I see literature as transcending them. The feeling I should like to leave with the reader is that literature is political even when it seems most removed from politics; and that it escapes politics even when it directly discusses them.

The dialogue with history is different. Barthes speaks of a resistance to history rather than an escape from it, and I'm not sure what an escape would mean, what unhistorical place one could escape to. One of the most interesting misreadings of deconstruction concerns just this question. Frank Lentricchia writes of de Man's "nostalgic definition of literature," which "points us away from history as an undesirable condition." It's true that de Man, with good reason, thought history was an undesirable condition, but the definition that Lentricchia quotes doesn't sound too nostalgic, and it points us not away from history but desperately, ineluctably back into it: "The distinctive character of literature thus becomes manifest as an inability to escape from a condition that is felt to be undesirable." This seems to me altogether too grim to be a convincing representation of the distinctive character of literature, or of history for that matter, but it has the merit of seeing that history is not going to go away.

But I don't think resistance is quite the word for literature's relation to history. Literature is too close to (the writing of) history to resist it, and quite often it just *is* history, taking a figurative form. Yet there is a fragile autonomy in literature, an element of privacy and play which falls well short of transcendence but matters all the more for that reason. It is the literary equivalent of what Said, thinking of Brahms, calls "the music of his music." Literature, let's say, entertains history, the way we entertain an idea; it also entertains itself, never at a loss for conversation or amusement; and in its more radical forms it invites history to think again. Who could be timely enough to think they were their own, or indeed anyone else's, contemporary?

ONE
Maps of Fiction

Can I call this book a novel?   —Marcel Proust, *Jean Santeuil*

I start from things and I give names, even worn-out ones.
                                            —Roland Barthes, *Writer Sollers*

2. *The Kindness of Novels*

The Ancient City

Writing about novels, Roland Barthes seems to respond directly (if not intentionally) to Auden's request that critics should define their idea of Eden. The
novel for Barthes is a lost paradise, finally less a genre than a moral ideal, a
model of human kindness. It's not that novels necessarily depict these things;
they enact them, the kindness is a particular inflection or arrangement of the relation between words and readers. Not all novels achieve such effects, of
course. But nothing that is not a novel comes near it.

Barthes's ideas about novels are interesting in their own right and because
they suggest an intricate criss-crossing between theory and practice; because
they articulate a gifted contemporary critic's dream of a particular form of
fiction; and because they are, in a sense to be explored, a variety of fiction
themselves. Barthes's way of addressing the genre is striking too, but not
unique. It is a recognizable (though not often recognized) form of critical
practice; earlier discussions of the novel are littered with seemingly loose talk
of the same kind.

At the end of his *Theory of the Novel*, a lofty exploration of the narrative
form that succeeded the epic—"The novel is the epic of a world that has been
abandoned by God"—Lukács rather startlingly explains why Dostoyevsky has
not entered into his consideration. "Dostoyevsky did not write novels." We
may well wonder, in a pedestrian but not entirely stupid way, just what Dostoyevsky was doing instead. After all, we know what a novel is, or at least we
know what common usage suggests it is: a prose narrative of a certain length

concerning imaginary people (usually living in real places); or more simply, a work of fiction of a certain length. Dostoyevsky certainly wrote that. Lukács himself came to something like this view in later years, and regarded his earlier remark as a youthful folly, a sort of Hegelian prank. But it was more than that, and alongside our pedestrian response, if we had it, we probably had another one: that of curiosity. Lukács is using the word *novel* in a special way, a way that excludes the work of Dostoyevsky. It isn't just a matter of deciding on labels, of allowing some novelists into the class and keeping others out—as if the novel were a club, the sort of place Groucho Marx didn't want to join because they might let him in. The interest must lie in our hesitation about the label, in why we are ready to classify one work in this way and not another; what it means to apply the label here, refuse it there. Like a riddle: when is a novel not a novel? When it's *The Idiot*. When it belongs, as Lukács says, "to the new world," the world that has overcome guilt, melancholy, irony, division.

Lukács was writing a book with *Theory* in its title, and what we now call theory quite often works in this manner: as a sort of quarrel, only sometimes amiable, with common usage, an attempt to ground or to get beyond common usage, to reach the sort of clarity or articulation common usage doesn't afford. When Henry James speaks of theory, for example, he lines the word up with "conviction" and "consciousness," closely followed by "faith," "choice," and "comparison" ("It had no air of having a theory, a conviction, a consciousness of itself behind it—of being the expression of an artistic faith, the result of choice and comparison"). Theory may want to mark its distance from the common indication by inventing an entire vocabulary of its own. Much scientific and philosophical theory does this, and so does some recent literary theory: no confusion with common usage, I almost said with common sense, is possible. We are then in what Wittgenstein called the suburbs of language, the straight streets of unequivocal, or would-be unequivocal discourse:

> Our language can be seen as an ancient city: a maze of little streets and squares, old and new houses, and of houses with additions from various periods; and this surrounded by a multitude of new boroughs with straight regular streets and uniform houses.

The attraction of this image is that it reminds us of something we often forget, or remembering, get exactly upside down. It is the specialized vocabulary that is direct and simple, common usage that is winding and cluttered. "Only that which has no history can be defined," Nietzsche says, a remark that invites us not necessarily to rewrite our dictionaries but certainly to rethink our use of them. In practice, the word novel is going to mean everything people have meant by it and been understood.

The kind of theory I am interested in here, which is also a kind of criticism, lives in the ancient city, among words like *novel* and, indeed, *theory*. It uses old words in new or restricted ways, seeks to specialize them, to carve a particular meaning out of the historical litter of language; but also—and this is perhaps more important—it aims to hang on to the ordinary, littered meaning of words too; reserves the right to travel back to it; asserts a continuity of meaning between specialised and ordinary senses. It is as if we were to clear the old city for a particular purpose, say a car or cycle race. After the race it reverts to its intricate life as a world of shops, bars, sidewalks, cinemas, etc.; but we remember it as the scene of a race. Just as during the race we may think of it as an inhabited, busy space. A confusion with common usage is not only possible but desirable here, and sometimes, mischievously or even unconsciously, this kind of writing actually implies that the special sense just is the ordinary sense, pretends not to know there is anything complicated going on. The effect is then that of a very sophisticated sort of innocence, or mock-primitivism, a style that says, "Who, me? I'm not using words in special ways."

Roland Barthes was not an innocent or a primitive, but he did travel swiftly and expertly between the ordinary and the less ordinary meanings of words. And he thought about such travel. He liked to play around with etymologies, for example, not because he thought they offered the true meanings of words, or because he cared about linguistic origins, but because he liked the "effect of the superimposed image: the word is seen as a palimpsest: I seem to have ideas at the level of language itself"—*à même la langue*. When a word has two meanings, Barthes likes to keep both fully in view, "as if one were winking at the other, and the meaning of the word were in that wink." This is strictly—more strictly than I myself would want—a matter of ambiguity, of double rather than multiple meanings. "The wish/the dream (*le fantasme*) is not to hear everything (anything), it is to hear *something else* (in that I am more classical than the theory of the text which I defend)." The notion of such travel among meanings is very useful to us, I think, since it allows us to see theory as a form of practice; and practice as aspiring to a theoretical consciousness. It also allows us to talk to each other more than we otherwise might manage.

Before looking more closely at Barthes, though, I'd like to glance at another distinguished example of theory using ordinary words, living its complicated and confused life in the old critical city. This a very familiar example, but never fails to surprise and amuse me. The mind of the critic here begins to look like Chaplin in *The Circus*: always about to fall into a bucket of water, miraculously escaping; and even when finally falling, still composed, still Chaplin, more a dancer than a clown. T. S. Eliot, like Lukács, is telling us that something we thought was a novel is not one. Or rather, he is telling us why *Ulysses*, if it isn't a novel, couldn't really have been one anyway:

> If it is not a novel, that is simply because the novel is a form which will no longer serve; it is because the novel, instead of being a form, was simply the expression of an age which had not sufficiently lost all form to feel the need of something stricter.

The head spins. Those two *simply*'s are extraordinary. Eliot always says *simply* when he is about to propose something unmanageable, rather as in the poems, he says *only* about things that matter deeply to him: master of the mournful throwaway. But what is he proposing here? He is using the word *novel* quite consistently, but in a special way, like Lukács—that is, with a different meaning, but with something like the same degree of specialization. The novel is not any sort of lengthy narrative, it is the kind of narrative that *Ulysses* is not. It is less strict than *Ulysses*, the sort of work we can't usefully write any more—it "will no longer serve," it won't do; it may be *lisible*, in Barthes's terms, but it isn't *scriptible*. But the word *form* is a little more protean here; it astonishingly gets used in three quite different ways within this single sentence. Anyone else would have fallen into the bucket of water at the first turn.

First, *form* has its ordinary, quite broad sense: a form is any sort of literary genre or mode, of which the novel is an example: "the novel is a form." Next, it appears in a specialized, theoretical sense, the sense a formalist might want to give to it, or even Henry James, thinking of much of the fiction of his time: the novel is not a form in this sense, being too baggy, too casual, too much a direct reflection of the world it lives in. And third, *form* seems to mean a social and historical arrangement or habit, something resembling Wittgenstein's "form of life": the previous age, it seems, had not lost its form in this sense (and so it could have novels); we have lost ours, and so need strict non-novels, like *Ulysses*, to provide the shape that life now lacks, being as it is (to quote a sentence from a little later in the same essay) "an immense panorama of futility and anarchy." Some very questionable things are being said here, of course, but I'm interested at the moment in the critical performance as performance: ordinary meanings jostle with special meanings, there are no signposts at all for what turns out to be quite heavy traffic, and a severe formalist seems to cohabit quite comfortably with a committed historicist. The comfort is illusory probably, as far as Eliot is concerned, but the possibilities are interesting, and the comfort is perhaps not illusory for everyone.

My examples are meant to suggest a way of reading criticism (and theory) with patience and irony, with the imagination; and more emphatically, to suggest that we shall lose a lot if we don't know how to do this. Criticism and theory won't always talk straight to us, any more than the old city will look like the up-to-date suburb, but they may have very interesting bent things to say, and not always old things. I'm not quite implying, as Geoffrey Hartman and others have, that we should read everything as if it were a poem or a novel, although this might in many cases be worth a try. I'm implying that reading, whether of poems or novels or criticism, requires both a close attention to the words and also a permission for the words to moonlight, a willingness to let them live several lives. When we ask them if they are specialists, some of them will just say yes; others will say yes and no; and some won't answer at all.

Roman/Romanesque

White on black, reproduced in Roland Barthes's handwriting, inside the front cover of a book called *Roland Barthes/by Roland Barthes* (*Roland Barthes par Roland Barthes*, 1975), and later repeated in print within the text, are these words: "All this must be considered as spoken by a character in a novel" (*Tout ceci doit être considéré comme dit par un personnage de roman*). All this: the book we are about to read. Barthes may mean simply that this is not a confessional work: "a character in a novel" is just a fictional character. But I should like to put a little more pressure on the phrase; a *personnage de roman*, in Barthes, is not likely to be a simple figure. Does this novel have a plot? Does the character change? Is there, could there be, a sequel? This is what Barthes himself, or his character, the one who has borrowed his handwriting, asks on the last page of the book, inside the back cover, white on black again. "And now?" The response is a brief dialogue:

—What to write, now? Will you be able to write anything else?
—One writes with one's desire, and I have not finished desiring.

Some kind of sequel, then; but not much of a plot, and a character too elusive to be seen as changing—too elusive to be a character in any ordinary sense. But then what does Barthes mean by *novel*? The answer to this question takes us on a longish journey through Barthes's critical career.

In *Roland Barthes/by Roland Barthes* the word *novel* and its derivatives are used to suggest a well-worn territory of fiction, a comfortable, readerly place: *un chateau de roman, du genre romanesque*. Nothing problematic there. Barthes's mention of a *roman familial* is a little more complicated, since this seems in context to mean a family novel, a modest French *Buddenbrooks* or *Forsyte Saga*, the implied narrative of any contemplated genealogy. But the phrase could also be translated as family romance, and Barthes must have been aware of (must have been amused by) the ambiguity. I shall return to this edging of the novel, and especially the French novel, toward romance.

But of course we are not asked to believe that the person who speaks in *Roland Barthes/by Roland Barthes* is a character in a novel, only to think of him as if he were. The novel in question is manifestly metaphorical, and Barthes himself becomes a metaphorical or imaginary novelist, the author of a project for the genre rather than of instances of it; the theorist, if you like, of an impossible novel. If this writer were a character in a novel, would this take him back into the old world before Dostoyevsky and Joyce? If it did, could we follow him? Would we want to?

Early in his career Barthes uses the word *novel* as roughly synonymous with narrative, and after a brilliantly lurid chapter in *Writing Degree Zero* (*Le Degré zéro de l'écriture*, 1953)—"The Novel is a Death: it transforms life into destiny, a memory into a useful act, duration into an orientated and meaningful time"—usually settles for the second term. He looks mainly at short texts, where narrative structures and manoeuvres can be closely analysed; and between narrative on the one hand and textuality on the other, with writing, *écriture*, running the gauntlet in the middle, the novel pretty much gets lost. When the novel returns in Barthes's criticism, it appears not (at first) as the work he wanted to write but as a category of thought he can't do without, a term he needs for thinking about literature.

Barthes's earlier work insisted on the novel's betrayal of reality; but he was also struck, early and late, by the quantities and kinds of reality caught in novels, and he resolved his dilemma, for a while at least, by means of an elegant opposition between the novel and what novels are made of—my crude translation of the terms *roman* and *romanesque*. This was a formula Barthes came back to again and again, as if it were a kind of salvation. The *romanesque*, he claimed, is "quite different" from the *roman*. The *romanesque* is an unstructured set of sections or divisions, *un simple découpage instructuré*, a dissemination of forms. No novel here, he said of *A Lover's Discourse* (*Fragments d'un discours amoureux*, 1977) but plenty of the sort of material novels go in for, *aucun roman (mais beaucoup de romanesque)*. The writerly, the *scriptible*, is among other things, *le romanesque sans le roman.* "I like the novelistic (*romanesque*)," Barthes said, "but I know the novel (*roman*) is dead." As you can see, he is using both the novel and the novelistic the way Lukács and Eliot used *novel*: to mean what has gone, what isn't there, and to signal a project, a new or remaining world. The difference is that where Lukács and Eliot put the novel in the past, Barthes puts it in the past and the present—and as we shall see, converts it into a kind of paradise. And then he realizes that the separation is not really durable or satisfying. Even critically, he must renounce the disseminated fragment, collapse the free-floating *romanesque* back into the order of a *roman*; or at least accept that the *romanesque* depends on the *roman*, is not really opposed to it. Can't have one without the other, as an old Sinatra song says on another subject, and as Barthes must always have known.

But what is the novel Barthes finally projects for us; the novel that waits not in his work, even as a concept, but just beyond it? A novel, he says in a late lecture (1978), is what he is calling "any Form which is new in relation to my past practice, to my past discourse." New to him as a writer, that is; old to him as a reader; new-old in that it builds a bridge between writing and reading. Barthes is not enough of an anglophone to be intending a pun on the word *novel* here, but language is full of such odd historical ambushes. Is such a novel possible? Probably not: it is *fantasmé, et probablement impossible*. The question is not whether Barthes could write such a novel, or why not, but whether anyone could, whether such a novel is writable. Neither a readerly nor a writerly text, then, but a phantom text: impossible. The impossible, though, as Barthes says elsewhere, can be conceived; and often needs to be conceived. To get at all close to this impossibility, though, we need to explore the *roman* and the *romanesque* a little further, and this is where we hit a little trouble with the cross-cultural meanings of the words.

Roman is *novel* in English all right, but the translation doesn't sit quite as comfortably as it seems to, since there is an echo of romance in the French word. One of the dictionary's extended meanings for *roman* is *récit dénué de vraisemblance*, as in the sentence *Cela m'a tout l'air d'un roman*. Novels in English are made up, but usually rather soberly, and they very often pretend not to be made up at all. The colloquial English for that phrase would probably be to say the thing was a fairy tale, or a fabrication. The novel in this sense has a tinge of the fantastic to it, and it is partly in this sense, I take it, that Proust wondered whether he could call *Jean Santeuil* a novel—because it had been accumulated, deposited by life; and then harvested, as he says, not made (*Ce livre n'a jamais été fait, il a été récolté*). *Romanesque* is novelistic, but that feels wrong in most contexts—mainly, no doubt, because it's not a word we use much, or have much use for. It feels fairly technical, but is there anything technical it describes? More often, the appropriate word is *romantic*—but then it means romantic in our sense, and also in the sense of behaving like a character in a novel. Larousse gives two instances. One from Rousseau: *Il se fit des hommes et de la société des idées romanesques* ("He had romantic/novelistic ideas about men and society"). Romantic ideas, and also ideas derived from novels—or ideas which are romantic because they are derived from novels. The other instance is from Proust: *un restaurant . . . où maintenant il n'allait plus que pour une de ces raisons, à la fois mystiques et saugrenues, qu'on appelle romanesques* ("a restaurant . . . to which he now went only because of one of those mysterious and ludicrous reasons we call romantic/novelistic"). Romantic reasons, sentimental reasons— the reasons novels are full of. Certainly Barthes's *romanesque* is closer to novelistic than this, but it's also romantic, and you can see some of the possibilities of slither. There is, as far as I know, just one mischievous precedent for translating *romanesque* as . . . romanesque: it appears in Nabokov's *Ada*, where a man called James Jones ("a formula whose complete lack of connotation made an ideal pseudonym despite its happening to be his real name") is described as a "romanesque private detective." This is a good joke, but not much comfort; and doesn't work at all unless you already know the French word, or are thinking about architecture.

These difficulties of language would be bad news if they weren't such a help; if they didn't turn out to confirm the drift of what I am trying to say about ordinary words and their relation to theory. Even within a language translation is approximate, scarcely ever possible from word to word; works through paraphrase and unraveling; through the addition of long sentences, even of gestures. The best translation of words we have is not into other words, either in our own or another language, but into practice. We use words, and show ourselves and others that we know what they mean.

In this sense the difficulty of getting meaning to travel from language to language is a precious, enormously useful one. Each language divides reality differently, and we learn about language and reality by looking at the differences. This is what Benjamin meant, I take it, when he said languages "are not strangers to one another, but are . . . interrelated in what they want to express." Interrelated but not twinned, since kinship, as Benjamin goes on to say, "does not necessarily involve likeness." The words *Brot* and *pain*, he says, " 'intend' the same object, but the modes of this intention are not the same." I would suggest that they don't even quite intend the same object, since French bread and German bread are quite different, but that reinforces rather than weakens the point. We are back with our riddle. When is a novel not a novel? When it's a *roman*. Well, fortunately, even if words don't intend the same object they do quite often hit the same object. The novel, we could say, is a vast patch of literary territory, with Tolstoy and Balzac in the middle of it; and so is the *roman*. But the map drawn by the words isn't the same color, and doesn't convey quite the same sort of information.

Barthes's first book, *Writing Degree Zero*, has a well-known bravura passage, full of wild simplifications and gallocentrism, but splendid stuff all the same:

> [The preterite, the past historic] is the ideal instrument for every construction of a world; it is the unreal tense of cosmogonies, myths, History and Novels. It presupposes a world which is constructed, elaborated, self-sufficient, reduced to significant lines, and not one which has been sent sprawling before us, for us to take or leave (*non un monde jeté, étalé, offert*). Behind the preterite there always lurks a demiurge, a God or a reciter. The world is not unexplained since it is told like a story; each one of its accidents is but a circumstance, and the preterite is precisely this operative sign whereby the narrator reduces the exploded reality to a slim and pure verb (*ramène l'éclatement de la réalité à un verbe mince et pur*) without density, without volume, without spread.

We may feel, I certainly feel, that Barthes brilliantly tells slightly less than half the story. Novels, it seems to me, are characteristically composed of imperfect tenses, whole lives and societies presented as occupying a continuing past—so thoroughly continuous that a present tense is possible, and frequent, as in "All happy families are alike, but an unhappy family is unhappy after its own fashion." The mood shifts into the pluperfect—"Everything had gone wrong in the Oblonsky household"—and direct action, when it comes, falls on this world like a raid. Balzac's *Lost Illusions* opens with a page and a half of imperfects, several presents, and one perfect (which is a sort of back-formation from the present: The mechanical presses of today have . . . made us forget); then arrives at a rush of preterites with a date: in 1793 our man David Séchard found himself married, escaped conscription, remained alone at the printing works. Without a habit of this sort of interplay of perfect and imperfect tenses, there would be no shock in Proust's amazing opening sentence, reporting a single completed action as if it were a continuous occurrence. *Longtemps je me suis couché de bonne heure*: as if we were to say, For a long time I went to bed early one day. Dickens's *Little Dorrit*, indeed, opens with just such an effect: "Thirty years ago, Marseilles lay burning in the sun, one day." The point of this pedantry is not to quibble with Barthes's bravura, but to shift its ground. The reduction of the sprawling world, the imposition of an unreal and too tidy coherence on a dispersed reality, takes place not between writing and lived experience but on the page. The novel is the record of this whole activity. We can accept what we might call the ethical drift of Barthes's remark, its defence of reality's profusion against a narrowing order, but we need to see that the reality, in this case, is in the novel too, that that is where Barthes gets it from. It is the rambling imperfect that suffers the military regime of the past historic. In looking at novels in this way, we are putting to use the terminology of the *roman* and the *romanesque*: good novels, we might say, are made of their fights and reconciliations.

Here is an example from Barthes's own prose:

> There I was (*j'allais ainsi*), alone in the apartment where she had died, looking at these pictures of my mother, one by one, under the lamp, gradually moving back in time with her, looking for the truth of the face I had loved. And I found it. (Or I found her: *Et je la découvris*).

What this passage suggests, I think, is not that *Camera Lucida (La Chambre claire*, 1980) is a novel but that pieces of novel can crop up almost anywhere. Frédéric Berthet nicely says that Barthes wrote "some novel" but not "a novel," *du roman* but not *un roman*, borrowing this use of the partitive from Barthes himself, who speaks of identifying *du langage* but not *un langage*. You can't say this in French any more than you can in English, or at least not without sounding like a parody of a linguistic philosopher, but it's a very useful distinction. The example also shows very beautifully how the *roman* (the plot, the past historic, the event) and the *romanesque* (the apartment, the lamp, all the wrong photographs, the "waste sad time") need each other, come together in a novel, or a piece of novel, *du roman*.

In a late Barthes text called "Soirées de Paris" (1979), generally rather tame and desultory, there are flickering moments of quite touching life. These occur not when the writing is better, or when something happens in the narration, but when we clearly see the character Roland Barthes, a man getting older, learning the long, slow business of renunciation. "All this must be considered as spoken by . . . ." A friend is hesitating about whether to go spend some time at Hyères. The friend wants to go, Barthes doesn't want him to, but perversely (and successfully) persuades him to leave. Barthes is acting, as he says, out of pique, generosity, fatalism, a sort of aristocratic showing-off (*forfanterie seigneuriale*), and no doubt plenty of other feelings are in play. Why do I think this is a piece of novel, and that its being so is what makes the scene stay in the mind? It's not the complexity of the motive or the situation—we often find more complexity in short stories. A question of the extent and density of the implied plot, perhaps, of the long imagined roads we have to travel to arrive at this scene, and to move on from it.

The *roman*, then, is the past historic, it is visible, excessive plot; it is proper nouns, representing rounded identities, fixed, stable characters. A biography, Barthes said, is a novel that dare not speak its name—that is, a confection of plot and character masquerading as history. A novel is "a story endowed with characters, with tenses"—*une histoire dotée de personnages, de temps*. Novels have conclusions for Barthes, they are closed systems. They are unlikely, picking up the implication of *roman* we have already looked at. Barthes uses the phrase "purely novelistic" in a sequence of words which includes "untenable" and "impossible"; and there is a memorable moment in *S/Z* where Barthes invites us to imagine a live person performing a trill, actually saying Addio in the way Balzac has her say it. "She added to the final syllable a marvelously well-executed trill, but in a soft voice, as if to give poetic expression to the emotions in her heart." It can't be done, Barthes says, reality in novels is not operable (*le réel romanesque n'est pas opérable*). Barthes pursues a similar notion in relation to Sade: it's all beyond human nature, we should need several arms, several skins, acrobats' bodies, and an infinitely renewable capacity for orgasm. This is in a section of *Sade, Fourier, Loyola* (1971) called "Impossibilia," and it is where Barthes says that written shit doesn't smell. The *roman* begins to veer toward an unorthodox utopia, the range of meanings widens to include rebellious details as well as authoritarian plot. The *roman* in other words edges toward the *romanesque*, Barthes's antithesis doesn't work every day or in every corner.

The *romanesque* is a novelistic attention to details, a gathering of contingency's litter. Barthes is drawn to what he calls the "novelistic surface of life":

> In daily life, I feel a sort of curiosity for everything I see and hear, almost an intellectual affection, of the kind that belongs to novels (*qui est de l'ordre du romanesque*). A century ago, I suppose I would have wandered about (*me serais . . . promené dans la vie*) with the notebook of a realist novelist.

In this sense then we might say not that *Camera Lucida*, his book on photography, is a novel, but that photography was a novel for him, a curious new art of the past historic, which doesn't summarize or subordinate, in which the world is seen as horribly mortal, once and for all, but not available for myth or cosmogony.

> What Photography reproduces to infinity has occurred only once . . . the event is never transcended for the sake of something else: Photography always leads

the corpus I need back to the body I see (*ramène toujours le corpus dont j'ai besoin au corps que je vois*); it is the absolute Particular, sovereign Contingency, matte and somehow stupid. . . . A photograph cannot be transformed (spoken) philosophically, it is wholly ballasted by the contingency of which it is the weightless, transparent envelope.

Let's leave aside the question of whether this is true of photography. It's an evocative picture, not of the imperfect tense invaded by a regimenting preterite but of a disarmed, undomineering preterite, a preterite in disarray. Similarly, anthropology offers to Barthes a sort of ideal (*romanesque*) novel, an infinitely rich novel full of sharply focused details, entirely (or almost entirely) lacking in plot. There is a splendid passage in *Roland Barthes/by Roland Barthes* where Barthes associates the work of Michelet and Sade, the novels of Balzac, Zola, Proust, and his own unscrambling of the surfaces of French life in *Mythologies* (1957), with the labors of ethnographers. "The ethnographical work has all the powers of any book we love: it is an encyclopaedia, noting and classifying all of reality, even its most futile, most sensual parts."

The Truth of Banality

The novel is system and what opposes system; meaning and what escapes meaning. The narrative voice in *Middlemarch*, for example, has interests that are different from those of the novel's metaphors—the metaphors are meaner, tougher, less programmatically tolerant. We could be depressed by the voice, as Yeats was; or cheered by the metaphors. So we might translate both *roman* and *romanesque* as novel, and leave the two meanings to fight it out. That would mean we would have to get along without the adjective, unless we fancy *novel-ish*. Thus in the following sentence we would no longer look for special, iso-latable senses for *romanesque* but we would remember our linguistic trouble—remember it as a gain, I hope, rather than a bad trip. "He would have liked to produce, not a comedy of the intellect, but the novel of the intellect" (*Il aurait voulu produire, non une comédie de l'Intellect, mais son romanesque*). This is the best brief description I know of Barthes's whole writing project. The context is his suggestion that criticism is an art, or more precisely that writing like his is an art that combines "theory, critical combat and pleasure"—not the most familiar of combinations in the Anglo-Saxon world. "We submit the objects of knowledge and scholarship—as in all art—no longer to an instance of truth, but to a consideration of effects." It is the aesthetic of Flaubert and Proust, their theory of the novel, applied to criticism.

Of course the sentence I have just quoted, about the novel and the intellect, is amazingly oblique: it is written in the third person, in the conditional, includes a negative, and arrives only at the *romanesque*, not quite at the *roman*. Even so, the remark allows us to ask some quite direct questions and to make some strong, even some surprising connections.

Barthes's imagined work is not a comedy, perhaps, because Beckett has already written the intellect's comedy, the comedy of the mind at the end of what may or may not be its tether. And the imagined work is not a full-blown modern novel, a *roman*, the novel that is still around after the devastations of Dostoyevsky and Joyce, because that novel just is the novel of the intellect, what else would it be? After Musil and Mann, after Gide and Kafka, what is left? No, what Barthes wanted to produce was the nineteenth-century novel of the twentieth-century intellect, a work in which the adventures of a mind might move us, not as the adventures of minds move us (they do, they do) but as characters in Tolstoy and Proust move us. This is, it seems to me, the novel that Barthes metaphorically wrote in *Roland Barthes/by Roland Barthes*—the character touches us as if there were a novel for him to be in—and literally wrote here and there, in scraps, fragments, moments of mere novel.

Barthes's lecture "Longtemps je me suis couché de bonne heure . . ." allows us to sharpen the focus on the questions we have been asking. Barthes calls for a theory of pathos in the novel (*une théorie ou une histoire pathétique du Roman*). Pathos occurs when we are gripped by what he calls (rather feebly, I'm afraid) "moments of truth" in a novel—nothing to do with realism and "absent from every theory of the novel." Absent, that is, from every theory Barthes is likely to think of. Most older theories have nothing but this pathos in them—unless we think of such approaches to the genre as somehow pretheoretical? Instances of moments of truth for Barthes: the death of Prince Bolkonski in *War and Peace*; the death of the narrator's grandmother in *Remembrance of Things Past*.

Is that all? This is what countless readers have habitually found in novels, and maybe only an advanced intellectual could have taken so long to get here. Let's not dodge the banality and sentimentality of Barthes's thought. But let's not miss its interest either; for it is here, if anywhere, down among the these dim and familiar notions, in the shabby and crowded streets of the old linguistic city, that we may learn something of the form Dostoyevsky abandoned, the form that wasn't a form for T. S. Eliot.

Barthes suggests that the novel (the one he reads, the one he may or may not be able to write) is animated by a feeling that "has something do with love." Can this feeling be named? Barthes tries kindness (*bonté*); generosity; charity;

pity. He doesn't settle the question—just as well, since pity is really disturb-ing—but asks of such a past and future novel three things:

1. that it tell or say loved ones, express them, remember them; say them like a sentence rather than (lyrically) saying sentences to them;
2. that it represent emotions fully but never directly—this is what Barthes means by pathos;
3. ("and perhaps especially") that it put no pressure on the reader, that it have none of the aggressiveness and arrogance and assertiveness of criticism.

In one sense this is very familiar. It's as if Barthes were a pacified D. H. Lawrence pronouncing on the novel; a Lawrence with old-world Proustian manners. In another sense Barthes's argument is less familiar. We are watching a gifted writer groping for the deep truth of a banality—not the *banalité cor-rigée* that Barthes elsewhere says is his method but banality itself, the dull dis-course of everyone. He is looking for what I should like to call, provisionally at least, the kindness of novels.

Perhaps it's absurd to moralize a genre in this way. Well, certainly it's ab-surd, but it is where our tracing of Barthes's tracks gets us. It's not uninhabit-ed country, though, there are quite a few people here. There is Nabokov, for example, defining "aesthetic bliss" as "a sense of being somehow, somewhere, connected with other states of being where art . . . is the norm." In parenthesis after art: "curiosity, tenderness, kindness, ecstasy": analogues for art, or per-haps a definition of art, which in context can only be an art of the novel. The country also contains Lionel Trilling, telling us that the novel "was the literary form to which the emotions of understanding and forgiveness were indige-nous, as if by the definition of the form itself" (note the past tense: the time is 1947). I once tried to set this quotation as a question in an M.A. examination at Columbia, Trilling's university. My colleagues, who didn't recognise the quo-tation, thought it was meaningless. They were probably right about the exam-ination question, but I would hope that Trilling's formulation, allied to the strikingly similar thoughts of Nabokov and Barthes, can be seen to make seri-ous, if still elusive sense. It's slackly phrased—*indigenous* can't be the word he wants, and understanding and forgiveness are not emotions—but it points to a real insight.

Here are quite a few words from the old city; from the same part of the old city: kindness, generosity; tenderness; understanding, forgiveness; the novel. What if we can't write novels without kindness? What if we have learned too well the Brechtian lesson about the "terrible temptation to kindness" and don't even feel the temptation? I'm not going to answer these questions, and I want to resist the nostalgia that seems to be tugging at them, so let me bluntly say that I do not think kindness is the only virtue, or the greatest of virtues. If I have to choose among virtues, I have to say I prefer truthfulness, even if unkind. We need to see too that great unkindnesses were masked and made acceptable by the kindness of nineteenth-century novels.

Even so, kindness is a virtue, and we must miss it if it's gone. And we do seem now to have a fuller answer to our riddle. When is a novel not a novel? When the streets of the city get too rough for kindness—too rough for kindness to be plausible or practical. When the novel Barthes wants really is unwritable. Or to answer the riddle yet again as we've already answered it: when the novel is *The Idiot*. When perfect kindness produces only madness and despair. In this sense Jane Austen didn't write novels because she didn't want to; and Kafka didn't write novels because he couldn't. Barthes's logic, followed out in this way, repeats the extravagant critical gesture of Lukács and Eliot, since many novels must fall short of what Barthes asks them to be and quite a few of them are not even trying to qualify. We glimpse, I hope, something of the historical urgency of what seemed at first to be a largely formal question. Barthes the novelist, Barthes the imaginary, metaphorical, fragmentary novelist, is important to us because, unlike most novelists, he was finally quite impossible.

Now we must choose, said Mercier
    Between what? said Camier
    Ruin and collapse, said Mercier
    Could we not somehow combine them? said Camier.
                —Samuel Beckett, *Mercier and Camier*

2. *The Comedy of Ignorance*

The comedy of the intellect, for Samuel Beckett, is a comedy of ignorance, the sign of our striving to know what we don't we know—that is, to know the things that we don't and perhaps can't know; and in the absence of any detectable success in this direction, to know the rich extent of our lack of knowledge. Beckett's paradoxical project is to say how little we can say, or more precisely to catch us in the act of saying it—of saying too much about it, since whatever we say turns out to be excessive, a form of hubris, an extravagant claim on the unclaimable. Far from full to start with, the world of Beckett's work emptied itself out over the years, but never to the point of absolute depletion. In the virtual silence there was still a voice—when no one was there, someone was heard saying "No one is here"—and in the apparently unpopulated darkness there were remnants of bodies, flickers of light.

Beckett's work is always delicately adapted to the mode of its performance, so that the distance of the theater in *Not I* (1972), for example, a small mouth in a large curtain, becomes a vast mouth eerily filling the screen in the television version of the same play (the mouth is that of Billie Whitelaw, an actress who worked closely with Beckett on a number of occasions). The angle of the camera in *Film* (1969) is itself a principle of vision within the imagined story. Footfalls sound in the radio play *Footfalls* (1976), and the loneliness of reading and writing is always an intimate part of the movement and effect of Beckett's prose fiction. But in all of these modes we meet a desperate loyalty to ignorance, as if it couldn't possibly be our salvation but might be our truth, if we were up to it. I concentrate here on the later fiction, because its modulations of ignorance seem to me so wonderfully revealing, but it's worth pointing out the

consistency of Beckett's imagined territory, with all its greater and lesser de-
pletions. It is resolutely mental and metaphorical, but it is also represented as
stubbornly if pallidly material—like the world of an empty nineteenth-century novel, let's say, *le roman sans le roman*, rather than the shifting writerly ter-
rain of experimentalists such as Philippe Sollers or Severo Sarduy.

Beckett's favorite setting is the one he names in *Krapp's Last Tape* (1958): "A
late evening in the future." The future is not a place and not much of a time; it
is a guess, a possibility, a threat. We could say it is in the head, and that is where
Beckett's characters often think they are: in an "imaginary head," "we are
needless to say in a skull"; "in the madhouse of the skull and nowhere else";
"perhaps we're in a head, it's as dark as in a head before the worms get at it,
ivory dungeon." But this head is not a place either. It is a metaphor, a spatial-
ization of the unseeable mind, and it is important not to be taken in by the familiarity of the figure. "How physical all this is," the narrator of *The Unnameable* (1953) moans as he tries to picture what cannot be pictured.

Another name, another metaphor for this nonplace is limbo, the home of
"those nor for God nor for his enemies," as Beckett puts it, quoting Dante. Yet
Beckett's fictional universe is a limbo not because of the neutrality of its inhabitants (although this may well be part of Beckett's strict judgment on himself) but because it is imagined and knows itself to be imagined. It is a domain
just off the edge of life, late in the future, an ending order peopled by decaying or immobile creatures who lose the use of their limbs the way others lose
their car keys. "It is in the tranquillity of decomposition," Molloy writes elegantly, "that I remember the long confused emotion which was my life. . . . To
decompose is to live too, I know, I know, don't torment me."

And yet a good deal of mimesis remains in Beckett. However broken or
derelict, schematic, unlikely or cruel, a *world* is being imagined or remembered
or both, and then imitated in words. It is because it is a writer's world, alterable
by a flick of the pen, that it seems so airless and arbitrary. "Unable, unable, it's
easy to talk about being unable," Moran writes in *Molloy* (1951), "whereas in
reality nothing is more difficult." It is because the writer himself seems more
often than not to be at the mercy of the images that present themselves to him
that it also has the feel of an observed or described world. "Perhaps I invented
him," Moran says of Molloy, "I mean found him ready-made in my head."

This world, implicitly or explicitly figurative, persists in Beckett's work, a
rickety or fragmentary externalization of the reason-ridden consciousness. But
it is less immediately recognizable in the later writing, less of a shared world,
and less likely to generate characters and stories. Belacqua, in *More Pricks Than
Kicks* (1934), inhabits a historical Dublin, complete with pubs, place names, and

Malahide murderer. Murphy, in the novel of that name (1938), sits in a mews in West Brompton. The landscapes of *Watt* (1953) and of *Molloy, Malone Dies* (1951), and *The Unnameable* are scarcely realistic, but they resemble our world in striking ways and can be reached from it. Malone has been to London, and Moran mentions Goering.

Above all, these personages are *characters*, caught up in stories, and eager storytellers themselves. They, and with them Beckett, equate stories with shape, meaning, and even a modest, if ultimately defeated, hope. This is what changes. "No need of a story," Beckett writes prophetically in *Texts for Nothing* (1955), "a story is not compulsory, just a life." In most of the later prose— *Imagination Dead Imagine* (1965), *Ping* (1966), *Lessness* (1969), *The Lost Ones* (1971), *For to End Yet Again* (1975), *Company* (1980), *Ill Seen Ill Said* (1981), *Worstward Ho* (1983), *Stirrings Still* (1988)—there are no characters, only closely watched creatures, and no stories, only stark images, obsessively focused and refocused. The scene is still a world, but it holds even less than "just a life"; holds only the starved imagination and its meager contents:

> No trace anywhere of life, you say, pah, no difficulty there, imagination not dead yet, yes, dead, good, imagination dead imagine. Islands, waters, azure, verdure, one glimpse and vanished, endlessly, omit.

Life dies, and then the imagination, the one that deals in islands, water, azure, and verdure. But even then *something* remains, imagination's ghost or residue, the indefatigable spook of the writer, who cannot *not* see things, who has to name what he omits, and who cannot give up trying to arrange in words what he sees. In this case, in *Imagination Dead Imagine*, the spook sees and describes a white sealed rotunda ("No way in, go in, measure") containing two human bodies, male and female, curled up, back to back, not moving, not asleep, not dead. The temperature in the rotunda rises and falls, light comes and goes. And then the spook's "eye of prey" perceives an "infinitesimal shudder" and abandons the image:

> Leave them there, sweating and icy, there is better elsewhere. No, life ends and no, there is nothing elsewhere, and no question now of ever finding again that white speck lost in whiteness, to see if they lie still in the stress of that storm, or of a worse storm, or in the black dark for good, or the great whiteness unchanging, and if not what they are doing.

Beckett's later fiction returns again and again to the spectral visions of what he calls "dead imagining":

For to end yet again [as the piece of that title opens] skull alone in a dark place
pent bowed on a board to begin. Long thus to begin, till the place fades, followed
by the board long after.

The place fades, and a gray world appears. A gray little body stands ankle
deep in sand pale as dust, the ruins of what is called its refuge sinking around
it. The figure is approached by two white dwarfs carrying a litter, a pair of
long-armed Keystone Cops trotting into a bleached nightmare. They do not
reach the figure, who falls headlong on his face and stays there. The dwarfs
then seem to freeze or die, the litter left lying between them:

> is this then its last state all set for always litter and dwarfs ruins and little body
> gray cloudless sky glutted dust verge upon verge hell air not a breath.

No, it is not the last state, or the last image, that will haunt this bowed skull.
There is always more in the remorseless mind, the afterlife of the imagination
is like Hamlet's sleep after death, perpetually startled by dreams.

All Strange Away was written in 1963–1964. Longer than most of the prose
pieces that follow it, it reveals more clearly the writer's hand, arranging and re-
arranging the images that beset him:

> Imagination dead imagine [it starts]. A place, that again. Never another ques-
> tion. A place, then someone in it, that again. . . . Out of the door and down the
> road in the old hat and coat like after the war, no, not that again. Five foot square,
> six high, no way in, none out, try for him there. Stool, bare walls when the light
> comes on, women's faces on the walls when the light comes on. . . . Light off and
> let him be, on the stool, talking to himself in the last person.

Light and darkness continue to alternate in this pictured place; the writer makes
the room smaller, takes the man's stool away, converts the images of women on
the walls to images of parts of one woman, Emma; changes the sex of the figure in the room, or rather defines it as female, "since sex not seen so far"; has
her lie down and corrects his text retroactively ("Let her lie so from now on,
have always lain so"). He cuts the size of the room still further and then converts it into a diminutive rotunda; lends Emma nightmares that fill her with
"dread of demons," adding cheerfully "perhaps some glimpse of demons
later"; and leaves the figure there, faintly sighing, moved by a dim memory.
"So little by little," the writer says, "all strange away."

This is a world very close to that of *Imagination Dead Imagine*, as the verbal echo suggests, a space that is cramped and inhuman but "proof against en-

during tumult." Or at least aspiring to such immunity. "For in the cylinder alone," Beckett says in *The Lost Ones*, where two-hundred-odd forlorn creatures, denizens of a flattened rubber cylinder fifty meters round by eighteen high, search unceasingly for their one and only counterparts, "are certitudes to be found and without nothing but mystery." The quest for a sure and surpriseless universe has dogged Beckett's characters from Murphy and Watt through Molloy and on to any number of later figures. The narrator of "The End" cannot bear the sea, "its splashing and heaving, its tides and general convulsiveness." "Closed place," Beckett writes in *Fizzles*. "All needed to be known for say is known. There is nothing but what is said. Beyond what is said there is nothing."

The repeating joke, of course, is that convulsiveness is everywhere, and entirely stable certitudes are not to be had, however ruthlessly we slash at the variables. Are not to be had and, short of suicide, cannot be *wanted* as much as we think we want them, since the only perfect accomplishment of "all strange away" would be death. "One's own death is unimaginable," Christopher Ricks comments, "since the imagination is itself a principle of life and an exercising of life." But exercising is not far from exorcizing, as Ricks would be the first to see, and it is possible that, as he says, "the one thing worse than not living for ever would be living for ever." What this suggests, though, is that even the simplest death wish may not be a wish precisely for death; and death in any case, in Beckett, is as elusive as certainty. Molloy, after patiently constructing a complex system for sucking sixteen pebbles in what he regards as a properly impeccable order, simply leaves the pebbles on the beach.

Company (1980) and *Ill Seen Ill Said* (1981) represent Beckett's most important work, if that dubious adjective is allowed, after *How It Is* (1961), and both are a good deal more accessible than that oblique and violent text. *Company* was written in English, but originally published in French, in Beckett's translation; and then revised for its English publication. *Ill Seen Ill Said* was written in French, then translated by Beckett into English.

At first sight *Company* appears to continue the vein of *All Strange Away*. It situates a figure in space and watches him, flat out and immobile except for the opening and closing of his eyes. But it returns us as well to the worlds of *The Unnameable* and *Malone Dies* and *Molloy*, since a voice speaks to the prostrate figure, offering him a sheaf of memories it insists are his own. "A voice comes to one in the dark," the text begins. "Imagine." But there is someone else here, someone saying these things. "And in another dark or in the same another devising it all for company. Quick leave him." "For company" is a kind of pun, meaning for us, the readers, and for himself, to keep himself company. The writer returns to this worry. "For why or? Why in another dark or the same? And whose voice asking this? Who asks, Whose voice asking this?"

The writer reaches a provisional, slightly bewildered answer to these unnerving questions:

> Deviser of the voice and of its hearer and of himself. Deviser of himself for company. Leave it at that. He speaks of himself as of another. He says speaking of himself, He speaks of himself as of another. Himself he devises too for company. Leave it at that. Confusion too is company up to a point.

But then he finds himself with a new character on his hands, and new authorial decisions to make. Is this figure (or "figment" as Beckett calls him) in the same dark as the voice and the hearer, or in a different dark? Is he "standing or sitting or lying or in some other position?" The writer settles for the same dark and crawling, but wonders what the status of these decisions is—can he cancel them if they don't work out, what are the obligations of a deviser to a character once devised? And who is asking the questions now? Another figment? "Yet another then. Of whom nothing. Devising figments to temper his nothingness. Quick leave him." Later the writer, in the grip of an infinite regress, finds he needs another figment still. "Yet another still? Devising it all for company. What a further addition to company that would be.'

But the company finally collapses. There is only the figure on his back in the dark, and all the rest, the proliferating figments, the writer concealed behind them, the shadowy readers, and the historical person of Samuel Beckett vanishing down a tunnel of perspective, is fictive elaboration, inference. Of course, the figure in the dark is probably fiction too, but it's impossible to say what world of fact he has departed from. The voice ends, saying, "And you as you always were. Alone." A pure premise; as bereft of consequences as he is of company.

These quotations will hardly have given an idea of how funny this gloomy-sounding stuff can be. "Might not the hearer be improved? Made more companionable if not downright human?" Beckett has often spoken of his characters as company for each other—in *The Unnameable*, in *How It Is*, in *Texts for Nothing*—but never with this tone of amused helplessness, with this sense of solitude longing for an inconceivable Dickensian jollity: "The test is company. Which of the two darks is the better company. Which of all imaginable positions has the most to offer in the way of company." Company, in this rather old-fashioned usage, suggests not conglomerates or corporations but polite visits, tea-times, a cosy Victorian parlor, as in "to receive company.'

The fact that there is *no* company here, that the prostrate figure doesn't speak, that he can't or won't acknowledge the past proposed to him as his own, plunges the text into unrelieved gloom at the end. But the work as a whole, like all of Beckett's best writing, is made up of gloom *and* irony, and a note of bravery sounds throughout the narrative. Writing is a mode of hiding for the writer—hiding while seeming to be seen. "Quick leave him." The writer can no more admit his actual presence on the page that the silent figure can lay claim to his past. But he can admit the absurdity of his unmanageable activity; he can take his textual tumbles, and smile himself at his narrative scrapes. "A dead rat. What an addition to company that would be."

The memories presented to the figure in the dark are another strand in the text. They are highly personal, and appear in several cases to be autobiographical, Beckett's own:

A small boy you come out of Connolly's Stores holding your mother by the hand. . . . It is late afternoon and after some hundred paces the sun appears above the crest of the rise. Looking up at the blue sky and then at your mother's face you break the silence asking her if it is not in reality much more distant than it appears. The sky that is. The blue sky. Receiving no answer you mentally reframe your question and some hundred paces later look up at her face again and ask her if it does not appear much less distant than in reality it is. For some reason you could never fathom this question must have angered her exceedingly. For she shook off your little hand and made you a cutting retort you have never forgotten.

Malone, in *Malone Dies*, recalls asking a similar question of his mother, who told him the sky was exactly as far away as it appeared to be. Other memories in *Company* include the child throwing himself repeatedly from a high fir tree, the great boughs breaking his fall; the child saving a hedgehog from hostile nature, only to have it decay and die in the old hatbox he has provided for it; moments of romance in "the bloom of adulthood" ("Imagine a whiff of that," the voice says); the child become an old man losing heart one day on a walk in the snow; and this striking epiphany, as Stephen Dedalus would have called it:

You stand at the tip of the high board. High above the sea. In it your father's upturned face. Upturned to you. You look down to the loved trusted face. He calls to you to jump. He calls, Be a brave boy. The red round face. The thick mustache. The greying hair. The swell sways it under and sways it up again. The far call again, Be a brave boy. Many eyes upon you. From the water and from the bathing place.

These memories are sharply realized, stripped of all nostalgia, and ultimately unowned. They cannot be claimed by the figure in the darkness, because he, like the women in *Rockaby* (1981) and *Not I*, like Molloy, Moran, Malone, and many other Beckett characters, has withdrawn from his dwindling world and life. They do not, in this context, properly belong to Beckett; and still less to us. Beckett's art here turns into something like the excruciating reverse of Proust's. Time is not recaptured, it is held up at an immeasurable distance, as if seen through the wrong end of a telescope. We perceive it so clearly *because* we can't have it back. Beckett consigns his character to solitude, and himself and us to "labour lost and silence." And yet the *writing* remains, a conquest not of time but of the pain of memory and the cruelty of a dead but unforgiving imagination.

Like many of these late texts, *Ill Seen Ill Said* rests on a melancholy equivocation. Less bleak than "imagination dead imagine," the formulation here suggests someone more simply undone; equally at a loss but less cerebrally so. The equivocal phrase is "How need in the end? But how? How need in the end?" or slightly more explicitly in the French, how to need anything, or to be in need, *Comment avoir besoin à la fin? Mais comment? Comment avoir besoin à la fin?* Meaning, I take it, both how could one possibly do it, since it obviously can't be done, and how might one, desperately, manage it after all. You would have to allow yourself to need, and you would have to know what you needed: both exorbitant prospects in Beckett's world.

The only company the closely watched creature has in *Ill Seen Ill Said* is the creaking of the cabin she sits in—"And every now and then a real creak. Her company." Or more precisely, this is the only company she knows about, since this old woman is watched throughout this wonderful and desolate little narrative by an eye that corresponds roughly to the voice that comes to the one in the dark in *Company*. The eye is kinder than the voice, makes no ferocious demands on memory, and foregrounds its own fictionalizing less. It watches the old woman sitting at her window; lying on her bed; walking across a chalky landscape to a graveyard. She is scarcely distinguishable from the stone she visits, a confusion much helped by a common gender in French:

> See them again side by side. Not quite touching. Lit aslant by the latest last rays they cast east-north-east their long parallel shadows. . . . Undistinguishable the twin shadows. Till one at length more dense as if of a body better opaque.

The stone is a little more solid than a frail old woman, especially when the frail old woman is a ghost, as this one probably is. The text secretes a series of delicate, mournful clues. It speaks of her twice in a lyrical past conditional: "As had she the misfortune to be still of this world"—*Comme si elle avait le malheur d'être encore en vie*. The woman is said to be "alive as she alone knows how neither more nor less. Less! Compared to true stone." She appears and disappears like a phantom, surprising the watcher by her sudden returns, abruptly leaving the watcher with only her old chair to look at. But it's not at first clear whether all this means that she is a ghost or that she is a memory best evoked in a language of ghostliness; and indeed whether she is dead or merely living a shadowy existence Beckett is reluctant to call life. In the end it seems that she is being evoked as still alive *and* already dead, caught up simultaneously in conditions that necessarily follow one upon the other for all of us. Two particularly obscure passages cry out for interpretation here:

> No shock were she already dead. As of course she is. But in the meantime more convenient not. Still living then she lies hidden.

And:

> If only she could be pure figment. Unalloyed. This old so dying woman. So dead. In the madhouse of the skull and nowhere else. . . . If only all could be pure figment. Neither be nor been nor by any shift to be.

One could spend years unpacking these economically compounded sentences, but at the very least they must mean that an unnamed dead woman is being remembered or represented as being alive, the question of whether she is a fictional (i.e., once alive and now dead within a fictional universe) or historical being left in dizzying abeyance; and that it would be altogether more comfortable if she were only fictional, could be guaranteed to have had only a fictional existence. We don't have to assume the historical Samuel Beckett is thinking of his mother, or take that thought as an explanation. We have only to wonder whether there are such things as pure figments, creations of the imagination trailing no historical baggage, and whether Beckett is perhaps thinking of my mother, although he doesn't know her. "How does language hook on to the world?" the young Wittgenstein wanted to know. Beckett is asking, without much hope, how fiction could cut itself loose.

Ill Seen Ill Said is a fine title in English but doesn't quite have the intimations of miniaturized social comedy you get from the French *Mal vu mal dit*. What's *mal vu* is what's not proper, not the done thing. *Mal dit* is close to *maudit*, accursed, and to *médire*, to speak ill of. Beckett's text insists on the literal, unidiomatic meaning of these phrases—seeing badly, describing wrongly—and indeed makes the negative marking, the sense of automatic failure, into something like the ordinary meaning of them. "Such the dwelling ill seen ill said"; "Scrapped all the ill seen ill said." To see just *is* to see badly, to describe just *is* to describe wrongly, what else did we expect? It's as if a stage Frenchman were to keep saying not, "How you say?" but "How you missay?" *Pour pouvoir reprendre. Reprendre le—comment dire? Comment mal dire?* This language reaches a spectacular climax—as spectacular as anything can be in these misty and darkened regions—in the following attempt to talk about the real and whatever its opposite may be:

> On resumption the head is covered. No matter. No matter now. Such the confusion now between real and—how say its contrary? No matter. That old tandem. Such now the confusion between them once so twain. And such the farrago from eye to mind. For it to make what sad sense of it may. No matter now. Such equal liars both. Real and—how ill say its contrary? The counter-poison.

"Once so twain" is a brilliantly tangled translation of the tangled *les deux si deux jadis*; but "farrago" seems to be a sign of Beckett's deciding, on second thoughts, to hide himself a little further away. The French deprecatingly but rather more clearly evokes the owner of the eye and the disarray that is all the eye can signal to him: *au compère chargé du triste savoir l'oeil ne signale plus guére que désarroi.* Who charged or burdened this fellow with the task of knowing? We have the answer. A figment who is not only, or not quite a figment. Quick leave him.

"They give birth astride of a grave," Pozzo says in *Godot*, "the light gleams an instant, then it's night once more." Vladimir amplifies this to: "Astride of a grave and a difficult birth. Down in the hole, lingeringly, the grave-digger puts on the forceps." This is so lugubrious (and funny—note how *lingeringly* slows down the pace and hints at an exaggeration) that Beckett cannot be out to demonstrate the *truth* of such propositions. He must mean to make us see how attractive they are, how comically irresistible, how we fall for them and relish them. Like Belacqua Shuah in *More Pricks Than Kicks* we are eager to put on "a long face" and readily welcome "a lachrymose philosopher," and still more when he is "obscure at the same time." This tone should warn us to tread softly when we look for large meanings in Beckett. "This is becoming really insignificant," Vladimir says. Estragon replies, "Not enough."

There is an edge to Beckett's jokes that queers their mournful content—doesn't shade it, as Beckett's critics often suggest, but gives it a different sense altogether—and there is a characteristic Beckett joke. "Personally, I have no bone to pick with graveyards"; "This is awful, awful, at least there's that to be thankful for"; "Nothing like breathing your last to put new life into you"; "when my comfort was at stake there was no trouble I would not go to." Perhaps the most haunting and moving instance of the joke occurs in *Molloy*. Moran has been told that his boss, one Youdi, has remarked that life is a thing of beauty and a joy forever—in the original French *une bien belle chose, une chose inouïe*. Moran, puzzled, tentatively asks his informant, "Do you think he meant human life?"

It is not that the joke cancels its dark substance. A good irony never cancels anything. The joke offers its gloom as a temptation, as an excess of philosophy or despair, and its wit not as a consolation but as the mark of an impossibility. This *cannot* be said seriously, even if, as it must often have been for Beckett, it is just what we feel. The joke ruins generality, leave us only with awkward particular cases, all refusing to meet our shapely (or morose) specifications. "The silence at times is such," Malone says at one point in *Malone Dies*, "that the earth sees to be uninhabited. That is what comes of the taste for generalization. You have only to hear nothing for a few days, in your hole, nothing but the sounds of things, and you begin to fancy yourself the last of human kind."

Gags are rarer in Beckett's later writing, although they do recur in *Company* and *Ill Seen Ill Said*. "God is love. Yes or no? No." "A moor would have better met the case. Were there a case better to meet"; "unchanged for the worse." Perhaps he came to see them as a form of whistling in the dark: not an answer to pain but an attempt to pretend that it is less grueling than it is, a version of fraud. The only form to be found in his work, he told Harold Pinter, is that of a scream. Without the gags Beckett's writing is purer, and we must respect the austerity that pares them away. But purity has its dangers. Colm Tóibín distinguishes between the fiction and the plays in this respect, and I can't do better than quote him on this subject:

> These late masterpieces have not been helped by Beckett's later works for the theatre, which often seem flat and embarrassing parodies of his supposed views. Since both the plays and the fiction insist on brevity and lessness, it is easy to feel that they come from the same impulse and should be taken as part of the same process. But the late fictions are written with a sympathy for the human voice which is not in the later plays. It is a broken voice, full of memory, fresh thought and insight, and only too willing to stop and start, to offer us more words, further statements, the rhythm repetitious and mesmerizing. The prose is modulated with care: there is no time now for jokes or casual ironies.

No time for the style of the earlier jokes, and Beckett's ironies were never casual. As Ricks says, "Beckett's engagement is not with life's little ironies, but with death's large ones." But a lingering, spectral joke is there even in the sparest of pieces, inseparable from Beckett's identity as a writer. It doesn't humanize him, but it does remind us of what he is not saying. Even a phrase such as "imagination dead imagine" gets its late little flutter of cliché and music: "Imagination at wit's end spreads its sad wings." The joke, early or late, is not the icing on the solemn existential cake, it is an expression of one of Beckett's few necessary truths: We can't take ourselves seriously without getting ourselves wrong, but how else are we to take ourselves, given the seriousness of our plight? Beckett, to borrow two of his own wonderful phrases, was a dream-eaten, ghost-forsaken man, who wrote the human, almost inhuman comedy of ignorance; the master, as Dante did not say, of those who do not know.

At the hour of his death, if there is time and lucidity, Lucas will
ask to hear two things: Mozart's last quintet and a certain piano
solo on the theme of "I Ain't Got Nobody." If he feels there
won't be enough time, he'll only ask for the piano record. . . .
Out of the depths of time, Earl Hines will accompany him.

—Julio Cortázar, *A Certain Lucas*

3. *Politics in Paradise*

The Forgetting of Eden

The novel for Barthes looks back beyond the unkindnesses of twentieth-
century history, while history in Beckett dwindles to a world of scarcely identifiable echoes, from Goering and Dublin to Connolly's Stores and the make
of an ancient car. For Latin American writers history speaks loud and clear
and unkind, and it has two principal names: oppression and Cuba. After Castro's revolution in 1959, those names were antonyms for a while, and for Julio
Cortázar, for instance, they remained so. For other writers they became gris-
ly synonyms, and it is no doubt not an accident that the most emphatic of
these writers were Cubans.

Julio Cortázar's socialism was so full of mischief and so romantic that his
critics often wondered whether it was socialism at all. What are we to make of
terrorists who kidnap a penguin, as a group does in *A Manual for Manuel* (*Libro
de Manuel*, 1973)? Cortázar's implicit reply was a version of Orwell's argument
on the same theme: we don't make bitter sacrifices in order to build a world
even grimmer and more humorless than the one we have ruined.

Cortázar died in February 1984. He had become for many, as he said of his
own departed heroes, Chaplin, Cocteau, Duke Ellington, Stravinsky, a person
in whose death one dies a little. The death of the author was a metaphor for
Roland Barthes, and an illuminating one, meant to dethrone a gloomy and demanding (and mainly French) monarch, a tyrant of interpretation. But when
an author literally dies (when Roland Barthes died), we miss not his dark rule
but all the words that won't get written, all the thoughts that can't now come

into being. We still feel this, curiously, when we know quite well that a writer has dried up, did his or her best work long ago.

This aspect of loss was particularly marked in the case of Cortázar because he was such a restless and inquisitive writer. He published volumes of epigrams, memories, poems, fantasies. His novels often read like notebooks, full of gags and quotations and fugitive ideas. Only in his short stories did he immerse himself thoroughly in his imagined worlds, adopt the often slangy and elliptical idioms of his various characters with the amazing range and fluency he could call up when he wanted. For this reason his stories, or the best of his stories, seem to be his most substantial achievement. But his other writings matter too. In them he eloquently lived—as Barthes once said he hoped to— the contradictions of his time. Cortázar saw the writer not only as an artist but as a witness, partial, human, willing to learn, and he suggested that we need to see our world in the mirror of minds that care about it; that enjoy it, I want to add, as Cortázar enjoyed jazz, whisky, Robert Musil, politics, friendship, writing, particular forms of insolence or provocation. In *A Certain Lucas* (*Un tal Lucas*, 1979), Cortázar's central character attends a concert where a pianist throws himself "with his hands full of Khatchaturian at a completely defenseless keyboard," provoking rapturous enthusiasm in the audience. Lucas meanwhile is groping on the floor, searching under the seats. Asked by a lady what he has lost, he replies, "The music, madam."

Like all Latin American writers in the second half of this century, and more than most because he was Argentinian, Cortázar was influenced by Borges. He took from Borges a sense of the world as radically provisional, a flimsy structure both terribly unsound and strikingly durable. But where Borges is interested in the swaying edifice, the dizziness of order, Cortázar is concerned with everything the order excludes. He dreams, as many writers have, of *others*: twins, doubles, the rejected, the buried, the forgotten. Yet he dreams of them not in fear but with a welcoming generosity that becomes part of his signature. In "Distances," one of his finest stories, a well-off girl in warm Buenos Aires is haunted by and finally changes places with a ragged second self in Budapest, snow filling up her broken shoes as she trudges off across a bridge: schizophrenia as a redistribution of goods and sorrows.

Paradise is loss for Cortázar as for Borges (and for everyone else), but it is a loss construed not as an infinite and universal pathos but as an incipient politics, a promise of resistance to the world that is left to us. Horacio Oliveira, the central character in *Hopscotch* (*Rayuela*, 1963), offers the invention of Eden as a symptom of our continuing unease, a proof that the march of progress is not as straight as we think, that language and history and science may be masks we have made for our comfort. In the Spanish version of the game of hopscotch the space at the top of the chalk pattern is called "heaven," and the force of the figure in the novel lies in the fact that heaven, in this game, lies "on the same plane" as earth, distant perhaps but not theologically segregated, *allá lejos pero en el mismo plano*. The problem is that even in the game almost no one learns how to get to heaven before their childhood (and therefore the game) is over. Heaven lingers, like paradise, not only as the name of a real longing but as a longing for the real, for a sense of what political and personal life could be beyond the trivial mess we happen to have made of it.

This is not an easy vision—Cortázar, along with his writer-character Morelli, accepts the argument that most paradises are merely refusals of a current, available, disobliging world, of everything we dislike about the faces of power. The vision to be pursued is the fragile, disreputable insistence of the person who believes, against the odds, that other lives are historically possible, not simply an ideal or a fantasy. When Oliveira thinks of what he call his "kibbutz of desire," he accepts that he may well die without reaching it, but the kibbutz is there, distant but still there—*estaba allí, lejos pero estaba*. This is a paradise and a utopia; but more paradise than utopia, more a memory or a haunting than a plan. The utopia (still to be built) would need to be faithful to the memory and everything it represented. Here is the difficulty, the all but irresistible temptation to forget, and in the most dazzling and beautiful of the meditations on paradise contained in *Hopscotch*, Cortázar evokes Masaccio's Adam covering his face as he leaves the garden, because he realizes that his punishment includes not only the loss of Eden but the loss of the very memory of the place. The rather too casual and far too lofty joke at the end of the passage (about the drawbacks of labor and the boredom of paid holidays) suggests Oliveira's (or Cortázar's) edginess about his eloquence, but doesn't dilute what that eloquence says to us:

> I suddenly understand better the frightening gesture of Masaccio's Adam. He covers his face to protect his vision, what had been his; he preserves in that small manual night (*esa pequeña noche manual*) the last landscape of his paradise. And he cries (because the gesture is also one that accompanies weeping) when he realizes that it is useless, that the real punishment is about to begin: the forgetting of Eden, that is to say, bovine conformity, the cheap and dirty joy of work and sweat of the brow and paid vacations.

"The sign of a great short story," Cortázar says, "is what we might call its autarchy." And again: "It seems to me a form of vanity to wish to intervene in a story with something other than the story itself." Cortázar's own stories are closed, independent, "spherical," in his image; and they are even more delicate than these comments suggest, since he has the remarkable gift of seeming interested in everything except the twist or point of his tales, of lavishing such democratic care on every detail that nothing seems to be there simply to move the story along. Conversely, the frequent extravagances of these works are systematically underplayed.

An early piece called "Bestiary," for example, depicts a long sad summer on an Argentinian estate, three adults and two children locked in an apparent tedium that ripples with half-submerged threats and dangers, the whole thing recounted with Jamesian finesse from the point of view of one of the children. But the crucial fact, which Cortázar mentions only a few times, and in the most offhand way possible, is the tiger that lives on the estate and roams the house at will, taking whole floors and rooms out of use as it goes:

> Almost always it was Rema who went to see if they could go into the dining room with the crystal chandelier. The second day she came to the big living room and said they would have to wait. It was a long time before a farmhand came to tell them that the tiger was in the clover garden, then Rema took the children's hands, and everyone went in to eat.

In a later story, "Apocalypse at Solentiname," the narrator, in the person of Julio Cortázar, much travelled writer, recounts a visit to Costa Rica and Nicaragua:

> press conference with the usual business, why don't you live in your own country, why was *Blow-Up* so different from your short story, do you think the writer must be involved? At this point I know I shall be interviewed for the last time at the gates of hell, and the questions will obviously be the same, and if by chance I end up chez St Peter it won't be any different, don't you think that down there you wrote stuff that was too hermetic for the people?

Cortázar spends a day at Solentiname, a community founded by the poet and priest Ernesto Cardenal, and, much taken with some paintings the peasants there have done—fishes, lakes, horses, churches, infants—he photographs them. Back in Paris he projects the slides in his apartment and sees in horror, not Solentiname, but the other face of Latin America, shot after shot of torture, murder, terror, corpses, fleeing women, dying children. When his friend Claudine comes in and runs the slides through again, he can't watch, but the shock doesn't happen for her, she sees only pictures of the primitive, beautiful paintings he originally photographed. "They came out so well," she says, *Que bonitas te salieron.*

The chief sign of the delicacy of these stories, and of their power, is the avoidance of allegory where it seems virtually unavoidable. The prowling tiger, the dark side of the Latin American pastoral—these are the "meanings" in the stories, their paraphrasable point. But their movement doesn't really yield emblems or statements, tigers of anguish or lessons of contemporary history. It suggests rather the diffuse fragility of dining rooms and idylls, the possibility that the screens that shield us from historical and psychological horror could crack at any minute. What matters in the later story, for example, is not only what the slides show in Paris but the uncanny intimation that they could show anything, that the camera could pull such switches. Looking at faces as they emerge on polaroid prints in Nicaragua, for example, Cortázar wonders what would happen if other faces or figures were to appear, such as Napoleon on horseback.

As against the concentration and selection of the stories, Cortázar's novels are magnets that attract all kinds of random pieces of his life and reading: quotations, clippings, afterthoughts, memories, jokes, parallels. "In the years of *Hopscotch*," he wrote in an essay,

> the saturation was such that the only honest thing to do was simply to accept this torrent of meteorites which came in from the street, books, conversations, day-to-day accidents, and convert them into passages, fragments, necessary or optional chapters.

Similarly *A Manual for Manuel* is full of newspaper cuttings and statistics. "No one should be surprised," Cortázar says in his preface,

> by the frequent inclusion of news stories that were being read as the book was taking shape: stimulating coincidences and analogies caused me from the start to accept a most simple rule of the game, having the characters take part in those daily readings of Latin American and French newspapers.

62: A Model Kit (*62: Modelo para armar*, 1968), is a novel that Cortázar kept deliberately free of such intrusions—"anyone who knows me will realize how hard it was," he remarks—but then once the book was finished he wrote, with visible relief, an essay that brought out all the missing allusions and connections, the other life of the writing mind: Aragon, Nabokov, Rimbaud, an inscription found on a house close to Lake Como, essays by Bachelard and Merleau-Ponty.

In Cortázar's stories, fears, failures and illuminations are presented as facts, pieces of a puzzle that have fallen out into memorable configurations. In the novels the same things are argued about, converted into problems and negotiations, and at times one feels that Cortázar is seeking an alibi for a certain parsimony or restraint of sentiment, indeed perhaps for the clarity and austerity that allows him to write the stories as he does. It was right to hang back, to refuse that person, that passion, that cause, that devouring demand on your independence. Not that Cortázar refused all such demands; his politics prove that he didn't. But the novels are haunted, almost dominated by an anxiety about commitment. In *Hopscotch* a form of emotional avarice is presented as half-heroic, the stand of Stephen Dedalus against the ensnaring forces of church and state and family and love. In *A Manual for Manuel* the same quality is depicted as distraction and cowardice, but even there it is given an enormous amount of space in which to make itself appealing and to underline the drawbacks of the engaged life.

A Manual for Manuel is in many ways a revision of *Hopscotch*. Here as in the earlier work, there is group of fast-talking cronies living in Paris, mostly Latin Americans; once again a man is caught between two women, trying to believe that his vacillation is freedom; again, there is a small child; and again, a rage for allusions, which in this case first run from Stockhausen and Henry James to Judy Garland and Joni Mitchell but begin to converge on the grim facts of torture in Latin America, soberly recited, scarcely discussed. This last feature indicates something of the difference between the two novels, the careful separation of similarities. The group of cronies is not debating jazz and literature, as in *Hopscotch*, it is planning an operation called the Fuck, prudently translated as the Screwery, which is to culminate in the kidnapping of a high Latin American official in Europe, and the death of Marcos, the most attractive and authoritative of the cronies. The small child in *Hopscotch* dies; in the later work the child not only lives but represents all the playful and humane future these engaging subversives may not be able to bring about. He is Manuel, and it is in this sense that the novel is a book for him, the legacy of an adventure and a generation.

More literally, Manuel's mother is making him a scrapbook of multilingual newspaper cuttings, which includes plenty of details of political oppression, but also an inspirational quotation from Paracelsus and a number of items describing things such as the theft of nine thousand wigs by a group of Latin American guerillas, the two-months' prison sentence of a young Argentinian for "disrespect for the national anthem," and the advantages of fried sandwiches for weekend excursions. And in the place of Morelli, the tired but brilliant experimental writer of *Hopscotch*, there is the novelist himself, named only as "the one I told you," making ghostly exits and entrances, collecting data for his book, talking to his characters not as their author but as their friend and chronicler. The one I told you is said to have disappeared before the text reaches the form in which we read it, and the final compilation appears to have been made by one of the characters. The effect of this complicated, shifting confession of artifice is not to suggest that everything is fiction but to make us wonder what is and what isn't.

At the end of the book Marcos, dead, lies in the morgue where his close friend works. The friend says,

> Look at the way we came to meet here, nobody's going to believe it, nobody's going to believe any of all this. It had to be us, that's for certain, you there and me with this sponge, you were so right, they're going to think we made it all up.

These are the last words of the novel. The bitter coincidence, the occasion for the artful soliloquy, are made up, that is what we think. And the preliminaries to the grand kidnapping, which include a series of "microagitations" such as screaming in a Paris cinema just when Brigitte Bardot is about to display what the audience came to see, or eating standing up in a fancy restaurant, or importing a turquoise penguin from Argentina, ostensibly as a gift to the zoo at Vincennes, do not strike one exactly as bits of documentary truth. But then neither Cortázar nor his characters nor the one I told you made up Brazilian prisons, or American military and paramilitary aid to Latin America, or the urgency of the struggle against the uninvented miseries of half the globe. "We may need," the philosopher J. L. Austin once said, "the grace to be torn between simply disparate ideals." We could be torn, we are torn, between an ideal justice and an ideal lightness of heart.

Cortázar, I suspect, was enough of a metaphysician not to accept the line about disparate ideals. The whole direction of his work denies such divisions, the Screwery implies a liberation from every oppression that weighs on us, sexual, political, cultural, the rest. It is his sense of how much confusion and multiplicity an authentic revolution would have to accommodate that makes Marcos such a commanding figure, and that same sense governs Cortázar's novel, which is a running plea for frivolity in the midst of serious concerns. Thus screams in a cinema and the jet flight of a penguin lead directly to a risky kidnapping; practical jokes and political agitation are not to be locked away in separate zones; screwing and the Screwery are part of the same grand scheme:

> So much is done in jest and because of what we think is jest, and then the other thing begins afterwards and underneath there is a kind of surreptitious recurrence of the jest or the pun or the gratuitous act.

At one point, Marcos's friend from the morgue insists that everyone leave their solemn plotting and come to watch his poisonous mushroom grow. It is only the elect of the novel, like Marcos and one or two others, who understand the importance of this "idiotic comedy':

> In this idiotic comedy there was for Marcos something like a hope, that of not falling into too complete a specialization, that of keeping a little play, a little Manuel, in one's conduct.

This way, Cortázar's implication goes, the victorious revolution stands a chance of avoiding the repressions of tomorrow, of fending off all the Robespierres and Stalins who lurk behind the deadly earnest faces of today's good guys, those "fascists of the revolution," as another character calls them.

This is an attractive argument, and many fallen revolutionary regimes might have learned from it. A man who makes puns, a character in Stendhal says, cannot be an assassin, *le calembour est incompatible avec l'assassinat*. It depends on the puns, perhaps. The truth of this charming view is horribly incomplete—for every redeeming joke in the world there must be four or five assassins making puns as they go about their business—and it is not in the end a political view, or it is only the beginning of one. Robespierre and Stalin lacked a sense of humor, no doubt, but that was hardly their chief lack. Similarly, I suspect that the metaphysical union of all our longings into the Great Screwery is not only a strategic error but a possible aid to oppression. If everything has to be liberated at once, if paradise is the only alternative to what we have, many people will stay at home in their prejudices, daunted by the dizzying dimensions of the task or the travel. Sexual and political freedoms, for example, may have to be fought for on very different fronts. We do need the grace to be torn by disparate ideals, and never more so than when the distance between them seems endless.

Odor or Ardor

"Any resemblance between literature and history," Guillermo Cabrera Infante writes, "is accidental." He means, of course, to offer the familiar disclaimer of fiction, particularly since his novel *Three Trapped Tigers* (*Tres tristes tigres*, 1967), the work to which the remark is attached, mixes the names of living persons with those of transposed or invented characters: a Havana stew. But he also means to offer a provocation, a sly and long-armed distinction. History for Cabrera Infante is the domain of power and preening ambition, a nightmare into which countless people can't wait to hurl themselves and from which many will escape only into death. Is there such a thing, he wondered in an article published in 1983, as "the tedium of power," a weariness of history's heights? The question was rhetorical since he was suggesting that suicide has become a political ideology in Cuba, the result of a combination of hubris and disappointment. "Absolute power disillusions absolutely."

Literature on the other hand is a form of freedom, not because it deals with the imaginary but because it reconstructs the real in the mind, which is a protectable playground, a place that can (sometimes) be whisked out of the clutches of political practice. "Do you believe in writing or in scripture," a character asks in *Three Trapped Tigers*, *en la escritura o en las escrituras?* "I believe," his writer friend answers, "in writers," *en los escritores*. He believes, as Cabrera Infante himself says in *Infante's Inferno* (*La Habana para un Infante Difunto*, 1979), in "the flesh made Word." But then this makes the writer a very curious creature, a voluntary inhabitant not of Dante's hell but of Derrida's limbo, a paltry scribbling Plato to a host of voluble versions of Socrates. The writer is important not because he can write but because he can listen, and his job, Cabrera Infante says, is "to catch the human voice in flight." The epigraph to *Three Trapped Tigers* comes from *Alice in Wonderland*: "And she tried to fancy what the flame of a candle is like after it is blown out."

Writing is itself a memorial of loss for Cabrera Infante. It appears to trail along helplessly—actually it's far from helpless—after all the talk and song that he wants to celebrate, the noisy, irreverent Havana of the days before Castro. The pages of *Three Trapped Tigers* are full of phonetically transcribed chatter, rather in the manner of Raymond Queneau, one of Cabrera Infante's masters. T's are dropped as in Cuban speech, words and phrases are contracted, and American phrases and film stars (weekend, thank you, Bette Davis) appear in strange guises—*wikén, senkiu, Betedavi*. The effect is delicate, more complicated than it perhaps looks. We hear the voices we can't hear (because we're not there, because they're fictional, because writing is made of marks not sounds); we imagine or create them, develop an auditory world out of visual intimations. But then we do this only to register the overwhelming absence of the world we have just created, the flimsy and abstract poverty of any mixture of mere letters compared with the agility of the most humdrum human voice. Cabrera is not reinstating what Derrida would call the heresy of voice and presence, or at least he's not always doing that, and he is not denigrating writing. Writing is neither a lapse from authenticity nor a redemption of loss, it is a work of allusion to a necessarily absent life. Absent because this is writing, because we wouldn't be writing it if we were living it; but then this absence is a rehearsal for many others.

And yet writing too has its life. Even the character in *Three Trapped Tigers* who is repeatedly asked why he doesn't write turns out to be a writer—writing pieces of this book, no less, since he speaks of "this page I am writing"—and a central character's praise of unwritten literature, which he calls writing in the air, is accompanied by a love of graphic puzzles and gags that work only in writing. You can't say a palindrome backward; it sounds just the same as it did forward.

This ambiguity is beautifully caught in the two accounts of a record, which is all that remains now of the black singer La Estrella. She is alive here, one character thinks, in "that voice which the worms would never have for lunch because here it was singing now on the record, a perfect and ectoplasmic facsimile, dimensionless as a specter. . . . This is the original voice." Another character thinks the record is "mediocre," and that "this is definitely not La Estrella, and the dead voice of that godawful record has nothing to do with her own live voice." Who is right? Could they both be right? Is being right an issue, or a possibility? The second speaker is a writer, and the first is a musician.

It may be that the musician is the better writer here; that the record of La Estrella's voice is (a record of) her voice only if we recognize that it can't be. Writing and sound recording don't fail to catch human voices, and don't succeed either. They are what we have instead of or alongside voices, and they too are ephemeral, or ephemeral enough. Mechanically reproducible, repeatable; but also destructible, by time or violence or other more subtle forms of exclusion and suppression.

These voluble characters are doubly dead, then, because they die in the story, and in any case could only be whispers in a book, the flesh made alphabet. Yet this same sad tale may be a triumph of memory and continuing affection, a means of preserving treasures where history sees only trash. It is very much in this spirit that Cabrera Infante, in exile first in Brussels and now in London, reinvents his Cuba, which is mainly Havana, an excited, talkative, many-layered city, a scene of mauve and yellow light, of trolley cars and the gleaming sea, of rainstorms and stopped traffic and palm trees and a seemingly endless supply of beautiful women. As early as 1894, I learn from an old and rather prim *Encyclopaedia Britannica*, the city was famous for its hectic pursuit of pleasure:

> Cafes, restaurants, clubs, and casinos are both exceedingly numerous and largely frequented, forming a good indication of that general absence of domestic life . . . which surprises the European visitant.

The sentence might be an epigraph for *Three Trapped Tigers*, a celebration of interminable nights on the town. In *Infante's Inferno*, we do see something of

Cuban domesticity, the other side of a busy coin, and we spend a lot of time in the city's myriad movie houses.

Cabrera Infante was born in 1929, in Oriente province, which also nurtured Batista and Castro. His parents were committed communists, and he himself was active in the early days of Castro's revolution. He had already by that time become a film critic and founded the Cuban cinemathèque—later he wrote the script for a very good American film, *Vanishing Point*. From 1959 to 1961 he edited a magazine called *Lunés de revolución*, and a volume of stories called *In Peace as in War* (*Así en la paz como en la guerra*, 1960) brought him a substantial Cuban and European reputation. With *Three Trapped Tigers* he won a major Spanish prize and entered the front rank of Latin American novelists. The book belongs with Cortázar's *Hopscotch*, García Márquez' *One Hundred Years of Solitude* (*Cien años de soledad*, 1967), and Donoso's *The Obscene Bird of Night* (*El obscene pájaro de noche*, 1970), works that opened up a whole culture both to us and to its isolated or unwitting possessors, and made much of the writing in the rest of the world look rather skimpy. Cabrera Infante had meanwhile fallen foul of the censorship in Castro's Cuba and been sent out of harm's way to be cultural attaché in Brussels. Later he severed all connection with the Cuban government and became a British citizen, or subject, as we still quaintly put it.

He likes, he told Rita Guibert in *Seven Voices*, Bogart's trembling hands in *The Maltese Falcon*, Henry Fonda in *My Darling Clementine*, Marlene Dietrich as Catherine the Great, "Conrad's rancid prose," "Carroll's dream-language," "the radiance of the city in some pages of Fitzgerald," the music of Bach, Vivaldi, Wagner, Mozart, "the exact moment when Charlie Parker begins to play a solo," and "above all, the privilege of memory, without which none of the above would have any meaning." I am selecting from a much longer and very lively list. Characteristically, one of Cabrera Infante's complaints against Castro is that he has forced a loquacious people to become laconic.

"He didn't understand," the writer in *Three Trapped Tigers* says of a friend's response to a story. "He didn't understand that it was not an ethical fable, that I told it for the sake of telling it, in order to pass on a luminous memory, that it was an exercise in nostalgia. Without rancour towards the past." Cabrera Infante uses the last phrase earlier in the book, and it is a clue both to the particular qualities of his longer works of fiction and to the pleasure that reading them provides. Both *Three Trapped Tigers* and *Infante's Inferno* seem aimless and unstructured, the second even more so than the first, but they don't produce the irritation or boredom such appearances often promise. This is partly a matter of the frantically active language, to which I shall turn in a moment, but it is also a matter of the tone of remembrance, the way in which the imagination is used to animate old places and distant people.

Rancor toward the past is very common. If we feel it, we either can't talk about the past at all or can't look at it straight, can't stop rewriting it. Sometimes we are in love with the past, as Proust was, but then we need to be Proust in order to prevent it from slipping through our overeager fingers. Cabrera Infante is not anxious about his past, and he has nothing against it. His impulse is not exactly nostalgia, even though that is what his character in *Three Trapped Tigers* claims. His attention to the past is brighter and more energetic than nostalgia ever manages to be. He treats the past simply as if it were the present, as if it had never been away, as if all those now demolished movie houses and now dispersed friends and Havana itself had found a permanent home in his prodigious memory. His master is surely not Proust but Nabokov—"odor or ardor," Cabrera Infante wisecracks at one moment on the subject of his difficulties with loved women who give off too high a smell—for whom the past came when it was called, obedient, more than presentable, all its magical details intact. "The Past," Van Veen writes in *Ada, or Ardor*, "is a constant accumulation of images. It can be easily contemplated and listened to, tested and tasted at random." And without rancor.

This tender, circumstantial recreation is even more a feature of *Infante's Inferno* than of *Three Trapped Tigers*. "She flew away," Cabrera Infante writes of one woman, "and into my memory"; and of another he says, "It wasn't the last time I saw her—it's never the last time one sees anybody." The book begins,

> It was the first time I climbed a staircase. Few houses in our town had more than one floor, and those that did were inaccessible. This is my inaugural memory of Havana: climbing marble steps. . . . A breeze moved the coloured curtains that hid the various households: even though it was midsummer, it was cool in the early morning and drafts came from within the rooms. Time stopped at that vision . . . I had stepped from childhood into adolescence on a staircase.

We know quite a few things about this book without going any further. It is very well written, the work of a stylist; we may get a whiff of (not quite) rancid Conrad in the prose ("Only the young have such moments," he says in *The Shadow Line*). When Rita Guibert asked Cabrera Infante if he corrected much, he said "eternally." The focus of the writing is on a personal past, historical in the widest sense but likely to bear only tangential, or accidental resemblances to what we usually call history. Carlos Franqui appears frequently, for example, as an old friend of Cabrera Infante's, and a great mover in his Havana circle, but the overlap between this figure and the renowned political activist is very slim. The book's main character is a boy from the provinces, dazzled by the big city, and we learn before long that he will always be dazzled by it, is dazzled even now as he writes, and that if the city is no longer the heroine of the book, as it is in *Three Trapped Tigers*, it is still a major protagonist. "The city spoke another language," the boy thinks. "The streetlamps were so poor back home that they couldn't afford moths."

Infante's Inferno was translated into English by Suzanne Jill Levine in collaboration with Cabrera Infante, who cut out large chunks of the Spanish text and made all kinds of English additions, mainly jokes but sometimes afterthoughts. The English title itself is a new gag to replace the unmanageable Spanish original, which relies not only on Ravel and the similarity between *pavane* and Havana but also on the fact that the French for *infanta* is *infante*. The book takes the form of the discursive, erotic memoirs of the country boy, now grown up, a Cuban Casanova, at least in longing and memory, and occasionally, it seems, in practice. The boy is twelve when he arrives in the tenement with the imposing staircase, in his twenties and married by the end of the book. Cuba still belongs to Batista. Our hero meets girls and women among his neighbors; discovers surprising homosexual inclinations in a respectable man; glimpses sexual paradise in a window across a passage, thereby anticipating his later career as a (near-sighted) voyeur. He writes lyrically of masturbation, comically of his first fiasco in a brothel, associates Debussy with various dreams of seduction, describes in baroque and sometimes moving detail his pursuit of women in cinemas, his high hopes of clutches and nudges in the conspiratorial dark:

> My finger brushed the back of her seat, a few centimetres—less, millimetres—beneath the girl's bare back . . . I again passed my finger from left to right along the surf of her skin, going a little higher but not enough for her to feel the shadow of my hand. I don't remember her hair nor can I say why I didn't stay until she got up . . . but this back that night in the Alkazar pleasure palace presents itself as a unique vision. Surely life has mistreated her, time soiling, spoiling her splendour, the years disfiguring her face, but they can't age the memory: that back will always be on my mind.

He wasn't always as discreet as this at the movies, and the book ends with a brilliant fantasy on the subject, a mixture of Rabelais, Jules Verne, and a schoolboy joke. Groping in the lower depths of a woman in the appropriately called Fausto Theatre—a free-ranging exploration, unlike many other "sour gropes," as Cabrera Infante calls them—he loses first his wedding ring, then his watch, then his cuff links. They have fallen into the well of loneliness, and our narrator, flashlight in hand, goes in after them, Gulliver in another country, a journey to the center of the birth, and wakes from his dream, if it is a dream, with the moviegoer's familiar cry: "Here's where I came in."

Cabrera Infante and his Havana friends, once out of adolescence, were "crazy for culture," he says, and always making puns, "suffering insufferably from paranomasia as not only an incurable but contagious disease . . . mad echolalia." The years have not eased the illness, and Cabrera Infante continues unrepentantly to mangle language and to hop from one tongue to another like a cat on several hot tin roofs. Some of these jokes are so terrible that they seem heroic, make Groucho Marx and S. J. Perelman look like sedate defenders of the dictionary. "There was an old saw back home that said, 'The grass is where it's green.' It must be a rusty saw by now because I haven't heard it in ages"; "Whatever Zola wants, Zola gets," "lecher de main," "Daguerre c'est Daguerre." Other jokes are so cumbersome, so fiendishly worked for, that the noise of grinding machinery deafens all chance of laughter. Cabrera Infante's character admires Alida Valli and meets a young girl who resembles her. This permits him to say, "How green was my Valli." He likes the proximity of glance and glans so much that he mentions it twice. The "aisle of Rite" will perhaps be intelligible to those who have looked at maps of the South coast of England recently, and "a coup de data to abolish chaff" depends on Mallarmé's *Un coup de dés jamais n'abolira le hasard* turning into English (abolish chance) halfway through.

Still other gags seem wildly compulsive, a form of fiddling with the text, a buzzing that can't let things be, and they can be a genuine distraction. Why would we want to think of a "baptism of pale fire," or associate vacillation with vaseline? At other times the gags make wonderful, surprising sense, and whole worlds come tumbling down on top of each other, as they always do in the best of puns: "pathetic fellacy," "Billy the Kitsch." It is as if Humbert Humbert had got hold of all of Nabokov's prose and wouldn't let go.

Finally, though, Cabrera Infante's writing offers us a mixture of passionate memory and reckless athletics of language, time regained in an avalanche of associations. "Our works," Carlos Fuentes wrote, thinking of Cabrera Infante and one or two other contemporaries, "must be works of disorder: that is, works of a possible order, contrary to the present one." Cabrera Infante's disorder is that of the intelligence overwhelmed by gags that go to the head like drink; his possible order is that of the evoked past, a period that comes so thoroughly alive that its squandering by the present is itself a judgment on the reigning power, the reproach, without rancor, that literature makes to history.

Another Hell

Skunk hour, in Robert Lowell's well-known poem, is a time of jaunty, disreputable defiance. The skunks march up Main Street, ready to take over the town. They are the scavenger's answer to the poet's Miltonic despair. "My mind's not right," the poet says, and "I myself am Hell." The skunks don't say anything, they just dive into the trash, making both mind and Hell seem irrelevant, almost an indulgence. The human skunks in Reinaldo Arenas's novel *The Palace of the White Skunks* (*El palacio de las blanquísimas mofetas*, 1980) are too depressed and depleted for any such bravado. Survival for them is not defiance, it is part of the penance, what they are condemned to. For them the torment of Hell is not its pain or disorder but its obdurate sameness. Even another Hell would be a comfort, but there is no other:

> Another hell, another hell, maybe more monotonous, maybe even more suffocating, maybe even more disgusting and reprehensible than this one, but another one, at least. Now I see that hell is always what you can't reject. What's just simply there.

And yet there is a lurid life in the writing of these disasters, a genuine exuberance in the detailing of miseries. It's as if a Cuban version of Buñuel's *Los Olvidados* had been shot in brilliant technicolor.

Reinaldo Arenas was born in 1943, in rural Oriente Province, Cuba, and died in New York at the beginning of December 1990. At the age of fifteen he left home to join Castro's revolt against Batista, and in the early years of the revolution his literary talent was quickly recognized by established writers such as Lezama Lima and Piñera. He published a novel, *Celestino before Dawn* (*Celestino antes del alba*, 1967), revised and retitled as *Singing from the Well* (*Cantando en el pozo*, 1982). He wrote a second novel, *Hallucinations* (*El mundo alucinante*, 1970), but couldn't get it printed in Cuba, because of its treatment of homosexuality. The book appeared in Mexico in 1969 and was rapidly translated into French, English, German, Portuguese, Dutch, Italian, and Japanese. At this point Arenas was an international celebrity and virtually unknown at home. He published a book of short stories in Uruguay; he was arrested in Cuba on charges of immorality and corruption of minors, causing a public scandal and other, rather more baroque crimes, such as being "extravagant."

He escaped from prison but was arrested again and sent to a correctional camp for two years. Released, he lived in anonymity in Havana. He escaped from Cuba in 1980 and was able to rewrite and publish his confiscated work, notably two further volumes of the projected five-volume sequence begun with *Singing from the Well*: a *pentagonía*, as Arenas called it, a pentagony, an agony in five parts. *The Palace of the White Skunks* is the second novel in the sequence; *Farewell to the Sea* (*Otra vez el mar*, 1982) is the third. The fourth and fifth, *The Color of Summer* (*El color del verano*) and *The Assault* (*El asalto* were published in Spanish in the year of his death. Arenas lectured in the United States and elsewhere, while writing essays and a new novel, *The Doorman* (*El portero*, 1987). He still lived in considerable poverty on New York's West Side, then finally contracted AIDS, and committed suicide. Since his death a number of further works have been published, including an autobiography, *Before Night Falls* (*Antes que anochezca*, 1992). He was a profuse, imaginative, well-read, and disturbing writer, a traitor to silence, as he says of one of his characters; a novelist who sought to give voices to the voiceless, and not only the obviously voiceless, the visibly suppressed but also those victims and sufferers whose distress eludes us, perhaps because they are too many or because we can't read their muted style. In Arenas's fiction even the most cramped or muffled minds are lent a fabulous fluency: no sorrow is left unturned.

Old Rosa (*La vieja Rosa*), composed of two novellas written in 1966 and 1971, is described as a novel in two stories, and this is, in miniature, a picture of how Arenas's whole fictional opus works: consciousness flows from book to book, characters change, die, disappear, but the story continues. Severo Sarduy writes of Arenas's "recurrent and musical" narrative, of his novels as one "long uninterrupted sentence," but also insists on the play of different voices, each character having his/her own rhetoric and images and obsessions. The author is a ventriloquist, projecting his life into a tissue of other, imagined minds, but those minds are possibilities, extensions of a plight, not mere duplications in another key. One thinks of Lorca depicting a house full of desperate women in *The House of Bernarda Alba*; the desperation was theirs and his, and indeed in one register the desperation of a whole country. It is in this sense that Arenas's claim that he is writing "the secret history of the Cuban people" is not as extravagant as it looks. The secret is not in the events but in the mentalities. Similarly, when Arenas says his novel *Hallucinations* recounts the life of the Mexican monk Fray Servando Teresa de Mier "as it was, as it may have been, as I should have liked it to have been," he is not offering those perspectives as alternatives. The book aims for all three, and this is why Arenas can say he wants it to be, rather than a historical or a biographical novel, simply a novel. His pentagony is both a sequence of autobiographical novels and a sequence of . . . novels.

The old Rosa of the title story is a land-owner who sets fire to her house and herself in a rage of frustration at a world that has escaped her control. Rosa is tough and pious, and drives her husband to suicide by rejecting, after her third child, all his sexual approaches; her very prayers are said to sound like orders. But now the Cuban Revolution has taken her fields and her elder son; her daughter has married a black man and gone to live in the city; her younger, favorite son is gay. She meets, in the shape of an encroaching hallucination, an angel who represents all the desire and grace and happiness she has refused in her life, and refused, she now sees, for nothing. She thinks the angel may be the Devil come to mock her, feels she has "been swindled all her life," grasps "the dimensions of an immeasurable solitude." But then she recognizes the rigidity and hollowness even of her renunciation, the way her religion has allowed her to deceive herself. The angel is a more intimate, less official enemy, a Catholic's version of Henry James's beast in the jungle, which turns out to be sheer emptiness, the terrible adventure of having no life at all: "But you're not the Devil she said finally, and now her words seemed to stumble upon the terrifying answer. You are something worse. You are nothing." At this moment the house begins to burn and Rosa and the angel are consumed together: "the figures . . . no longer were distinguishable."

The opening of "Old Rosa" affords a very good glimpse of Arenas's style:

> In the end she went out to the yard, almost enveloped in flames, leaned against the tamarind tree, and began to cry in such a way that the tears seemed never to have begun, but to have been there always, flooding her eyes, producing that creaking noise, like the noise of the house at the moment when the flames made the strongest posts totter and the flashing frame came down in an enormous crackling that pierced the night like a volley of fireworks.

There is quite a bit more than we need here—the fireworks weaken the picture rather than strengthen it, and the "enormous crackling" seems mere bombast compared to the discreet, domestic "creaking noise"—but the ancient weeping and the transfer of the creaking from fire to tears, masked as a simple simile, are very powerful, and Arenas prolongs this scene with a string of conditional, bifurcating notions that place us both inside and outside it. Rosa looks like a little girl in the sort of story "she had never read;" if a neighbor had passed, he/she would have seen that this was Old Rosa; but if Rosa had screamed, no one would have heard her for the sound of the fire. Rosa might have thought,

My God, this is hell, and she might have prayed, but she didn't. The effect is to set up fleeting, parallel fictions, other Rosas; to make writer and reader Rosa's allies but also to remind them of their difference from her, the books they have read, what they themselves might have thought, their safety from the fire.

Arturo, in the second story in the book, is Rosa's youngest child, now in a Cuban camp for homosexuals. Like Rosa, he is dying as the story begins and ends. He has been shot while trying to escape, and the text recounts his various strategies for survival in the camp, and meditates on the strange collusions that power exacts from weakness. Arturo separates himself mentally from the other prisoners, from what he sees as "their world . . . their repulsive lives . . . their endless, stupid conversations, with their exaggerated, effeminate, affected, ar-tificial, false, gross, grotesque posturings," but the very language suggests the fragility and anxiousness of the separation, and we learn that Arturo has be-come an expert mime of every stereotyped gay gesture because he thinks "it's easy to fit in anywhere, slip into any reality at all, as long as you don't take it seriously, as long as you secretly scorn it":

> Arturo did begin to use that affected, dizzying slang of theirs, begin to cackle
> and howl with laughter like any ordinary queen, to sing, pose, shadow his eyes
> and dye his hair . . . until he had mastered, come to possess, all the cant, every
> typical movement and feature of the imprisoned gay world.

But does Arturo scorn this world? Can he, should he? What bothers him about "them," the other prisoners, is their agile complicity with the system that persecutes them, their ability to "trivialize the pain":

> they would do anything, suffer any terror, turn the other cheek to any insult, and
> immediately incorporate it into the folklore, the customs, the daily calamities,
> yes, they had a gift for transforming terror into familiar ritual.

One hardly knows whether to admire or despair of such a gift. "Leopards break into the temple," Kafka wrote in a parable Arenas is perhaps thinking of here, "and drink to the dregs what is in the sacrificial pitchers; this is repeated over and over again; finally it can be calculated in advance, and it becomes part of the ceremony."

Like Rosa, Arturo sees an angel, only this is a benign figure, an ideal future companion, the prince who will one day redeem all the dross and mess of or-dinary, disfigured life. Arturo has found an escape in writing, in imagining a fabulous alternative world where there are brilliant, precious palaces and fountains and music, and rows of stately elephants; a dwelling worthy of the angel. But is this an escape? Don't all such escapes confirm the very prison they seek to deny? Where else but in penury would one dream up such riches? These are the questions the story is designed to pose. Is it true, for example, that "reality lies not in the terror one feels and suffers but in the creations that overpower that terror, and wipe it out," and who could answer this question for us? Or is the dead, tortured body of a fellow prisoner the ultimate, absolute real, erasing all fond fantasies and visions? Is time another such reality, "aggressive, fixed, unyielding, unbearable"? We can't deny the second, harsher reality; can't want to undersell the power and freedom of the imagination, even harassed, even imprisoned. Not too long before his internment Arturo was "still convinced that a cluster of signs, a cadence of images perfectly described—words— might save him." The tense suggests he is no longer convinced, but the signs are what he has, and he dies having "reached the monumental row of stately, regal elephants" that frames this story like a frieze formed of Arturo's writing. He has died, that is, into his fantasy; not saved but not simply canceled.

The two stories make a novel not just because they narrate the ends of two members of the same family, and not just because Arturo, about to be killed, confuses the brutal camp lieutenant with his mother, places her at the head of the shooting party. She is "the only person who had ever loved him," but she had also tried to kill him on discovering his sexual orientation. She is the un- avoidable, the prison behind the prison. But the novel puts the two characters together on another, non-narrative plane. They meet different angels, but em- body the same despair, the same feeling of being "condemned to live in a world where only frustration made sense and had a place."

This world is historical, not some eternalized human condition; but it is not simply Cuba in the 1950s and 1960s. It is every (historical) world that regu- larises repression, makes difference and deviance routinely punishable. Many of Arenas's commentators and fans cheerfully insist on the counterrevolution- ary, antiprogressive tendency of his writing, as if it was all right to be a florid reactionary as long as you were against Castro. But it is the subversive quality of the writing that seems to me most notable, its refusal not of progress or rev- olution but of a rigid correctness, of sentimentality and bullying. It is writing that seeks to construct, as Juan Goytisolo says, "a habitable mental space" against the political and moral odds. The mere possibility of such a space is enough to make many people, on the left and on the right, want to invade it, abolish it.

All of Arenas's skunks dream and some of them dream novels, pour their imaginations on to paper. Their minds are not right, but their world is not right either; their very unhappiness is a form of protest. At the center of *The Palace of the White Skunks* is Fortunato, a boy who, like Arenas, runs off to join the rebels in 1958. Like Arturo, Fortunato has discovered in writing a promise of salvation; but not only for himself. He is "like a lightning rod for terror," he thinks, "for terror in all its variety," and he insists that he has been all the members of his desolate family, that he is the emissary of their song, their isolation. Thus he has been his bitter grandfather, a Spaniard who emigrated to Cuba from the Canary Isles; his pious, crazed grandmother; his spinster aunt, interminably locked in the bathroom; his married aunt, abandoned by her husband, returned home with two children to care for; those two precocious, misbehaving children themselves; his other aunt, haunted by her dead daughter, who committed suicide at thirteen; that daughter too. "Many times—all the time really—he had been all of them, and he had suffered for them, and perhaps when he had been them (for he had more imagination than they did, he could go beyond the mere here-and-now) he had suffered more than they, deep within himself, deep within his own, invariable terror." The one person he hasn't been, can't be, is his mother, who has gone off to work in the United States. She is Fortunato's betrayer and only fixed resource; he would love her if his resentment would let him.

"All the time really" is a Nabokovian gag, reminding us that all these creatures are written, inhabitants of the imagination of Fortunato/Arenas, since he is, doubly, the only voice they have: because their pain would otherwise go unrecorded, and because they are fictional anyway. Fictional, but not without live counterparts, and most of them drawn, I assume, from models found in Arenas's childhood in the Cuban countryside and in the town of Holguín. Like Arenas's Mexican monk, Fortunato's family is both inside and outside the mind of the memorialist: as it is, as it might have been, and as he revamps it. There is of course something self-serving and self-deluding in Fortunato's sense of his mission: how could he suffer more than the others do? He is too much in love with his job as scapegoat, and his "deep, invariable terror" seems overwritten, however genuine and constant the terror might basically be. But then he is young, and Arenas hasn't written him ironically.

He hasn't written any of this book ironically, he has written it lyrically ("The moon, soundlessly, silvers the edge of the blinds, makes pale tracery on the photographs"), making excess and stylistic risk a kind of signature. Certainly there has to be a danger of coyness in a novel that begins "Death is out there in the backyard, playing with the wheel off a bicycle." What staves off the coyness, leaves us with just the danger, is the intensity and detail of the evoked reality (the broken, once much-ridden bicycle rather than the allegorical reaper) and the intelligence of the narrator's reflections on what is happening, the sense of a mind trying to make sense of miserably fragmented lives, battered by poverty and strangled desire. "But what was God for them? God was above all the possibility of crying their lamentations, their only real possibility. God offered them the occasion, which all men and women need if they are not to become absolute monsters, of being children from time to time, with their whining and their complaints, their anger, their fits of tears." There are grim jokes too, as when the grandmother is described as "screaming 'I can't take it anymore' till you can't take it anymore." Arenas has been reading Joyce and Rimbaud, makes a whole section of the work a phantasmagoric play in the manner of the "Circe" chapter of *Ulysses*, echoes the prose poems of *Illuminations*. He plays with the layout of the page, inserting paragraphs of comment from the characters in small corners of different print; quotes film announcements and beauty advice; reworks revolutionary bulletins from late 1950s.

Fortunato also has the nightmare I have associated with Henry James—"the certainty that nothing, not even something terrible, would ever truly happen to him"—and one of his aunts longs for "the consolation of some terrible disgrace, some awful misery, some unbearable bad luck." Fortunato/Arenas grants her her wish, sends her patrolling the streets looking in vain for a man, has her beaten, robbed, thoroughly humiliated. And Arenas saves Fortunato from his nightmare by having him arrested by Batista's troops, tortured, allowed to run free, and then shot and hanged. This is a place where "the interpreting ceases," Fortunato thinks. "And all the games vanish, and all the flights, all the escapes crash into each other and fuse, burst, and form a hard brick wall." Except that they don't, at least not in fiction, and not in the mind of anyone prepared to remember or imagine the missing. Everyone dies many times, and Arenas allows Fortunato and his young cousin a talkative life after death, so he knows that something terrible has happened to him; and will go on happening to him, since hell is all there is and ever was. Even happy or beautiful moments feed the horror. "Everything becomes golden, fleeting, glorious," the narrator reflects, "so that one would think the world was made to be lost." But then it is made (again and again) before it is lost, and Arenas's writing offers us the drama of the making as well as the document of the ruin.

Farewell to the Sea is part prose, part free verse, full of parody and phantasmagoria; a successor to Lezama Lima's novel *Paradiso*, a sort of Cuban cousin of Pound's *Cantos*, and it also draws quite heavily on Joyce's *Ulysses*. Its energy lies in the tortured consciousness of its two main characters and also in its profuse spray of language, its harsh and mocking incantation of sorrows and pains, life in the world that is being lost.

Hector, a diffident, disaffected veteran of the final struggle against Batista, and his unnamed, loving, frustrated wife have taken a cabin by the sea for a week. Their eight-month old baby is with them, they want to spend time away from the crowding and routine and hopelessness of life in Havana. The date is 1969. First we learn of the wife's thoughts through a long, sinuous interior monologue, full of cramped memories and violent, unsatisfying dreams—at one point she turns a scene from the *Iliad* into a wild sexual orgy, heroic phalluses everywhere. She has sudden, evanescent moments of happiness too, and her perceptions are captured very precisely:

> The sky and the smell of time, the smell of leaves, the singed smell of earth that was waiting today too for a cooling shower, for rain. Perfume. The smell of trees that take darkness as a comfort. The smell of ocean and pine trees, the imperceptible fragrance of oleanders, the smell of almond trees. The smell of the ocean . . .
>
> But what I would really like to preserve, have, is exactly that which vanishes—the brief violet of evening on the water, the last gleam of the pines, the moment when a yagrumo leaf flutters and falls, a smile of my mother's that I never saw again afterward.

But mainly this woman is defeated, uncertain, anxious for a consolation she only half believes in. "Somewhere there must be more than this violence and loneliness, this stupidity, laziness, chaos, and stupor which are killing us." "The terrible," she thinks in a memorable phrase, "becomes merely monotonous." "Real disaster never comes suddenly, because it's always happening." She understands though that in Cuba as elsewhere it is possible to blame public events for private griefs:

> We take advantage of the horrible state of affairs to avoid our own horrible situation . . . we denounce the implacable censorship so as not to discuss our own silences.

Neither she nor Hector believes in words—"There are no words, there are no words, there definitely are no words"—and yet words are all they have, the silent, mental spinning out of their loneliness.

Hector is a poet—or was before he lost his hope or his will and stopped writing—and his portion of the book is a buzzing mixture of verse and prose, of rhetoric and self-scrutiny. "All she wants," he thinks of his wife, "is for you to want her. She is so tender, so unbearable." He plays happily with his child, launches great diatribes against the Cuban situation. He has an encounter with a handsome boy on the beach, and then afterward makes a grim, self-lacerating prophecy:

> You will live your whole life pleading, begging pardon of the whole world for a crime you haven't committed, and doesn't even exist. . . . You will always be the safety valve, in a way, for any era—for all eras . . . you will be the world's shame. And the world will use you to justify its failures and discharge its fury. . . . For you there are only jail cells and work camps where you'll meet people like yourself, but much worse—and you will, of course, have to become like them.

The boy later commits suicide by throwing himself from a cliff.

Hector has milder lyrical moments, usually associated with the sea—"for the sea is the memory of some holy thing which we cannot comprehend," the sea is "unsmirched by legends, curses or offerings"—and he has his memorable phrases too—"all that is not trivial is damned." But mainly his thoughts are "offensive and offended," as his wife thinks his speech is. He often sounds like a hysterical version of Eliot's Prufrock, whom he both quotes and parodies:

> Let's go, then
> hand in hand, to take
> a walk, make a face, and babble
> nonsense, dancing the jig
> around this emptiness.

He arraigns Whitman for his easy hope—

> Ah, Whitman, ah, Whitman,
> how could you not have seen the hypocrisy
> behind the mask of an act of mercy? . . .
> I refute your poetry by that single and eternal disproportion
> between what is possessed and what is desired

—but he also has more local, particular complaints, bitterly listing what he calls the privileges of the present system in Cuba:

> Writing a book on cutting sugarcane and winning the National Poetry Prize;
> Writing a book of poetry and being sent to cut sugarcane for five years . . .
> Concentration camps exclusively for homosexuals . . .
> Song festivals without singers . . .
> The child as a field of police experimentation . . .

Tamarind trees felled to plant tamarind trees;
Betrayal of ourselves as the only means of survival . . .

How closely are we to associate Hector with Arenas? I take it Arenas wants
us to note the shrillness of Hector's thoughts, their whining tone, his self-pity
and his failure to distinguish, in itemizing his complaints, between hurt flesh
and wounded vanity. Arenas wants us to see too that some of what Hector
finds in Cuba are only what he grimly calls "the era's standard adornments:
bombs, shots, arguments, shouts, threats, torture, humiliation, fear, hunger"—not confined to Cuba, but not banished from Cuba either. As with the
passage on Whitman ("that single and eternal disproportion"), an elegant parody of the chorus from a Greek tragedy puts part of the blame not on politics
but on the species:

> Man
> is of all vermin the most loathsome,
> for convinced that all things
> go to irrevocable death,
> he kills . . .
> Ah, man
> a doubtful, laughable thing
> that merits our most suspicious
> observation—having invented God, philosophy,
> and other punishable crimes . . .

The point, finally, is not that Hector must be right or wrong but that he must
be heard; if he can't be heard he is already more than halfway right, evidence
for his own exorbitant case. Unhappiness can be unjust, wild in its accusations,
a skunk's idea of hell. But it can scarcely be unfelt, and it is an impeccable argument against paradise.

an obscure world

> Of things that would never be quite expressed,
> Where you yourself were never quite yourself
> And did not want or have to be . . .
>> —Wallace Stevens, "The Motive for Metaphor"

Like parodies of themselves, theological notions are reflected in
the triviality of our lives.   —Milan Kundera, *Slowness*

4. *The Motive for Metaphor*

The word *idyll*, Milan Kundera says, in *The Art of the Novel* (1986) is "rarely
used in France but a concept important to Hegel, Goethe, Schiller: the condition of the world before the first conflict; or beyond conflicts; or with conflicts
that are only misunderstandings, thus false conflicts." It's an admirable notion,
Kundera thinks, but only on condition that we do not attempt to realize it. Once
we do that we enter a realm of terrible deceptions and repressions, and actually reverse the meaning of the term, since we create a world that is *all* conflict,
but conflict unacknowledged, inadmissible. In *The Book of Laughter and Forgetting* (1979) Kundera identifies as an "idyll" an attempt to recreate a "garden
where nightingales sing, a realm of harmony where the world does not rise up
as a stranger against man nor man against other men." And where anyone who
doesn't like the garden must be a traitor, has to be put in one of the garden's increasing number of prisons, "caught and squashed between the fingers like an
insect." This simile alone—insects presumably had full rights of residence in
Eden—hints at the garden's problems and at its ignorance of its own contradictory ecology. The Prague Spring of 1968, Kundera suggests, was an attempt
to revoke this idyll, to deny and rewrite this grotesque and premature grasping
at Eden.

In *The Unbearable Lightness of Being* (1984) Kundera looks at the word *idyll*
in another context and ponders its connection to paradise:

> Raised as we are on the mythology of the Old Testament, we might say that an
> idyll is an image that has remained with us like a memory of Paradise.

And paradise is the capacity to be happy, not bored, with monotony, with repetition. As animals are, "because only animals were not expelled from Paradise." "The longing for Paradise is man's longing not to be man." Paradise then is not exactly a longing for repetition but a longing for another, nonhuman relation to repetition; a world without repetition's alternative, without knowledge of the irrevocable, of the once-and-for-all changes that are the very condition of our conscious (and indeed our physical) life. These changes occur to animals too, of course, but (we assume) they don't interpret them as we do. They think perhaps, they interpret behavior; but they don't register change or time, or they register them lightly, merely as the necessary means of measuring continuity and return. Paradise is theirs and can't be ours; the Fall is not the fruit of sin, it is mere mortality and the consciousness of it; the world of the forgiving novelist.

The novelist does more than forgive, in Kundera's view. He remembers, but is attached neither to Eden nor its opposite. He discovers "dimensions of existence" that are at risk, buried or banished by a busy progressive world. His first incarnations are Rabelais and Cervantes, and he is almost always a European, although North Americans and Mexicans are allowed as nonresident contributors (Kundera defines a European as "one who is nostalgic for Europe"). Since the novel is "grounded in the relativity and ambiguity of things human, the novel is incompatible with the totalitarian universe." No novels are written under totalitarian governments? Yes, but they are not novels in Kundera's sense, because "they fail to participate in the *sequence of discoveries* that for me constitutes the history of the novel" (Kundera's italics). "The novel's spirit is the spirit of complexity." It is "by definition, the ironic art." In a novel, Kundera says, sounding like Philip Sidney, "no one affirms." "Once it is part of a novel, reflection changes its essence: a dogmatic thought turns hypothetical." A novel sets "different emotional spaces side by side" and creates a "fascinating realm where no one owns the truth and everyone has the right to be understood." Doesn't this begin to sound a bit like an idyll? Where are the conflicts, the dogmas even, that would make this place something other than a heaven of intellectual laissez-faire, that would test the tolerances that are being so happily praised?

In a later book of essays, *Testaments Betrayed* (1993), written directly in French, Kundera says, "Suspending moral judgement is not the immorality of the novel, it is its morality"—or its moral, or its morale, since the French word is *morale*. There is no room for hatred in a novel, which is—Kundera is speaking of Rushdie's *Satanic Verses*—an "immense carnival of relativity." The novel is again always ironic, nonaffirmative:

Irony means: none of the affirmations found in a novel can be taken by itself each of them stands in a complex and contradictory juxtaposition with other assertions, other situations, other gestures, other ideas, other events.

This all sounds very familiar, like a reinvention of Lionel Trilling's *Liberal Imagination*; entirely understandable, given Kundera's experience of a totalitarian world, but not going beyond a certain allegory of freedom of speech. Two further thoughts, however, give this argument an edge and take it into interesting new territory, an undisputed but ill-defined strip of culture placed somewhere between literature and philosophy.

The first thought is that the novel is this sense is not just dying, in the East as in the West, but is dead without our having noticed, as God dies in Nietzsche's fable about the madman:

> The death of the novel is not just a fanciful idea. It has already happened. And we now know *how* the novel dies: it's not that it disappears; it falls away from its history. Its death occurs quietly, unnoticed, and no one is outraged.

Lukács and Eliot would have been quite at home with this language. There are novels still, but they are not novels. They don't live up to what novels were or could be; and the fault is ours. But Kundera doesn't believe the novel is actually dead, he's just trying to scare us:

> If the novel should really disappear, it will do so not because it has exhausted its powers but because it exists in a world grown alien to it.

We get, or shall get, the non-novels we deserve.

And this is not just because we are insufficiently tolerant or ironic and have lost our sense of humor, as Kundera repeatedly asserts. It is because we have become deaf to the one really interesting task of the novel as Kundera defines it, which is indeed a task that most contemporary stories, with their dedication to surprise and marvel and mystery, cannot do for us. The novel since Flaubert is a refusal of theatricality, an evocation of what is "banal, ordinary, quotidian," what is "random, or mere atmosphere." If novels exist to remind us of what we forget, *this* is what we forget best. We don't know the present moment as it passes but only once it is past. And what we then remember is something else. "The present moment is not like the memory of it. Memory is not the negative of forgetfulness. Remembering is a form of forgetting." In this context it is the novel's business, its "ontological mission" to recover for us what Kundera beautifully calls "the prose of life': "there is nothing so thoroughly disputed as the prose of life." The novel can do this, Kundera suggests, without the old apparatus of nineteenth-century realism, and without succumbing to the merely psychological:

> But understand me: If I locate myself outside the so-called psychological novel, that does not mean that I wish to deprive my characters of an interior life. It means only that there are other enigmas, other questions that my novels pursue primarily.

If a novel has an ontological mission, does it become philosophy? Kundera finds the notion of philosophy "inappropriate": "Philosophy develops its thought in an abstract realm, without characters, without situations." But then his discussions of Nietzsche, in *Testaments Betrayed* and elsewhere, make philosophy sound just like a novel. Kundera says he looks for particular words (tenderness, vertigo), turns them over, defines them in relation to his characters: tenderness is "the fear instilled by adulthood," the creation of "a tiny artificial space in which it is mutually agreed that we would treat others as children"; vertigo is "the intoxication of the weak." He calls the business of investigating words (and characters and situations) "meditative interrogation" or "interrogative meditation." Sounds more like philosophy than like many a good novel. Kundera goes on to say his narrative/verbal "definitions" are "neither sociological nor aesthetic nor psychological." His interviewer proposes "phenomenological" as a possibility, which Kundera courteously says is not bad, but refuses all the same.

We are left, I think, with fiction that must be philosophical in some sense but won't call itself that. Kundera attributes to Hermann Broch "a new art of the *specifically novelistic essay* . . . hypothetical, playful or ironic" (Kundera's italics). Tone is very important in this context—Kundera calls his own tone playful and ironic, like Broch's, and adds "provocative, experimental, or inquiring." His essay on Kitsch in the sixth part of *The Unbearable Lightness of Being* is, he says, not only part of the novel but "unthinkable" outside a novel: "there is a great deal of reflection, experience, study, even passion behind it, but the tone is never serious." What is seriousness? It is, Kundera suggests in his introduction to his play *Jacques and His Master*, what literary critics can't do without, the ingredient whose absence drives them to panic. But fiction, in Kundera's terms, can't be serious. "Serious is what someone is who believes what he makes others believe." A novelist who was serious in this sense would be in bad shape: "no novel worthy of the name takes the world seriously." Kundera's distinction between writers and novelists, likely to prove rickety in any detailed or strenuous development, is helpful here. A writer, he says, has "original ideas and an inimitable voice." He may write novels but whatever he writes, those ideas and that voice are what matter. The novelist "makes no great issue of his ideas" and is interested not in his voice but in the interplay between form and whatever aspects of existence he is anxious to explore. Rousseau, Goethe, Chateaubriand, Gide, Camus are writers in this theory. Fielding, Sterne, Flaubert, Proust, Faulkner, Calvino are novelists, and we know where to place Kundera, even if Calvino, in spite of Kundera's naming him here, begins to slip away from the fold. The appeal and the challenge, as Kundera says, thinking of Musil and Broch, would be "not to transform the novel into philosophy" but to bring to bear on the novel "a sovereign and radiant intelligence." We may think of Musil's "essayists," who are both personality types and possible writers:

> Their domain lies between religion and knowledge, between example and doctrine, between amor intellectualis and poetry, they are saints with and without religion, and sometimes too they are simply men who have gone out on an adventure and lost their way.

In a 1983 interview reproduced in *The Art of the Novel*, Kundera revealed many of the secrets of the confection of his work: approach to character, use of ellipsis and counterpoint, themes that are said to function in the manner of Schoenberg's tone-row, fondness for seven-part structures and for early announcements of the deaths of his central figures. The talk seemed to be an analytic farewell to fiction. Surely the speaker was about to enter a monastery, return to music, devote himself entirely to literary criticism. After such knowledge, what creativity? In fact, he had just finished *The Unbearable Lightness of Being* and was about to embark on another novel, unashamedly constructed on the same principles as the earlier work, full of ellipsis, counterpoint, recurring theme-words, announcing a death long before the end, and divided into seven parts. The result, *Immortality* (1991), allowing for a little excessive winsomeness here and there and a dip or two into shallow pop sociology, is a triumph, a proof that novelists don't need to keep secrets from themselves. Or that self-consciousness doesn't have to be crippling, opposed to an awareness of the world.

Characters in Kundera acquire psychologies and histories, but they start out and continue to function chiefly as images, provocations: a man staring at a wall, or repeating a phrase; a woman arguing, putting on her glasses, shaking her head; a girl sitting in the middle of a major road amidst rushing traffic.

These images are not illustrations of preformed thoughts, but neither are they simply pieces of novelistic behavior. They are meetings between persons and notions, or, more precisely, written, recreated, invented records of such meetings. "I have been thinking about Tomas for many years. But only in the light of these reflections did I see him clearly. I saw him standing at the window of his flat." An elderly woman leaving a swimming pool makes a young woman's gesture of goodbye:

> Her arm rose with bewitching ease. It was as if she were playfully tossing a brightly coloured ball to her lover. . . . The instant she turned, smiled and waved . . . she was unaware of her age. The essence of her charm, independent of time, revealed itself for a second in that gesture and dazzled me. I was strangely moved. And then the word Agnes entered my mind. Agnes. I had never known a woman by that name.

Who are Agnes and Tomas? Who is "I"? Well, "I" is a textual version of Milan Kundera, author of the novel we are reading and of other, mentioned novels—*Life Is Elsewhere* (1973), for example. He is not of course writing before our very eyes, and he is not exactly reporting on the way he writes. He is miming the art of the novel, producing for us a picture of the sort of interest a character has for him; not unraveling fictions but showing us how they get raveled, why he cares about them and why we might care too. It is an old realist prejudice, a strategy now worn thin and seen to be unnecessary, to claim that we can't weep for characters we know to be invented. What matters about characters, in and out fiction, is whether their needs are real to us, whether we are able to imagine their lives.

Agnes and Tomas are not mere projections of Kundera, other selves or masks of Kundera, in spite of his saying that the characters in his novels are his own "unrealized possibilities": "A character is . . . an imaginary being. An experimental self." The experiment, as the rest of Kundera's discussion makes clear, concerns selves other than the writer's, sympathetic guesses at what goes on in other minds and hearts. Nor are Agnes and Tomas mere compilations of people Kundera has known; or pure fictions (whatever that might mean). They are explicitly what characters in novels implicitly always are: ways of acting and understanding brought together in a story, given names. They are possibilities of conduct, as Kundera also suggests, but they are more than possibilities, since the word may imply an indulgence in unanchored speculation, the unbearable lightness of sheer frivolity. There are things to be said in defense of frivolity, and Kundera says them well; but we shouldn't undersell fiction in this respect. Agnes and Tomas, like all memorable characters in novels, are fragments of history, real and imagined, collected and recomposed in language. They resemble people we have met and, better still, people we have yet to meet.

Kundera, or "Kundera," expounds a theory about character in *Immortality*, suitably wrapped in irony and questionable context but powerful all the same. He distinguishes between the Latin notion of reason (*ratio, raison, ragione*) as inescapable rationality and the German *Grund* (ground, basis). We have reasons for our actions, Kundera is suggesting, we inspect motives and causes, but we also have grounds, deeper, irrational inscriptions governing much of our behavior. A Freudian would wonder why Kundera was avoiding the notion of the unconscious, and various jokes about Jacques Lacan in this novel suggest the evasion is deliberate. The answer, I think, is that a ground could be intuitively understood—in a fiction, for example—while analysis might never take us beyond reasons, however buried they initially seemed. "I am trying," Kundera the novelist says, "to grasp the *Grund* hidden at the bottom of each of my characters and I am convinced more and more that it has the nature of a metaphor." His companion, the portly and eccentric Professor Avenarius, says "Your idea escapes me," and Kundera replies, "Too bad. It is the most important thought that ever occurred to me."

The tactic here is the double bluff, with complications. This can't be the most important thought that has ever occurred to Kundera, or even to "Kundera," and it is in any case absurd to speak of your own thought as important, especially when it doesn't look better than a bright idea, isn't even sketchily worked out. The dramatized implication, though, is not that the idea isn't important but that Kundera, quite properly, doesn't know how important it is. Metaphors, in this argument, are means of comprehension rather than decoration or escape; perhaps the only means we have. This is a self-interested claim for a novelist to make, a defense of the trade, but it is not a self-absorbed claim. It states, I think rightly, that if we can't imagine others ("Imagine me," Humbert Humbert cries to his readers in *Lolita*, "I shall not exist if you do not imagine me"), if we are not in some modest way novelists in our daily lives (historical novelists perhaps), we shall not understand much of anything.

Kundera pictures the girl sitting in the middle of the road, for example, as having felt herself to be unheard by others, become anxious to assert her presence in a world that refuses to acknowledge her.

Or another image: she is at the dentist's, sitting in a crowded waiting room; a new patient enters, walks to the couch where she is seated, and sits down on her lap; he didn't do it intentionally, he simply saw an empty seat on the couch; she protests and tries to push him away, shouting: "Sir! Can't you see? This seat is taken! I am sitting here!" but the man doesn't hear her, he sits comfortably on top of her and cheerfully chats with another waiting patient.

When Richard Rorty writes of philosophy's turning to narrative and the imagination, pointing us toward solidarity through "the imaginative ability to see strange people as fellow sufferers," he must mean something very much like the novelist's picturing of this lonely girl. It's a generous project, even an "important" one. But we have to see, as Kundera so clearly does, how flimsy it is as well. Better to guess at the girl's feelings than to have no feeling for her. But what if we learn that she felt nothing of the kind? Some writers of fiction will say it doesn't matter, but most will try another metaphor.

Tomas is a character in *The Unbearable Lightness of Being*, Agnes in *Immortality*. There is a strong connection between the two novels, spoofed in the later work in a fine, multistoreyed joke. Kundera tells Avenarius he is writing a new novel (this novel) and announces what will happen (what does happen) in the next section. Avenarius thinks the promised novel sounds pretty boring, but he wants to be polite and asks "in a kindly voice" what it is to be called. Kundera doesn't hesitate:

> "*The Unbearable Lightness of Being*"
> "I think somebody has already written that."
> "I did! But I was wrong about the title then. That title was supposed to belong to the novel I'm writing right now."

In the earlier novel Kundera invited us to wonder, with Nietzsche, how we would behave if everything we did were to be repeated, were loaded with the weight of return. Here we are to think of gestures prolonged into immortality, like words and phrases and motions dropped into the infinite memory of Funes, in a famous story by Borges. Would we do it all again? What wouldn't we do again? Would we—here is the hard question—wish to stay even with the people we love? Could we admit that we might not wish to? Agnes loves her husband Paul and her daughter Brigitte but not as much as she loves the memory of her dead father and the peace she finds in certain places away from her job and family and ordinary life. She is not unhappy with marriage, or France in the 1980s, but she wouldn't want them for eternity. One of the most poignant and ambiguously beautiful moments in the novel records Agnes's death, a compound of horror, waste, and a kind of grace. Agnes has been fatally injured in a car crash (caused by the girl sitting in the middle of the road, who herself walked away uninjured). Her husband, desperate to be at her bedside, has been delayed by an absurdist twist in the apparently absent plot: Avenarius, given to randomly slashing tires at night as a gesture against the drift of the world toward order and repression, has disabled Paul's car. Paul arrives too late, finds his grief baffled by an "unknown smile" on Agnes's dead face: "it was meant for someone he did not know and it said something he did not understand." It was meant for no one, which is precisely what Paul cannot grasp. Agnes had not wanted anyone to see her dying or to die into anyone's world. She had longed for a realm without faces and believes she has found such a realm as she dies. She seems to hear the words, "No, they don't have faces there." Her smile reflects her gratitude or her illusion; a happy end, unhappy only for the excluded Paul.

Others who worry about immortality in this novel are Goethe and Bettina von Arnim, whose relationship is fancifully recreated and analyzed; Napoleon, posing for posterity as if our cameramen were already there; Beethoven, refusing to doff his hat for an empress; Hemingway, chatting to Goethe in the afterworld; and, above all, a series of fictional characters in contemporary Paris: Agnes and Paul; Agnes's sister Laura and her lover Bernard, who is a fashionable and self-conscious radio interviewer; Agnes's lover Rubens, whose nickname mocks his abandoned artistic ambitions. The central and most interesting figures are Agnes and Laura, affectionate, intelligent, often distraught women who are alike and unalike, both born of the old lady's young gesture as she leaves the swimming pool. "The gesture revealed nothing of that woman's essence, one could rather say that the woman revealed to me the charm of a gesture," a gesture Kundera later compares to "a finished work of art." This is the gesture he lends to Agnes, who he says copied it from her father's secretary. Laura copies it from Agnes, but the old lady at the swimming pool hasn't copied it from anyone we or Kundera know, and the gesture thus stands for many acts and motions that travel the world, creating a sort of community of performance, an anonymous immortality, a flight from time and error into continuing physical grace. Of course there are graceless gestures too, so not even this immortality is safe. "All gestures," Kundera says in his novel *Slowness* (1995), "have a meaning that exceeds the intention of those who make them."

Kundera himself must be anxious about the test of eternity—would he want to spend it writing novels, or writing these novels?—and amusingly gets his characters to bite back at him. He invents Agnes and Paul and then, much later, meets Paul, drunk and mildly abusive, a disappointment but not now dismissible. Professor Avenarius circulates freely between worlds, has lunch with Kundera, but also (probably) sleeps with Laura. The girl who sits down in the roadway has a similar double life: she appears as a news item on Kundera's radio (and possibly on ours) and is then incorporated into the novel he is writing and we are reading. She is in a sense the most important figure in the book: the one we understand least and who causes the most havoc, an image for the limits of reason.

There is nothing metaphysical or spiritualist about Kundera's toying with immortality: it is a question put to mortals, not a consolation or a theosophy. He is interested in the irrational and the metaphorical but remains in many respects an entirely unreconstructed rationalist. What is new in *Immortality*, I think, is a certain chastening in the novelist, both as character and author. He is less exuberant, although still witty ("Napoleon was a true Frenchman in that he was not satisfied with sending hundreds of thousands to their death but wanted in addition to be admired by writers"). He is kinder to his characters, more worried about the way they hurt. He continues to want to know what human beings want and why they lie to themselves so much. His answer, insofar as he has an answer, is often that they want to get away—his characters, he says, are all "in some fashion withdrawing from the world"—to be relieved not of life but of the burden of living. "Living: carrying one's painful self through the world." Or again: "What is unbearable in life is not *being* but *being one's self*." He suggests more clearly than before that they can't at best do more than begin their retreat, and that they usually don't even understand their need, because they are caught up in the dream of sentiment and personality, the celebration of vanity, the great obligation to be someone, which seems to be coextensive with modern European culture, East and West.

Some of Kundera's best pages, here and in earlier work, are dedicated to the dry, grimly comic deconstruction of what he calls *homo sentimentalis*. "*Homo sentimentalis* cannot be defined as a man with feelings (for we all have feelings), but as a man who has raised feelings to a category of value." This is the world of kitsch, the world where we worship emotion, and then worship our worship of it, charmed by the delicacy of our own tears. "In the realm of kitsch, the dictatorship of the heart reigns supreme." Dostoyevsky is Kundera's touchstone in this respect, the great, perilous teacher of the authority of suffering; and Mahler is the last great European composer who "naively and directly" wanted to move us:

> I think, therefore I am is the statement of an intellectual who underrates toothaches. I feel, therefore I am is a truth much more universally valid. . . . Suffering is the university of egocentrism.

This austere joke is quite complicated. We are being teased, Kundera is asking us to think not about the dignity or reality of suffering but about the way we abase ourselves before it. There would be both lucid and self-mutilating ways of loving Mahler and Dostoyevsky. Descartes, in *The Unbearable Lightness of Being*, is attacked for denying that animals have souls, and Nietzsche, embracing a whipped horse in Turin before his last madness descended on him, is memorably said to be "trying to apologize to the horse for Descartes." In *Immortality* Descartes's presumed ignoring of toothaches seems not only cerebral but stylish, a moment of light before Europe plunged itself into an orgy of boastful suffering. The shift nicely illustrates Kundera's claim that philosophy is necessarily playful in novels, that dogma must become hypothesis. Philosophers themselves become characters with changing roles: "Descartes" here is not René Descartes the person and not the corpus or reach of Descartes's philosophical work; not even Descartes's general reputation. He is a pair of famous remarks and the images they evoke; a miniature colleague of Agnes and Tomas.

Kundera's humor is often so ascetic as to be scarcely visible. As with Borges, it wouldn't be hard to mistake his games with philosophy for philosophy itself, and we can already imagine the scholarly works that will reliteralize his speculations, smudge their contexts, and mislay their irony. With discreet mock pedantry Kundera classifies coincidences (mute, poetic, contrapuntal, story-producing, morbid), builds a whole taxonomy of immortality (minor, major, ridiculous—this last category including Tycho Brahe, who wouldn't get up from an imperial dinner to go to the lavatory; Robert Musil, who died while lifting weights; and very nearly Jimmy Carter, who came close to immortality as a jogger rather than a president). At other times, as if to compensate for the austerity and slyness of the jokes, Kundera's manner becomes both coy and lumbering—in the conversations between Goethe and Hemingway, for example, in *Immortality*. There are passages on the reign of images in the Western world and the rise of the journalist in France that read like fussy and half-hearted social comment, as if Marshall McLuhan had arrived a little late for the party or, rather, as if Kundera had arrived after McLuhan had left.

However, there is a terrible and beautiful casualness in a phrase such as "our century of optimism and massacres," and Kundera's general remarks on coincidence are light and deep. Coincidences are everywhere in ordinary life but can't happen in fiction, where they can only be mimed. When they are well mimed (or interrogated), their apparent triviality may blossom into a kind of anguish. A coincidence is the crossing of two or more unconnected stories, chains of causality. If a girl, absorbed in her own loneliness and distress, sits down on a busy highway and brings about the deaths of three sets of people, this is precisely what we call an accident. If the girl does this in a novel, the accident is a metaphor, a *Grund* not for character but for the way we experience the order and disorder of our lives. It suggests, as intricately plotted events in novels always do, that no man or woman is an island; and also, as novels more rarely suggest, that this fact is dangerous, a new and unmanageable feature of our crowded, modernized planet. We seem to meet a crazed and disreputable form of fate, a last, ironic, impossible master narrative.

Marco Polo describes a bridge, stone by stone.

"But which is the stone that supports the bridge?" Kublai Khan asks.

"The bridge is not supported by one stone or another," Marco answers, "but by the line of the arch that they form."

Kublai Khan remains silent, reflecting. Then he adds: "Why do you speak to me of the stones? It is only the arch that matters to me."

Polo answers: "Without stones there is no arch."

—Italo Calvino, *Invisible Cities*

5. *The Promised Land*

Silent Destinies

Marco Polo and Kublai Khan converse among the fountains and magnolias of the Khan's hanging garden. At first, the Venetian is unable to speak the Khan's language and can recount his travels in the Empire only with gestures, leaps, and cries, and by exhibiting various objects he has brought back with him. He also resorts to pantomime:

> One city was depicted by the leap of a fish escaping the cormorant's beak to fall into a net; another city by a naked man running through fire unscorched; a third by a skull, its teeth green with mold, clenching a round, white pearl. The Great Khan deciphered the signs, but the connection between them and the places visited remained uncertain; he never knew whether Marco wished to enact an adventure that had befallen him on his journey, an exploit of the city's founder, the prophecy of an astrologer, a rebus or a charade to indicate a name. But, obscure or obvious as it might be, everything Marco displayed had the power of emblems, which, once seen, cannot be forgotten or confused.

Before long Marco masters the Tartar idiom (or the Emperor begins to understand Italian), and the dialogue proceeds with greater precision. But then a certain nostalgia for the emblem sets in: "you would have said communication between them was less happy than in the past."

These encounters and this lapse into language occur in Italo Calvino's *Invisible Cities* (*Le città invisibili*, 1972), and the writer seems to be thinking of a passage in Rousseau's *Essay on the Origin of Languages*, where the eloquence of emblems is preferred to the poor specificity of speech. But the preoccupation with silent discourse is very much Calvino's own. In the frame story, in both frame stories, of *The Castle of Crossed Destinies* (*Il castello dei destini incrociati*, 1973) a group of travelers is struck dumb by some terrible, unnamed experience, and each can tell his or her story only by pointing to and arranging in sequence certain cards of the tarot pack.

In one sense this situation is *only* a frame, a pretext for "reading" pictures, so we shouldn't overload it with meaning. But we shouldn't see it simply as a trick either, because it offers us, delicately and obliquely, a narrative metaphor that plainly matters a great deal to Calvino. The attraction of images, as opposed to words in their everyday, functional guise, is that they are rich and equivocal: they tell, or suggest, many stories but never tell any single story for sure. Yet it seems that we can abstain from the excessive and illusory clarities of verbal language only through some sort of calamity, as in this book, or through a shift beyond our own linguistic boundaries, like Marco Polo's travels to China (or Roland Barthes's experiences in Japan, pictured in *Empire of Signs* as a place where everything means something and yet nothing is understood). In *The Castle of Crossed Destinies* Calvino reinforces this implication by retaining all the noises around the travelers—"the drumming of spoons, the rattle of goblets and crockery . . . the sounds of chewing and the smacking of lips gulping wine"—so that we understand that speech is what is lost, not sound. These are people, we may say, not without language but without a language, without the language they think of as their own, without what we mostly think of as language.

The tarot cards "conceal more things than they tell," we learn at one point, but they tell plenty, and the travelers are eager to get hold of them, to signal and recount their own adventures:

> As soon as a card says more [more than it might seem to, more than some more neutral-looking card?], other hands immediately try to pull it in their direction, to fit it into a different story. One perhaps begins to tell a tale on his own, with cards that seem to belong solely to him, and all of a sudden the conclusion comes in a rush, overlapping that of other stories in the same catastrophic pictures.

"Pull it in their direction" is a literal move on the table, of course, but also a metaphor for how these stories go. The urge to tell stories survives language, finds languages of its own. The ambiguity of the images on the cards is an opportunity, not just a compensation or replacement for the speech that is lost but a new field, a place where stories glitter and mingle as they cannot do in other modes. "Each story runs into another story," Calvino says, and "the same cards, presented in a different order, often change their meaning." The besieged city represented in the tarot of the World, for instance, is both Paris and Troy, a celestial city in yet another story, and a subterranean city in still another.

The tarots, widely used in fortune-telling and rather casually employed in *The Waste Land* ("I'm not familiar with the exact constitution of the tarot pack," Eliot said), are a deck of cards with twenty-one picture cards in addition to four full suits (cups, coins, swords, staves). There is also a card called the Fool, which corresponds to the Joker in other packs. The picture cards, or Arcana, portray, among other things, Eliot's Hanged Man, the Devil, Death, Strength, Temperance, the World, the Moon, the Hermit, the Broken Tower, and most mysteriously of all, a female Pope (or perhaps a Pope's wife). The pack, Calvino says, is "a machine for constructing stories," and he allows the look of the cards, rather than any occult meaning, to speak to him. He sees forests, for example, wherever crossed staves begin to look thick on the ground, and the King of Swords followed by the Ten of Swords produces this wonderful effect:

> Our eyes seemed suddenly blinded by the great dust cloud of battles: we heard the blare of trumpets, already the shattered spears were flying; already the clashing horses' muzzles were drenched in iridescent foam; already the swords, with the flat or the cutting edge, were striking against the flat or cutting edge of other swords.

Calvino is working with two versions of the pack: the sumptuous Visconti deck painted by Bembo and the fairly common Marseilles deck, which can be bought in any decent occultist's shop. For the first deck, he imagines travelers staying at a castle, or perhaps an inn—the place is rather too grand for an inn and rather too disorderly for a castle. Their stories are those of an unfaithful lover, of an unpunished grave robber, of a man who met the Devil's bride. We also hear of Faust, and of Roland as he is portrayed in Ariosto. The narrator's interpretations of the cards as they are displayed are confident but frankly speculative, articulated through phrases such as "our fellow guest probably wished to inform us," "this row of cards . . . surely announced," and "we could only venture some guesses"; and when he needs the story of Astolpho, the English knight in Ariosto who recovers Roland's wits for him, he seems simply to conscript a fellow guest who "might well be that English knight." The narrator doesn't tell us his own tale, but it is there, he says, buried in the pattern the cards make on the table once several criss-crossing stories have been dealt out. More precisely, he says his story is there but he can "no longer say which it is," and a little later announces that he has "lost" his story, "confused it in the dust of the tales, become freed of it." The hint, an echo of Borges perhaps, is that everyone has a story but that those who tell many stories lose their own, not because it is buried or repressed but because it is dispersed, played out in all kinds of figurative or displaced forms. "A man," Borges writes,

> sets himself the task of sketching the world. Through the years he peoples a space with images of provinces, kingdoms, mountains, bays, ships, islands, fishes, rooms, instruments, stars, horses and persons. Shortly before dying, he discovers that this patient labyrinth of lines traces the image of his face.

For the second deck Calvino imagines another set of silent travelers, but they seem more clearly to be at an inn, as befits the less aristocratic nature of the cards themselves, and for some reason the stories deduced from these cards are much more vivid and ingenious. They include the tale of the waverer, a narrative that finds impossible choices at every turn of the card, and also the stories of Faust (again) and Parsifal, and of Hamlet, Macbeth, and Lear. At one point Calvino decides to interpret the picture card of the Pope as signifying a latinized Freud, "the great shepherd of souls and interpreter of dreams Sigismund of Vindobona," and starts to look for, and of course soon finds, the story of Oedipus in the pack, "that story which, according to the teachings of [Sigismund's] doctrine, is hidden in the warp of all stories." In this deck the writer does dig out his own tale, but it is a tale of writing, not a confession of worldly adventures or sentimental secrets. Among his cards are the Devil, because "the raw material of writing" is "a rising to the surface of hairy claws, cur-like scratching, goat's goring, repressed violences that grope in the darkness," and the Juggler, a figure "who arranges on a stand at a fair a certain number of objects and, shifting them, connecting them, interchanging them, achieves a certain number of effects." Among his models are Stendhal and the Marquis de Sade, because "in writing, what speaks is what is repressed." If we are lucky. Calvino worries a little about the portentousness of some of this—"will I not have been too pontifical?" (*troppo edificante*) he says a little later—and has his narrator deflate his own claims even as he makes them. "Writing, in short, has a subsoil which belongs to the species, or at least to civilization, or at least to certain income brackets."

In such a view, or in such an income bracket, the tarot pack is not only a machine for constructing stories, it is a labyrinth where all the world's stories can be found. But they have to be found, and finding them, it seems, does not interfere with the inexhaustible mystery of the labyrinth itself, which is organized, Calvino says, around "the chaotic heart of things, the center of the square of the cards and of the world, the point of intersection of all possible orders." Calvino experiments briefly (and brilliantly) with "reading" other pictures in the same way—famous paintings of St Jerome and St George, for example—and he says he thought of completing his "Castle of Crossed Destinies" (the Visconti pack) and "Tavern of Crossed Destinies" (the Marseilles pack) with a "Motel of Crossed Destinies," in which the mute survivors of an unnamed catastrophe would tell their tales by pointing to the various frames of the comics page of a scorched newspaper.

In the last chapter of *The Castle of Crossed Destinies* Calvino "discovers" the stories of Hamlet, Macbeth, and King Lear, described as "Three Tales of Madness and Destruction," lurking among the tarot cards already laid out, already used for other stories. He can do this, of course, only if he and we are willing to believe that almost any story can be found in the tarot deck, and if we know these stories already, so the idea of reading takes an interesting turn here. The images of the cards no longer suggest to us stories we do not know and must piece together, or stories we have lived and wish to communicate to others, but stories we can, with a little ingenuity, recognize in the images set before us; stories we literally discover, or discover again.

The stories are "told" by, attributed to, members of the company in the tavern of crossed destinies, who are identified first as "a young man," "a lady," and "an old man," later as Hamlet, Lady Macbeth, and Lear. The attribution of the Macbeth story to Lady Macbeth—she is the one who thinks about the witches and their prophecies, sees Banquo's ghost, it is her life, more lucid than her husband's, that the witches make nonsense of—is a delicate shift, consistent with the focusing on madness in these narratives. The card of the Ruined Tower is Elsinore, and its haunted battlements in the night; it is Dunsinane, Birnam Wood advancing upon it; it is Lear's castle, from which he has been driven, "emptied from the walls like a can of rubbish"—the card shows figures falling, a tilted crown at the top of the tower, a feather licking at the broken edifice, perhaps representing lightning, perhaps an emblematic suggestion of how lightly the agencies of destruction may seem to proceed. The card of the Moon is the night in which Hamlet's father's ghost walks; the night the witches invoke and in which they work; the blasted landscape that is all Lear has left of his possessions. The card of the Hermit is Polonius in the arras, Banquo's ghost, or perhaps even Macbeth himself, the man "who has murdered sleep" and stalks the guest rooms of his castle; and Lear on the heath, with the Fool (another card) as "his only support and mirror of his madness." The card of the Star, which depicts a set of stars and a naked woman pouring water from two pitchers, is Ophelia gone mad; Lady Macbeth seeking to wash away the stain that nothing will remove; and (in a little riff Calvino has added to the story, or found in the cards) Cordelia in exile, "drinking water from the ditches" and depending on the birds for her nourishment. The Chariot, finally, is Fortinbras come to clear up the mess in Elsinore; Malcolm arriving to assume his rightful place on the throne of Scotland; and the King of France, Cordelia's husband, crossing the channel a little too late to save the mad king and his murdered daughter.

Other cards overlap in two of the three stories—Hamlet plays the Fool and meditates on the Fool's skull; Temperance, represented by another lady with pitchers, this time pouring water from one into the other, is both Ophelia and the virtue that Lear has lost, perhaps the daughter he has lost for lack of that virtue—and some cards appear in only one story. The whole thing is a virtuoso exercise on Calvino's part, lightly done, full of mischief and amusement. Hamlet's method in his madness becomes, "If this is neurosis, there is a method in it, and in every method, neurosis." Both Hamlet and Lear are seen as plays about problems between the generations, the young haunted by the authority of the old, the old beset by everything the young refuse to bury. "With daughters, whatever a father does is wrong: authoritarian or permissive, parents can never expect to be thanked." The Macbeth marriage is one of equals: "they have shared the roles like a devoted couple, marriage is the encounter of two egoisms that grind each other reciprocally and from which spread the cracks in the foundations of civilized society." The suggestion of anachronism, of twentieth-century tackiness creeping up on these august old tales, mocks us gently for thinking we could tame and understand such wildnesses. We have found the stories, they are stories we know; but in what sense do we know them?

The largest suggestion here though—and Calvino's placing of this material at the end of his book is important—is that these stories, found in this way, take us deeper into reading than we have probably been before, deeper into what reading is. Two elements of this proposition seem particularly important. First, Calvino's interpretations are not simply imposed on the cards—not any cards would do for any story—but they are not simply taken from the cards either. The stories are familiar already, but still need finding, and finding is itself a notion we now need to linger over a little. To discover the (very different) watery associations of Ophelia and Lady Macbeth in a particular card, as Calvino elsewhere finds the figure of the writer in the King of Clubs, who does indeed, in the Marseilles pack, seem to be holding something that looks like a ballpoint pen, is not to read these cards according to an intention ascribed to them, it is to make associations, whether theatrical and Shakespearean or technical and twentieth-century. The associations may operate as a joke, like the ballpoint pen, or as an extension of a metaphorical universe, like the water in the card of the Star.

There is a sense here of the curious, punning crossover between fiction and fiction, or between fiction and fact, which we meet when characters from novels by Cortázar and Fuentes show up in a novel by García Márquez, or when we read about the Gents' Outfitters shop in Dublin, both Joyce's and history's, which is called Henry and James. The names are common enough in the second case, there is no mystery here; but for a moment the city seems mischievously to refer to a famous writer, to make a literary joke, and Joyce didn't miss it. On the contrary, he recorded it for us, precisely, since the shop has gone and the text remains. There is a more elaborate instance of such interplay between given and taken associations in Pynchon's *Gravity's Rainbow*. The German pronunciation of the letter V is *fau* (rhymes with how), so that the names of the v-1 and v-2 rockets sound like the word for a peacock, a *Pfau*; whose tail when spread has the color of the rainbow, and the shape of the rainbow and of the trajectory of those rockets as they fly from North Germany to England: gravity's rainbow. The deliberate construction of such a network of associations, either by the novelist or by the critic, would be an absurd piece of pedantry. As it is, it would be pretty pedantic to brood on it much. But there surely is an eerie little shock here, as if we had stumbled on an order we had not suspected and that is not ours. The German language, or a pun that is lurking in this language and not in others, seems to connect the rocket with the peacock and to bring natural and technical shapes and colors together in the wake of this connection. Dublin similarly, not Joyce, made the joke Joyce found.

Yet of course Joyce, or someone, had to find it. What I am suggesting here, what I read in these images of reading, is that both writing and reading are larger affairs than our narrow notions of communication allow; and that reading understood as finding pieces of a world, as distinct from imagining whole worlds, assembled, disassembled, reassembled, has a peculiar richness of its own. We can't dispense with the imagination of course—there is no reading without it, and not much life of any kind—but we shouldn't allow it all the honors, exclusively. The world as it is has surprises for us too; to impose, as Stevens said, is not to discover.

Second, it's important that single cards can be read in so many different ways. Again, not an infinite number of ways, we are still talking about reading rather than daydreaming. Here I interpret Calvino as suggesting—I interpret his text as allowing us to think—that the images of the tarot pack may not only remind us of everything articulated language flattens and misses, and not only invite us to pick up the dialogue between image and speech so beautifully dramatized in Marco Polo's reading of the Great Khan's chessboard, to which I shall return. They may also picture for us language itself in its most ordinary sense: what words are like. They are not just the pale and harassed servants we push around when we want to get things, ask for directions, food, love. Words, even the smallest, most insignificant-seeming, most abused of them, are pictures of life; they have histories and complications and multiple uses. When you say "tower" you might mean a card in the tarot pack, or a structure in Paris, or Blackpool, or London; just as the card may mean Elsinore or Dunsinane or the castle Lear has lost. Words are cards, you can play them in functional sentences, you can tell fortunes in them and tell stories; you can read stories in them, above all, in this context, the stories that hide in or accompany the stories ostensibly being told. "In writing, what speaks is what is repressed." We don't have to hold Calvino to this remark as to a declaration of faith. But "writing" here might be taken as a metaphor borrowed from Derrida. Writing, whether materially set down, or spoken aloud, or mentally pursued, is looking at words so as to see the pictures in them, to glimpse the other, possible stories they offer, as well as the stories they have been conscripted to tell.

The question of the language, or languages, used by the Great Khan and Marco Polo reminds us of the irony that is lurking everywhere in *The Castle of Crossed Destinies*: we are not reading the stories in the tarot cards, we are not even in the room with the narrator who is reading them. The narrator has translated the mute speech of the cards into Italian, and Calvino has reported his activities in print—and we have read the whole thing in English. The silence of the cards is repeated in the silence of the page and (perhaps) in the silence of the room in which we read. But the pictorial ambiguities of the cards, their worlds of possibility, have been turned into consecutive, grammatical language. The celebration of emblems must leave the realm of emblems behind, cannot do without the supplementary clues and markings of language in its most familiar sense. There is a dialogue, in other words, between the riches of imagery and the directedness of speech or writing, and it is the dialogue that matters rather than the riches or the directedness on their own. Or we need images as a reminder of everything language simplifies or misses, and we may believe that a language that remembered this would be different and renewed. But can an articulated language remember this? The example of the merchant and the emperor in *Invisible Cities* is not encouraging at first.

Spoken Cities

"You would have said communication between them was less happy than in the past." Marco Polo and the Great Khan shift from gestures to words but experience this chiefly as a loss. Words are more precise, of course, "more useful than objects or gestures in listing the most important things of every province and city," but Marco Polo finds he can't put the daily life of those places into words, and goes back to "gestures, grimaces, glances."

So, for each city, after the fundamental information given in precise words, he followed with a mute commentary, holding up his hands, palms out, or backs, or sideways, in straight or oblique movements, spasmodic or slow. A new kind of dialogue was established: the Great Khan's white hands, heavy with rings, answered with stately movements the sinewy, agile hands of the merchant.

But then this language in turn becomes stable, conventional, closed. "The pleasure of falling back on it also diminished in both; in their conversations, most of the time, they remained silent and immobile."

We must guard against too literal a reading of this situation. The decay of dialogue is part of the beautifully elegiac and speculative movement of the whole of *Invisible Cities*, which begins with the Khan seeing his vast empire as a sumptuous, corrupt ruin and takes us deeper and deeper into his melancholy, his "sense of emptiness" and loss. We are repeatedly invited to wonder whether anything of what we read is actually happening, even within the world of the fiction. Do the Khan and Marco Polo, historical figures already thoroughly reimagined in the mind of the writer, really communicate with each other in this story, or do they dream they do? "The foreigner had learned to speak the emperor's language or the emperor to understand the language of the foreigner." This is to say they had turned to words, but not to whose words. And the supposed communication is often located more openly within the minds of the characters: "Marco Polo imagined answering (or Kublai Khan imagined his answer)"; "Kublai Khan interrupted him or imagined interrupting him, or Marco Polo imagined himself interrupted"; "Marco Polo could explain or imagine explaining or be imagined explaining or succeed finally in explaining to himself." The characters imagine themselves to be in dialogue, which is a way of saying that we have to imagine them at it, and that it is the dialogue we imagine that matters. The book raises further doubts about the (fictional) reality of the speakers, by having them wonder philosophically who and where they are. "Perhaps," Marco Polo says, "this garden exists only in the shadow of our lowered eyelids, and we have never stopped: you, from raising dust on the fields of battle; and I, from bargaining for sacks of pepper in distant bazaars." "Perhaps," Kublai Khan replies, "this dialogue of ours is taking place between two beggars nicknamed Kublai Khan and Marco Polo; as they sift through a rubbish heap, piling up rusted flotsam, scraps of cloth, wastepaper, while drunk on the few sips of bad wine, they see all the treasures of the East shine around them."

There are fabulous cities here, architectural dreams, haunting conclusions to scarcely imaginable journeys. Each city is a story—"Tell me another city," the Great Khan says to Marco Polo at one point. There are cities of intricate memory—"the special quality of this city for the man who arrives there on a September evening . . . is that he feels envy toward those who now believe they have once before lived an evening identical to this and who think they were happy, that time"—cities of desire, cities of signs, cities of the living and the dead. There is a city you can't arrive in, which is only the city you see as you approach; there is a city that "knows only departures"; another that is all outskirts, which has no center that anyone can reach.

Certain cities have an ecological look, or the look of an ecological parody. Leonia discards so much rubbish that it piles up like mountains on all sides of the city. This rubbish would take over the globe if other cities were not doing just as Leonia does. "Perhaps the whole world, beyond Leonia's boundaries, is covered by craters of rubbish, each surrounding a metropolis in constant eruption. The boundaries between the alien, hostile cites are infected ramparts where the detritus of both support each other, overlap, mingle." The situation is dangerous: "a tin can, an old tire, an unraveled wine flask, if it rolls toward Leonia, is enough to bring with it an avalanche of unmated shoes, calendars of bygone years, withered flowers, submerging the city in its own past."

Procopia has such a population explosion that each time the traveler returns, the landscape outside his inn is fuller and fuller of faces, one, three, six, sixteen, twenty-nine, forty-seven, until at last nothing but faces can be seen from the window. It's not too comfortable inside the inn either:

> There are twenty-six of us lodged in my room: to shift my feet I have to disturb those crouching on the floor, I force my way among the knees of those seated on the chest of drawers and the elbows of those taking turns leaning on the bed: all very polite people, luckily.

Above all there are cities within cities, implied or invisible or unknown second worlds within or alongside second worlds, dreams within dreams. The city of Valdrada, for instance, is built on the shores of a lake, and the traveler always sees the city and its exact reflection. "Nothing exists or happens in the one Valdrada that the other Valdrada does not repeat, because the city was so constructed that its every point would be reflected in its mirror." When the inhabitants of the shoreside city make love or murder each other those gestures are repeated in the lake, and "it is not so much their copulating or murdering that matters as the copulating or murdering of the images, limpid and cold in the mirror." Of course the mirror image is not exactly the same: it is a symmetrical inversion. "The two Valdradas live for each other, their eyes interlocked; but there is no love between them." Another double city allows Marco Polo (and Calvino) a light and perfectly placed gag, a simple reversal but one we are not ready for. "Sophronia is made up of two half-cities": the fairground city, with its roller coaster, Ferris wheel, circus tent; the solid city of "stone and marble and cement," with its bank, factories, palaces, slaughterhouse, school.

> One of the half-cities is permanent, the other is temporary, and when the period of its sojourn is over, they uproot it, dismantle it, and take it off, transplanting it to the vacant lots of another half-city.
>
> And so every year the day comes when the workmen remove the marble pediments, lower the stone walls, the cement pylons, take down the Ministry, the monument, the docks, the petroleum refinery, the hospital, load them on trailers.

The situation of the city of Beersheba is more complicated. Its inhabitants believe that their terrestrial city is shadowed by a celestial one where all their "most elevated virtues and sentiments" are stored, and by a subterranean one, "the receptacle of everything base and unworthy that happens to them." They are right about the two shadow cities but wrong in their identification of them: the supposed celestial city is really infernal, driven only by "a grim mania to fill the empty vessel of itself"; the supposed infernal city, a place of waste and neglect and refusal, is the real celestial city, representing the "only moments of generous abandon" known to Beersheba, "a city which only when it shits, is not miserly, calculating, greedy." Similarly, although in a different register, the city of Raissa is full of sadness and doesn't recognize the scattered moments of happiness that are also part of its fabric, the "invisible thread that binds one living being to another, then unravels, then is stretched again between moving points as it draws new and rapid patterns so that at every second the unhappy city contains a happy city unaware of its own existence."

There is also Perinthia, whose astronomers designed the city according to all the most favorable conjunctions of the stars, only to see the place develop into the home of every kind of deformity and horror:

Perinthia's astronomers are faced with a difficult choice. Either they must admit that all their calculations were wrong and their figures are unable to describe the heavens, or else they must reveal that the order of the gods is reflected exactly in the city of monsters.

And there is Andria, similarly built according to a celestial pattern. Its denizens live, the traveler assumes, in an unchanging world, an elegant reflection of the "meticulous clockwork" of heaven. He is right about the reflection, but the inhabitants are astonished that he should think the place doesn't change. They point to the ceaseless shifts and new buildings of the city. But then what about the matching with the stars? "Our city and the sky correspond so perfectly," they answered, "that any change in Andria involves some novelty among the stars." The astronomers, after each change takes place in Andria, peer into their telescopes and report a nova's explosion, or a remote point in the firmament's change of color from orange to yellow, the expansion of a nebula, the bending of a spiral of the Milky Way. Each change implies a sequence of other changes, in Andria as among the stars: the city and the sky never remain the same. This is why the inhabitants or Andria are so confident and so prudent. "Convinced that every innovation in the city influences the sky's pattern, before taking any decision they calculate the risks and advantages for themselves and for the city and for all worlds."

In the city of Eudoxia the mirror and secret design of the place is found in a carpet. This is at first sight surprising, since the city is full of "winding alleys, dead ends," refusals of straight lines and symmetry:

> At first sight nothing seems to resemble Eudoxia less than the design of that carpet. . . . But if you pause and examine it carefully, you become convinced that each place in the carpet corresponds to a place in the city and all the things contained in the city are included in the design, arranged according to their true relationship, which escapes your eye distracted by the bustle, the throngs, the shoving.

The stars are part of this city's sense of itself too. When an oracle was asked about the mysterious resemblance of the carpet and the city it said one of those objects had "the form the gods gave the starry sky and the orbits in which the worlds revolve," while the other was "an approximate reflection, like every human creation." For some time the interpreters were sure that the carpet mirrored the work of the gods and the city represented human labor.

> But you could, similarly, come to the opposite conclusion: that the true map of the universe is the city of Eudoxia, just as it is, a stain that spreads out shape-

lessly, with crooked streets, houses that crumble one upon the other amid clouds of dust, fires, screams in the darkness.

No city seems to be able to live without some sort of refraction of perfection as its opposite or model or echo. This is clearest of all in the last two cities Marco Polo describes. Theodora banishes, destroys the whole animal kingdom, leaving no other species than man in existence. If anyone wants to know about the old fauna, they will have to look them up in one of Theodora's well stocked libraries. And yet. The animals return: not the former animals, but the wildest animals in the books, leaping from the pages in the library, perching on the edge of the citizens' sleep. "Sphinxes, griffons, chimera, dragons, hirocervi, harpies, hydras, unicorns, basilisks were resuming possession of their city." Berenice is described as "the unjust city," but it contains a just city within it, the hope of to-morrow. Yet that city in turn will contain the seeds of its opposite, injustice stirring in the heart of justice itself. The cities are not sequential, however:

> From my words you will have reached the conclusion that the real Berenice is a temporal succession of different cities, alternately just and unjust. But what I wanted to warn you about is something else: all the future Berenices are already present in this instant, wrapped one within the other, confined, crammed, inextricable.

Marco Polo's warning anticipates the wonderful last words of this book. The Khan thinks this quest for cities is finally hopeless. The perfect city will never be found, even by putting some sort of ideal city together from the pieces of all the rest. The real city, "the last landing place," "can only be the infernal city." Marco Polo doesn't disagree but replaces all the implicit worries about paradise with the stronger, more practical suggestion of a resistance to hell. The inferno, he says, if there is one, is where we already live, "what is already here": why this is hell nor are we out of it, as Marlowe's Mephistopheles says. There are two ways to escape the sufferings of hell, Polo suggests:

> The first is easy for many: accept the inferno and become such a part of it that you can no longer see it. The second is risky and demands constant vigilance and apprehension: seek and learn to recognize who and what, in the midst of the inferno, are not inferno, then make them endure, give them space.

We Don't Know What They Mean

But even if we are careful not to take too literally the question of language in *Invisible Cities*, we still need to attend to the remarkable moment when Marco

Polo rescues the Khan's empire from a desolate and terminal abstraction by "reading" his chessboard. The situation anticipates that of *The Castle of Crossed Destinies* but then shifts the dialogue between image and articulated interpretation several stages further.

> Returning from his last mission, Marco Polo found the Khan awaiting him, seated at a chessboard. With a gesture he invited the Venetian to sit opposite him and describe, with the help only of the chessmen, the cities he had visited. Marco did not lose heart. The Great Khan's chessmen were huge pieces of polished ivory: arranging on the board looming rooks and sulky knights, assembling swarms of pawns, drawing straight or oblique avenues like a queen's progress, Marco recreated the perspective and the spaces of black and white cities on moonlit nights.
>
> Now Kublai Khan no longer had to send Marco Polo on distant expeditions: he kept him playing endless games of chess.

The empire becomes a game; a game is an empire. But what is a game? "Each game ends in a gain or a loss," the Khan thinks, "but of what? What were the true stakes?"

> By disembodying his conquests to reduce them to the essential, Kublai had arrived at the extreme operation: the definitive conquest, of which the empire's multiform treasures were only illusory envelopes. It was reduced to a square of planed wood: nothingness.

At this point, for the only time in the book, the linguistic situation is made perfectly clear: Marco Polo fluently speaks the language of the Khan. Yet it is not the fluency that amazes the Emperor but what that fluency permits: an extraordinary combination of vision and articulation. Without the vision, there would be nothing to say; without the articulation, almost nothing of this vision could be evoked, since it is a vision of absence, of just what images cannot show. They can show the traces of absent people and things, of course, but the reading of those traces requires a syntax, a logic that goes beyond that of visual juxtaposition or sequence. This is as true of film as it is of tarot cards or paintings, or any other of our favorite mute rebukes to the noisiness of verbal language. Even in Poussin's marvelous "Cephalus and Aurora," the young man's absent wife is represented by a picture of her: her material absence figured in the presence of a reproduction.

What Marco Polo sees in the chessboard, to be more precise, is not exactly an absence but a presence filled with other, older presences, the past of the present case, what was there (here) before the chessboard became what it now is:

"Your chessboard, sire, is inlaid with two woods: ebony and maple. The square on which your enlightened gaze is fixed was cut from the ring of a trunk that grew in a year of drought: you see how its fibers are arranged? . . . Here is a thicker pore: perhaps it was a larvum's nest; not a woodworm, because, once born it would have begun to dig, but a caterpillar that gnawed the leaves and was the cause of the tree's being chosen for chopping down. . . . This edge was scored by the wood carver with his gouge so that it would adhere to the next square, more protruding . . ."

The quantity of things that could be read in a little piece of smooth and empty wood overwhelmed Kublai; Polo was already talking about ebony forests, about rafts laden with logs that come down the rivers, of docks, of women at the windows.

In his lectures, *Six Memos for the Next Millennium* (1988), Calvino speaks of *Invisible Cities* as "the book in which I think I managed to say most." He achieves this, as I hope my discussion has suggested, in the face of the most scrupulous sense of the difficulty of saying anything—as distinct, for example, from merely asserting things or announcing them, or pretending you have said them. Calvino loves and distrusts and displaces language; drives it to its limits and beyond them; devises tests and defeats for it. It would be a mistake, I think, not to take seriously his conviction that language is often a form of failure rather than success. "When you kill, you always kill the wrong man," he says in a gloss on the story of Hamlet in *The Castle of Crossed Destinies*. It's not that Hamlet is "incapable of killing": "Why, that is the only thing he succeeds in doing!" First Polonius, then Rosencrantz and Guildenstern, then Laertes, finally Claudius. Is Claudius the wrong man? Well, if he's the right man, he comes pretty late in the series. And Calvino's fiction, with its dazzled and dazzling allusions to the denser meanings of the visible world, is a monument to one of literature's most important half-truths. When you write, you always write the wrong book; the book that betrays silence, the book that suffers from the simple fact that a book is what it is. Of course, you have to write pretty well for this proposition to make any interesting sense, and the other half of the truth is that the wrong book can also be just right. There are failures and failures. Some are too easy, effects of our laziness. Some are too hard, sheer impossibilities in disguise. And some are subtle forms of success.

Calvino's failure is substantial and willed, a discreet and calculated punctuation of silence:

In fact, silence can also be considered a kind of speech, since it is a rejection of the use to which others put words; but the meaning of this silent speech lies in its interruptions, in what is, from time to time, actually said, giving a meaning to what is unsaid.

The central character of Calvino's *Mr. Palomar* (*Palomar*, 1983) "hopes always that silence contains something more than what language can say," but then wonders, "what if language were really the goal towards which everything in existence tends?" Mr. Palomar, shopping, wants the rich foods to speak to him: "He would like the duck and hare pâtés, from their platters, to show they prefer him to the others . . . No, nothing vibrates . . . Perhaps, for all the sincerity of his love of galantines, galantines do not love him." If everything in existence did tend toward language, it would be toward a language scarcely to be spoken or written, an idiom quite different from most of the idioms that fill our talk and our books and our documents.

Even so, Calvino can also speak, in *Six Memos for the Next Millennium*, of literature as "the Promised Land in which language becomes what it really ought to be." This means, I think, that literature remains a promise rather than a practice, it is what writing seeks but perhaps can only seek. Indeed Calvino says later that "literature remains alive only if we set ourselves immeasurable goals, far beyond all hope of achievement." But it also means that all language, written or spoken, has a Promised Land as its elusive inheritance, an imaginable paradise that resembles the heaven to be gained at the end of the game in Cortázar's *Hopscotch*; and this corresponds exactly to Calvino's understanding of "the use of words": "as a perpetual pursuit of things, as a perpetual adjustment to their infinite variety." The quest alone for the Promised Land will take us a long way from the misery of seeing and not telling, or not seeing because we don't know how to tell. You could look at the inlay and fibers and scorings of the chessboard without needing words—although you might have needed words to learn some of the things that helped you to look closely enough. But you couldn't read the board's richness without words, or make clear that your reading was a reading. It is only in words that you would be able to speak of the "trunk that grew in a year of drought," and a long dead caterpillar and a probably dead wood carver, and the rafts and logs and docks of the past, and the imagined women at the windows of the mind.

Mr. Palomar would like to learn a modest lesson or two from the unexplained world. But of course, as we have seen, the simplest things and creatures shimmer with complication when you look at them closely. What was richness and restoration of the world for Marco Polo will seem like invasive human history, or depredation by self-consciousness, if you are trying to get back to nature. This is how we meet Mr. Palomar, on the first page of the book:

The sea is barely wrinkled, and little waves strike the sandy shore. Mr. Palomar is standing on the shore, looking at a wave. Not that he is lost in contemplation of the waves. He is not lost, because he is quite aware of what he is doing: he wants to look at a wave and he is looking at it. He is not contemplating, because for contemplation you need the right temperament, the right mood, and the right combination of exterior circumstances . . . Finally it is not "the waves" that he means to look at, but just one individual wave.

Mr. Palomar "vacillates at length," Calvino says, and indeed the character's life on the page consists of lengthy, strenuous vacillation. But then Calvino's patience with Mr. Palomar's amiable pedantry—or rather Calvino's ironic invention of Palomar and pedantry and the precise and relaxed prose that pursues them—produces wonderful effects. The individual wave is lost, but an indirect, unexpectedly beautiful description of the sea takes its place:

> And so the wave continues to grow and gain strength until the clash with contrary waves gradually dulls it and makes it disappear, or else twists it until it is confused in one of the many dynasties of oblique waves slammed, with them, against the shore.

Mr. Palomar has a swim, thinks about naked bosoms on beaches—is it a sign of prejudice to avert your eyes? He listens to a pair of blackbirds and wonders whether their signals are very different from those he exchanges with his wife. "The equal whistle of man and blackbird now seems to him a bridge thrown over the abyss." An albino gorilla, lost in his biological loneliness, hugs a rubber tire as if he knew what a symbol was. This, Mr. Palomar thinks, is how we seek to escape from "the dismay of living: investing oneself in things, recognizing oneself in signs."

The albino gorilla is a type nature has produced but not preferred, "sole exemplar in the world of a form not chosen, not loved"; even his mate and his offspring are black like other gorillas. "Mr. Palomar feels he understands the gorilla perfectly," Calvino tells us, inviting us to smile at his hero's presumption; but it is likely that Mr. Palomar does understand, if not the gorilla, then something of the gorilla's condition as extravagant remnant of a road not taken: a possibility actualized once and only once. It is this strange dialogue with possibility that draws Mr. Palomar to the reptile house in the Jardin des Plantes in Paris. The iguana, for instance, looks like "a sample-case of forms available in the animal kingdom and perhaps also in other kingdoms: too much stuff for one animal to bear." If the gorilla is (almost) no one, the iguana is everyone. The whole reptile house suggests to Mr. Palomar "a squandering of forms without style and without plan, where all is possible." But then only certain forms—"perhaps actually the most incredible"—become finally fixed and identifiable in natural history, classifiable in the cases of a zoo. They are that history, "the order of the world," and it may be that what Mr. Palomar likes is the thought of "the world as it was before man, or after"; the chance, as he thinks, to be someone "who peers out beyond the human." But of course every sample in the zoo is torn from whatever life it lived in nature and preserved in an artificial climate. Far from being the order of the world before or after man, this is the very order of the human, the place where the world is our representation and our hypothesis. It's at this point that the smell of the reptile house becomes unbearable to Mr. Palomar, and he gives up wondering about the appeal of the iguanas. They are replaced (in his immediate experience, in the bestiary of his mind) by a group of brilliantly described, inscrutable crocodiles.

> Is theirs a boundless patience, or a desperation without end? What are they waiting for, or what have they given up waiting for? In what time are they immersed? In that of the species, removed from the course of the hours that race from the birth to the death of the individual? Or in the time of geological eras that shifts continents and solidifies the crust of emerged lands? Or in the slow cooling of the rays of the sun? The thought of a time outside our experience is intolerable. Mr. Palomar hurries to leave the snake house.

Mr. Palomar takes himself to the edge of the human, finds there more humanity than he wants, and then encounters a darker, more frightening sense of the world without us. The human is in one sense inescapable, in another it is what we cannot bear the thought of escaping from: the first because of the second, perhaps. Knowledge for Calvino means seeing what we have done to the world, how littered it is with our decisions and interpretations; but it also means giving up our grasp of the world, fostering a loyalty to that which persists beyond or beneath or apart from our interpretations. This intractable stuff wouldn't necessarily be blank or uninterpreted, purely natural—it's actually quite hard to see what the notion would mean, since the concept of nature is itself the product of ancient and proliferating assumptions. But it would elude our interpretations, there are whole universes, large and small, to remind us of the fullness rather than the emptiness of silence.

Perhaps the deepest and funniest moment in *Mr. Palomar* occurs in the account of our hero's visit to a prehispanic ruin in at Tula, in Mexico. His Mexican friend is "an impassioned and eloquent expert," full of stories about Quetzalcoatl, the god-king who takes the form of a plumed serpent; and about extravagant coyotes and jaguars. "Mr. Palomar's friend pauses at each stone, transforms it into a cosmic tale, an allegory, a moral reflection." At the same time a group of schoolboys is being taken round the ruins. At each stone, or pyramid, or statue, their teacher provides copious factual details—date, civilization, building material—and adds each time "We don't know what it means." Mr. Palomar "is fascinated by his friend's wealth of mythological references: the play of interpretation, allegorical readings, have always seemed to him a supreme exercise of the mind. But there is a humility of the mind too and Mr. Palomar is also drawn to what he takes to be the teacher's position, a "refusal to comprehend more than what the stones show us," which is "perhaps the only way to evince respect for their secret."

The teacher leads the boys to the beautiful Wall of the Serpents. "This is the wall of the serpents. Each serpent has a skull in its mouth. We don't know what they mean." Mr. Palomar's friend can stand it no longer, and cries, "Yes, we do! It's the continuity of life and death; the serpents are life, the skulls are death. Life is life because it bears death with it, and death is death because there is no life without death." The boys listen, astonished. Mr. Palomar thinks his friend's interpretation is still in need of an interpretation ("What did death, life, continuity, passage mean for the ancient Toltecs?") but knows that "not to interpret is impossible, as refraining from thinking is impossible." Impossible for us, that is. Once the school group is round the corner, the teacher says, "No es verdad, it is not true, what the señor said. We don't know what they mean."

We don't know; we do know; we can't bear not to know; all knowledge is frayed with ignorance, tilted over absences or further questions. "I am accustomed to consider literature a search for knowledge," Calvino says in one of his lectures, and Mr. Palomar is the fictional embodiment of this condition; not exactly a character, as I called him earlier, but not an abstraction either. More like an animated hypothesis, a theory with a wife and children and funny habits. It's as if Valéry's Monsieur Teste, that dream of the marooned intellect, had been rigged out with the gait and posture of Tati's Monsieur Hulot. "Why is such a person impossible?" Valéry asked, not expecting an answer. The question *turns us into Monsieur Teste*, he then rather alarmingly said. Teste is the demon of possibility, Valéry added, *il n'est point autre que le démon même de la possibilité*; and one of the great virtues of fiction is that it regularly makes us wonder what we have done with the notion of the possible.

TWO
Other Times

It belonged to time now; to history; was past
the touch and control of the living.

—Virginia Woolf, *Orlando*

6. A Postmodernist Romance

Time Flies

Modernism was among other things a weirdly troubled quarrel with time and history. The modernists were uneasy about the present; sought to reject the immediate past and the linear time that led straight to it; loved the idea of raiding the remote past for models and arguments; and preferred, when they thought about time at all, to think of it as cyclical or broken and irregular, like a season or an echo or a prophecy; not like a clock or a day or a year. Time itself was a kind of fall; paradise half regainable through an intense selectivity of cultural memory.

Of course the quarrel with time doesn't have to be nostalgic. Gabriel García Márquez's *One Hundred Years of Solitude* (*Cien Años de Soledad*, 1967) mimes a certain nostalgia in order to dispose of it, invites us to rethink Latin American history so that we can revive a more attractive, a more active present, a way out of the cage of a self-celebrating loneliness. But it is clear that these modernist preoccupations are very much present in this novel, and in García Márquez's later work. They are combined, however, with something else.

We know quite a bit about García Márquez's reading, and the role the Anglo-American modernists played in it, but one or two quotations may help to give some body to these generalities. García Márquez himself says for example that a sentence in *Mrs. Dalloway* "completely transformed" his "sense of time." His conversation with Plinio Apuleyo Mendoza gives us a charming picture of our writer at twenty, selling encyclopedias in the Goajira in Colombia, sitting in seedy hotel rooms at night, "swatting mosquitoes and dying of heat"; and reading about Bond Street and the passage there of some mysterious famous person. This situation itself mirrors the sort of displacement and incongruity García Márquez liked so much in Woolf. The sentence which remained in his mind, so that he still quotes it from memory, makes Woolf into an early version of Melquíades, the sage and magician of *One Hundred Years of Solitude*, author of a mysterious, prophetic manuscript. "I saw in a flash," García Márquez says, "the whole process of decomposition of Macondo and its final destiny":

> But there could be no doubt that greatness . . . was passing, hidden, down Bond Street, removed only by a hand's-breadth from ordinary people who might now, for the first time and last, be within speaking distance of the majesty of England, of the enduring symbol of the state which will be known to curious antiquaries, sifting the ruins of time, when London is a grass-grown path and all those hurrying along the pavement this Wednesday morning are but bones with a few wedding rings mixed up in their dust and the gold stoppings of innumerable decayed teeth.

The beginning of the passage seems recognizably Woolf's, but Borges (or Harold Bloom) would surely say García Márquez's hand shows in that "Wednesday morning" dropped so neatly into millennial history, as well as in the details of the gold and decayed teeth. We might add that Woolf does think that the identity of the person in the car will in the end be cleared up for good. No one knows now whether it is the Queen or a prince or the Prime Minister, but when London is a grass-grown path, Woolf's next sentence says, "The face in the motor car will . . . be known." García Márquez is more of a modernist than she is in this respect, and of Macondo we know only what memory and the imagination can devise. The answer to history is not a final revelation of the truth but the best that fiction can do.

Another quotation:

> Quentin had grown up with that; the mere names were interchangeable and almost myriad. His childhood was full of them; his very body was an empty hall echoing with sonorous defeated names; he was not a being, an entity, he was a commonwealth. He was a barracks filled with stubborn back-looking ghosts still recovering, even forty-three years afterward, from the fever which had cured the disease, waking from the fever without even knowing that it had been the fever itself which they had fought against and not the sickness, looking with stubborn recalcitrance backward beyond the fever and into the disease with actual regret, weak from the fever yet free of the disease and not even aware that the freedom was that of impotence.

This passage cries out for a commentary that would take us too far afield, but let us at least note the interchangeable names and the sense of time as specific (forty-three years—the time now, we have just learned, is 1909) and yet oddly flattened, a single block of haunted pastness. We note too that knowledge—of impotence, disease, history—is available to someone, author, reader, anonymous consciousness, but not to the character. This text too is a version of Melquíades's manuscript.

Or it is an anticipation of the textual tapestry of *Autumn of the Patriarch* (*El otoño del patriarca*, 1975):

> He was condemned not to know life except from the other side, condemned to decipher the seams and straighten the threads of the woof and warp of the tapestry of illusions of reality without suspecting even too late that the only livable life was one of show, the one we saw from this side which wasn't his general sir, this poor people's side with the trail of yellow leaves of misfortune and our ungraspable instants of happiness, where love was contaminated by the seeds of death but was all love general sir, where you yourself were only an uncertain vision of pitiful eyes through the dusty peepholes of a train.

"Condemned" implies the gloomy wisdom of an author or prophet, who knows what the character doesn't even suspect, not even "too late"; although the voice shifts swiftly and brilliantly from a slightly solemn third person to a garrulous and complaining first personal plural. "He do the Police in different voices" was Eliot's tentative title for *The Waste Land*. García Márquez do the dictator and his mother and the people and the literary novelist.

There is more, of course; much more of the same. García Márquez's relation to the modernist tradition is intricate and rich. But there is also more and different. There is clearly something missing in what I've been saying so far, a tone, a sound, an accent, an idiom we do not find among the modernists. The modernists were often very funny—Woolf in particular I think is an underrated comic writer—but they were not often playful and almost never casual. Time, for instance, was too important a topic, too big an enemy, to permit them to joke about it; and García Márquez's jokes about time therefore become an interesting index, a sign either of a distinctly personal touch or of a later moment in history, when the old enemy has become familiar: not less frightening, or less haunting but not in a position to claim the old respect. Or both: a personal signature and a historical trace. There is a wonderful, repeated exchange in *One Hundred Years of Solitude*. In each case a character is surprised by the sight of change in what seemed an unchanging place. "What did you expect," another character says, "time passes." "So it does," the first character agrees, "but not as much as that"—*Así es, pero no tanto*. Or again, in *Autumn of the Patriarch* the apparently deathless tyrant celebrates his hundredth year in power with a remark along the lines of "Seems like only yesterday": "A hundred years already, God damn it, a hundred years already, the way time passes."

Time flies. We are in the realm now not of a quarrel with time or history but of familiar cliché, the sort of stuff we hear (and say) every day. If we don't reflect much on these matters, we are perhaps inclined to think that clichés are simply a bad habit, something that educated and intelligent people—and, still more, writers—don't really use. A little thought (a little modesty) will makes us realize that we all use clichés pretty much all the time, and that the tricky question is not whether but which. It is a mark of much of the best of contemporary writing that it not only understands this truth about cliché but is at home with it. There is a lugubrious story about Flaubert at the end of his life, looking at a settled bourgeois family of the kind he had spent his career excoriating and saying "they have it right *(Ils sont dans le vrai)*." For Flaubert this is a horrible moment, a sort of recantation. If we can imagine the same insight accepted, still ruefully but with a kind of warmth, a welcome, we shall understand a great deal about our writers; and about a shift in our attitude to time. "Make it new," the modernist slogan, makes it hard for clichés; makes it hard for old things in general; spares only those new/old pieces of the past we have decided to revive. Clichés, we might say, belong to yesterday and today. Modernism's main interests were the day before yesterday and the day after tomorrow.

There is a broad progression here. Flaubert was a great collector of clichés; Joyce was the master of the artistic use of them—like Stravinsky using jazz, say; Nabokov was a magician of the mangled cliché, the fiendish excavator of all the clichés we thought were safely buried. But García Márquez, and Raymond Queneau and Manuel Puig, say, and Angela Carter (and in another mode John Ashbery) are cliché's friends, actually fond of them, happy to live among them, as we all must.

There is a movement too within the work of García Márquez, which repeats part of the progression I have just described. It's not chronological but goes, so to speak, from high to low, from literature to popular romance, and at the same time from modernism to something else. *Autumn of the Patriarch* uses clichés beautifully and inventively, but in the high modernist manner, as part of a weave of voices, the brilliant act of a ventriloquist. The ventriloquist/author remains at some distance from the language being used, the way Joyce remains hidden, even aloof, behind his many styles and voices. García Márquez says this is his "most important" book "from a literary point of view," and so it is;

"a much more important literary achievement" than *One Hundred Years of Solitude*. But we may perhaps see, as García Márquez did not at that time (1982), something slightly restrictive in the phrase "literary achievement."

One Hundred Years of Solitude itself, García Márquez told Plinio Apuleyo Mendoza, was "like a bolero": "on a knife's edge between the sublime and the vulgar." Like the boleros that begin to become fashionable in *Love in the Time of Cholera* (*El amor en los tiempos del cólera*, 1985): "the first boleros that were just beginning to break hearts (*astillar corazones*) in those days. *Astillar corazones*, literally "to splinter hearts," is itself a phrase that might come from a bolero; but García Márquez offers it without quotation marks, as an unsignaled, uninflected piece of his own prose. Apuleyo Mendoza's description of the bolero helps here. It is:

> the most authentically Latin American music. It seems overly sentimental but is also ironic, its exaggeration worn with humor and with a sense of "don't take it too literally" which apparently only we Latin Americans understand. Like the adjectives of Borges.

I'm not sure either Borges or the Trio Los Panchos would be too happy with that connection. What I like most in this evocation is the "also." Apuleyo Mendoza seems at first sight to be saying that the bolero looks sentimental but isn't, it's ironic. What he is actually saying, if I read him right, is that the bolero looks sentimental, and is; *and also* is funny, and not to be taken too literally. It's an interesting mixture and leads us a long way into the later work of García Márquez. *One Hundred Years of Solitude* is more intimate with clichés than *Autumn of the Patriarch* is, but there is still a certain distance, a disavowal in the tone, as García Márquez's remark about the sublime and the vulgar suggests. The whole thrust of the writing in *Love in the Time of Cholera* is to imply that what we think vulgar often is sublime, or that the vulgar actually doesn't exist, except as a fantasy in the minds of people who think it is what they are not.

Reading Dazzle

The most casual reader of García Márquez notes his fondness for numbers. There are one hundred years of solitude, and in the novel of that name the rain pours down on Macondo for exactly four years, eleven months, and two days. A traveler circles the earth sixty-five times. Gargantuan eaters consume for breakfast eight quarts of coffee, thirty raw eggs, and the juice of forty oranges. The numbers call up an air of legend, a precision that mildly mocks the idea of precision. But numbers can also suggest patience, an intimacy with the slow seepage of time. Closer to the numerical flavor of *Love in the Time of Cholera*, the sad and long-suffering hero of *No One Writes to the Colonel* (*El coronel no tiene quien le escriba* (1961) needs, we are told, every counted minute of the seventy-five years of his life to arrive at the simple word that summarizes both his defeats and his dignity, his refusal to accept the unacceptable. He is a courteous, old-fashioned man and has earlier rebuked a group of local youths for swearing. At last, however, nothing short of rude anger will do. The simple word is shit, *Mierda*.

Love in the Time of Cholera ends on a milder phrase, but one that has been similarly stored, one that similarly reflects an arithmetic of obstinacy and concentration. A captain asks how long he can be expected to keep his boat going up and down a tropical river, and the answer he receives has been brewing for "fifty-three years, seven months, and eleven days and nights." It is an answer that looks forward as well as backward: "Forever" (*Toda la vida*).

It takes the reader some time to get here too, and on my first reading of this novel I found myself counting pages now and then, the way the characters count years and months. Good stories are best told slowly, Thomas Mann says, but it is possible to have too much of a good thing, and Mann may not be the ideal witness in such a cause. García Márquez really needs the snail's pace he sets, I think, but we need a little patience to understand his need. Or some of us do: the book's huge commercial success suggests that slow telling is making a comeback.

The book begins with a corpse, and the scent of almonds that indicates death by cyanide. "It was inevitable," the doctor thinks who is examining the body, "the scent of bitter almonds always reminded him of the fate of unrequited love." Inevitable, fate, love: we are reading the opening sentence of the book, and we seem already to be deep in an old-fashioned romantic novel. So we are, but we are also caught in the first of García Márquez's narrative lures. What is inevitable is not that deaths by cyanide should be those of lovers but that the doctor should think of such deaths. This one in fact is the first cyanide death he can recall that has nothing to do with love, unrequited or requited. It is not an exception that proves the rule but an unruly event that makes us wonder whether we know what the game is. The doctor himself unfortunately doesn't have much time to wonder, since he dies later the same day in a ridiculous accident, trying to recapture an escaped parrot. And this is the second narrative lure we have already stumbled into. The story we hear at length in the first part of the book is not that of the corpse, as the initial plot moves seem to promise, but that of the doctor and his city and his day. In the rest of the book we hear little more of the corpse or of its earlier life but a great deal more about the doctor, and his wife/widow, and the indefatigable, obsessive fellow who has been in love with her for the amount of time so carefully detailed before the pronunciation of the word "Forever." The corpse is that of Jeremiah de Saint-Amour, an escaped convict turned photographer, who killed himself at the age of sixty because he had decided long ago that he did not want to live beyond that age. Sadly, at the end he found himself regretting his resolve but couldn't think of changing it—"as the date approached he had gradually succumbed to despair as if his death had been not his own decision but an inexorable destiny." This is an important phrase. *Love in the Time of Cholera*, like García Márquez's other novels, is an exploration of destiny, but of this kind of destiny: the kind we invent and displace and fear and desperately live up to or die for.

The setting of the novel is an ancient city on the Caribbean coast of Latin America, the former favorite residence of the viceroys of New Granada. The city is not named but is a composite picture, García Márquez has said, of Cartagena, Santa Marta, and Baranquilla, places in Colombia where he spent much of his early life. It has a cathedral, a former slave quarter, and a grim colonial building that once housed the Inquisition and now (a detail that perhaps nods toward the shade of Buñuel) is occupied by a severely Catholic girls' school. The place resembles Haiti and Cuba because of the sea and the heat and the tropic and the life of the port; it is connected to a colder, mountainous Latin America through its language and its history of empire and independence and civil war. There is much talk of river navigation, of manatees and caimans sporting on the muddy banks of the Magdalena, as well as of ships passing for New Orleans, and of fabulous galleons sunk by English pirates as late as the early eighteenth century. Joseph Conrad is mentioned as involved in an arms deal; the doctor studies in Paris with Dr. Adrien Proust, the father of the novelist. We hear of Dreyfus, the new waltzes of Johann Strauss, the premiere of *The Tales of Hoffman*, the screening of a film called *Cabiria*.

The country is not named either, but it has Colombia's Liberals and Conservatives (the only difference between a Liberal president and a Conservative president, a character says, sounding like Colonel Aureliano Buendia in *One Hundred Years of Solitude*, is that the Liberal is not as well dressed), its War of the Thousand Days, which took place in 1899–1902, and plenty of towns and rivers that would allow us to find our way on an actual map of Colombia. It even anticipates the terrible peacetime violence for which Colombia has become notorious since 1947, a chaotic, wholesale murdering by crooks and guerillas and the police and the army, a butchery that lacks even the historical shape of a civil war but is none the less real for that. When the Violence (as it is simply, sparely called) was taken to be more or less under control, in 1962 there were still some two hundred civilian deaths occurring each month. It appears here grimly, casually, almost silently, as it does in García Márquez's other books, this time in the shape of corpses floating down river toward the sea, a strange, unaccountable sight, "for there were no more wars or epidemics." Like many other words in this book, and in the historical Latin America it evokes, this clause is both true and deceptive. There are no more epidemics, and we are near the end of the novel. But cholera still exists, even if only endemically, so the time of cholera does continue. There is nothing going on that can really be called a war, unless we insist on the "larval wars that governments were bent on hiding with distracted decrees." But there is random killing, a plague as lethal as any other.

The time of the novel is the later nineteenth and earlier twentieth centuries. A recent event is a showing of the movie *All Quiet on the Western Front*, which was released in 1930 but may have reached Latin America a little later. More precisely, the present of the novel is just under two years in the 1930s, when all the principal characters are quite old, a lot older than Jeremiah de Saint-Amour, and have no thought of taking his view of things; and there are extensive flashbacks that give us the youth and backgrounds and long lives of these people. The book has been compared to a Naturalist novel and to a photograph album. It's a lot more like the second than like the first, but we might like to pause over the idea of a sophisticated, affectionate Naturalist novel, an evocation of an old, grubby, rigid world for its own sad and charming sake and not for any grim demonstration it might permit. This is a place where an old-fashioned mother can castigate even the contents of her daughter-in-law's sleep: "A decent woman cannot have that kind of dream." The doctor, returning to the city from a long stay in Europe, can hate its filth and its rats and its disease and its backwardness but still love it enough to look at it straight:

> "How noble this city must be," he would say, "for we have spent four hundred years trying to finish it off and we still have not succeeded."

From the paupers' cemetery, one can look down on

> the entire historic city, the broken roofs and the decaying walls, the rubble of fortresses among the brambles, the trail of islands in the bay, the hovels of the poor around the swamps, the immense Caribbean.

This is not a romantic vision, but it is a way one might talk of home.

There is a variety of suspense García Márquez has very much made his own. It consists in giving away conclusions and leaving the reader to guess at how they are reached. The trick characteristically involves removing most of the plausible narrative props, making us dizzily wonder whether already reached conclusions actually can be reached. It is another way of playing with destiny. Liberty creeps into unlikely human spaces, even what has happened seems doubtful, and hindsight, surely the safest of all forms of prophecy, turns risky. Thus we know in this novel that the couple I have just evoked do not marry when young, since we first meet them at the ludicrous death of her husband, the doctor. The suitor is now seventy-six, the woman is seventy-two. He has been waiting, since she first turned him down, for "fifty-one years, nine months, and four days"—a little less than two years short of the final count we have already seen. We learn of their courtship, his numerous affairs, her marriage to the doctor, the doctor's single, scared infidelity, the lovers' happy, belated, foolish reconciliation, old skeletons still able to dance and get frightened at their feelings—though then we are told, in a fine phrase, that they wonder what they are doing "so far from their youth," and that their relation is "beyond love," because it is "beyond the pitfalls of passion, beyond the brutal mockery of hope and the phantoms of disillusion"—*desengaño*, one of those great Spanish words we find both in Baroque poems and lingering as the names of modern streets and lanes, caught up again in an ancient rhetoric of suspicion of the world. What we can't picture, what we must follow page by page, is how any of this can actually come about, how obstacles are removed, how people can bring themselves to say and act as they must to ensure the named developments. García Márquez's formality is impeccable here, a slow joke in its own right. He almost always refers to the doctor by his full name and title, for example: Dr. Juvenal Urbino. His wife invariably appears under her Christian name and maiden name, Fermina Daza; her stubborn lover under his Christian and family name, Florentino Ariza. No modern intimacies of appellation.

The text is not solemn, there are sly gags, fantastic images, and abrupt violences: a group of brothers called after popes (Leon XII, Pius V, and so on); a baby carried around in a bird cage; a woman discovered in adultery and murdered by her husband without a word; a ghost who waves from the river bank; a black doll that silently, eerily grows, becoming too big for its dress and its shoes; a suicide for love (with laudanum, though, another blow to the doctor's theory). But the prose is unruffled, affects not to notice anything untoward. This is a stylistic act, of course, but the chief feature of the act is its discretion. Irony would be too strong a word for the almost invisible humor, the scent of skepticism in the following sentence: "He was a perfect husband: he never picked up anything from the floor, or turned out a light, or closed a door." Such a husband is perfect because there is no chink between him and the myth.

The time of cholera, which is over and not over, is the time of romantic love. Love is like cholera, we are told several times in the book—even its physical symptoms, dizziness, nausea, fever, and the rest, can be the same. Like cholera, love is mortal, exclusive (because it separates us from our world) and undiscriminating (because it doesn't care what kind of victims it gets). García Márquez is fond of telling interviewers that the book he took with him when he first left Colombia for Europe was Defoe's *Journal of the Plague Year*—a story that, apart from doubtless being true, suggests an interest in communities doomed to clinical isolation. The community here is the teeming Caribbean city, not the backland of Macondo, but it is also the community of all those, in Latin America and elsewhere, who are perhaps too keen on morbid metaphors of love. Love is a disease in this book, and this is a romantic novel; but the disease is one of the self-deluding, stubborn will, a fruit of mythology and obstinacy rather than any fate beyond ourselves. Indeed the word itself becomes subject to a kind of creative disintegration or dissemination. At first and most prominently used to evoke the unique, histrionic, weepy passion, the endless topic of soap operas and their predecessors, the kind of the thing that drives people to death through cyanide, it gradually attaches itself to quite various human activities and affections: a long marriage, for example, begun without love, and then finding it and losing it and finding it; the "emergency love," the "hurried love" peddled in brothels; the "loveless love" of desperate people; love for a city, as we have seen; the love of children, love of food, love for life. The first of Florentino Ariza's many mistresses teaches him that "nothing one does in bed is immoral if it helps to perpetuate love." Florentino Ariza himself thinks at one point, "My heart has more rooms than a whorehouse," a secular twist on the rumored many mansions of heaven. The heart: home of sentiment and dream and nostalgia, but also of more erratic, unpredictable emotions, the place where life itself can always turn up and surprise us. Love is the name for attractive and disreputable impulses as well as for all the noble enchantments and illusions, the *engaños* and *encantos* with which we garnish our insufficiently romantic times. If love were always and only a disease, it could only be because life is. Writers have suggested this, but García Márquez is not one of those writers.

In interviews García Márquez has described *Love in the Time of Cholera* not as like a bolero but as "practically a telenovela, a soap opera" and also as a nineteenth-century *feuilleton*, the serial novel that was the soap opera's literary antecedent. It is important to see that García Márquez's novel is not a pastiche of these genres, and still less a parody. It doesn't criticize or condescend to the genres, it seeks, as Stephen Minta has very well said, for "the truths about emotional life which . . . are . . . solidly embedded in the language of the popular imagination." And yet. The clichés are clichés, however much we may feel at home among them. What are we to do with a discourse that is certainly straight-faced but not entirely straight; something less than ironic; certainly not figurative, indeed devoted to the meticulous reconstruction of a historical world, but still not entirely literal?

There is an answer, I think, suggested chiefly by the behavior of the characters in the novel itself, but first we need to look a little more closely at the stealth of García Márquez's style, and his relation to his soapy sources. There is much discussion of reading in the book, of the doctor's European culture (he is a fan of Loti and Anatole France), of poetry competitions, and above all of the sentimental romances and poems through which so many people conduct so much of their imaginative lives—*versos y folletines de lágrimas*, "verses and tearful serialized love stories." Florentino Ariza immerses himself in books, reads everything from Homer to the lousiest local poets:

> But he made no distinctions: he read whatever came his way, as if it had been ordained by fate, and despite his many years of reading he still could not judge what was good and what was not in all that he read. The only thing clear to him was that he preferred verse to prose, and in verse he preferred love poems.

García Márquez's implication, I take it, is not exactly that this is an ideal reader, but that there are many worse, and that serious, critical readers are often the worst of all.

The language of the book itself, then, is that of fate and broken hearts and eternal passions; of "mists of grief" and the "quicksand" of old age; of a "private hell" and "the wasteland of . . . insomnia"; of blood pounding in the veins and "night eternal over the dark sea." Yet the effect, as I have suggested, is neither pastiche nor straight imitation but a form of homage to popular literature, a friendly glance at its often lurid prose. And the prose here is not itself lurid, in spite of the phrases I've just quoted; it is stately, a graceful orchestration of old verbal tunes. What distinguishes this novel from the sentimental work it continuously alludes to is not irony or distance but a certain persistent lucidity. This is not a tearful text; just scrupulously loyal to tearful stories, only occasionally murmuring words such as "fallacy" and "illusion." If it moved faster it would have to judge summarily, settle issues, could hardly avoid the recourse to irony. As it is, time and our patience situate the events and the characters.

Fermina Daza when young, for example, is suddenly sure that what she thought was love is nothing of the kind. She looks at the suitor she has not seen for some time and feels not the passion she has been diligently nurturing but only an "abyss of disenchantment," *desencanto*, another of those great Spanish names for cheated desire. Is she right, or is her disenchantment just ordinary disappointment, of the kind lovers often feel after absences? She is probably wrong, and the text, much later, hints that she is. For the moment, though, she is sure she is right, acts on her feeling, condemns her suitor to a lifetime's despair; more, since she is not a person who can admit mistakes, she will in her own terms always have been right, whatever shifts of feeling may take place in what this novel calls her heart. When García Márquez writes of the "revelation" she experiences, and of the "correctness" of her decision, the words are simple and clear, but several meanings have piled up in them. They point, among other things, to a conviction that alters reality and then takes that alteration as proof of the conviction's justice. A form of destiny. Conversely, Florentino Ariza thinks of himself as doggedly faithful to his one love, in spite of the fact that he has slept with hundreds of other women (he has a note of 622, but there are other affairs too casual to be registered) and even loved some of them. His fidelity is like her certainty, clear to its possessor, questionable to others. By fidelity he means being unable to forget or replace his first love and being able to ensure that news of his apparent infidelities doesn't reach her.

The characters in fact are better guides to meaning than the narrator; better readers of their world and better teachers of reading. Like the characters in García Márquez's earlier novels, indeed like all of us, they are subject to bad luck. We could any of us fall from a ladder and die while trying to rescue a parrot. But they are not, these characters, the victims of fate, prisoners of an author's plot. They write their own lines; they choose their own interpretations of the lines of others; and they are very skillful at both activities.

Florentino Ariza, as a young man of eighteen, brings his first love letter to Fermina Daza. She is sitting sewing outside her house, under the trees, and this is how the occasion is described:

> He took the letter out of his inside jacket pocket and held it before the eyes of the troubled embroiderer, who had still not dared to look at him. She saw the blue envelope trembling in a hand petrified with terror, and she raised the embroidery frame so he could put the letter on it, for she could not admit that she had noticed the trembling of his fingers. Then it happened [*Entonces occurió*]: a bird shook himself among the leaves of the almond trees, and his droppings fell right on the embroidery. Fermina Daza moved the frame out of the way, hid it

behind the chair so that he would not notice what had happened [*lo que había pasado*], and looked at him for the first time, her face aflame. Florentino Ariza was impassive as he held the letter in his hand and said, "It's good luck." She thanked him with her first smile and almost snatched the letter away from him.

If this had been a passage in Flaubert, the birdshit would have been a comment on life and love, a sort of visual epigram; if this had been a telenovela, the birdshit wouldn't have appeared at all, would have been edited out or simply not thought of. The interesting point is that Flaubert and the soap opera are in agreement about the incompatibility of birdshit and romance, and García Márquez's narrator, with his ominous narrative signal ("Then it happened") seems ready to feel the same. Until the characters absorb the shit into the romance without breaking step; thereby teaching the narrator, and us, a needed lesson about compatibilities.

Throughout the book we are invited to read language (and the language of gestures) the way the characters do; but I don't know how well we do this. Florentino declares his love to Fermina—his "eternal fidelity and everlasting love," after a fifty-one-year wait—but before he speaks he places his hat over his heart, or more precisely, where his heart is, *en el sitio del corazón*. We can't laugh at the gesture, and we can't patronize him, call him quaint or cute; but we are aware that the gesture itself is empty, an ancient formality rendered moving by the crazy, formless passion that has borrowed its face. Florentino's whole appearance is like this:

He was what he seemed: a useful and serious old man. His body was bony and erect, his skin dark and clean-shaven, his eyes avid behind round spectacles in silver frames, and he wore a romantic, old fashioned [*un poco tardío para la época*] mustache with waxed tips. He combed the last tufts of his hair at his temples upward and plastered them with brilliantine to the middle of his shining skull as a solution to total baldness. His natural gallantry and languid manner were immediately charming, but they were also considered suspect virtues in a confirmed bachelor. He had spent a great deal of money, ingenuity, and willpower to disguise the seventy-six years he had completed in March, and he was convinced in the solitude of his soul that he had loved in silence for a much longer time than anyone else in this world ever had.

This paragraph ends in a swirl of clichés, which must represent (faithfully, the way Joyce represents Gertie MacDowell's consciousness in the thirteenth chapter of *Ulysses*) Florentino's view of himself. We have in our minds the belated moustache and the unequal fight against baldness. Is this what Romeo would have looked like, if he had lived to seventy-six and moved to Colombia? There is also the odd, uncompromising directness of the paragraph's first sentence: "He was what he seemed to be: a useful and serious old man," *un anciano servicial y serio*. What do we get when we put together the straight talk, the old-fashioned style, the romantic sense of self? Something rather grand, I think, but also something rather oblique, in spite of the direct start. Something like the absurd (but real) grandeur of his claim about being a virgin, which I shall discuss in a moment. We like his style but not on the terms on which that style offers itself. We accept him but not on his valuation. And not, oddly, on the narrator's either, since the narrator's voice becomes a contribution not a summary. This fellow is an *anciano servicial y serio*, sure, but he's also more than that.

The characters take each other seriously but not always literally; they know what clichés mean but can't always say. When Florentino and Fermina get together, at the end of novel, she expresses her surprise that in all the years of their separation—fifty-three years, seven months, eleven days—he has not been known to have a woman, and this in a city where gossip knows everything "even before it's happened." This is too good a chance to miss, a place for the bolero to blossom. "I've remained a virgin for you," Florentino says, *Es que me he conservado virgen para ti*. The likely options for a writer here seem to be the soggy score, a prose of soaring violins, or a knowing wink to the reader: sentimentality or parody. What García Márquez gives us is the character's skepticism. And her belief. And invites in us at the same time a complex implied respect for both characters. Fermina doesn't think this absurd sentence is true, and we know it's not, since we have been told how many women Florentino has slept with, but she likes its style, "the spirited way in which he said it," *el coraje con que lo dijo*.

Fermina is not moved by the thought or the sentiment of the florid claim, although she knows Florentino's emotion to be deep and genuine, in spite of the banality and untruth of the words. She likes the unashamed way in which he assumes the language of romance, the fiction no one believes in, no one needs to believe in, since its function is not to transmit a declared meaning but to allow certain feelings and prowesses to circulate. It is her sense of this function, indeed, which causes Fermina to doubt the truth of Florentino's claim—she doesn't have the information the reader has. "She would not have believed it in any event, even if it had been true, because his love letters were composed of similar phrases whose meaning mattered less than their brilliance," *que no valían por su sentido sino por su poder de deslumbramiento*. Their dazzle. She isn't dazzled, but she likes the dazzle; she can read the dazzle. I think of a remark of

Chomsky's in which he expresses surprise that linguists (or anyone) should think of conveying information as the characteristic business of language. "Human language can be used to inform or mislead, to clarify one's own thoughts or to display one's cleverness, or simply for play." And for much else.

The implication here reverses one of modernism's major claims about language and replaces it with something a good deal more optimistic and democratic. Pound quite explicitly and most of the modernists implicitly associate debased or banal language with debased or banal thinking. The kindest option is a sort of uneasy sympathy. When we leaf through the sentimental prose of the Gertie Macdowell chapter of *Ulysses*, we may feel sorry she has no better means of expressing her longings than the trashy idioms of what she reads, we hardly feel at all that she has expressed her longings, still less that these trashy idioms could in any way become an adequate or lively vehicle for them. Yet this is just what García Márquez is proposing, and the move, oddly, brings him close to Henry James, a writer he doesn't mention and perhaps hasn't read. James lends his intelligence to his characters in just the way García Márquez does; not because he has more intelligence but because his intelligence is different and will translate into a more discursive currency. He speaks the reader's language, while the characters speak only their own. Or to put that less obscurely, Fermina doesn't need fancy words, or any words, for her understanding of how language works—she merely needs to know how to act on her understanding. Her understanding is very subtle, however; and so, the suggestion goes, is the understanding of many apparently unsophisticated or unliterary people. The writer needs all the subtlety (and discretion) he/she can muster to get anywhere near it.

There are two kinds of time in García Márquez—at least two. There is the magical, stagnant, modernist time, which scarcely seems to pass; and there is the cumulative, devouring time, which is always passing. Both times are constantly in play—as we see in the famous image of the wheel and the axle in *One Hundred Years of Solitude*, the wheel turning in what looks like cyclical time while the axle wears away according to linear succession—but not always equally accented. We might contrast the time of the Buendías, for example, with the time of the Colonel to whom no one writes.

Love in the Time of Cholera inhabits the Colonel's time but without his despair and ultimate rage. We can't really say that time is accepted here, or that the characters are resigned to it. We have only to think of Florentino's hairdo; of Fermina's wrinkled shoulders, fallen breasts; of these two comically ancient lovers generally, baffled by their renewed romance. Their age is part of what makes them touching, not quite ridiculous but always on the edge of being so—as they themselves quite clearly know. Time is real and regrettable—but not a disaster. Time is the birdshit on the romance, but the romance can accommodate it. It has only to be treated the way many contemporary writers treat clichés—to be treated as the cliché it is. It is possible to make a style out of its banality rather than our despair. If the modernists had been able to do this, their ghosts—Quentin Compson's Southerners, the dictator who doesn't know, even too late, what he is missing, many more—would have been not laid to rest but freed, released from their narrow haunts. Paradise would have been neither lost nor regained but deserted, left to its own devices. It is precisely through this metaphor that Alan Wilde figures the shift from modernism to postmodernism, the second moment releasing, as he puts it, the humanity of the first: "paradise, once lost, is now abandoned." That is, the pathos of loss is abandoned, we make peace with the losses (and gains) of everyday living. In such a view the modernists, staying on, surviving their old anguishes, would have learned the lesson that their anxiety about time hid so thoroughly from them: that we domesticate time, come to terms with it, not by mythifying it but by counting it; not by tearing the hands off our watches, as Quentin Compson does in *The Sound and the Fury*, but by looking steadily at the hands as they go round. And round.

She needs nothing. Nothing utterable.
—Samuel Beckett, *Ill Seen Ill Said*

7. *The Mind Has Mountains*

Every week . . . a paper laid bare the bones of some broken woman. Man kills wife. Eight accused of rape dismissed. Woman and girl victims of. Woman commits suicide. White attackers indicted. Five women caught. Woman says man beat. In jealous rage man.

This particular compilation of bad news appears in Toni Morrison's novel *Jazz* (1992). Are these broken women mere victims? "Natural prey? Easy pickings? . . . I don't think so," Morrison's character repeats as she reads this news and meditates on it. Some are, no doubt, and the novel tells us the story of one of them, a girl who likes to push people into "something scary" and who, when shot by a man she has driven too far, allows herself to die. But other black women are arming themselves, physically and mentally, and in this they have caught a current of the times, a not always visible indignation that says enough is enough and that is glimpsed in new forms of protest and political organization and heard in the freedom and sadness and hunger of jazz. There are extended flashbacks in the novel, but its main "times" are the 1920s, or rather a period Morrison dates from 1917, the year of major riots in East Saint Louis and a commemorative march in New York. The novel's most intimate, violent events occur in January 1926. There was a jazz age behind the Jazz Age.

The simplest of public incidents, the kind that make it into the newspapers, arise from complicated private stories, and stories of this kind, the connecting of blunt or bitter fact with its riddling context or history, have always been Morrison's business as a novelist. And not only as a novelist. In her introduction to a volume of essays on the Anita Hill/Clarence Thomas affair, Morrison distinguishes between "what took place" and "what happened," where the former is what can be briefly stated and the latter is what we might, after patient thought and considerable investigation, actually understand. We live in a world of what the narrator of *Jazz* calls "a crooked kind of mourning," and the phrase takes us a good way into Morrison's moral universe.

The mourning is often a grief for what suddenly and undeniably took place: a shooting, a rape, the killing of a child. The crookedness is part of what happened and keeps happening, and one of the special provinces of the imaginative writer. In *Playing in the Dark* (1992), Morrison speaks of "places where the imagination sabotages itself, locks its own gates, pollutes its vision," and her fiction is largely concerned with the geography and (possible) redemption of such places. The mind, for Morrison, could always be a friend but is often an enemy, as we learn in *Beloved* (1987), for instance, where an escaped slave is imprisoned in the horrors of memory, where even a place of torment has something of the flavor of home:

> She shook her head from side to side, resigned to her rebellious brain. Why was there nothing it refused? No misery, no regret, no hateful picture too rotten to accept? Like a greedy child it snatched up everything.

The physical beauty of the rural world compounds the problem, disguising the pain and disgrace of the remembered slave farm: "It never looked as terrible as it was and it made her wonder if hell was a pretty place too." It is horrifying, of course, that history should record as much material cruelty as it does, and even then forget the half of it; no less horrifying, perhaps, that the long legacy of such a history is an imagination often dedicated to self-sabotage, unable even to mourn except in crooked ways.

Morrison's lucid and eloquent first novel, *The Bluest Eye* (1970), portrays a poor black family who live in a run-down storefront in Lorain, Ohio. There is an important difference, Morrison's narrator insists, between living there and staying there:

> They lived there because they were poor and black, and they stayed there because they believed they were ugly. Although their poverty was traditional and stultifying, it was not unique. But their ugliness was unique. . . . You looked at them and wondered why they were so ugly; you looked closely and could not find the source. Then you realized it came from conviction, their conviction. It was as though some mysterious all-knowing master had given each one a cloak of ugliness to wear, and they had each accepted it without question.

Each member of the family interprets and acts out his or her ugliness differently, but none of them understands that the all-knowing master is not God but only history and habit; the projection of their own benumbed collusion with the mythology of beauty and ugliness that oppresses them beyond their already grim social oppression. Throughout Morrison's novels—those already mentioned but also *Sula* (1973), *Song of Solomon* (1977) and *Tar Baby* (1981)—variously trapped and bewildered characters fight against similar mythologies, alluring versions of what it means to be black or female or poor or free or respectable or southern. They fight with energy and dignity but usually without much success. The best they get is release from pain or haunting, or an understanding of the life they are about to lose.

The strongest moments in the novels represent what we might call the paradoxes of crookedness: rape as a form of love in extremis; infanticide as the deepest expression of a mother's care. The ugly father of the ugly family I have just described rapes his daughter, but at least, the narrator bleakly says, he "loved her enough to touch her." For the chief character in *Beloved* the killing of her baby in order to save her from a return to slavery is both simple and unforgivable, what she had to do and what she cannot forget, the direct result of a deformed history. "If I hadn't killed her," she says, "she would have died"; and the tangle of the thought is the exact image of the tangle of her heart and mind. In sharply evoked crookedness of this sort, tender, horrifying, passionate, and violent, Morrison finds a solution to the problem of severely registering the effects of oppression without making its victims seem only victims, less than human, precisely the passive, inferior beings their oppressors like to think they are.

In *Jazz*, for the first time in Morrison's fiction, there is a genuine escape from crookedness and sabotage, a defeat of mythology, and Morrison herself seems at a loss to describe what has happened—even if she knows precisely what has taken place. Perhaps Morrison is only miming disarray, and in one sense she must be. She has her narrator declare her surprise with her characters' behavior, as if they had just got away from her, as if they had managed to end up happy without her permission. "I was so sure, and they danced and walked all over me. Busy, they were, busy being original, changeable—human, I guess you'd say." I guess we'd rather not, and of course we can't linger too long over this old trope. When writers (or their surrogates) say their characters have a life of their own, we wonder both what they are actually up to and why they are resorting to this metaphor. But while Morrison's narrator is sentimentalizing her characters (it is human to be original and changeable, but no less human, alas, to be blinkered and monotonous), something else is happening, and to see what it is we need to return to the "facts" of the novel, what the newspapers might have reported for January 1926 on Lenox Avenue and thereabouts.

Middle-aged man shoots and kills an eighteen-year old girl, they might have said. Wife attempts to slash the face of the girl's corpse. Joe and Violet Trace have been living happily enough in New York City since they came up from Virginia in 1906, more happily (at first) than they ever expected to. They had heard a lot about Baltimore, and Violet at least was afraid New York might be "less lovely":

> Joe believed it would be perfect. When they arrived, carrying all of their be-longings in one valise, they both knew right away that perfect was not the word. It was better than that.

The narrator, a garrulous, intelligent, unnamed Harlem local ("Sth, I know that woman," she begins), has the same wide-eyed view of the excitements of the (always eagerly capitalized) City. "I'm crazy about this City," she says. "I like the way the City makes people think they can do what they want and get away with it'; and she likes the way it allows people to become "not so much new as themselves: their stronger, riskier selves":

> The City is smart at this: smelling and [sic] good and looking raunchy; sending secret messages disguised as public signs: this way, open here, danger to let col-ored only single men on sale woman wanted private room stop dog on premis-es absolutely no money down fresh chicken free delivery fast.

The City is one of the main characters of the novel, a strangely cheerful urban home for the "wildness" Morrison celebrates in the rural worlds of her other novels. "When I see this wildness gone in a person," she says in an interview, "it's sad." Wildness is a "special lack of restraint," clearly a virtue in those whose lives have been nearly all restraint. And indeed in *Jazz* too there is a rural wild zone, to be found in the Virginia the Traces have abandoned but not forgotten.

Yet of course you can't become your riskier self without taking risks, and even your stronger self may not be strong enough. Joe and Violet, in their dif-ferent ways, have got lost among the City's enchantments. Their happiness trickles away into aging, they scarcely speak to each other. Violet begins to think of the children she hasn't had and the meanings of her mother's long-ago suicide. What the narrator calls "cracks" begin to develop in Violet's con-sciousness, "dark fissures in the globe light of the day," moments when she loses her words and her meanings. And Joe, more traditionally, has the male midlife crisis, looks for his youth in a young girl; but then also, in rather too novelistic a contortion perhaps, seems to see in the girl a substitute for the mother he never knew. The girl herself finds a handsome arrogant boyfriend of her own age, clumsily dismisses Joe, and Joe kills her without knowing which piece of his life he is trying to erase or rearrange. He is not arrested, not even accused, "because nobody actually saw him do it, and the dead girl's aunt didn't want to throw money to helpless lawyers and laughing cops when she knew the expense wouldn't improve anything." Joe and Violet go on living together, miserable, silent, baffled.

All this matches the narrator's expectations. She has meanwhile been imagining lives for these people and others, giving them pasts, lending them voices: Joe, Violet, their courtship and life in Virginia; the girl, Dorcas, her parents killed in the riots in East Saint Louis; Dorcas's aunt, Alice Manfred, who after her niece's death strikes up an oddly austere and tender friendship with Violet; Dorcas's friend Felice, who gets to know and like the Traces, in spite of their strangeness and their sorrow. But the narrator is imagining all or most of this, a novelist within the novel. She's pretty happy with her performance and doesn't stint on self-praise:

> Risky, I'd say, trying to figure out anybody's state of mind. But worth the trouble if you're like me—curious, inventive and well-informed. . . . It's not hard to imagine what it must have been like.

It's not hard to imagine, but it's hard to get it right, and this is what our chastened narrator learns at the end of the novel. Not before she changes her personality (or at least her style) a couple of times and has a spell as a sort of Faulknerian memorialist. The prose gets worryingly close to parody here and certainly signals a frank shift to a grander literary gear—or signals perhaps the writer's need of the freedom to make such a shift. The chatty narrator saying, "I know just how she felt," and, "Good luck and let me know," becomes a theorist saying, "I have to be the language that wishes him well, speaks his name." And starts to devise sentences like this one:

> When he stopped the buggy, got out to tie the horse and walk back through the rain, perhaps it was because the awful-looking thing lying in wet weeds was everything he was not as well as a proper protection against and anodyne to what he believed his father to be, and therefore (if it could just be contained, identified)—himself.

"He" is a young mulatto Violet has heard about from her grandmother. He has discovered (from his white mother) that his father is black, and he has gone in search of him. The "thing" he meets on the way is a pregnant young black woman, who may or may not be Joe Trace's mother-to-be. The narrator is having a fine time evoking this ripely resonant stuff but does herself seem caught up in one of the very mythologies Morrison keeps trying to get her characters out of: race as trauma, suffered by the character but weirdly relished by the teller of the tale. Here as in certain moments in *Song of Solomon* and *Tar-Baby*, but not, as far as I can see, in the other novels, a certain talkiness in Morrison's language reflects an abstraction in her thought, a move to diagrams rather than the working-through of particular, problematic experiences.

Fortunately, the diagrams are never there for long, and the talkiness is more than answered by something like its reverse: a willingness on the novelist's part to inhabit language, to let it do the talking, to see it as itself, a freighted form of history rather than a mere means of making statements. The characters in *Jazz* are said to treat language like an "intricate, malleable toy designed for their play," and to enter a Toni Morrison novel is to enter a place where words and idioms tease each other and where what is said is richly shadowed by what is not. This is why she doesn't need to have her narrator announce "I want to be the language," and so on. When a character in *Song of Solomon* promises to "fly from Mercy," he literally means he is going to try and fly from the roof of Mercy Hospital in a city that I take to be Detroit, but we can hardly miss the suicidal sadness of his project, and mercy is what other characters in the novel long for, sing for, and (in scarcity) find. The very names of Morrison's characters are a mark of their history, in slavery or out, and the jokes they make about their names are a way of remembering that history and fighting it. "Names they got from yearnings, gestures, flaws, events, mistakes, weaknesses," we read in *Song of Solomon*. "Names that bore witness." A list of names follows, starting inside the fiction and moving into the public record: Macon Dead, First Corinthians Dead, Railroad Tommy, Empire State, Ice Man, Muddy Waters, Jelly Roll, T-Bone, Washboard, Gatemouth, Staggerlee, many others. Joe Trace, in *Jazz*, names himself on the basis of the story he hears about his parents disappearing "without a trace": he decides he is the Trace they disappeared without.

It is in the flowing, personal language of her conclusion that the narrator expresses her new-found humility about what she knows and doesn't know, but it is not exactly in language that she discovers it. What she learns is not only that her characters have cheated her expectations but that they have lived and continue to live in ways she needs to know more about; not just that they have escaped her, but that they are kinder and wiser and more resilient than she is. "I lived a long time, maybe too much, in my own mind," she says early on, but she is not really apologizing. Her story is skewed not because her mind is where she lives but because of how she lives there; because her mind has appetites she has not properly considered. "Pain," she says finally. "I seem to have an affection, a kind of sweettooth for it. Bolts of lightning, little rivulets of thunder. . . . What, I wonder, what would I be without a few brilliant spots of blood to ponder? Without aching words that set, then miss, the mark?" Morrison's narrator, like the narrator of Nabokov's *Pnin*, has thought harm is the norm, that unhappy endings are both true and what we want. She has seen her characters as "exotic" and "driven," that is, as characters:

> I was sure one would kill the other [she says of Joe and Violet]. I waited for it so I could describe it. I was so sure it would happen. The past was an abused record with no choice but to repeat itself at the crack.

As Morrison knows, and has shown in her novels, the past is such a record for many people, and their present is only this cracked repetition of the past. Yet Joe and Violet Trace finally walk away from misery and remorse into an ordinary, settled happiness and affection, a "whispering, old-time love." What Morrison is saying through this development, through her narrator's mea culpa and the defeat of her plausible if slightly too lip-smacking narrative predictions, is that forgiveness is (just) possible, and self-forgiveness too. The crooked cannot be made straight but it can be survived, left behind. The odds are not good, of course; poor in fiction, and worse in fact. But the odds are there, harm is not everything. *Beloved* was about the pain and necessity of remembering and forgetting; *Jazz* is about remembering all we can and yet knowing, when the time is right, how to change the record.

Talking to Dorcas's friend Felice some time after the murder, Violet Trace asks "What's the world for if you can't make it up the way you want it?" She can't make it up entirely, but she can make it again, and she has understood that your mind can be your friend as well as your enemy. Violet has messed up her life so far, she thinks, because she "forgot it":

> "Forgot?" [Felice asks]
> "Forgot it was mine. My life. I just ran up and down the streets wishing I was somebody else."
> "Who? Who'd you want to be?"
> "Not so much who as what. White. Light. Young again."
> "Now you don't?"
> "Now I want to be the woman my mother didn't stay around long enough to see. That one. The one she would have liked and the one I used to like before."

To be the woman her mother would have liked: it seems a modest enough goal, but it is precisely the goal so few of Morrison's earlier characters can reach. An old freed slave in *Beloved* asks "If my mother knew me would she like me," and we need to hear the measure of loss in such a question—in the possibility of such a question being asked—if we are to understand the strength of Violet's new confidence, and what the narrator (and we) can learn from her.

In *Playing in the Dark*, Morrison recalls a moment from Marie Cardinal's autobiographical book *The Words to Say It*, where a Louis Armstrong concert is said to provoke an anxiety attack in the white woman who is the main character. Morrison says she smiled at the passage when she read it, partly in admiration of the clarity with which the experience of the music was evoked and partly because she (mischievously) wondered what Armstrong was playing that could have had such a wild effect ("Gripped by panic at the idea of dying there in the middle of spasms, stomping feet, and the crowd howling, I ran into the street like someone possessed"). Of course, as Morrison goes on to suggest and as the tone of Cardinal's language makes clear, it wasn't Armstrong or the number that released the anxiety but the expression in terms of jazz and improvisation of a submerged myth of otherness. "Would an Edith Piaf concert or a Dvorak composition have had the same effect?" Morrison agrees they could have. But they didn't, and she must be right in feeling that Armstrong's color and the black origins of jazz have a part to play in this version of the myth.

What Morrison calls Africanism is a "trope" and a "virus," it is the way white Americans take over and mystify the life of the "unsettled and unsettling population" they can neither accept nor ignore. Thus American slaves, who all but disappear in white literature as historical victims, reemerge as "surrogate selves for meditation on problems of human freedom." There is a "thunderous, theatrical presence of black surrogacy" in American writing that generations of critics have somehow contrived to miss.

> How could one speak of profit, economy, labor, progress, suffragism, Christianity, the frontier, the formation of new states, the acquisition of new lands, education, transportation (freight and passengers), neighborhoods, the military—of almost anything a country concerns itself with—without having as a referent, at the heart of the discourse, at the heart of definition, the presence of Africans and their descendants?

Morrison's case here is not angry and partial, as some have thought, but global and slightly wishful. "Africanism is inextricable from the definition of

Americanness," she says. It should be, on the grounds that a fudged acceptance of historical responsibility is better than a blank refusal. But is it inextricable? The proposition assumes that the occluded thought of slavery looms as large as it ought to in white minds, and that American blacks derive a secret power from the suffering of their ancestors. This is a noble story, but it isn't a story Morrison tells in any of her novels.

The story she does tell in *Jazz* has a similar generosity, but it has a nuance and a complication that are lacking in *Playing in the Dark*. This is not only because good fiction says more than even the most intelligent discursive prose. The story itself is different. It concerns not the black haunting of white minds but the slow and difficult liberation of black minds from black and white oppression, from complicity with the all-knowing master of ugliness. Morrison's chief metaphor for this movement is in her title. This is not a novel about jazz, or based on jazz, and I think reviewers' comments about the improvisatory quality of the writing underestimated what feels like the careful premeditation of the work. Morrison would say, I suspect, that jazz itself thrives on a sort of deferred premeditation, or at least on an interplay of form and freedom. Each chapter after the first, for example, picks up an image or other cue from the preceding one, and takes it into new territories: caged birds, hot weather, a hat, spring in the city, the phrase "state of mind," a look, a person, the words *heart* or *pain*. This is musical and elegant, as if a tune were to be shifted into a new arrangement, but what it borrows from jazz is a sense of flight and variation, not a simple liberation from the rules.

The novel is dedicated to the taste and the air of jazz, to what jazz says to people who care for it. No one in this book would have an anxiety attack at a Louis Armstrong concert, even supposing they got to a concert. "Race music," as jazz used to be called, and as a character once calls it here, is the recognizable music of desire, the sound of the hopes and dangers of this community. Jazz is risky, like the city, but its risk is its charm. Dorcas's severe aunt hears "a complicated anger in it" but also an "appetite," a "careless hunger." "Come," she hears it saying. "Come and do wrong." Later in the book the narrator listens to young men on the Harlem rooftops playing trumpets and clarinets and gets a different, easier feeling: "You would have thought everything had been forgiven the way they played." You would have thought: only an impression, perhaps an illusion, but one of jazz's real gifts to us. Fiction and forgiveness come together once again.

There is no binary division to be made between what one says
and what one does not say.

—Michel Foucault, *The History of Sexuality*

8. *Tigers and Mirrors*

Do You Go to the Cinema Often?

"I like anything that flickers," Angela Carter said. She was thinking of old
movies and the uncertain light of vaudeville; of the lost, stagy life to which her
last two novels, *Nights at the Circus* (1984) and *Wise Children* (1991), are so lovingly dedicated. But she also uses the image in her first novel, *Shadow Dance*
(1966)—"Henry Glass seemed to flicker as he walked, like a silent film, as if his
continuity was awry"—so the liking goes back some time, and the phrase says
something about Carter's prose style too. She writes as if stability and death are
identical, her tone always flickering, aiming to unsettle; her diction always on
the edge of parody (and of self-parody) because it is so delicately attuned to a
world aware of its lateness. Fashion, whether in literature or furniture or architecture or clothes or youth culture, is where we came in; we have been here
before. "The bar was a mock-up," the same novel begins, "a forgery, a fake; an
ad-man's crazy dream of a Spanish patio." "He could only say he was sorry,"
we learn of a character in this book, "by pretending he was a sorry somebody
else." A handsome Palladian mansion, now a mental hospital, strikes a character in Carter's novel *Love* (1971), "by the witty irrelevance of its grandeur to its
purpose." The building isn't trying to be witty. Time and history have replaced
what might have been pathos with an elegant joke: past pretensions turn not to
dust but to the helpless ornaments of madness.

Carter has been seen as a female Salman Rushdie, an English Italo Calvino,
proof that magical realism begins at home, that fairy stories didn't die in
France in the eighteenth century or in Germany in the nineteenth. She loved

fairy stories, but her vein was not so much magic realism as a fictional psy-
chopathology of everyday life. Her sense of flicker pointed her not to the fantastic nature of the real but to the persistent, lurid reality of so many fantasies:
unsteady but also unkillable. She liked tales, she said—"Gothic tales, cruel
tales, tales of wonder, tales of terror"—because they can "deal directly with
the imagery of the unconscious." "The tale does not log everyday experience
as the short story does; it interprets everyday experience through a system of
imagery derived from subterranean areas behind everyday experience." In this
sense all Carter's short works are tales, and her longer works are extended tales,
or novels with a tale at their hearts.

The chief setting of Carter's early novels is an unnamed city that much resembles Bristol: large but provincial, a university town, handsome, slightly decaying. Her characters inhabit various fringes or interstices of city life, hanging
out in pubs and cafes and desolate flats. They are tramps, prostitutes, unsuc-
cessful painters and writers, would-be antique dealers; or they work in hospitals
or offices or schools. The swinging England (which was mainly a swinging London and Liverpool) of the 1960s passes them by, except that they sometimes find
themselves in music, and their motley styles of clothes and make-up look like an
eerie prediction of punk. "In 1969," Carter later said of a violent, near-psy-
chotic character in *Love*, "Buzz was still waiting for his historic moment . . . he
was simply waiting for punk to happen." Carter also wrote of what she came to
feel was the "penetrating aroma of unhappiness" in this novel, and this aroma,
spliced strangely with a vivid and perky prose manner, an unmistakable happiness in the writing, defines all of her early work. Madness and death, damage
and guilt, are its obsessive themes; but the writing seems to be dancing. The
principal partners are the crazy girl and the alarmingly beautiful boy.

Shadow Dance opens with the appearance of a once lovely, now hideously
scarred girl in a pub, and it ends with her death in a sort of ritual game—as if
the scar was only paint and death only a tableau. In between these moments, the
various men who have slept with her skitter with guilt, another woman commits suicide, and various sturdier women find ways of getting on with their
lives. Aloof from all this, prince of this marginal kingdom, is the alluring, sex-
ually ambiguous, entirely amoral Honeybuzzard, who has cut the girl up in the
first place and kills her in the end. He has a way of frightening everyone and
making everything seem all right, like a child whose charm hides his danger. Or
perhaps his charm is his danger:

> Honeybuzzard had the soft, squashy-nosed, full-lipped face one associates with
> angels blowing glad, delirious trumpets in early Florentine pictures of the Na-

tivity; a nectarine face, bruisable and somehow juicy, covered with a close, golden fuzz that thickened into a soft, furry, animal down on his jaw but never coalesced into a beard. . . . He had a pair of perfectly pointed ears, such as fauns have and, curiously, these were also covered with down. . . . It was impossible to look at the full, rich lines of his dark red mouth without thinking: "This man eats meat."

"They are all shadows," Honeybuzzard says to his nervous sidekick Morris, who says he feels sorry for their sad pub companions. "How can you be sorry for shadows?" Honeybuzzard's strength is his ability to see others as shadows; their weakness is their inability to insist that he is wrong. What proves him wrong is a series of flesh-and-blood risks and disasters. People are not shadows, however flickering their grip on life; but you may have to enter the world of real shadows to find this out.

Films and photographs are recurring images in these novels. "It was easier . . . to face the fact of Uncle Philip if she saw him as a character in a film, possibly played by Orson Welles." "He wavered as he walked as if he were a piece of trick photography and might suddenly disappear altogether, so discreetly the air would not even be disturbed by his passage." Photographs are "frozen memories of the moment of sight," and the following disturbing conversation takes place between a grieving young husband and a woman who is a hospital psychiatrist. The psychiatrist's implicit recognition of the visual world in question is almost eerier than the husband's anxious allusion:

"A kind of expressionist effect," he said.
   "Pardon?"
   "Everything is subtly out of alignment. Shadows fall awry and light no longer issues from expected sources."
   "Do you go to the cinema often?"

What all this suggests is not only a culture saturated in movies and déja vu but a group of people who are afraid both of finding reality and of losing it. They are "connoisseurs of unreality," as Carter calls one couple. They wear their facial expressions like clothes ("Mentally he wandered through his wardrobe of smiles, wondering which one to wear to suit this ambiguous occasion"), but they have trouble linking yesterday's self to anything in today's life: "There seemed no connecting logic between the various states of his life, as if each had been attained, not by organic growth but by a kind of convulsive leap from condition to condition." One young woman lives so thoroughly by the mythic, magical assumptions of her fears that she has never "suspected that everyday, sensuous human practice might shape the real world. When she did discover that such a thing was possible, it proved the beginning of the end for her for how could she possess any notion of the ordinary?" To possess a notion of the ordinary would be to be able to leave the cinema (or the movie) if you wanted to; to see your Uncle Philip as if he wasn't Orson Welles; or, less psychologically, more pragmatically, to have an uncle you didn't have to turn mentally into Orson Welles.

If *Shadow Dance*, in its sense of damage and danger, is the most striking of Carter's early novels, *Love* is the novel where the mood of the shadow city is most hauntingly caught. It is a "Surrealist poem for the forlorn daughter," Sue Roe says, "a poem which cannot take Annabel as its subject, except as *peinture-poésie*, photomontage, *cadavre exquis*, collage." Annabel is a suicidal young woman, who finally commits suicide. Before she does this, she marries Lee, or, more precisely marries into the ménage of Lee and Buzz, two brothers so severely damaged by their mother's madness that they have made a homeland out of their relationship to each other and can scarcely connect to the world outside it. Lee is apparently well-adjusted, another of Carter's wonderful-looking men, Buzz is malign and violent; but both are sheltering from old fall-out. They are pretty good at telling themselves stories, though:

> When Lee attained the age of reason and acquired his aunt's pride, he was glad his mother had gone mad in style. There could be no mistaking her intention nor could her behaviour be explained in any other terms than the onset of a spectacular psychosis in the grand, traditional style of the old-fashioned Bedlamite. She progressed to unreason via no neurotic back alleyway nor let any slow night of silence and darkness descend upon her; she chose the high road, operatically stripping off her clothes and screaming to the morning: I am the whore of Babylon.

Carter herself spoke of "the ornate formalism of the style" of this book, as well as of "its icy treatment of the mad girl"; but there is a sense in which everyone delights in style here, author, mad mother, remembering son, mad girl. Style is not an antidote to unhappiness, rather the reverse. But it is where almost everyone's energy comes from, as if the high road had all the virtues, even if it leads only to death and despair.

Annabel is destroyed not by her relationship with the brothers but by her attempt to escape from her solipsism into the world. Like Honeybuzzard, she sees everyone except herself as a shadow, but unlike him, she cannot manipulate others, cannot register them as real enough to be manipulated. When she demands that Lee have her name tattooed over his heart, he thinks she means to humiliate him, to take revenge for his infidelity to her. But this isn't so, couldn't be so, since she "was hardly capable of devising a revenge which required a knowledge of human feeling to perfect it." When she and Buzz make love, because Buzz inhabits her fantasy in way that Lee doesn't, the event is a fiasco. "It is always a dangerous experiment to act out a fantasy; they had undertaken the experiment rashly and had failed, but Annabel suffered the worst for she had been trying to convince herself she was alive." She is left to "wander off alone through the dark streets, a fragile, flimsy thing whose body had betrayed both their imaginations." Her suicide is her retreat from this body and this betrayal, and takes place in atmosphere of distressing serenity, as if it were simply the accomplishment of the logic of her sense of her life:

> She left no notes or messages. She felt no fear or pain for now she was content. She did not spare a thought or waste any pity on the people who loved her for she had never regarded them as anything more than facets of the self she was now about to obliterate so, in a sense, she took them with her to the grave and it was only natural they should now behave as if they had never known her.

Our Poor Symbols

Rilke is wrong, we are told in the opening pages of *The Passion of New Eve* (1977), to believe that our symbols are inadequate. They are what we have, perfectly adequate to our inadequacy:

> Our external symbols must always express the life within us with absolute precision; how could they do otherwise, since that life has generated them? Therefore we must not blame our poor symbols if they take forms that seem trivial to us, or absurd. . . . A critique of these symbols is a critique of our lives.

Carter is expertly parodying a certain type of cultural commentary, but her defense of the "poor symbols" is not itself a parody. It is an invitation to look again at our icons and statues and pieties, whether they seem trivial or grand. At D. H. Lawrence, for instance: "It is impossible for any English writer in this century to evade the great fact of D. H. Lawrence, but taking him seriously as a novelist is one thing, and taking him seriously as a moralist is quite another." Or at the city of Bath, "built to be happy in, which accounts for its innocence and its ineradicable melancholy." This is not just a joke about the scarcity of happiness, in Bath or anywhere, it reminds us what happiness costs and sees it as an actual cause of sadness. Similarly, when Carter compares the same city to Marilyn Monroe, a whole world of stardom and sorrow and memory infiltrates the famous, stately architecture:

> Marvellous, hallucinatory Bath has almost the quality of concretised memory; its beauty has a curiously second-order quality, most beautiful when remembered, the wistfulness of all professional beauties, such as that of the unfortunate Marilyn Monroe whom nobody wanted for herself but everybody wanted to have slept with.

"A joke need not be funny to give pleasure," Carter astutely says, but almost all her jokes are funny, and she doesn't, in her later work, go many sentences without a joke. "So we did not quite fit in, thank goodness," Carter remarks of her family; "alienated is the only way to be, after all." "Maybe Yorkshire never really left the Third World." "At times, Bradford hardly seems an English city at all, since it is inhabited, in the main, by (to all appearances) extras from the Gorki trilogy, huddled in shapeless coats." "It won't be much *fun* after the Revolution, people say. (Yes; but it's not all that much fun now.)"

But these jokes are also a form of criticism, a way of thinking about alternatives. "In the pursuit of magnificence," Carter writes of Pete Townshend of The Who, "nothing is sacred," and she took the title for a book of essays. The sheer ease of the phrase, what one might think of as a happiness of cliché, allows her both to admire and to smile at the wrecker of expectations and decorum, to align herself with rebellion and to mock the predictability of the counterculture. Disrespect is a fine tonic, but it's not that magnificent to smash your guitar. Myths lead off in all directions here, as in Roland Barthes's *Mythologies*, and Carter obviously learned a lot from that subtle and mischievous book. "Myth deals in false universals" she says in *The Sadeian Woman* (1978), "to dull the pain of particular circumstances." And: "The notion of the universality of human experience is a confidence trick and the notion of a universality of female experience is a clever confidence trick."

This is to say that there was in 1978 (and still is in 1998) a lot of cultural work to be done. Carter's first move in her book on Sade is to distinguish between the oppressive, demeaning enterprise pornography currently is and the liberation that a "moral pornographer" might promote. This figure wouldn't be any more respectable or any less violent and nasty than the other kind of pornographer, but he would be "a terrorist of the imagination, a sexual guerilla," and would expose, by the sheer extremity of his inventions, the realities that underlie our sexual mythologies. "Sade became a terrorist of the imagination in this way, turning the unacknowledged truths of the encounters of sexuality into a cruel festival at which women are the prime sacrificial victims when they are not the ritual murderesses themselves."

The pornographer as terrorist may not think of himself as a friend of women; that may be the last thing on his mind. But he will always be our unconscious ally because he begins to approach some kind of emblematic truth.

Does Carter believe this? Not quite. Her book on Sade, she says, "is an exercise of the lateral imagination." "Sade remains a monstrous and daunting cultural edifice; yet I would like to think that he put pornography in the service of women." What she shows is that pornography's insistence on sex is the twin of respectability's denial of it and that between the innocent Justine and the diabolical Juliette, Sade's antithetical heroines, the one all sacrifice and the other all pleasure and will, we should always, if we have any respect for our bodies and our desire, choose Juliette. Justine is the grandmother of the bewildered and suffering Marilyn Monroe—"she cannot envisage a benign sexuality," she is "the persecuted maiden whose virginity is perpetually refreshed by rape," just as Monroe fails to realize that "her flesh is sacred because it is as good as money"—and her life, Carter says, "was doomed to disappointment before it began, like that of a woman who wishes for nothing better than a happy marriage." Juliette is the scary sexual predator, the "moral of [her] life suggests the paradox of the hangman—in a country where the hangman rules, only the hangman escapes punishment for his crimes." This is a way of saying, as Carter also says, that "a free woman in an unfree society will be a monster." And although she says she doesn't really want Juliette to renew her world, any more than she really thinks Sade was on the side of women, it is important to see that the imaginary wreckage caused by Juliette, the real wreckage that could be caused by a woman who would resist hypocrisy in the way she does, "will have removed a repressive and authoritarian structure that has prevented a good deal of the work of renewal." Women (and men) need to understand the grammar of passivity—"To be the object of desire is to be defined in the passive case. To exist in the passive case is to die in the passive case—that is, to be killed"—and to recognize that the pornographer, whether as terrorist or exploiter, is as frightened as we are, and of the same thing. In his fear we see our fear for what it is, the "perfect, immaculate terror" of love: "It is in this holy terror of love that we find, in both men and women themselves, the source of all opposition to the emancipation of women."

"If Little Red Riding Hood had laughed at the wolf and passed on, the wolf could never have eaten her," Colette says, and Carter literalizes precisely this argument in one of the ten dazzling fairy tales of *The Bloody Chamber* (1979). "Since her fear did her no good," we read of the girl who is now alone with the wolf who has eaten her grandmother, "she ceased to be afraid." The wolf tries to act his oppressive part, and responds in the proper way to the ritual comment on his teeth. "What big teeth you have!" "All the better to eat you with." But the girl just bursts out laughing: "she knew she was nobody's meat." She and the wolf get into bed together and look to be set to live happily ever after. "See! sweet and sound she sleeps in granny's bed, between the paws of the tender wolf." It remains true that the tender wolf has eaten grandma; but since when were fairy tales dedicated to kindness all round? "The tiger will never lie down with the lamb; he acknowledges no pact that is not reciprocal. The lamb must learn to run with the tigers." The imagery here recalls a wonderful Nietzschean joke in *The Sadeian Woman*: "The lamb . . . is hampered by the natural ignorance of the herbivore, who does not even know it is possible to eat meat. The lamb could understand easily enough how mint sauce might be delicious but it does not have the mental apparatus to appreciate that its own hindquarters are also nourishing food if suitably cooked."

Of course Carter knows it's not so easy to give up your fear just because it doesn't do you any good; and she knows that the ferocity of male wolves, human and bestial, is not only a projection of female fear. To believe that would be to accept a sort of nursery school version of Dr. Hoffman's theories of desire and the world (The titular figure of *The Infernal Desire Machines of Dr. Hoffman* [1972] is a cross between Dr. Caligari, Dr. Mabuse, and any number of mad scientists out of Hollywood B-movies, whose theory is that "everything it is possible to imagine can also exist," and that "the world exists only as a medium in which we execute our desires"). But that is how Carter wants the fairy tale to work. It sketches out an idea of the possible—in this case the possible irrelevance of fear, the possibility that fear is the cause of the problem not a reaction to it—and invites us to compare it with our own most cherished assumptions about reality. The fairy tale humanizes terror, just as pornography terrorizes humans, but its simplifications are so striking that the banished complications of the world cling to them like shadows. In a tale called "The Werewolf" Carter shows us how cruel these simplifications can be—Sade begins to look positively friendly compared with this picture of folk culture. "It is a northern country," we read; "they have cold weather, they have cold hearts." Natural enough, the implication seems to be. These people have "a hard life"; "harsh, brief lives." Are they superstitious? Of course. Wouldn't you be in their situation?

To these upland woodsmen, the Devil is as real as you or I. More so; they have not seen us nor even know that we exist, but the Devil they glimpse often in graveyards. . . . At midnight, especially on Walpurgisnacht, the Devil holds picnics in the graveyards and invites the witches; then they dig up fresh corpses, and eat them. Anyone will tell you that.

Except for the last sentence, where a hint of sarcasm seems to have crept in, this description remains sympathetic to the local beliefs—who are we to judge them, we are all anthropologists these days. Then we learn what these cold-hearted folks do to the women they take to be witches—their cold hearts do not preclude a real enthusiasm for persecution.

When they discover a witch—some old woman whose cheeses ripen when her neighbours' do not, another old woman whose black cat, oh, sinister! *follows her about all the time*, they strip the crone, search for the marks, for the supernumerary nipple her familiar sucks. They soon find it. Then they stone her to death. (Carter's italics)

The coolness of the writing here means the reader is likely to be startled by the conclusion of the paragraph, by the implicit outrage in the prose. "They soon find it" is like the writing of white anger. Not: they imagine they find it, or they find something like it, or even though they find nothing they still decide she is a witch. But: there is nothing there (of course), but they find it anyway, for the same reasons that they keep seeing the Devil. It is a hard life. Fairy tales are not liberating in themselves, although the reading of them may be.

From Carter's very earliest fiction onward, her young women characters think of themselves as caught in Bluebeard's castle, potentially willing victims of violent men and of their own curiosity. Even when they are about to be killed, they are capable of feeling "a terrified pity" for their murderer and exclaiming at "the atrocious loneliness of that monster." "Bluebeard's castle, it was," Melanie thinks of Uncle Philip's house in *The Magic Toyshop* (1967). In *Shadow Dance* one of Honeybuzzard's girlfriends casts herself in the same story:

"I found this key in one of his trouser pockets, see, and I thought, you know, of Bluebeard."
"Bluebeard?"
"Bluebeard. And the locked room."

Bluebeard is the killer all husbands might be. He is the awe and danger of sex, what is objectively to be feared in men; and also an image of false fear, the nightmare form of fear itself. He is the wolf who devours and the toothless wolf turned into a terror by old wives' warnings and young girls' imaginings. In the title story of *The Bloody Chamber* he is also a connoisseur of torture, a relative of the sado-cinematic Count young Desiderio meets in *The Infernal Desire Machines of Dr. Hoffman*. He talks like a French novel, since much of his dialogue, and most of the furnishings of his world, have been lovingly borrowed from Colette. The writing here, with its modulation from high camp to low proverb to striking double metaphor, shows Carter at her inventive, allusive, and irreverent best. "My virgin of the arpeggios, prepare yourself for martyrdom," the marquis has improbably said—the girl is an accomplished pianist. But then she escapes from the axe.

> The Marquis stood transfixed, utterly dazed, at a loss. It must have been as if he had been watching his beloved Tristan for the twelfth, the thirteenth time and Tristan stirred, then leapt from his bier in the last act, announced in a jaunty aria interposed from Verdi that bygones were bygones, crying over spilt milk did nobody any good and, as for himself, he proposed to live happily ever after. The puppet master, open-mouthed, wide-eyed, impotent at the last, saw his dolls break free of their strings, abandon the rituals he had ordained for them since time began and start to live for themselves; the king, aghast, witnesses the revolt of his pawns.

There Are No Monsters

Nights at the Circus opens in raucous stage cockney, as if Eliza Doolittle had never met Professor Higgins:

> "Lor' love you, sir!" Fevvers sang out in a voice that clanged like dustbin lids. "As to my place of birth, why, I first saw light of day right here in smoky old London, didn't I! Not billed the 'Cockney Venus' for nothing, sir."

"Nobody talks like that," as Tony Curtis says in *Some Like It Hot*, during his memorable impersonation of Cary Grant, who did talk like that. Nobody outside of novels and movies, that is. Inside a novel or a movie, such open embraces of the expected produce a quality of unrepentant playfulness, a sense of the banishment of anything that looks like accepted or acceptable taste. Fevvers's very name is a phonetic mauling of the word "feathers," a reference to the fact that, unlike most ordinary, unmythological women, she has wings, but also a sign of cockneyness so stereotyped it has to be a joke. Fevvers has all kinds of adventures, in a sprawling picaresque mode—this is Carter's longest work by far—and travels from London to Petersburg to Siberia with a "Grand Imperial Circus." She is brought up in a brothel run by a one-eyed Madame called Ma Nelson, after the admiral who is supposed to have put his telescope to his blind eye in order not to see a signal he wished to ignore; she is assigned to Madame Schreck's museum of female monsters; teams up with and then escapes from a wealthy magus who has designs on her as a human sacrifice. In Russia she encounters bandits, shamans, revolutionaries. But the most persistent adventures in the book are linguistic, Fevvers's and others' knockabout recountings of her life to the American journalist Jack Walser, who follows her across the world, lured by the enigma of her wings—are they real or not? Fevvers at the end seems to say they are not: " 'To think I really fooled you!' she marvelled. 'It just goes to show there's nothing like confidence.' " But she may be referring to her virginity rather than her wings, and reality in Carter is always a matter of faith and desire. Not that faith and desire can simply, directly alter the literal world; only that the literal world is always already infiltrated by faith and desire, so that the possession (or not) of wings is not strictly the question. The question is can you fly, or do people see you fly? Fevvers is a metaphor for the New Woman, or, rather, a blatant but sympathetic parody of the idea of the New Woman—the novel is set in the last months of the nineteenth century—and is described as "the pure child of the century that just now is waiting in the wings, the New Age in which no woman will be bound down to the ground." "And once the old world has turned on its axle," Fevvers says, "so that the new dawn can dawn, then, ah, then! all the women will have wings, the same as I." "Waiting in the wings" is an excruciating pun in the context, and Fevvers probably means "axis" rather than "axle." "Same as I" is Fevvers being posh, her little stab at being ladylike.

But then her language is like this, a patchwork of mismatched idioms and an emblem of Carter's dedication to the abolition of old stylistic decorums. Even the notion of parody doesn't quite catch what she and Fevvers are doing. "Like any young girl," Fevvers says, "I was much possessed with the marvellous blooming of my until then reticent and undemanding flesh." But she also says "Nobility of spirit hand in hand with absence of analysis, that's what's always buggered up the working class," and "This is some kind of heretical possibly Manichean version of neo-Platonic Rosicrucianism, thinks I to myself." The last phrase comes out of old songs and music-hall routines; "much possessed" comes from T. S. Eliot's "Whispers of Immortality"; and the rest comes from various stations between Lukács, Sade, and the local pub. The suggestion, I think, is not so much that language or culture does the writing, takes over from the writer, as that all language is dialect, and the best a writer can do is understand the futility of all attempts at settled style. The apparent (and often real) lack of control in Carter's writing is itself a political gesture; not an abandonment of responsibility or hard work but an act of resistance to any coherence that can be felt as a coercion—as almost all coherences can, Carter would say. The uncertainty of her early characters, unable to keep track of their moral or psychological selves from day to day but wonderfully adept at inventing new stylistic selves by the minutes, has become a principle. If you know who you are, you must be the wrong person, and there is no greater temptation for the writer, Carter is suggesting, than to award yourself the Olympian security your characters—and not only your characters, but you yourself, and everyone you know outside of fiction—so desperately lack. The narrative voices of this text, Lorna Sage says, "are generously endowed with the kind of dubious plausibility that comes from the suspicion that they are making it up as they go along, *just like the author*." Carter's style, "sinuous and ramshackle," as she describes the movements of one of her fictional young men, is a form of solidarity with the shaky but often hilarious world we have inherited and hope to change. It is a style that breeds laughter, and it is infectious:

> Fevvers' laughter seeped through the gaps in the window-frame and cracks in the door-frames of all the houses in the village. . . . It seemed this laughter of the happy young woman rose up from the wilderness in a spiral and began to twist and shudder across Siberia. . . . The spiralling tornado of Fevvers' laughter began to twist and shudder across the entire globe, as if a spontaneous response to the giant comedy that endlessly unfolded beneath it, until everything that lived and breathed, everywhere, was laughing.

In *Nights at the Circus* a group of chimps are seen practicing their act, a laughable simulation of children in a classroom. There is a professor chimp with black suit, watch-chain and mortarboard; there are twelve attentive, silent pupils, boys and girls, all in sailor suits, "each with a slate and slate pencil clutched in their leathery hands." "How irresistibly comic," Jack Walser thinks, watching them. But then he looks closer. Is that writing on the blackboard? Are the chimps perhaps asking real questions, actually learning, writing something down? When Walser stumbles and reveals his presence, the professor instantly wipes the blackboard clean, and the chimps start fooling around, gibbering and shooting ink pellets, doing their "apes at school" number. Walser's eyes meet those of the professor, and he never forgets "this first, intimate exchange with one of these beings whose life ran parallel to his, this inhabitant of the magic circle of difference, unreachable . . . but not unknowable."

Difference is Carter's great theme. We can know other creatures, including humans, but only if we know their difference. "I didn't know his God," D. H. Lawrence says of a fish. Carter would say we probably wouldn't be any wiser if we did, but she shares Lawrence's sense of what otherness is like and how much our perception of it matters. That is why there are so many beasts, and images of beasts, in her fiction. The beast is absolutely other, what we are not. He is Blake's tiger, burning bright—Carter's work is littered with references to this extraordinary icon of ferocity and innocence. But he is not caged except by us, and beastliness is not a final, unshakable category, beyond transformation. Beasts are also what we could become, like Alice crossing into the world beyond the mirror to discover a place that is not a reflection of her own. And beasts can become human, as Carter's tales repeatedly show. So there are no monsters, there is only difference. The delicate, spiraling mystery of Carter's work lies in this complicated separation and interaction of kinds, men and women, young and old, human and other animals. Difference is total but not final; essential but not absolute. Parallel lives are unreachable (unless you cease to be yourself) but not unknowable.

The Princess of Abyssinia (born in Marseilles, of a West Indian mother and a Brazilian father) is a tiger-tamer who doesn't usually brood on the thoughts of her animal charges but always has a moment, as her act begins, when she remembers what these unreachable creatures might do: "Just for that moment, while she knew they wondered what on earth they were doing, when her vulnerable back was turned towards them and her speaking eyes away from them, the Princess felt a little scared, and, perhaps, more fully human than she was used to feeling." "Perhaps" is very subtle; but the princess "knows" what the tigers are wondering. The tigers' own experience is evoked in this way:

The cats . . . leapt on to the semi-circle of pedestals placed ready for them and sat there on their haunches, panting, pleased with themselves for their obedience. And then it would come to them, always with a fresh surprise no matter how often they performed, that they did not obey in freedom but had exchanged one cage for a larger cage. Then, for just one unprotected moment, they pondered the mystery of their obedience and were astonished by it.

Two later images in the same novel repeat this mood with an inflection of magical threat. When the circus train crashes in the steppes, "a great wonder" occurs. The tigers have become mirror tigers, and have broken when the mirrors broke:

They had frozen into their own reflections and been shattered, too. . . . As if that burning energy you glimpsed between the bars of their pelts had convulsed in a great response to the energy released in fire around us and, in exploding, they scattered their appearances upon that glass in which they had been breeding sterile reduplications. On one broken fragment of mirror, a paw with the claws out; on another, a snarl. When I picked up a section of flank, the glass burned my fingers and I dropped it.

A little later, another set of tigers appear, this time explicitly associated with Blake:

We saw the house was roofed with tigers. Authentic, fearfully symmetric tigers burning as brightly as those who had been lost. . . . They stretched out across the tiles like abandoned greatcoats, laid low by pleasure, and you could see how the tails that dropped down over the eaves like icicles of fur were throbbing with marvellous sympathy. Their eyes, gold as the background to a holy picture, had summoned up the sun that glazed their pelts until they looked unutterably precious.

The last phrase is a little feeble, as if Carter can't find all the words for the vision she wants us to see. But "like greatcoats" is wonderfully casual, military and human; and "roofed with tigers" takes us into a world resembling that of Chagall. The mirror tigers make vividly metaphorical the implications of the mysterious acquiescence of their antecedents. They are beautiful, broken, and still dangerous. Anything that flickers can also burn. They are the magic of otherness, entirely unlike us. Except that we too, perhaps, in occasional unprotected moments, ponder the mystery of our obedience and are astonished by it.

We can take these apes and tigers in *Nights at the Circus* not only as summarizing continuing preoccupations in Angela Carter's work but also as evoking essential features of her historical moment. Angela Carter's Britain—she remains a very English writer in spite of her cosmopolitan reading and her total lack of "English" reserve—is a multiracial, multicultural society that has great difficulty in recognizing and respecting its internal differences. The moral attraction of Carter's writing is that it thrives on difference—to a greater degree even than that of Salman Rushdie, since if he has a whole other culture behind him, she has behind her the full panoply of her own unremitting individuality: difference as a kind of habitat.

The obedience of the tigers can be read as a metaphor for social submission, the readiness of wild creatures to accept the unreasonable routines of so-called civilization. The British, like the tigers, have long been "pleased with themselves for their obedience," regarding it as a cultural triumph—as if their remarkable circus performance were all they had ever wanted to achieve and circus tigers were all they had ever been. Carter is not arguing that this submission is a mistake or that the tigers should go wild again at once. She is a radical, but not an anarchist, and like Joseph Conrad she admires the strange self-confidence of the country she needs also to criticize. But she is saying that the tigers' obedience was always a mystery and could be revoked.

That was when he felt his entire structure of organized thought
begin to slide slowly toward some dark abyss.

> —Stephen King, *The Langoliers*

9. *All the Rage*

Stephen King has become a household name in at least three senses. He is a
writer pretty much everyone in the English-speaking world has heard of, if
they have heard of writers at all. He is regularly read by many people who
don't read many other writers. And along with Danielle Steele and a few others, he is taken, by the posher punters, to represent everything that is wrong
with contemporary publishing, that engine of junk that pushes serious literature out of our minds and our bookstores. The English writer Clive Barker has
said, "There are apparently two books in every American household—one of
them is the Bible and the other one is probably by Stephen King." I don't know
what Barker's source is for this claim, but I wonder about the Bible.

Do we know what popular literature is? When is it not junk? Is it ever (just)
junk? Who is to say? What is the alternative to popular literature? Serious,
highbrow, literary, or merely . . . unpopular literature? Stephen King responded with eloquent anger in an argument over these issues conducted in
the PEN newsletter in 1991. He thought best-selling authors came in all kinds.
He said he found James Michener, Robert Ludlum, John Le Carré, and Fred-
erick Forsyth unreadable but enjoyed (among others) Elmore Leonard, Sara
Paretsky, Jonathan Kellerman, and Joyce Carol Oates. This seems sound
enough to me, although I have to confess to liking Ludlum and Le Carré as
well. "Some of these," King continued, "are writers whose work I think of as
sometimes or often literary, and all are writers who can be counted on to tell a
good story, one that takes me away from the humdrum passages of life . . . and
enriches my leisure time as well. Such work has always seemed honorable to
me, even noble."

What had made King angry was the term "better" fiction, which Ursula Perrin had used in an open letter to PEN ("I am a writer of 'better' fiction, by which I mean that I don't write romance or horror or mystery"), complaining about the profusion of worse fiction in the bookstores—"this rising sea of trash" were her words. "Ursula Perrin's use of the word 'better,' " King says, "which she keeps putting in quotation marks, makes me feel like baying at the moon." The rest of Perrin's letter suggests that King was right not to see any irony or skepticism in the use of the quotation marks, only a slight disappointment at the lack of a more appropriate term—Perrin's examples of writers of "better" fiction were John Updike, Kurt Vonnegut Jr., and Alice Hoffman.

But King was wrong, I think, to assume that Perrin's argument could only rest on snobbery—he himself owes his success not to some all-purpose skill in entertainment but to his skill in a particular genre and to his readers' expectations of that genre. There is a real difficulty with the rigidity and exclusivity of our literary groupings; but it is no solution to say that exclusivity is the problem. What happens maybe is that the tricky task of deciding whether a piece of writing (of any kind) is any good is repeatedly replaced by the easier habit of deciding which slabs or modes of writing we can ignore. Even King, who not only should but does know better, confuses fiction that is popular with popular fiction, best-sellers with genres, and his line about the humdrum passages of life and the enrichment of leisure time is as condescending in its mock-demotic way as the idea of "better" fiction. No one would read Stephen King if that was all he managed to do.

There can't be a single category of fiction that is just *not* romance or horror or mystery, and I doubt whether those categories themselves will serve as much more than a guide to the shelves in the bookshop. But genres do exist, and the work they do is honorable, even noble. When we say writers have transcended their genre, we often mean they have abandoned or betrayed it. Genres have long and complicated histories, richer and poorer, better and worse. They may be in touch with ancient and unresolved imaginative energies, or whatever haunts the back of a culture's mind; and they permit and occasionally insist on allusions the writer may have no thought of making. Stephen King, however, *has* thought of making allusions, and thought of it more and more, as the classical excursions of *Rose Madder* (1995) make very clear.

What's interesting about *Carrie*, King's first novel, published in 1974, is the way it sustains and complicates its problems, gives us grounds for judgment and takes them away. The genre here (within the horror genre) is the mutant disaster story, which in more recent years has become the virus novel or movie. Sixteen-year old Carietta White has inherited awe-inspiring telekinetic powers, and in a fit of fury wipes out whole portions of the Maine town where she lives, causing a death toll of well over four hundred. Carrie has always been awkward and strange, cruelly mocked by her companions at school and liked by no one. Her mother is a morbid fundamentalist Christian who thinks that sex even within marriage is evil. The town itself is full of rancor and hypocrisy and pretention—the sort of place where the prettiest girl is also the meanest, the local hoodlums have everyone terrorized, and the assistant principal of the school has a ceramic ashtray in the form of Rodin's *Thinker* on his desk—so that without any supernatural intervention at all there's plenty to go wrong and plenty of people to blame. Carrie's terrible gift for willing physical destruction is an accident, the result of a recessive gene that could come up in anyone, and the novel makes much play with the idea of little Carries quietly multiplying all over the United States, like bombs rather than children. The last image in the novel is of a two-year-old in Tennessee who is able to move marbles around without touching them, and this is the portentous question the novel pretends to address: "What happens if there are others like her? What happens to the world?"

This is a big question, but it's not as important as it looks, because apart from being unanswerable in the absence of any knowledge of the characters and lives of the "others like her," it mainly serves to mask another question, which is the most urgent question of the horror genre as Stephen King practices it: what difference does the supernatural or fanciful element make, whether it's telekinesis or death-in-life? What if it's only a lurid metaphor for what's already there? Carrie White is not a monster, even if her mother is. Carrie has been baited endlessly, and when someone finally is nice to her and takes her to the high school prom, the evening ends in nightmare: pig's blood is poured all over her and her partner, a sickening echo and travesty of the opening scene in the novel, where Carrie discovers in the shower room that she is menstruating and doesn't know what is happening to her. Human folly and nastiness take care of all of this region of the plot, and Carrie's distress and rage are what anyone but a saint would feel. But then she has her powers. The difference is not in the rage but in what she can do about it, and this is where contemporary horror stories, like old tales of magic, speak most clearly to our fears and desires.

Edward Ingebretsen, S.J., in a work whose subtitle ("Religious Terror as Memory from the Puritans to Stephen King") confirms King's status even in the academic household, speaks of religion where I am speaking of magic. "Once-religious imperatives," Ingebretsen says, "can be traced across the variety of American genres, modes, and texts." "The deflective energies of a largely forgotten metaphysical history live on, not only in churches, but in a myriad other centers of displaced worship." Ingebretsen has a nice sense of irony—I hope it's irony—dark and oblique like his subject: "A major comfort of the Christian tradition is the terror it generates and presupposes." He certainly understands how King, while seeming to offer escape from the humdrum passages of life, shows us the weird bestiary lurking in those apparently anodyne places. "Change the focus slightly and King's horror novel [in this case *Salem's Lot* (1975)] reintroduces the horrific, although the horrific as it routinely exists in the real and the probable." "Routinely" is excellent.

It's true that religious hauntings are everywhere in American life, but because they are everywhere, they don't really help us to see the edge in modern horror stories, the way these stories suggest that we have returned, on some not entirely serious, not entirely playful level, to the notion that superstitions are right after all, that they offer us a more plausible picture of the world than any organized religion or any of our secular promises. It's not only that the old religion is still with us but that even older ideas have returned to currency. This is a very complicated question, but the concept of magic will allow us to make a start on it.

Magic is the power to convert wishes into deeds without passing through the cumbersome procedures of material reality, taking planes, hiring assassins, waiting for the news, going to jail. It bypasses physics, connects the mind directly to the world. All of Stephen King's novels that I have read involve magic in this sense, even where nothing supernatural occurs, where the only magic is the freedom of fiction to move when it wants to from thought to act. Would you, if you could, immediately and violently get rid of anyone and anything you dislike? If you were provoked enough? And could be sure of getting away with it? The quick response, of course, is that you know you shouldn't and probably wouldn't. The long response is the same, but meanwhile, if you're not really thinking about it, you probably let it all happen in your head, which is a way of saying yes to the fantasy of immense violence while feeling scared about it.

This must be a large part of the delight of this kind of horror fiction. Is this really all right, even in a novel? There's a relish in the thought of Carrie's destroying her miserable town, we can't wait for another gas station to go up. But there's also an ugly comfort in feeling Carrie's an alien and a freak, not one of us, and above all in knowing, at the end, that she's dead. At the heart of *Carrie* is a conversation between Susan, the one girl in town who worries about Carrie, and Susan's amiable boyfriend, who dies for his attempt at niceness. They have no idea of what's going to happen; they know only that everyone's always been mean to Carrie.

> "You were kids," he said. "Kids don't know what they're doing. Kids don't even know their reactions really, actually hurt other people . . ."
> She found herself struggling to express the thought this called up in her, for it suddenly seemed basic, bulking over the shower-room incident the way the sky bulks over mountains.
> "But hardly *anybody* ever finds out that their actions really, actually hurt other people! People don't get better, they just get smarter. When you get smarter you don't stop pulling the wings off flies, you just think of better reasons for doing it."

And what if, the question about magic continues, you grant to these people, without improving their moral awareness in any significant degree, inconceivable powers to hurt? To wipe out cities or abuse their wives? It wouldn't matter whether you called these powers telekinesis or Mephistopheles. Carrie's relative innocence—she's not smart and she doesn't pull the wings off flies—helps to focus the question but makes the powers all the scarier. Fortunately it's only a fantasy.

If we want to see what a genre novel looks like when it's barely in touch with any imaginative energies, either ancient or modern, we can look at King's *The Langoliers*, a short work published in *Four Past Midnight* and then adapted as a lumbering miniseries for television. The genre here is the end-of-the-world-as-we-know-it story, combined with a disaster in technology (airplane, ocean liner, skyscraper). The codes are so threadbare that the characters themselves keep complaining about the genre they're stuck in. A plane leaves Los Angeles and flies through a fold in time into the past—or rather into an alternative world that the present has abandoned, into the past as it would be if it vanished the moment we turned our backs on it. The plane lands at Bangor, Maine, which turns out to be deserted, nothing but stale air and tasteless food. Fortunately the plane can refuel and manages to fly back through the time fold. There is a nasty moment when it arrives in Los Angeles too early—this is the future, just as deserted as the past but not as dead and tasteless, and the good news is that you have only to wait a while for the present to catch up.

There are possibilities here, and the hint of a genuine anxiety about the fading past, a sort of mixture of disbeliefs about it: that it's still there, that it's actually gone. King writes engagingly in his introduction of "the essential conundrum of time"—"so perfect that even such jejune observations as the one

I have just made retain an odd, plangent resonance"—but he hasn't worked all that hard at this version of it. He obviously felt his novel needed something more, which he provided in the shape of huge bouncing balls that are eating away the earth—well, not just the earth, but reality itself. The balls are black and red, they have faces and mouths and teeth; they are "sort of like beachballs, but balls which rippled and contracted and expanded again." "Reality peeled away in narrow strips beneath them, peeled away wherever and whatever they touched." Apart from telekinesis, King has done vampires, rabid dogs, cats back from the dead, zombies, a demon automobile, and a whole barrage of ghosties and ghoulies. But sort of like beachballs?

The novel and the movie called *Dolores Claiborne* (1992, 1994) are good illustrations of the way in which the same story can be told twice and mean different things each time. The novel is all about what people do when there's nowhere to go. The movie is about doing what you can but still having nowhere to go, and every image in it—the sea and the sky, the bare landscape, the half-abandoned houses—reinforces this feeling. I don't think the movie intends to be depressing. It intends to be beautiful and uplifting, all about courage and coming through, and Kathy Bates, as Dolores Claiborne, is full of fight and dignity. But she can't compete with all those images, which in another context might well suggest freedom or an unspoiled world.

Still, it is the same story, in spite of the different tilts of meaning and of obvious and extensive changes in the development of characters and their part in the plot. Dolores Claiborne, accused of two murders, has committed one but not the other. In the second case, where she is innocent, the evidence is damning. She was seen with a rolling pin raised above the head of the aged and now dead woman whose housekeeper she was, and she has inherited a fortune through the woman's death. In the first case, when she killed her husband nearly thirty years ago, the evidence was sparse because she took care to get rid of most of it—of all of it that she could find. She killed him, not just because he was a drunk and because he beat her, and not just to be free of him, but because he was molesting their daughter and she cold see no future for any of them in the world as long as he was alive. Obliquely but unmistakably instructed by her employer (" 'An accident,' she says in a clear voice almost like a schoolteacher's, 'is sometimes an unhappy woman's best friend' "), Dolores arranges for her drunken husband to fall down an old well he can't get out of. Like all bad characters in good horror stories, he takes a long time dying, indeed seems virtually unkillable. The same trope animates a battered and dying bad guy in *The Langoliers*: "There was something monstrous and unkillable and insectile about his horrible vitality.'

This may remind us that murder in fiction is almost always too easy or too hard—that it is a fiction, a picture not of killing but of the way we feel about killing. Will Dolores, guilty the first time, be convicted the second time? Will her daughter, who suspects her of murder, ever trust her again? Would her daughter understand if she heard the whole story? Both the novel and the movie answer these questions, and both use the total eclipse of the sun in 1963 as their dominant visual image. This is the day of the murder of the husband, ostensibly a good time to get away with it but really (that is, figuratively) a time of strange darkness when all bets are off and all rules suspended: this is the magic of the story, the moral telekinesis. Dolores doesn't need supernatural aid to kill her husband, she just needs, magically, for a few hours, to be someone else.

We are back in the world of *Carrie*, where rage is both understandable and terrifying. Carrie can read minds as well as move objects, and a phrase used about her helps us to see something else these novels are about: "the awful totality of perfect knowledge." The novels don't have perfect knowledge, or imagine anyone has it, except by magic. But then the magic, as well as giving anger a field day, would also give us a glimpse of the inside of anger, as if it we could read it, as if it could be perfectly known. We might then want to say not that to understand everything is to forgive everything but that to understand everything is unbearable.

Stephen King is still asking his question about magic in *Rose Madder*. It takes two forms here, or finds two instances. One involves a psychopathic cop, Norman Daniels, addicted to torturing his wife but shrewd enough to stop before she dies or before the evidence points only to him. He is also a killer, but even his wife doesn't know how crazy he is until she leaves him. Yet he's thought to be a good guy down at the station, recently promoted for his role in a big drug bust. His wife thinks every policeman is probably on his side, if not actually like him. Until King introduces a good cop around page 300, it looks as if the police force itself is the psychopath's version of telekinesis, what moves the world for him. There is a disturbing moment at the beginning of the novel, borrowed from Hitchcock but subtly and swiftly used, when Norman, having beaten his wife badly enough to cause a miscarriage, decides to call the hospital. "Her first thought is that he's calling the police. Ridiculous, of course—he *is* the police."

The other, more elaborate form of the question concerns Norman's wife, Rose. She finally finds the nerve to run away, after fourteen years of what King describes as sleep:

The concept of dreaming is known to the waking mind but to the dreamer there is no waking, no real world, no sanity; there is only the screaming bedlam of sleep. Rose McLendon Daniels slept within her husband's madness for nine more years.

Rose starts a new life in a distant city; makes new friends, gets a job reading thrillers for a radio station. You will have guessed that Norman goes after her and catches up with her at the climax of the novel and that there is much maiming and murder and fright along the way, and you will have guessed right. The violence is inventive and nasty, and Norman is as truly scary a fictional character as you could wish to keep you awake at night. He owes a certain amount to the Robert de Niro character in *Taxi Driver* (1977), but when King himself refers to the actor and the movie—he pays his dues—the gesture isn't merely cute, it's amusing, and polite, a casual tip of the hat. Norman is madder than the de Niro figure, his murder score is much higher, and—this is really distressing—he is often funny. Norman glances at a picture of Lincoln, for example, and thinks he looks "quite a bit like a man he had once arrested for strangling his wife and all four of his children."

What you won't have guessed is that the novel has a classical streak and that King is quite consciously connecting his own modern mythology to a well-known ancient one. Rose buys a painting—it's called *Rose Madder*, after the color of the dress of the woman who is the chief figure in it, but the title, for us, also plays on the double meaning of "mad," on Rose's need to get angry and the craziness that may result—and discovers that she can step into it, become part of its world and have adventures there. The picture appears to be a mediocre classical landscape, with ruined temple and vines, and thunderheads in the sky. What's going on there, as Rose learns when she visits, is a mixture of the myths of the Minotaur in the maze and of Demeter looking for Persephone, her daughter by Zeus, after Persephone has been abducted into the underworld.

The creature in the maze isn't exactly the Minotaur, since it's all bull, and it's called Erinyes, a name that means fury and is one of Demeter's epithets. Later the bull becomes Norman, or Norman becomes the bull: the monster is a metaphor for the less than human male. It's an engaging feature of King's play with these images that he doesn't forget the risks he's taking, and when Rose sees a pile of creaturely crap in the mythological maze she knows what it is: "After fourteen years of listening to Norman and Harley and all their friends, you'd have to be pretty stupid not to know bullshit when you see it."

The mother seeking her child is not exactly Demeter either, since Rose is told she is "not quite a goddess," and Demeter was undoubtedly the real thing.

The mother is also decaying, having "drunk of the waters of youth" without getting immortality to go with it; and she is not only, or not always a woman. She is a feminine principle, Carrie's anger in a calm disguise, telekinesis in a classical garb, and sometimes she looks like a spider or a fox. A literal vixen and cubs introduced in another part of the novel—in the world that is not that of the painting—sets up the idea of rabies, whose name means rage, and whose name *is* rage in several European languages. "It's a kind of rabies," Rose thinks, picturing some mythological equivalent of the disease, a consuming anger that could destroy a near-goddess. "She's being eaten up with it, all her shapes and magics and glamours trembling at the outer edge of her control now, soon it's all going to crumble."

This woman is a figure for the anger Rose may not be able to control or return from. The last pages of the novel are like an afterword to *Carrie*. Rose knows the power of her anger, but her anger also knows her and won't let her go. In a trivial quarrel in her happy new life, after the gruesome and entirely satisfactory mangling of Norman in the spooky world of the painting—not only in that world, though, Norman's not coming back—Rose has to make "an almost frantic effort" not to throw a pot of boiling water at her harmless second husband's head. She finds peace in an encounter, not with the near goddess of the picture but with the vixen of the American countryside, with the puzzle of rabies in that clever female face. "Rose looks for madness or sanity in those eyes . . . and sees both." But only sanity is actually there—a matter of luck, no doubt, of the way the disease ran among the local wildlife—and when she sees the vixen much later Rose has become confident of her own resistance to the power to hurt, knows the madness (or the magic) has faded. These are the last words of the book: "Her black eyes as she stands there communicate no clear thought to Rosie, but it is impossible to mistake the essential sanity of the old and clever brain behind them."

King writes very well at times: "Her shadow stretched across the stoop and the pale new grass like something cut from black construction paper with a sharp pair of scissors"; "Huge sunflowers with yellowy, fibrous stalks, brown centers, and curling, faded petals towered over everything else, like diseased turnkeys in a prison where all the inmates have died." The second example is a bit ripe, but it's effective. But then we also get "riding through a dream lined with cotton," "shards of glass twinkling beside a country road," and "what she felt like was a tiny fleck of flotsam in the middle of a trackless ocean." This is not popular writing, it's yesterday's posh writing, and it's consistent with Rose's thinking of *Madame Bovary* and Norman's muttering a line from *Hamlet*. Perhaps this is "better" fiction after all.

But of course what we are looking for in Stephen King is not felicity of phrase but invention and despatch, and racking fictional anxiety, and King supplies them in good measure. He also gives us a pretty generous clue as to what he is up to with his mythology. Within the world of the painting the bull gets out of the maze, and Rose worries that this may mean not only that the bull is loose but that the world has become his maze. The world of the painting, at least. A voice in her head, eager to help King out, takes her thought further. "This world, all worlds. And many bulls in each one. These myths hum with truth, Rosie. That's their power. That's why they survive." This is heavy-handed as explanation but doesn't really hamper the functioning of the myth. The magical picture of *Rose Madder* does what the beachballs of *The Langoliers* just won't do: it reminds us through fantasy how fantastic the unimagined everyday world can be. The trouble, in such a scenario, is not that dreams don't come true but that we are already living with them.

THREE
Stories and Silences

20. *Lost Paradises*

Counterpoint

What redeems certain empires, or perhaps only the British, according to Conrad's Marlow, what saves them from mere rapacity, from being "just robbery with violence, aggravated murder on a great scale," is "the idea only. An idea at the back of it; not a sentimental pretence but an idea; and an unselfish belief in the idea—something you can set up, and bow down before, and offer a sacrifice to." At this point in *Heart of Darkness* Marlow is said to break off. It is "only after a long silence" and "in a hesitating voice" that he speaks again and starts to tell the story of his journey to Africa and his meeting with the mysterious and dying Kurtz.

Marlow stops speaking, presumably, because he is troubled by the metaphor he has stumbled into. Bowing down and offering a sacrifice don't sound like the activities of an organized and enlightened Western mind. They sound like idolatry, even if the recipient is an idea rather than a barbarous deity. The very thing that (perhaps genuinely) distinguished the British from the ancient Roman and modern Belgian empires identifies it with the supposed savages it is unselfishly dispossessing of their land, and worse still, with Kurtz himself, the European who has gone native, whose house is surrounded by human skulls, and who has himself become someone to bow down before and offer a sacrifice to. African chiefs are said to "crawl" to him. As so often in Conrad, an argument begins to collapse into its opposite. There is a slippage at the heart of empire, a crack in its definition of itself.

Marlow's argument breaks down when the world of the story overtakes it.

But other features of empire are intact and unthreatened in *Heart of Darkness*, and even Conrad seems quite untroubled by them. We might start our quotation a little earlier:

> The conquest of the earth, which mostly means the taking it away from those who have a different complexion or slightly flatter noses than ourselves, is not a pretty sight when you look into it too much. What redeems it is the idea only. An idea at the back of it.

As the carefully understated irony makes clear—"slightly flatter" is particularly stealthy—Conrad was not a racist in the most obvious and virulent sense; he did not believe in the superiority of one race over another and repeatedly mocks the very notion. But he did believe in the loaded concept of race itself, as almost everyone did until more recently than we care to remember. Conrad welcomed the stereotype of the African savage, even if he thought (or because he thought) we were all savages at heart. He could see that Europeans might be as wild and morally benighted as Africans, or even more so, because of the veneer of their hypocrisy and refinement; he could not see that Africans might have their own enlightenment and civilization.

This is an effect of culture as we have come to understand it, or rather of power experienced as a cultural inflection, and the exploration of this effect is the business of Edward Said's *Culture and Imperialism* (1993). But culture doesn't simply respond to power; it shapes the moral world in which power is exercised and encountered. Culture decides on the eminence or obsolescence of competing stories, tells us what to take for granted, to imagine we always already knew. In one sense *Culture and Imperialism* is a sequel to Said's enormously influential *Orientalism* (1978); in another it is, as he says, "an attempt to do something else." Like *Orientalism*, the later work describes a culture of dominance, the way realities of power are both registered and masked in language and behavior; but it also explores cultural resistance, talking back, counterstories, the ways in which an ancient or emerging culture can speak within and against domination:

> No longer does the logos dwell exclusively, as it were, in London and Paris. No longer does history run unilaterally, as Hegel believed, from east to west, or from south to north, becoming more sophisticated and developed, less primitive and backward as it goes.

The new perspective requires not a denial of what comparative literature used to be in the grand old days of German philologists like Spitzer, Auerbach, and

Curtius but an extension of its interest to works of historical and sociological learning, and a reexamination of its old hierarchies, its (sometimes) implicit but (always) unmistakable Eurocentrism.

The real hero of Said's book is anonymous and collective; everyone who has been silenced or misrepresented by an empire but who has said enough, or left marks enough, to encourage the chance of liberation. Frantz Fanon comes close to being the named hero, the bearer of a "cultural energy" that could move us beyond nationalism, seen as the continuing grip of empire's hand, into an authentic humanism, a term to be stripped of its conservative and self-congratulating intonation. "It is a misreading of Fanon," Said suggests, "not to see in him something considerably beyond a celebration of violent conflict." I'm sure this is right, although Said's dismissal of Fanon's support of armed struggle as "at most tactical" is a little swift—it was more than that—and doesn't even evoke "the justified violence of the oppressed," a phrase Said uses elsewhere.

However, Said's topic at this point is not violence but nationalism, and he already has enough difficulties on his hands. He doesn't want to refuse nationalism its legitimacy as a mode of resistance to imperial domination; he wants us to see that there are many forms of nationalism, courageous as well as crazy and tyrannical ones. But he also wants nationalism to be critical of itself. Only in this way can it modulate into liberation and put an end to the ghosts of empire. At this point, words such as *universal* might make a comeback, because they would represent not the projection into time and space of whatever our civilization happens to be but the discovery of authentically shared human grounds, old and new.

It will be more difficult to rehabilitate *objective*, a word often found in the same lexicon, not because there are no common truths or because subjectivity is all we have left but because *objectivity* has served too many forms of Realpolitik, has too often meant merely an insufficient curiosity about the status quo, as when the facts (our facts) are assumed to take care of all argument. Said quotes Fanon as saying that "for the native, objectivity is always directed against him." There are other objectivities, of course, which may be helpful to the native, or may be the native's own, as when an investigation reveals the lies and distortions of an oppressor. But even there, even when a relative objectivity can be substantiated and agreed on, there are also passion and polemic, not the mere, aloof disinterestedness the word *objectivity* mostly seems to proclaim.

This is a delicate matter, which haunts all of Said's work—indeed haunts much modern scholarship in all kinds of fields. He acknowledges the force of various Nietzschean skepticisms about the possibility of truth and knowledge but clings to the idea that "there is such a thing as knowledge that is less, rather than more partial than the individual . . . who produces it" and that what he calls "the seductive degradation of knowledge" can be resisted. All knowledge is potentially political, we might say; it doesn't have to be, shouldn't be politicized. The trouble is that when it calls itself objective, it is often hiding its politics, as if politics couldn't even be a question. Fanon's native might well claim to speak the truth; would not have the imperial comfort of believing the truth simply speaks for itself.

Taking a cue from Raymond Williams, Said describes the elaborate involvement of culture in empire as "a structure of attitude and reference." This capacious phrase, almost obsessively repeated, begins to wear a little thin or to look more like a talisman than a concept. Is there anything that won't go into this baggy container? Like Williams, and like Lukács, his other *maître à penser*, Said deals frequently in the very broadest of propositions. The difficulty with them is not that we can't assent to them but that we can scarcely see what it would mean not to.

Said himself is certainly aware of this problem, and in an earlier book speaks of the risk of "soupy" designations and "sloppy" notions. In *Culture and Imperialism* he writes of the "unacceptable vagueness" that may attend words such as *imperialism* (or *culture* for that matter), and offers two responses to this concern: we do need to look at the details and differences concealed by the general term; we must not use these details and differences to avoid the hard realities lurking in the vagueness itself. This is persuasive, and in the case of empire the vagueness is a product of the sheer size of the phenomenon, of the fact, say, cited by Said, that by 1914 "Europe held a grand total of roughly 86 per cent of the earth as colonies, protectorates, dependencies, dominions, and commonwealths." As a result, empire lingers almost everywhere, in economies and in minds, even when it is supposed to have gone, and Said can plausibly speak of our political "context" as still "primarily imperial." We need to remember that the culture of empire often includes a magisterial denial of the possession of anything like an empire, or an interest in any such thing, as when the interventions of the United States in Asia and Latin America are pictured not as imperial adventures but as humble, even altruistic acts of peace-keeping. Or when the British and the Belgians indulged in the metaphor of bringing light to darkness that so caught Conrad's attention.

Said invites us to a "contrapuntal reading" of works of literature: a reading in which ordinarily separate histories are allowed to play against each other, to produce not harmony but a complicated polyphony. What is important about this invitation is not its occasional bluntness or its sometimes overstated claims but the range of insight and argument it makes possible. It is not only a matter, as Said too modestly says, of provoking "a newly engaged interest" in canonical texts, or of making them "more valuable as works of art." It is a matter of learning how to find, in literature and elsewhere, what Said calls "a heightened form of historical experience." I take this to mean finding history in places where it ought not to have been lost, amid our favorite formalisms and decorums, for example.

This is what Said's demanding discussions of Camus, Flaubert, Forster, Gide, Yeats, Césaire, Neruda, and many others do for us. The point, to parody Marx, is not to appreciate the world but to understand it. We see the "strengths" and "limitations" of works we care about—Conrad's *Nostromo* for instance; we catch the references they themselves make to things we have forgotten, as I shall suggest in a moment in relation to Jane Austen; we gain or regain a "sense of the human community and the actual contests" that go into the formation of national and other histories, those of the British in India, say, and the Indians under the British; and we recognize in empire and its legacy "a compellingly important and interesting configuration in the world of power and nations." There is no exaggeration in such a claim, and by analogy we recognize other missed or displaced configurations too.

Culture and Imperialism is a hospitable book—surprisingly hospitable perhaps for a volume with such a turbulent topic and for an author with such a (well-earned) reputation for polemic. It is a work of prodigious learning, littered with warm acknowledgements of writers and titles. Its very pages look like an active community of scholarship, and Said speaks eloquently of the university as a "utopian space" where politics are (must be) an issue but where such issues are not "imposed or resolved." We may think of the space as wider than the university, as appearing wherever thought and argument are active, wherever criticism in Said's sense occurs. The "social goal" of criticism, he says in *The World, the Text, and the Critic* (1983) is "noncoercive knowledge produced in the interests of human freedom"; and he asks, in a rather Jamesian turn, "What is critical consciousness at bottom if not an unstoppable predilection for alternatives?"

Literature itself would be a utopia in this sense, as Barthes and Calvino and Kundera also suggest (Kundera: "the novel is incompatible with the totalitarian universe"). But then this same utopian, critical space, if much wider than the university, is still pretty slender overall in the world and is threatened even within the university, vulnerable to all sorts of conformities and always at risk when the predilection for alternatives, whichever way they run, is treated as treason.

Too Silent in the Evening Circle

There is an excellent example of regainable historical experience in Austen's *Mansfield Park*, which Said controversially discusses in *Culture and Imperialism*. Said's case seems at first sight very much overworked; a few mentions of Sir Thomas Bertram's possessions in Antigua support a whole structure of argument about empire and slavery. Said shows analogies between running an estate and writing a novel, and between restoring order at home, where the young folks have been putting on a play, and keeping order abroad, where the natives are no doubt restless. When he writes that "there is nothing in *Mansfield Park* that would contradict us" if we were to pursue such connections, skepticism begins to arise in some of us. This is how lawyers talk when their evidence is shaky.

But Said's evidence is not shaky, and he is if anything too discreet about it. He says, correctly but without quoting, that Austen continues to link colonial expansion with domestic morality "right up to the last sentence." If we turn to that last sentence with questions about slavery in our mind, we are likely to find it disconcerting. Should we have questions about slavery in our mind? Well, Austen had; it's her later readers who haven't.

In the last words of the novel we learn that the parsonage at Mansfield, the house where Fanny Bertram, married, now lives,

> which . . . Fanny had never been able to approach but with some painful sensation of restraint or alarm, soon grew as dear to her heart, and as thoroughly perfect in her eyes, as every thing else, within the view and patronage of Mansfield Park, had long been.

The restraint and alarm have to do with the former inhabitants of the parsonage, who include Fanny's meddling and snobbish aunt, her glittering rival for the love of her cousin Edmund, and a man who made her an offer it seemed she couldn't refuse; but "patronage" reaches out into a world beyond Fanny's immediate experiences and picks up discussions earlier in the novel. I don't think "patronage" can literally include Sir Thomas Bertram's overseas possessions, because it wouldn't be the right term for them, even by extension. But I do think Mansfield Park, the place and the idea, must include everything that sustains it, and that Austen invites us to remember the plantation in Antigua, even as she knows we will probably forget it. This is in part what her irony about "perfection" aims at.

For there must be a discreet smile in the phrase "thoroughly perfect," and a declared restriction in the phrase "in her eyes." The place is not perfect, because nowhere is. Austen has just said, in one of her milder relativizing touches, that "the happiness of the married cousins . . . must appear as secure as earthly happiness can be." How secure is that? How secure did Austen think it was? What is the word *appear* doing there? Austen goes on to specify by implication that this happiness involves "affection and comfort," and—a somber joke—the death of the incumbent at the parsonage, so the happy couple can move in. I don't think we should read Austen as sneering here, or doubting the happiness of the married cousins. But it is a worldly happiness, and the projected perfection, as Fanny herself quite unmistakably knows, includes slavery as one of its supports, if not one of its foundations.

Austen, like Conrad (and most other English novelists writing before this century), accepts the idea of overseas possession; she fails to express any considerable interest in the human objects of British colonial attention, undoubtedly caught up in the "recent losses" Sir Thomas Bertram has sustained "on his West India Estate," part of the "experience and anxiety" he met there, since "the Antigua estate" is making "such poor returns"—although indeed his losses and anxiety may well have to do with the approaching abolition of the British slave trade rather than its heartless flourishing.

But Austen does express unease, or allow space for unease, about the morality of the practice of overseas possession. Sir Thomas Bertram, having taken his mousy niece into his house as an act of kindness, is surprised, on his return from Antigua, to find she has grown into an attractive young woman. "Your uncle thinks you very pretty, dear Fanny," her cousin Edmund says. "You must really begin to harden yourself to the idea of being worth looking at. . . . You must try not to mind growing up into a pretty woman." Edmund means to be kind and has tried to frame his father's compliments with an appropriate moral reservation: "Though they may be chiefly on your person, you must put up with it, and trust to his seeing as much beauty of mind in time." Even so, "being worth looking at" is brutal enough, and "beauty of mind" here sounds like the stuff you get at question time in the Miss World contest.

But the real problem, which makes Fanny "distressed by more feelings than he was aware of," is that she is in love with Edmund, and we are to imagine the strange torture of hearing these things from his mouth but not from his mind and heart. Edmund, blind to all this and not yet in love with Fanny, says she needs to talk to her uncle more, she is "one of those who are too silent in the evening circle." At this point Austen makes an astonishing connection, which I certainly should not have seen without Said's invitation, between the question of women's worth and a more notorious commerce in human flesh. Fanny says:

"But I do talk to him more than I used. I'm sure I do. Did not you hear me ask him about the slave trade last night?"

"I did—and was in hopes the question would be followed up by others. It would have pleased your uncle to be inquired of farther."

"And I longed to do it—but there was such a dead silence."

Fanny goes on to explain her diffidence: she didn't want to seem more interested in her uncle's doings in the West Indies, or specifically his "information" about the place, than the man's own daughters were.

There is a lot of work for the reader to do here, and different readers will do different work. It's possible to see this moment as not *about* the slave trade at all; mention of it merely signals Fanny's seriousness and the empty-headedness of the Bertram girls. The dead silence is one of boredom. This is certainly how Edmund sees the matter, but his mind is not fully on it. He is thinking, as his next speech shows, about the charms of Mary Crawford, the woman he is currently attracted to. And can it be true that Sir Thomas would have been pleased by further questions about the slave trade? What was his answer to the first? Perhaps the dead silence was his, and Fanny describes her diffidence because she doesn't want to complain or argue. Or she is embarrassed at the memory: she didn't mean to cause trouble or seem like some sort of radical, she only wanted a wise and authoritative answer to her no doubt foolish qualms.

For Said the dead silence suggests that the cruelty of the West Indies could not be connected with the civility of places like Mansfield Park, "since there simply is no common language for both." This is certainly the effect of the silence, and it is certainly the way many (perhaps most) readers of Jane Austen see the matter. Several English reviewers of Said's book thought the notion that Austen might (or might not) have anything to say about slavery was his chief and most ridiculous idea, and their articles were illustrated with rather demure-looking prints of the novelist, as if she were a cultural icon to be saved from political desecration. But the silence in the novel must in practice be local, rather than a reflection of the culture at large. The British slave trade was abolished in 1807, and most commentators assume the novel (written 1811) to be set in the years just before that. The subject would have been much discussed, and might have been discussed even at places like Mansfield Park. Fanny was trying and failing to talk about the *news*. If the silence is Sir Thomas's, rather than that of general boredom, we still have to guess at its source. Is he an embarrassed anti-abolitionist, or does he just think women shouldn't talk about these things? Does he not know what to say, or is he fed up with all the talk about the slave trade? Or just too distressed to talk any more?

Of course, we can't take any of these questions very far without writing our own novel; but that is not a reason for dropping them entirely. Slavery is not attacked in such a scene; but it is remembered, and there is no comfortable place for a critic or reader to be. The writing is so understated, so delicately unforthcoming, that at first we can only note the presence in it of a question that in older, less contrapuntal readings, Fanny might be thought too frightened to ask and Austen might be thought too genteel to entertain.

Broken Narratives

Austen offers us several stories here, or several possibilities of story, and such a move in fiction invites us to think about Said's critical argument about narrative and power. "Narrative itself is the representation of power," he says in *Culture and Imperialism*, echoing an earlier essay called "Permission to Narrate" (1984). It's not that the powerless don't have stories, and it's not only that they don't get to tell the stories they have. It's that they are scarcely perceived as capable of having stories, their stories are not so much refused as ruled out, unimaginable as pieces of recognized history. "With no acceptable narrative to rely on, with no sustained permission to narrate, you feel crowded out and silenced."

It's true that the acceptance of official stories often leaves little room for anything else, and that a person who doesn't share the assumptions of those stories will often seem to be mute. But narrative is not always on the side of power, nor is it only the representation of power. There are narratives of resistance as well as of dominance; and narratives that slip past the guard of power, either through irony or through seeming too negligible for power's attention. The stories in Said's own work—his literary and cultural criticism, his writing on music, his polemical writing, his moving essay-memoir *After the Last Sky* (1986)—are often brief and submerged, sometimes only implied; but it is work full of stories.

Said writes at times of alternatives to narrative, of "lateral, non-narrative connections," or "anti-narrative energy," or "anti-narrativist waywardness." But these gestures and moments are themselves instances of narrative, other ways of telling, to adapt the title of one of John Berger's books. They are "broken narratives" in Said's own phrase, scraps of story, dissolutions or diversions of the tyrannical single narrative. *After the Last Sky* transcribes a grimly comic interview in which a captured Palestinian is questioned on Israeli radio:

"And what was your mission in South Lebanon?"
"My mission was terrorism . . . in other words, we would enter villages and

just terrorize. And wherever there were women and children, we would terrorize. Everything and all we did was terrorism . . ."

"What's your opinion of the terrorist Arafat?"

"I swear he's the greatest terrorist of all. . . . His whole life is terrorism."

At one point, Said indicates, the man being interviewed makes a terrible linguistic joke or slip. He belongs, he says, to the "Popular Front for the Liberation [*tahrir*]—I mean Terrorism [*takhrib*]—of Palestine."

What is happening here relates only indirectly or ironically to the actual horrors of terrorism and violence, on either side of the fearful situation in Israel and Palestine. Even if this man were a terrorist, his performance would be a parody, a caricature of a nightmare. Of course, he might just be frightened, not to say terrorized, into talking like this, and he might be just groveling. Or he might be brutally, blatantly cynical about an ugly truth. But the reading Said offers is the most persuasive one. The man lives inside a powerful story and can defend himself against it only by mockingly accepting everything it says. We have seen similar strategies in many very different situations. Here we are looking at a dominant myth in action, one that says that there is only one kind of terrorism ("theirs") and that all captured Palestinians are terrorists, what else could they be? You can't answer such a myth, you can't even tell a clear counterstory that anyone will believe. You can only travesty it, repeat it as if it were a mocking fable. Said says, "This story and several others like it circulate among Palestinians like epics; there are even cassettes of it available for an evening's entertainment." *That* story is scary too, of course. What if the parody turns back into a simplified, murderous version of the real thing?

Two of Said's broken narratives in particular help to focus his work, hang in the mind like elusive emblems of that work's most subtle stories. One concerns artists of great gifts, composers, novelists, critics, whose historical situation or relation to language becomes a cage or an impasse: their very achievements lead them to frustration, they demand more of the world and of themselves than either can give, and their immense successes are caught up in what feels to them like failure. Swift, Hopkins, Conrad, in Said's accounts of them, all enact versions of this grand but hard tale. There is also Yeats, struggling to "announce the contours of an imagined or ideal community" in the violent reverse of an ideal world. Put together, these glimpses of brilliant and baffled artistic careers begin to resemble Adorno's vision of modern music, finding an austere integrity in the dead end into which it drives itself. "Modern music sees absolute oblivion as its goal," Adorno encouragingly writes. "It is the surviving message of despair from the shipwrecked." Also lurking somewhere here perhaps is the example of Said's Princeton teacher R. P. Blackmur, who spoke of failure as "the expense of greatness" and said (of Henry Adams), "a genuine failure comes hard and slow, as in a tragedy, is only fully realized at the end."

Said is drawn to these careers, and his later writing returns again and again to Adorno in particular. But the story I hear in Said's work is finally less doomed and more dynamic than the one Adorno tells, more direct and less mournful than the one we meet in Blackmur. The artist is a hero not because he wins or loses but because he acts, because he is faithful against the odds to a difficult idea of the self and the world.

The other broken narrative is a version, or an anticipation, of the story of the obliging terrorist. It echoes through Said's writing in quite different contexts, early and late, and it is the implied story, the narrative behind the narrative, of *Orientalism*. This book is very emphatically about the "system of ideas" by which the West has mapped the East, and says it acknowledges only "tacitly" the "lives, histories, and customs" of those who actually live in so-called Eastern lands. Said insists that he doesn't believe in any "real or true Orient," "some Oriental essence" to be opposed to a set of essentially wrong Western views. It's the very invention of the Orient that is the problem; it allows learning and sympathy and literature and adventure but it always risks tumbling into myth. Said quotes the scholar Duncan Macdonald on the Oriental's "*liability* to be stampeded by a single idea" and comments on the liability of Macdonald and his colleagues to be stampeded by a single idea about the Orient. In one of the quietest and most telling moments in the book, Said suggests that the "difference is slight" between the history the West has given the Arab since 1940 and the history it has taken from him. Much is to be learned from the thought that a theft and a gift might, in certain contexts or perspectives, be almost the same.

But then there are real people in the imaginary East, and Said's tacit acknowledgement of actualities is louder than he perhaps thought it was at the time, since it embodies a genuine passion for the unrepresented, for those who can't speak but who flicker in the pages of *Orientalism* whenever Said invokes a neglected human history. He writes for example of "the disparity between texts and reality," of "the Islamic people as humans," of "individual Arabs with narratable life histories." What else but this reality, the untold story of this reality, would make Orientalism such a problem-filled enterprise? Just how narratable these neglected life histories are, and by whom, is of course the question we are looking at. Said doesn't want to speak for the silenced or the ignored—he thinks the Orientalists are already doing that—he wants their silence to be heard.

Not all Orientals are silent, of course, and not only Orientals are silenced; Said's broken narrative comes into play wherever representation overwhelms the represented, and we can all think of parallel examples. This is to say that the story, as a story, concerns a group or groups of people who are unable to represent themselves not because they cannot speak or have no stories, and not even because they have been repressed, although that is often also the case. It is not even chiefly a question of their access to the means of distribution of narrative, although that too is of course important. They cannot represent themselves, Said is saying, because they are already represented, like the interviewed terrorist. A monstrous imitation stands in their place and is worked like the chess-playing puppet Walter Benjamin evokes at the start of his "Theses on the Philosophy of History." They are different from us and their difference, usually but not always construed as inferiority, is who they are. They have no other life.

At the same time the silence of these peoples has a charm of its own and is a criticism of our noisy speech. This is not to justify their silencing but to say they are not only victims, and I find I want to associate the habits of secrecy Said attributes to the Palestinians in *After the Last Sky* ("We are a people of messages and signals, of allusions and indirect expression," there is "something withheld from an immediate deciphering") with what he calls the "reticence, mystery, or allusive silence" of music, the modesty of its wordlessness. These reticences are worlds apart, of course, but they share the sense of a realm that language can point to but cannot name, that only community or the art of listening can inherit. In *Musical Elaborations* Said quotes Proust on the subject of books as the work of solitude and the children of silence, and thinks of the phrase in relation to Brahms: "I found myself coming to a sort of unstatable, or inexpressible, aspect of his music, the music of his music, which I think anyone who listens to, plays, or thinks about music carries within oneself." This is not a retreat from the world, or a denial of worldliness. It is one of the ways, and among the most valuable, of living in the world. Solitude is part of who we are, and it can, in communities of trust, open out on to shared silences, the imagined music of our music.

Such communities are fragile and intermittent. They are places where allusions are enough and silences count as much as words; where words too still count but have been relieved of the burden of assertion and will. They are often more a memory than a fact, and sometimes not even a memory. They are like home as Said describes it at the end of *Culture and Imperialism*, evoking the exile of Erich Auerbach, who fell into the East at Istanbul and found in his mind the Europe he had lost. Said quotes Hugo of Saint Victor, who thought that love of home should give way to a love of "every soil," which in turn, for the person who had become "perfect," should yield to a sense that "the entire world is a foreign place." Said's comments on this passage are wonderfully delicate and subtle and can be seen as offering an original reading of Proust's suggestion that true paradises are lost paradises:

> Exile is predicated on the existence of, love for, and a real bond with one's native place; the universal truth of exile is not that one has lost that love or home, but that inherent in each is an unexpected, unwelcome loss. Regard experiences then as if they were about to disappear.

This is a truth for those who have lost their love and home, and for those who have not; and for those who have returned to them. Exile, as Said suggests earlier in this book, can be a happy and an unhappy condition, a chance of belonging "to more than one history." It can be suffered or sought, or imaginatively borrowed. It is a way of understanding loss and a way of knowing what there is to lose, the paradise that can't exist until it's gone.

No future in this. Alas yes.   —Samuel Beckett, *Worstward Ho*

22. *The Discourse of Others*

Music and Dreams

"Can you believe it? What am I supposed to do? They take so much for granted, all these people. What do they want me to do, on this night of all nights?"
You hear the whine in your voice, but you can't stop. Self-pity is a country
where everyone else is unreasonable, where your manifest innocence cries out
in perfect pitch. There is a horrible pleasure in visiting this country; but it's
hard to leave, the borders close behind you almost as soon as you get there.
"But it's the same as everywhere else," you say. "They expect everything from
me. They'll probably turn on me tonight, it wouldn't surprise me."

The voice I'm quoting is that of Ryder, the English concert pianist whose
dazed narrative constitutes Kazuo Ishiguro's *The Unconsoled* (1994), but I'm
also suggesting that its ghastly familiarity is all but irresistible. I'm sure there
are people who know nothing of self-pity and have never spoken like this, even
in their dreams; lucky them. But for the rest of us, Ryder's experience is like a
map of our plaintive, small-time self-dramatizing, a catalog of the postures we
adopt when we feel guilty but want to feel virtuous.

Ryder arrives in an unnamed German town to give a concert. He's hazy
about his schedule—he remembers reading it, but not what it said—but can't
bring himself to ask for clarification. He's to give a speech, apparently, as well
as perform some contemporary music, and the whole town's moral and perhaps economic well-being depends on a turn in cultural affairs over which
Ryder is to preside. The town has strongly supported one Christoff, a conduc-
tor now felt to be a charlatan. His shallow and dogmatic interpretations being

exposed, with Ryder himself administering the coup de grace, Christoff must give way to the disreputable but reformed Brodsky, a gifted musician who has dedicated himself to drink for the last twenty years. Ryder knows he ought to be surprised at this shift of his role from musician to musical authority, and indeed at the extreme penetration of musical life into the gossip and politics of the humdrum city, but he isn't, partly because he feels he must have agreed to the program even if he can't remember any of it, and partly because he's too busy being besieged by locals asking favors of him: will he look at a woman's album of cuttings, will he listen to a young pianist play, will he meet with concerned citizens, will he take a message to the porter's daughter? He also seems to relish the idea of his own cultural importance and talks complacently of "the crisis I had come to assess," as if his concert were a sideline.

Three features in particular make clear to us what strange territory Ryder and we are in. First, almost no one *approaches* Ryder. People appear at the moment he thinks of them or they are mentioned by someone else. He and a porter are in an elevator, for example, apparently alone. The porter talks of a Miss Hilde and Ryder finally asks who she is. "No sooner had I said this, I noticed the porter was gazing past my shoulder at some spot behind me. Turning, I saw with a start that we were not alone in the elevator. A small young woman in a neat business suit was standing pressed into the corner behind me." Second, almost everyone who meets Ryder launches into the narrative of his or her life, so that the porter, for example, tells a slow story of several pages, out of all proportion to the length of any imaginable elevator ride. The hotel manager tells the tale of his marriage, how he allowed his wife to believe, during their courtship, that he was a musician, and how he has been waiting for twenty years or more for the inevitable day when she will leave him. Certain pieces of Ryder's past have been transposed to this town, and he recognizes them as such, although always in the sudden, apparitional way he notices Miss Hilde. There are old schoolfriends, a girl from his village in Worcestershire; a room in his English aunt's house that has now become a room in a German hotel; an old car that used to belong to his parents in England and is now mysteriously abandoned outside an art gallery in Germany. But these material memories, so to speak, make up only a small part of Ryder's experience in the novel. He is traveling chiefly not to his past but to his scrambled and elusive present, to a present that seems endlessly deferred and out of reach. He meets new people, enters strange rooms, and then is invaded by the thought that he ought to know them; know them well. Memories creep up on him: "Sophie's face had come to seem steadily more familiar to me. . . . I found a faint recollection returning to me of listening to this same voice"; "I found myself remembering more of the argument I had had with Sophie"; "The room was by now growing steadily more familiar to me."

The strangers are no longer entirely strangers, but they are not part of Ryder's nameable history. On the contrary: they have no real history for him, their history is what he has lost. This is particularly painful in the case of Sophie and Boris, since Ryder appears to be in the middle of a turbulent and unhappy relationship with Sophie, and may be Boris's father. He seems to meet Boris for the first time near the beginning of the book but is soon calling him "My boy, Boris." At the end of the novel Sophie turns on Ryder, and says, "Leave us. You were always on the outside of our love." To the boy she says, "He'll never be one of us. You've got to understand that, Boris. He'll never love you like a real father." Ryder sobs with distress—he is sitting on a tram at the time—but with the inconsequentiality that marks every scene in this book and is the third identifying feature of this territory, cheers up instantly when he discovers that a splendid breakfast is being served on the tram itself. The most horrible events occur in this work, from deep embarrassments to death and mutilation, but they are always reinterpretable as small blips or snags. Ryder doesn't give the concert, or the speech, the whole book has been tending toward, because he has been distracted by one of the many other calls on his time. Dawn comes up, the audience is gone, but Ryder somehow sidesteps the disarray we feel he ought to feel. "I surveyed the scene around me and saw how needless had been my worries concerning my ability to cope with the various demands presented to me in this city. As ever, my experience and instincts had proved more than sufficient to see me through. Of course, I felt a certain disappointment about the evening, but then, as I thought about it further, I could see the inappropriateness of such feelings." The corollary to self-pity is this astonishing self-absolution. The last words of the novel, following shortly on Sophie's devastating dismissal, are these: "I filled my coffee cup almost to the brim. Then, holding it carefully in one hand, my generously laden plate in the other, I began making my way back to my seat."

A lot of people are sleepy in this novel, and all three sections after the first open with Ryder awaking from a nap. Is it all perhaps a version of one of those dreams in which you keep dreaming you are awake? It's tempting to think so, and the book is full of hallucinatory, often comic images that appear to have come from a surrealist repertoire revised by diffidence and guilt. When Ryder steps on to the stage to give his much delayed and infinitely discussed performance, he discovers that there is not only no audience but no seating. The floor of the auditorium is quite clear, "a vast, dark, empty space," and pieces of the ceiling have been removed for good measure, "allowing the daylight to come down in pale shafts onto the floor." It's as if we had wandered into a dream within a dream in Buñuel's *Discreet Charm of the Bourgeoisie*. The folded ironing-board, however, which serves the rehabilitated but injured Brodsky as a crutch, emerges from some delirious English domesticity, and the elaborate preparations for Ryder's talk sound as if Kafka had been coaching Pinter or Stoppard. The fussy speaker is the hotel manager, who is in charge of the whole event:

> The whole auditorium, for a single moment, will be plunged into blackness, during which time the curtains will open. And then a single spot will come on, revealing you standing at the center of the stage at the lectern. At that moment, obviously, the audience will burst into excited applause. Then, once the applause has subsided, before you have uttered a word—of course, this is so long as you are agreeable—a voice will boom out across the auditorium, pronouncing the first question. The voice will be that of Horst Jannings, this city's most senior actor. He will be up in the sound box speaking through the public address system. Horst has a fine rich baritone and he will read out each question slowly. And as he does so—this is my little idea, sir!—the words will be spelt out simultaneously on the electronic scoreboard fixed directly above your head. . . . The words on the scoreboard, dare I say, will help some of those present to remember the gravely important nature of the issues you are addressing. . . . Each question will be there in front of them spelt out in giant letters. . . . The first question will be announced, spelt out on the scoreboard, you will give your reply from the lectern, and once you have finished, Horst will read out the next question and so on. The only thing we would ask, Mr. Ryder, is that at the end of each reply, you leave the lectern and come to the edge of the stage and bow. The reasons for my requesting this is twofold. Firstly, because of the temporary nature of the electronic scoreboard, there are inevitably certain technical difficulties. . . . So you see, sir, by moving to the edge of the stage and bowing, thus provoking inevitable applause, we will avoid a series of awkward pauses punctuating the proceedings. . . . There is, sir, a further reason this strategy recommends itself. Your coming to the edge of the stage and bowing will tell the electrician, very unambiguously, that you have completed your answer.

It sounds like a recipe for a fiasco, even apart from its remoteness from what is normally expected of concert pianists; but Ryder, caught up in what he calls a "dreamy sense of unreality," wearily assents: "It all sounds splendid, Mr. Hoffman." Later he panics, and in the midst of the phrases I quoted at the beginning of this chapter, says "They've actually brought in an electronic scoreboard. Can you believe it?"

But I'm not sure it helps to think of the whole novel as the record of a dream. It's more like a long metaphor for deferred and displaced anxiety, and the point about anxiety is that it doesn't occur only in dreams. The German city is redrawn and repeopled by Ryder's preoccupations. Its geography is particularly fantastic, sprouting obstacles and distances at random, and its time frames are peculiarly flexible. But this is only to say that the novel takes the opportunity that fiction so often resists and pursues the darker logic of a world governed by our needs and worries rather than the laws of physics.

At the center of this unconsolable place are the unappeasable parents, the parents for whom no performance is good enough and whose mandate never dies. Ryder remembers his own parents quarreling when he was a child; they are supposed to come to his concert in Germany, but don't—have they ever been to one of his concerts? He says they are coming "to hear me perform for the very first time," but later says he is about "to perform once more before my parents." When he is sure they haven't come, he bursts into tears; and then is half-consoled by the news that his parents have visited this city in the past—as if the old visit and his current stay could be patched up in some other dimension. Ryder's dilemma is mirrored in that of the hotel manager's son, a pianist of talent whose parents have no faith in him, so that the very moment of his spectacular success seems to them a cruel mockery of their hope. The town itself has made a judgment about music the key to its self-esteem; and Ryder's failure with Sophie and Boris is a sacrifice of the family to a musical career—or would be, if Ryder could overcome his distractions and get back to his musical career. Music is how you try to justify yourself in this world; and also the reason your attempts at justification fail. Music is a challenge and a prowess; but every success breeds new doubts and peoples the world with judges. The slightest favor that is asked of you, as favors are asked of Ryder at every turn, is a chance of proving that you are not only a good musician but a good person. You can't resist the lure of this proof, but what would your niceness prove? "*Par délicatesse j'ai perdu ma vie,*" Rimbaud wrote. Niceness proves only that you want to be nice; and probably shows that an unmanageable guilt has spilled into the simplest encounters. Is music a crime? The mask of your necessary betrayal of your parents, or their unforgivable betrayal of you? Or is music an image of control, the very thing that turns to chaos once your anxiety gets the better of you? Ryder talks repeatedly, as well he may, of chaos descending on him and of the need to regain control of his time and his movements. Practicing a piece called *Asbestos and Fibre* he feels "in absolute control of every dimension of the composition." The novel, we may think, shows us just the reverse of this feeling, displays with eerie consistency what an absolute lack of control might look like, and how it might play itself out.

The Unconsoled itself is beautifully controlled, even-paced, deadpan in spite of all extravagances. Its determined equanimity of tone makes you drowsy, and sometimes you wonder if you'd notice if you dropped off to sleep while you were reading. But there is finally something haunting, even compelling, about the proliferation of obstacles and stories in this book. It's not that a sense of suspense or of climax is created, far from it. But there is a kind of excitement in Ryder's stumbling from errand to failed errand, as if nothing were certain in life except the interruption of whatever you are trying to do. We know he's not going to get anywhere, unravel his relationships, help his friends, please his parents, give his concert or his speech, sort out this terribly self-preoccupied town. But it's hard work not getting anywhere. Ryder's endless distraction from his multiplying purposes is so distracting that we can hardly bear it. His life is overwhelmed by irrelevance, buried under pointless but irresistible demands. That's when the novel ceases to feel like a dream, or only like a dream.

Oriental Silences

"I suppose I was perhaps the last guest down to breakfast," Ryder says, "but then again, I had had an exceptionally demanding night and saw no reason to feel any guilt about it." That's how all guilty people talk, Kafka would say. It's certainly how all Ishiguro's main characters talk. The least interesting of these characters is probably Stevens, the butler in *Remains of the Day* (1988). He uses his stuffy language to avoid whatever insights may be lurking in his starved and shriveled mind, and the text is a kind of tour de force of impersonation on Ishiguro's part. The trouble is that the work lacks the mystery of Ishiguro's other novels and that it's hard to believe that Stevens's repressions aren't a lot more fun than anything he could be repressing. This aspect of the novel is made luminously clear in James Ivory's movie version, where Anthony Hopkins is having such a high old time being a butler that you can't imagine him swapping the life for anything, least of all a dingy romance with that nice housekeeper, Emma Thompson. The central character in *An Artist of the Floating World* (1986) is a Japanese artist who doesn't know how much he should or can regret his prewar patriotism. Should he apologize for his complicity in that militarist world, or is the idea that he made any kind of contribution to the horrors of the time a sort of folie de grandeur, an exaggeration of his own role? Is he hiding from his past or inflating it? If you say you have no reason to feel any guilt, you're not bound to be guilty, but you're not bound to be innocent either. And whom are you saying it to? Whom should you be saying it to?

Ishiguro's first novel, *A Pale View of Hills* (1982), after many readings still seems to me a small masterpiece. Like *The Unconsoled* it concerns drastic denials and what happens when the denied material comes back to haunt you. *The Unconsoled* doesn't have the concentration of *A Pale View of Hills* or its violent and poignant historical background. But it does ask us to think about real and imaginary guilt, and when you realize, only a few pages into the book, that the porter who is going on about the nobility of the porter's vocation is parodying Stevens's line about the dignity of butlering in *The Remains of the Day*, you get an idea of Ishiguro's deepest subject: not the risks of repression but the comedy and the pathos and the sorrow of the stories we tell ourselves to keep other stories away.

Etsuko has left Japan and her Japanese husband to live in England. Her second, English husband is now dead; she has had a daughter from each marriage. A visit from her half-English daughter sparks off a series of memories, of mysterious but unavoidable connections between the years in Nagasaki after the war (after the bomb) and the recent suicide, in Manchester, of Etsuko's entirely Japanese daughter, the girl she brought with her from Japan. Etsuko sees herself, or rather determinedly refuses to see herself, even as she evokes the resemblance, in a Nagasaki friend who neglected her daughter and went off with an American. Almost everything is unspeakable here, and yet much gets spoken, or at least suggested. What is most memorable about the book is the calm of Etsuko's narrative, the sense that she is both acknowledging an enormous guilt and plausibly asking what else she could have done.

We could think of the unspeakable as having two different senses: the unutterably horrible or monstrous, and that which just can't be said. In practice the two senses, although distinguishable from each other, can't, I think, entirely stay out of each other's way. And it is possible to arrive at the unspeakable by way of the unspoken. What isn't spoken becomes, almost imperceptibly, what can't be spoken. In Ishiguro's (or anyone else's) Japan, these notions drop us directly into cultural stereotype: here are those subtle and silent, endlessly inscrutable Orientals so dear to the Western imagination. They are not altogether inscrutable, I want to suggest, even to us; although their subtleties and silences may be more varied than we think. The way out of stereotype, if there is one, may lead through stereotype. And of course, there are other, western countries of the unspeakable—the Germany that is the setting of *The Unconsoled*, for example.

"I was thinking about someone I knew once. A woman I knew once." These simple sentences from *A Pale View of Hills* are full of silence. Someone, a woman. We assume this someone is some *one*; a particular woman. This assumption seems right, because we are soon told about a woman called Sachiko, a friend of the narrator's, Etsuko's. But then the sheer bareness of the language is a kind of richness, since we also hear about other women, and Etsuko is manifestly thinking of them too: a woman, possibly imaginary, who haunts a little girl; a woman seen killing her child, of whom more in a moment; an unnamed and unapprehended child murderer, who hangs a little girl from a tree and might or might not be a woman; and Etsuko herself, that person of long ago, a woman she knew once.

The words come from the second page of the novel. They are followed by words that give us a relative time, and the name of a place. "I knew her when I was living in Nagasaki. . . . A long time ago." A little later we get the implication of a date. "The worst days were over by then. American soldiers were as numerous as ever—for there was fighting in Korea." We are in the early 1950s.

Nagasaki. Now it's the historical loading of the word that provides the richness, fills the silence, although the brevity, almost the deadness of the mention makes the signal very soft. The novel's cover tells us that Ishiguro was born there, in 1954; also that he moved to England in 1960. The *Britannica* tells us that you get a fine view of Nagasaki harbor from a mansion said to be the location of *Madame Butterfly*. None of this is irrelevant to the mood and idiom of this wonderful book; but it doesn't get us to the unspeakable. Nagasaki, if you weren't born there and are not thinking of Puccini, means only one thing, which is unspeakable in all kinds of crucial aspects: it is the place where the second atomic bomb was dropped, on August 9, 1945, inaugurating, along with the bomb dropped on Hiroshima three days earlier, entirely new possibilities of human harm. In the course of the novel Nagasaki comes to mean something very similar to what Hiroshima means in Marguerite Duras's and Alain Resnais's film *Hiroshima mon amour* (1959): not the dropping of the atomic bomb or the experience of its fall, not the politics or the morality or the shock of that, but the landscape of feeling created by the bomb, or more subtly, named by the bomb. A place where everyone has seen horrors, and no loss, large or small, can be properly mourned.

At the center of the novel, in an extraordinarily delicate set of narrative layers or abysses, we get this: a woman, who is a mother, tells a young woman, who is pregnant, about a little girl seeing another young woman drowning a baby in a canal.

> Mariko [the little girl] ran down an alleyway, and I followed after her. There was a canal at the end and the woman was kneeling there, up to her elbows in water. A young woman, very thin. I knew something was wrong as soon as I saw her. . . . I knew something was wrong and Mariko must have done too because she stopped running. At first I thought the woman was blind, she had that kind of look, her eyes didn't seem to actually see anything. Well, she brought her arms out of the

canal and showed us what she'd been holding under the water. It was a baby. I took hold of Mariko then and we came out of the alley.

We infer the baby's death from the past tense and from the fact that we don't hear any more about the case, except that a few days later the young woman kills herself. We also infer, for obvious reasons, that the young woman is the mother of the child, although this isn't actually said either. There are several kinds of silence here. Part of the peculiar horror, a feature of the writing rather than of the narrated instance, is that the young woman's killing of the baby seems strangely natural, almost ordinary, as deaths often do in novels, for reasons recently discussed by Margaret Anne Doody in *The True Story of the Novel*. We want to know how we, or anyone, could feel this, and what the consequences of such a feeling are. The fact that his scene takes place in Tokyo toward the end of the war—"I know it was a terrible thing that happened here in Nagasaki," the woman telling the story says. "But it was bad in Tokyo too"—makes it all the more interesting. Ishiguro has removed all causal connection to the Nagasaki bomb—he could have set the scene in Nagasaki if he had wanted to—but augmented the symbolic connection, everything not said by those banal, almost empty words *terrible* and *bad.*"

When Etsuko's daughter commits suicide in Manchester, the English newspapers insist on her being Japanese, and only on that:

> The English [Etsuko says] are fond of their idea that our race has an instinct for suicide, as if further explanations are unnecessary; for that was all they reported, that she was Japanese and that she had hung herself in her room.

We are deep in what Barthes calls the discourse of others here, the mire of stereotypes; and the noise of the unspoken is very loud. The English have their idea, they think the Japanese are a race, that they have a particular instinct. Is Etsuko saying all this is untrue? What is the Japanese view of the undeniable place of suicide in their culture? What Etsuko is saying, or rather what the silence around her words is saying, I think, is that the Japanese have no racial instinct for suicide, or she herself would be dead. The Japanese have a culture that can be changed, that has been changed. There are those who leave Japan, there are those who survive, and she is one. But then what about her daughter? How could her death not be connected to the culture of suicide, how could the English not be right on some wavelength, even if their crass formulations are all wrong. One can die of the discourse of others, Barthes says, and perhaps this young Japanese woman has.

The narrative question, then, since we hear of this suicide right at the beginning of the novel, is what does this death in Manchester in or around 1980 have to do with those days in Nagasaki in the 1950s? The answer is a relay of further questions and images, including the woman drowning the baby; and the child murderer on the loose; and also a dream of a child on a swing that turns out to be a dream of a hanged child; and a curiously unmotivated, dangling, piece of rope. We see the following scene twice. Are there two scenes, closely resembling each other? Or just one, obsessively repeated? Etsuko, the narrator, still young, and pregnant, looks for Sachiko's daughter, who has gone running off along a river bank. A rope gets caught around Etsuko's ankle, she takes it off, keeps it in her hand. The little girl, when found, is frightened, asks about the rope, why Etsuko is holding it. Etsuko doesn't answer this question, only says how the rope came to be in her hands:

> "Why have you got that?"
> "I told you, it's nothing. It just caught on to my foot." I took a step closer.
> "Why are you doing that, Mariko?"
> "Doing what?"
> "You were making a strange face just now."
> "I wasn't making a strange face. Why have you got the rope?"
> "You were making a strange face. It was a very strange face.
> "Why have you got the rope?"

Much later, the same scene is revised. The girl is still Mariko but she seems to have merged with Etsuko's own daughter, as Etsuko the mother merges with Mariko's mother, the "woman I knew once":

> The little girl was watching me closely. "Why are you holding that?" she asked.
> "This? It just caught around my sandal, that's all."
> "Why are you holding it?"
> "I told you. It caught around my foot. What's wrong with you?" I gave a short laugh. "Why are you looking at me like that? I'm not going to hurt you."

Is Etsuko the child murderer? Probably not, although the thought must cross our minds, because she has stepped visually into the murderer's posture; looks like a murderer, whether she is one or not. The novel is not very interested in settling this sort of question at the level of the literal. All Etsuko has done is leave Japan and her Japanese husband for an Englishman and England, taking her Japanese daughter with her, although she knows the girl will not be happy. "I knew all along," she says. "I knew all along she wouldn't be happy over here. But I decided to bring her just the same." Etsuko's friend Sachiko has similarly left Japan with an American, taking her Japanese daughter with her. Sachiko is even more emphatic. "Do you think I imagine for one moment that I'm a good mother to her?" Is Etsuko actually Sachiko? Is there one person here or two? Again, this is perhaps not quite the question. The question, I think, is how could Etsuko, in her memory and her distress, *not* be Sachiko, and the infanticide and the child murderer? Thinking of her hanged daughter, how could she *not* enter the blasted landscape where not being a good mother and killing your child are the same unspeakable thing, where it takes only one dead woman, not the 39,000 men and women massacred outright by the Nagasaki bomb, to turn the universe into an allegory. Etsuko's sanity, and the pathos of her story, rests on her denying that she has entered any such landscape. She is even sarcastic about the very idea that she is responsible for her daughter's death, and of course she is both right and wrong about this, as I suppose survivors always are in cases of suicide.

Etsuko's silence, the long denial that amounts, in all its terrible implications, to an avowal, corresponds of course to an English idea about Japanese delicacy and stoicism. My idea. But then I take it from Ishiguro as well as from my store of stereotypes. And his Japan, the place he left when he was six, must in large part be memory and legend, a sort of English idea itself. Things get really interesting if this English idea turns out to be a Japanese idea too, a piece of orientalism not confirmed by the Orient but occupying much the same semantic space as the Western cliché. The two ideas would still be different even if they sounded just the same, and neither would make the other less fictional or less mythological. But we would no longer be talking about simple imperial projection, the bare blunt fantasy of otherness. Rather, about the possibility of national fictions informing us rather than imprisoning us. We can't speak for others, and we can't be them; we can't even hear them as long as we're talking all the time. But there are silences where we may meet; it is possible to imagine others if we listen hard enough to their silence, and it is possible for them to recognize themselves in our imagining. Stereotypes can kill, but they can also, as I suggested about the clichés in *Love in the Time of Cholera*, provide an idiom for understandings they cannot name. The stereotype of silence, in Ishiguro's delicately orientalized Orient, hints at the kinder life that inhabits, under dispensations we still need to find, the silence of stereotypes.

We're cutting back History. . . . History will merge with General
Studies.   —Graham Swift, *Waterland*

12. *The Nightmare of Narrative*

I Thought You Were a Lesbian

We are still in a novel and we don't entirely leave words behind. But we almost
lose them in the ladderlike lines of a long fragment from a musical score. The
writing is for three voices and full orchestra, plenty of work for the horns and the
cellos. The language of the text is German, and given that the names of the
singing characters are the Marschallin, Octavian, and Sophie, even the operati-
cally challenged like myself don't have too much trouble in recognizing Strauss's
and Hoffmansthal's *Rosenkavalier*. If we did have trouble we could look at the
copyright acknowledgments at the front of the book and find the opera's title
there. The work that fades away into music in this manner—or more precisely,
fades away into the silence of written sound—is *Art and Lies* (1994), the fifth full-
length work of fiction by the English writer Jeanette Winterson.

   The book is subtitled "A piece for three voices and a bawd." The bawd is
Doll Sneerpiece, a character in an entertaining pastiche of a louche eighteenth-
century novel; the three voices are those of Handel, a Catholic (male) doctor,
Picasso, a young (woman) painter, and Sappho, variously the Greek poet and a
woman who likes to walk at night in twentieth-century London. The three of
them are on a train, looking for the lives they have mislaid or wasted or so far
failed to find. We piece their story together through their memories and, more
often, their remarks on the vacuous and self-satisfied world of their contemporaries. They arrive at the sea, which may be death and is almost certainly a new
beginning, and the book itself ends, or seems to end, with the words "It was not
too late." This ending is then signed with the word FIN, but the text continues,

without commentary and without further conclusions, with nine pages from *Der Rosenkavalier*.

We can read this aftertext in all kinds of ways. We can read the score as music (if we can read music), hear the sounds in our heads. We can put on a record and hear the music in our room. If we do either of these (especially the second), we shall hear Strauss's swooping melodic lines, three female voices woven into the most intricate of criss-crossing textures, and a wonderfully dense orchestration for a very large orchestra (four horns, three trumpets, three trombones, ten cellos, eight double basses, and so on, as well as sixteen first and sixteen second violins and twelve violas). We can read the score as a *sign* of music, a metaphor for the condition all art aspires to, according to Walter Pater, twice quoted in this text. It will then be like the foreign languages at the end of Eliot's *Waste Land*, which can be interpreted for what they say but also, more dramatically and perhaps more illuminatingly, as images of multiple foreignness, the Babel of tongues into which the helpless and unblessed modern world has fallen. Or we can remember that the score does have words too, that it comes from a famous and much-loved opera, with a story line and an infinitely fraught emotional context.

The fragment we have is the Trio from the close of the work. The Marschallin, a woman of thirty-two, is letting go her lover, Octavian, a boy of seventeen, because she knows she has to, because she has always known she would have to when he meets, as he now has, a girl his own age. "I promised myself I would love even his love for another," the Marschallin says, "but I didn't think I would have to do it so soon." Octavian feels things are going horribly wrong and wonderfully right, and the girl, Sophie, feels the Marschallin is simultaneously giving Octavian to her and taking him away, as indeed she is. Hoffmansthal, in a letter to Strauss, said that the whole point of the scene is that Octavian "falls for the *very first* little girl to turn up," which beautifully underlines the sense that time itself is the enemy rather than human inconstancy; age is both a form of behavior and a form of fate. In the book Winterson echoes this scene in the story of a castrato and his young lover, and the unorthodox sexual alignment glances at the casting (and scoring) of *Der Rosenkavalier*, where all three parts in the Trio are sung by women, and where Octavian, a young man sung and acted by a woman, twice dresses up as a pretty young maid. Winterson also makes her own the words the Marschallin sings immediately after those I have just quoted: "The majority of things in the world are such, that one would not believe them if one were told about them. Only those who experience it believe and do not know how." The Marschallin means it is possible to be desperately, painfully surprised by the very thing you have been expecting, but Winterson is giving the sentence a wider implication. The world itself is fantastic, she is saying, a universe of unbelievable stories—stories that are unbelievable until one of them happens to you. The whole tumbling context of time, sexuality, departing and arriving love is caught in the Marschallin's last words, which are also the last words of Winterson's book, apart from a brief stage direction: "In Gottes Namen," literally "In God's name," usually translated as "So be it" or "God be with you," but also readable as "For God's sake."

There is plenty of story here, but we seem to have come a long way from what used to be the novel. Winterson herself is very emphatic about this, and bluntly says, in her book of essays *Art (Objects)* (1995), "I do not write novels. The novel form is finished." It's not clear whether she doesn't write novels because the form is finished, or the form is finished because she, and by implication other contemporary writers who know what's what, don't write novels, but perhaps the causality is not the most interesting question. Certainly the remark sounds familiar, even ancient, and we don't have to go any further back than chapter 1 of this book to find T. S. Eliot telling us that if *Ulysses* "is not a novel, that is simply because the novel is a form which will no longer serve."

The connection of Winterson to Eliot is not accidental or antiquarian:

> I was in a bookshop recently and a young man came up to me and said
> "Is Sexing the Cherry a reading of Four Quartets?"
> "Yes," I said, and he kissed me.

The point of this little scene is Winterson's refutation of the idea that lesbian writers have to be interested (only or primarily) in other lesbian writers:

> I was in a bookshop recently when a young woman approached me.
> She told me she was writing an essay on my work and that of Radclyffe Hall. Could I help?
> "Yes," I said. "Our work has nothing in common."
> "I thought you were a lesbian," she said.

We note the kiss and the shift of sex in the meeting, but Eliot is not simply a sign for an established male writer, an indication of freedom from sexual correctness. The "yes" and the kiss are metaphors for the recognition of a good reading, sympathetic detection of the appropriate ghost. "There is at present," Winterson says directly, "no twentieth-century poem that means more to me than *Four Quartets*. I know it by heart . . . and it remains a vital influence on my life and on my work." The poem echoes through her works, its mournful, haunting phrases often subtly modified by their new contexts. "Ridiculous this waste sad time," the narrator thinks in *Written on the Body* (1992). There is an "unimaginable zero temperature" in *The Passion* (1987), an "unimaginable zero winter." "That which is only living can only die" is repeated three times in *Art and Lies*. Versions of the opening lines of "Burnt Norton" return again and again, in *The Passion* and in *Sexing the Cherry* (1989): "Without past and future, the present is partial. All time is eternally present and so all time is ours"; "If all time is eternally present, there is no reason why we should not step out of one present into another"; "The future is intact, still unredeemed, but the past is irredeemable." And occasionally another, earlier Eliot poem comes up—"Then human voices wake us and we drown"—or a line from *Four Quartets* is more substantially modified, so that Eliot's "Only through time time is conquered" becomes Winterson's "Through the body, the body is conquered." The voice is still there, but the thought could hardly be further from Eliot's anxiously ascetic world.

In her essays if not in her fiction, Winterson turns out to be more modernist than the modernists, dedicated to the mandarin exaltation of art and the free-flowing scorn for popular culture and the masses that Eliot and Woolf are regularly (and wrongly, in my view) accused of espousing. "Did the Modernists too far strain the relationship between reader and writer?" Winterson asks. "I think not." "To assume that Modernism has no real relevance to the way that we need to be developing fiction now, is to condemn writers and readers to a dingy Victorian twilight."

Winterson is certain that art must not speak "the language of shop assistants and tabloids," wishes to resist the "notional life" promoted by "governments, mass education and the mass media," and says, "Art always dresses for dinner. Does this seem stuffy in the jeans and T-shirt days of popular culture? Perhaps, but without a formal space art cannot do its work." Art certainly needs form, but the persistent snobbery in these analogies unravels a lot of Winterson's meaning. Art always dresses, perhaps; but it doesn't always dress conventionally or dress for dinner. "I know of no pain that art cannot assuage," Winterson writes. This is intended as a tribute to art, but it sounds like an ignorance of pain. Perhaps it's the difference between knowing and knowing of. A little chauvinism is stirred into the mixture for good measure. Foreigners "hate" the fact that English is "thick with the possibility of puns." Conrad is "the disciplined pedant, the Salieri of letters"; "a Pole who prided himself on his impeccable and proper English usage. He never understood that the glory of English is in its entirely improper gallops."

Winterson is prepared to countenance foreignness as a figure of speech, but the contradiction is not as large as it seems:

> Art, all art, not just painting, is a foreign city, and we deceive ourselves when we think it familiar. No-one is surprised to find that a foreign city follows its own customs and speaks its own language. . . . We have to recognise that the language of art, all art, is not our mother-tongue.

She is speaking as a reader and viewer here and endorsing the sentimental fable that surrounds all Mozarts with pathetic, unimprovable Salieris, mere readers who imagine themselves to be writers. The artist is the native speaker, the mistress of puns; the reader/viewer is the baffled but delighted foreigner—even when that person is on other days herself an artist. This is the split mythology of reading and writing that I look at in my last chapter; its interest here is that it so clearly aligns Winterson with yesterday's literary assumptions, the world of Auden and Eliot, not the world of Cortázar and Calvino.

But the full force of this attachment to the high places of modernism, in relation to Winterson's fiction, lies in an implied argument about time and narrative. We have seen a version of this argument in what I called García Márquez's postmodernist romance, where time is scrupulously counted rather than grandly refused or combatted. The consequence is a reinvestment in narrative, a return to a forgotten richness of story. Winterson wants to do something quite different, and in (rather erratically) managing to do it, she offers us a very different notion of what postmodernism may be. Her idea, as all the quotations from Eliot suggest, is to retain the high modernist hostility to time and plot and to get story to function pretty much as if it wasn't a story at all. Yet story, as she says again and again, and as the beautiful refrain of *The Passion* keeps telling us, is what she has to work with. "I'm telling you stories. Trust me."

> I am a writer who does not use plot as an engine or a foundation. What I do use are stories within stories within stories within stories. I am not particularly interested in folk tales or fairy tales, but I do have them about my person, and like Autolycus (*The Winter's Tale*), I find that they are assumed to be worth more than they are.

This is a little brutal and sells the stories short. Winterson doesn't just use them, as if she might have decided to use something else. But she is pointing to an important contemporary practice in fiction. To put this, for clarity, in its crudest but still fairly dizzying form, we have in Winterson a writer who retains story in order to reject narrative.

Is this possible? What would story mean in such a project? As a child, working at a public library in a northern provincial town, Winterson realized, she tells us,

> what I had known dimly; that plot was meaningless to me. This was a difficult admission for one whose body was tattooed with Bible stories, but I had to accept that my love affair was with language, and only incidentally with narrative.

The story of the tattooing with stories is told in Winterson's first book, *Oranges Are Not the Only Fruit* (1985), whose chapters are named after books of the Old Testament, and that recounts, in lively and bitter detail, a young girl's discovery of the forbidden pleasures of the love of women and her escape from a ferociously religious Lancashire upbringing into a London writing career. The girl is called Jeanette. "Is Oranges an autobiographical novel?" Winterson asks on our behalf in a preface written for a reprint of the book and answers, "No not at all and yes of course." The most significant insight in the book, perhaps, the one that frees Jeanette both from her actual mother and the mother she has internalized as an evangelical superego, is formulated in a phrase that Winterson herself cites again in *Art (Objects)*, calling it a form of wisdom: "not all dark places need light." "I have to remember that," Winterson's narrator adds. She does remember, and so does Winterson in what is probably her best book, *The Passion*, and intermittently in *Sexing the Cherry*. After that a sort of missionary impulse returns, an urge to bring light to dark corners, and all of the later fiction, to say nothing of the essays, is damaged to some degree by sermonizing, a regular badgering of the reader.

The worst offender in this respect is *Written on the Body*, a work in which an ambiguously gendered narrator, a person who may be a man or a woman but who has slept with both men and women, a sexual predator now turned faithful lover of a married female beauty, discovers that her/his loved one has an incurable form of cancer. The narrator abandons the loved woman, ostensibly for her own good, so that she can pursue her treatment in peace, but in fact because she/he is terrified of the disease and deeply in love with an intensely self-regarding notion of how noble he/she is finally being. The trouble is that the narrator arrives at an understanding of this self-deception some fifty pages or more after the slowest reader will have got there. She/he has to go to church to be jolted into thinking of "Louise in her own right, not as my lover, not as my grief," and even then lectures us about what went wrong:

> I had failed Louise and it was too late.

What right had I to decide how she should live? What right had I to decide how she should die?

No right at all, but the whole plot of the book rests on the idea that this right could at some stage of shock and distress have seemed plausible, not merely evasive:

> No-one can legislate love; it cannot be given orders or cajoled into service. Love belongs to itself, deaf to pleading and unmoved by violence. Love is not something you can negotiate.

This would be pretty flat and sappy even if it were true, as every instance in Winterson's books, this one and all the others, shows it is not. "Destiny is a worrying concept," the narrator says, and "Why are human beings so contradictory?" Not all commonplaces need to make it to the page, especially if the writer has no interest in the life of the commonplace. "It's the clichés that cause the trouble," the narrator of *Written on the Body* says several times. There is no trace of the hunch that we find in García Márquez, Carter, and Ishiguro, that clichés could get us out of trouble too.

However, even this weakness in Winterson's later fiction reinforces the initial point about story and narrative. In her most recent work, *Gut Symmetries* (1997), she twice speaks of "the nightmare of narrative" but also insists on the need to tell stories, even when the task is impossible: "Need to tell a story when no story can be told"; "And every story I begin to tell talks across a story I cannot tell." The central situation in this book is a love triangle with an added complication: the young mistress loves (differently) both the husband and the wife. Each is given a history and a cultural identity (Liverpool English, Italian American, American Jewish), and all three survive various disasters. The whole thing is loosely anchored to the tarot pack and argues vigorously against closed categories, the falsity of separation:

> The separateness of our lives is a sham. Physics, mathematics, music, painting, my politics, my love for you, my work, the star-dust of my body, the spirit that impels it, clocks diurnal, time perpetual, the roll, rough, tender, swamping, liberating, breathing, moving, thinking nature, human nature and the cosmos are patterned together.

There is some lively writing here, and there are some good jokes, and some excellent pages on the pain of betrayal—the sort of pain that art is not likely to assuage. "I understand that pain leapfrogs over language and lands in dumb growls beyond time." But there is also plenty of sermonizing, and there are some fairly grotesque attempts at making feeling real to us through metaphor. "Stella turned towards me and crumpled my heart in her hand"; "I would have been glad to climb into the plate and cover myself with clam sauce."

These stylistic gestures, and the lectures Winterson gives us in her fiction are a sign that she is "only incidentally" interested in narrative and that plot is meaningless to her. It is because the plot is meaningless that she has to tell us what it means. But then if she wrote only sermons we would have to pay attention to her, if at all, only as a sermonizer. Fortunately, she does more than this.

Winterson's stories are usually parables and/or pictures and scarcely ever come together in the larger scope of a plot. But they are not simply narrative images, and they are not simply dramatized propositions. If García Márquez and Morrison and others pick up the sense of sequence in narrative, the entanglement of people in irrefutable but variegated time, Winterson uses something like a ruse of narrative to ask questions about the way time is imagined, and the consequences of these strategies for our ideas of the possible. In this as in several other respects, and in spite of her old-fashioned theories about reading, she comes very close to Calvino, whose invisible cities both court and evade narrative. "I try to drive together lyric intensity and breadth of ideas," Winterson says. The notion of driving suggests the difficulty of the task but barely hints at the fact that stories are the places where the meeting occurs.

It seems incoherent for Winterson, in *Art (Objects)*, both to celebrate and diminish the concept of story, and certainly her argument is not tidily made. But I think she can reasonably say that "We mostly understand ourselves through an endless series of stories told to ourselves by ourselves and others" and also that "If prose-fiction is to survive it will have to do more than to tell a story." The echo of E. M. Forster ("Oh dear, yes, the novel tells a story") helps us to see where we are. Story in one sense enslaves us to time; in another it allows us to replay time and even take it back, invites us to rearrange and reinterpret what we have done and what happens to us. We understand ourselves through these arrangements, Winterson is saying, but her quiet use of *story* for the process suggests something precarious about this understanding. For her a story always contains the idea of being "taken in by someone"—tricked, that is, not given shelter. The refrain of *The Passion*—"I'm telling you stories. Trust me"—keeps shifting its context; sometimes it means that you can trust me because I'm not lying about the fact that I'm lying to you, and at other times that you would have to be mad to believe such far-fetched stuff. In *Gut Symmetries* we meet this elegant bit of dialogue:

SHE: What you see is not what you think you see.
ME: Sound science.
SHE: Doesn't that depend on the scientist?
ME: I wouldn't depend on the scientist.

What we understand about ourselves may be sheer fairy tale, and we need to correct this tale from time to time—if we don't, life or our friends will do it for us. But it's hard to see what form this (constant) correction could take except that of further stories, still susceptible to what now look like at least three or four different meanings of this easy and familiar word, as when we say "story line," meaning plot, or "news story," meaning report, or "At least that's my story," meaning my version, or "Have you been telling stories again?" meaning have you been telling lies. We need stories in all these senses, although we shall of course lean on some senses more than others at particular moments. Winterson writes:

> When we let ourselves respond to poetry, to music, to pictures, we are clearing a space where new stories can root, in effect we are clearing a space for new stories about ourselves.

Interesting that novels do not figure among the instances.

The Ghost of a Leopard

One of Winterson's favorite and most successful forms of story is the aphorism, that mode which always means more than it says and always hints at absent narratives. "He uses winter like a larder," we are told of Napoleon in *The Passion*. "The Bonapartes were ordering everything from cream to David"; "we got most of our meat from nameless regions and I suspect from animals Adam would not recognise." The narrator here is a Frenchman, Henri, onetime fan and servant of Napoleon, now locked away on a prison island near Venice for having committed a crime of passion—more precisely and more intricately, for having killed the obese and obscene husband of the Venetian Villanelle, the woman he loves but who in turn loves another woman. One wouldn't have thought either Venice or the Napoleonic Wars could have been evoked with such freshness at this stage of the century, but the speed and wit of Winterson's recreations of these familiar scenes are amazing. The moral of the book, subdued but visible enough, is that passion will save us from a lukewarm living death—the moral of all of Winterson's books, in short. But here she concentrates on the passion rather than on her easy scorn for the tepidities of the world, and the effect is to make passion itself come alive, even when it swings loose from narrative, and even when it is denied. Young soldiers, for instance, don't know how to "gather up their passion for life and make sense of it in the face of death . . . but they do know how to forget, and little by little they put aside the burning summer in their bodies and all they have instead is lust and rage." "Somewhere between fear and sex passion is," Winterson tells us repeatedly, and then returns to the soldiers' dilemma in another, older context, that of the survivors of Napoleon's march on Moscow:

> You can't make sense of your passion for life in the face of death, you can only give up your passion. Only then can you begin to survive.
> And if you refuse?

Passion is "desperate," whether it concerns a man or a woman or an emperor. It is a form of "obsession," and Winterson regularly compares it to gambling, which is one of Villanelle's chief pastimes in Venice and in life. "You play, you win, you play, you lose. You play." "We gamble with the hope of winning, but it's the thought of what we might lose that excites us." "It's the gambler's sense of losing that makes the winning an act of love." Except that the characters in Winterson's fiction always lose—or win, if at all, only through their losses. They see what they might have won, if they hadn't played safe. Unrequited love is the norm; death destroys sense. What "passion" means then is not only a reckless commitment, at least in theory, to the violence of obsession but a sort of principled rejection of psychic prudence, even as one gives in to it in practice. Winterson invents a fable. This is Villanelle thinking about her feelings for the elusive, married Venetian woman she loves. One could

> refuse the passion as one might sensibly refuse a leopard in the house, however tame it might seem at first. You might reason that you can easily feed a leopard and that your garden is big enough, but you will know in your dreams at least that no leopard is ever satisfied with what it's given. After nine nights must come ten and every desperate meeting only leaves you desperate for another. There is never enough to eat, never enough garden for your love.
> So you refuse and then you discover that your house is haunted by the ghost of a leopard.

The attraction of this fable and of the aphorisms about winter or Napoleon or Adam is that they provide a working model for a form of fiction that is neither the old novel nor the newly garrulous story, but a sort of vivid Brechtian abstract of an interesting situation: the appetite that would allow you to use winter like a larder; the subjects of the paintings the Bonapartes ordered like cream; the weird emergence of new animals subsequent to the creation. The situation is without flesh in all of these cases, and pretty much without suspense, but not without passion or consequence. We fill the story in, not because stories are all we have but because this is one of the things stories happily invite us to do. There are story-worlds, and there are novel-worlds, and there are also worlds still to be imagined, waiting at the edges of all those stories that are spare enough and swift enough to leave the details of the world-making to us. Villanelle thinks of her "other life, the parallel life," the one she might have lived with her beloved woman instead of with her fat and soon-to-be-dead husband. But she doesn't evoke this life for us in any sensuous or concrete way. She presents the pure romance of thought, the way Beckett writes the comedy of the intellect, and Barthes longs for the novel the intellect deserves. Scarcely a narrative at all, but certainly an extensive story, enough for several lifetimes:

> Is this the explanation then when we meet someone we do not know and feel straight away that we have always known them? That their habits will not be a surprise. Perhaps our lives spread out around us like a fan and we can only know one life but by mistake sense others.

The possibility is real, even familiar, but the excitement here lies all in the sense of it as possibility not as accomplished reality. "Every journey conceals another journey within its lines," we read on the second page of *Sexing the Cherry*, and much later in the same book: "Everyone remembers things which never happened. And it is common knowledge that people often forget things which did. . . . I have heard people say we are shaped by our childhood. But which one?"

"It is required you do awake your faith," is a phrase Winterson fondly repeats in her work. It is spoken in Shakespeare's *Winter's Tale* shortly before the occurrence of a miracle that is also a trick, a trick that is also a miracle, the return to life of a woman thought to be dead, and the awakening into life of a woman thought to be a statue. We might associate the phrase with the Marschallin's remark about the difficulty of believing in the things of the world and not knowing *how* one believes, even when one has experienced them. Faith is the opposite of proof, as believers and skeptics have always known. But it may be that the fullest encounter with reality, any reality, requires faith *and* proof, an ability to go on believing in the experience you have just had. And by extension, of course, to believe in experiences you haven't had, the authority of fiction. "I'm telling you stories. Trust me."

In *Gut Symmetries* Winterson repeats an image from *Sexing the Cherry*, a house that seems to have floated up out of one of Calvino's invisible cities. This is the earlier version:

> The family who lived in the house were dedicated to a strange custom. Not one of them would allow their feet to touch the floor. Open the doors off the hall and you will see, not floors, but bottomless pits. The furniture of the house is suspended on racks from the ceiling; the dining table supported by great chains, each link six inches thick. To dine here is a great curiosity, for the visitor must sit in a gilded chair and allow himself to be winched up to join his place setting. He comes last, the householders already seated and making merry, swinging their feet over the abyss where crocodiles live. Everyone who dines has a multiplicity of glasses and cutlery lest some should be dropped accidentally. Whatever food is left over at the end of the meal is scraped into the pit, from whence a fearful crunching can be heard.
>
> When everyone has eaten their fill, the gentlemen remain at table and the ladies walk in order of precedence across a tightrope to another room, where they may have biscuits and wine with water.

There is the feeling of a children's story about this image: high formality, danger, and a version of the aerial fantasy, the dream of life in a tree or in the air. But there is also, in this description that is only minimally narrative, an almost irresistible invitation to story-making, to an imagination of continuing life in this house, of how it got to be that way, what will happen to it. Not all houses are like this, although any house could be. As Roland Barthes says in *Camera Lucida* of the photograph of a rather nondescript street corner in rural Spain, "it is quite simply *there* that I should like to live." "For me," he adds, "photographs of landscape . . . must be *habitable*, not visitable. . . . Looking at these landscapes of predilection, it is as if *I were certain* of having been there or of going there." This is not how Calvino's cities affect us—we are drawn to the design of those cities, the secrets of their economy and architecture—but it is a large part of the appeal of Winterson's imagined places. Even when Winterson depicts, in *Sexing the Cherry*, a city that could hardly be closer to Calvino's vision, she finally espouses the fantasy of the residents rather than the traveler. This is a place

> whose inhabitants are so cunning that to escape the insistence of creditors they knock down their houses in a single night and rebuild them elsewhere. So the number of buildings in the city is always constant but they are never in the same place from one day to the next.

This custom "accounts for the longevity of the men and women who live there," but above all it enacts the fantasy of a home that is also elsewhere, as Barthes would say his street in Spain was, and as the mother's body must always be in psychoanalysis. "In the city the inhabitants have reconciled two discordant desires: to remain in one place and to leave it behind for ever."

Sexing the Cherry recounts the adventures, mainly set in the seventeenth century, of the foundling Jordan who becomes a great traveler, and the immense Dog-Woman, who rescued Jordan from the river (hence his name) and brought him up. The historical John Tradescant, collector and gardener, plays a significant role in Jordan's education, and provides the book with its title, since he specializes in grafting cherries, and teaches Jordan that even a cherry not born from seed can be sexed ("the cherry grew, and we have sexed it and it is female"). We may think of a passage that appears late in *Art and Lies* on the subject of the castrato:

"He was a man?"
"Yes, sweet boy."
"And he was a woman?"
"Yes."
"God has not made such things."
"God has made everything."

The point is not to cheat nature but to escape imprisoning mythologies, of nature or of anything else. "Language always betrays us," Winterson writes in *Sexing the Cherry*, "tells the truth when we want to lie, and dissolves into formlessness when we would most like to be precise." Both halves of this betrayal are important, and both return us to the notion of story. The story enacts the truth *and* our desire to lie, can scarcely do otherwise; it offers us a form of precision in spite of itself. "We cannot move back and forth in time," Winterson writes, "but we can experience it in a different way." The different way in this book involves twentieth-century incarnations of Jordan and the Dog-Woman, ghostly returns of old longings and appetites in new bodies. These visions are not entirely persuasive, but the idea of intertwined times is. We are back in Eliot's *Four Quartets* and may want to remember the poem's rejected epigraph from *The Pickwick Papers*: "What a rum thing time is, ain't it, Neddy?" Time passes, as we read (twice) in *One Hundred Years of Solitude*. So it does, *pero no tanto*, not as much as that. The nightmare of narrative offers moments of reprieve.

Those Eyes, That Smile

There is a splendid moment in Nabokov's *Pnin* (1957) when we learn that our bumbling hero is planning to teach a course on tyranny. "The history of man is the history of pain," Pnin says enthusiastically. His amiable boss taps him on the knee and says "You are a wonderful romantic, Timofey." Rather to my surprise I find I associate the casual darkness of this comedy, its light darkness so to speak, with the considerably more elaborate and visibly pain-filled history that Walter Benjamin's angel stares back on:

> His eyes are staring, his mouth is open, his wings are spread. This is how one pictures the angel of history. His face is turned toward the past. Where we perceive a chain of events, he sees one single catastrophe which keeps piling wreckage upon wreckage and hurls it in front of his feet. The angel would like to stay, to awaken the dead, and make whole what has been smashed. But a storm is blowing from Paradise; it has got caught in his wings with such violence that the angel can no longer close them. This storm irresistibly propels him into the future to which his back is turned, while the pile of debris before him grows skyward. This storm is what we call progress.

Pnin as the angel of history? Not quite. Pnin as the person who has taught himself not to see what the angel has to look at:

> In order to exist rationally, Pnin had taught himself, during the last ten years, never to remember Mira Belochkin—not because, in itself, the evocation of a

youthful love affair, banal and brief, threatened his peace of mind . . . but because, if one were quite sincere with oneself, no conscience, and hence no consciousness, could be expected to subsist in a world where such things as Mira's death were possible. One had to forget—because one could not live with the thought that this graceful, fragile, tender young woman with those eyes, that smile, those gardens and snows in the background, had been brought in a cattle car to an extermination camp and killed by an injection of phenol into the heart.

The point is not only that Nabokov and Benjamin, an unlikely pairing on any account, really do seem quite close here, attending to the same terrible historical and human debris, but that if this pairing makes any sense, then we must go beyond the names, the mere shorthand, and think about the assumptions, gestures, positions, loyalties that lurk behind the names, everything that the names allude to or focus for us. If the self-declared aesthete shares the world of the self-declared Marxist, if their (very real) differences are in this respect ones of strategy, not of perception or diagnosis, then there are all kinds of questions about aesthetics and history, aesthetics and politics that we shall have to revisit. Much of what looks like indifference or loftiness in Nabokov would be a form of discretion; and even his genuine indifference and his frequent political silliness would be readable as marks of damage. We might also mount a kind of *a fortiori* argument about literature and history, in which Nabokov would function as a kind of fulcrum or lever. If even the mandarin Nabokov can be shown to be so caught up in the darkness of his times, we shouldn't have too much trouble with the easier cases.

We can go further. It's not just that the talky Nabokov turns out to be an artist of silence, he actually takes on, in his own idiom, Adorno's anguished contentions about literature and culture's role in an irremediably damaged world—notably of course his assertion that "to write poetry after Auschwitz is barbaric." Pnin is saying that even remembering Buchenwald is barbaric. And Nabokov has found, against the odds, a form of writing that doesn't accept, but doesn't seek to evade, its own barbarism. And not only Nabokov. I am thinking also of scenes in Grass and García Márquez—of the onion cellar in *The Tin Drum*, where good Germans weep the tears they cannot otherwise find; of the massacre of people dressed as playing cards in *One Hundred Years of Solitude*— where the unspeakable comes across (initially) as affectless chatter. In the silence that is stolen from us by apparently bland reporting, the silence we keep imagining because of the busy but unsurprised noise of the horrors, a little piece of the history of pain gets told.

This talk of barbarism has a very particular history, though. "There is no document of civilization which is not at the same time a document of barbarism," Benjamin famously said—the very phrase that lurks behind Adorno's usage. *Es ist niemals ein Dokument der Kultur, ohne zugleich ein solches der Barbarei zu sein.* This is often taken to mean that culture is barbarism, once you've stripped it of its ideological pretensions, but that is not what the remark says. Indeed, it doesn't, on the face of it, say anything very exceptional. Macchu Pichu and the Egyptian pyramids required the nameless toil of thousands; great monuments are built at an exorbitant human cost. Benjamin is asking us to remember those thousands, that cost. More interestingly, we might take him as saying that we like to forget that cost, to think only of culture, because the cost was so high; and certainly he is saying that culture and barbarism belong together, that you can't have one without the other. This would mean not only that visible triumphs rest on invisible oppression but that culture and barbarism are different faces of a single moment, questions of perspective. Not identical, still opposed; but each entailing the other.

This is precisely what Adorno's remark about poems after Auschwitz says in context. "Cultural criticism finds itself faced with the final stage of the dialectic of culture and barbarism. To write poetry after Auschwitz is barbaric, and this corrodes even the knowledge (*frisst auch die Erkenntnis an*) of why it has become impossible to write poetry today." Here it is not only that a document of culture is also a document of barbarism; the very idea of culture, in certain contexts, becomes barbaric—because to argue for culture, or make culture's gestures, is to betray everything culture used to stand for, is as barbarous as any of culture's enemies have ever been. And even to say this is barbaric

In Nabokov's *Bend Sinister* (1947) a government official in a totalitarian state explains to a distraught father how his eight-year-old son has been taken to an Institute for Abnormal Children and tormented and abused there. The father doesn't yet know that his son is dead. What happens at the institute is that "the most interesting inmates" are given little orphans to work out on. "The theory . . . was that if once a week the really difficult patients could enjoy the possibility of venting in full their repressed yearnings (the exaggerated urge to hurt, to destroy, etc.) upon some little human creature of no value to the community, then, by degrees, the evil in them would be allowed to escape, would be, so to speak, 'effundated,' and eventually they would become good citizens." The unironic voice of the official comes to us in uninflected indirect speech. All the horror of the scene is left to us to animate, as we pick up the hints of nightmare in phrases such as "really difficult patients," "venting in full," "yearnings," "the exaggerated urge to hurt," "some little human creature of no value to the community." What is an unexaggerated urge to hurt? Who is speaking so blithely of this little human creature of no value? There is a tremendous outrage behind this writing but also a sense that outrage is helpless and inappropriate in the face of real enormity, the world where "such things as Mira's death" and such things as this sleazy sociological apology for torture are possible. It is barbaric to have created this world in the first place, historically; barbaric to recreate it in fiction; and more subtly barbaric to deplore it, as if it were only an error in taste, or as if our deploring it made any difference.

It takes a while to realize what Nabokov is doing in *Bend Sinister*. He is travestying Nazi and Stalinist terror through hyperbole—something one wouldn't have thought possible. And he is announcing, or at least exemplifying, the particular form of bleak, muted irony that allows writers as different as Toni Morrison and Kazuo Ishiguro to speak of historical horrors without softening them but also without claiming immunity from their contagion. He is making torture and thuggery sound even more pleased with themselves, even more recklessly dedicated to the enjoyment of the pain of others, than they probably were; and he has given them for their (implied) speech the vocabulary of modern social thought. Do the officials of this institution believe in all this cant about the social redemption of these murderous inmates? Well, which is worse? That they should or that they shouldn't? That they are brutal, educated fools, or that they are brutal, educated cynics? It is clear, though, that these people represent, in 1947, the year of *Bend Sinister*, not only an identifiable set of historical practices but also, to the extent that we can't get behind their language to the horror itself, our own helplessness and (all too often, I'm afraid) indifference to these practices and their ugly international relatives, early and late: the banality of not being surprised by the banality of evil.

Hidden in the Distance

The history of pain becomes the writing of silence—of many silences. This is one of the ways in which novels and stories may get history to think again. Everything depends on the tone and the timing with which a silence is broken and on the writer's fidelity to what words can't reach. But then what of the reader? Doesn't something happen to his or her comfort in the process?

Italo Calvino once wrote that he "spent more time with the books of others than with my own." He added, "I do not regret it." That must be an unusual remark for a writer to make, even a writer who worked in a publishing house. We may think of Mr. Cavedagna, in *If on a Winter's Night a Traveller*, who is described as "a little man, shrunken and bent," not because he is like that, or looks like that, or even because he seems to have emerged from a book where little men are always shrunken and bent. No: "He seems to have come from a world in which they still read books where you encounter 'little men, shrunken and bent.' "

It is Mr. Cavedagna who puts galley proofs on a table very gently, "as if the slightest jolt could upset the order of the printed letters." Much of Calvino's sense of literature lives in that small image; and not only of literature. "I still have the notion that to live in peace and freedom is a frail kind of good fortune that might be taken from me in an instant." An order may be a modest form of art, the model of the good society; or it may be thoroughly repressive. We don't always have the choice of orders, but we do have the choice of ways of thinking about them. "The ideal library," Calvino says,

> is one that gravitates towards the outside, toward the "apocryphal" books, in the etymological sense of the word: that is, "hidden" books. Literature is a search for the book hidden in the distance that alters the value and meaning of the known books; it is the pull toward the new apocryphal text still to be rediscovered or invented.

Rediscovered or invented. Read or written. Much of the fiction I have been considering conflates these two terms, as if reading regularly spilled over into writing, as if writers were always great readers and often great critics. It was not ever thus. Only yesterday writers were still boasting about how much they had lived and how little they had read. Of course contemporary writers don't simply invert these terms. They take tremendous pleasure in old and new fiction, but they don't oppose reading to life. They don't even challenge or seek to deconstruct the opposition, saying for instance that reading *is* life, or that life is a text that dare not speak its name. They just recognize the risks of reading; the very risks that writing has claimed for so long.

"It is now possible to say, quite seriously, that we need not histories of literature but histories of reading; a little while ago the observation would have seemed inane." The remark is Frank Kermode's and "now" was 1975. The symbolic center of the perceived shift was Barthes's 1968 essay "The Death of the Author," with its Frazerian last sentence: "the birth of the reader must be at the cost of (*doit se payer de*) the death of the Author." A year earlier Calvino had turned the author into a writing machine, at the same time handing over the life and creativity we associate with writing to the reader. "The author: that anachronistic personage, the bearer of messages, the director of consciences, the giver of lectures to cultural bodies . . . the author vanishes— that spoiled child of ignorance—to give place to a more thoughtful person, a person who will know that the author is a machine, and will know how this machine works."

Why would the observation about the history of reading have seemed inane "a little while ago"? What implied proposition about reading is being over-turned? The old proposition, I think, was that reading is (for some) difficult to learn, but once learned, unproblematic; like riding a bike. A rudimentary skill, of no theoretical interest. We all do it (those of us who can), it doesn't need talking about. The reader is therefore the uninteresting partner in the literary relation, the one who is always there, necessary, but not a locus of any serious promise of understanding. Reading is a passive, tame, quiet, sheltered activity. Auden, in a famous poem, contrasts reading and riding (along with fearing and faring, and horror and hearing):

> "O where are you going?" said reader to rider,
> "That valley is fatal where furnaces burn,
> Yonder's the midden whose odours will madden,
> That gap is the grave where the tall return."

> "O do you imagine," said fearer to farer,
> "That dusk will delay on your path to the pass,
> Your diligent looking discover the lacking,
> Your footsteps feel from granite to grass?"

> "O what was that bird," said horror to hearer,
> "Did you see that shape in the twisted trees?
> Behind you swiftly the figure comes softly,
> The spot on your skin is a shocking disease."

In the last stanza the three active characters (rider, farer, hearer) seem to melt into a single, answering, dismissive figure, although the questions, the fears re-main apart, plural:

> "Out of this house"—said rider to reader,
> "Yours never will"—said farer to fearer,
> "They're looking for you"—said hearer to horror,
> As he left them there, as he left them there.

It was Auden also who said, in an essay, that "the interests of a writer and the interests of his readers are never the same." Never? Well, not in the Auden poem I've just quoted, and in the world it implies. The mythology of writing that accompanied the old proposition about the reader was that it was a lonely, difficult, dangerous, desolate art; a mystery; an adventure. In that myth the reader was a mere stay-at-home; an armchair adventurer, beneficiary of the startling exploits of others. What happened, in or about 1967 or 1968, is that readers wanted their share of glamour and developed a new mythology of reading. The very mythology of writing, in fact: a lonely, difficult, dangerous, desolate art, and the rest. I think there is substantial truth in both myths, and I don't want to make too much fun of them. But as long as the myths just stare each other in the face, claiming all the thrills, or equal thrills, we can scarcely begin to understand them.

Readers achieved their share of glamour (if they have—the question is still open) only by understanding reading in a different way. In this sense the development we are looking at is recent only in its maturing, since it seems to be the fruition of a movement that began with Richards and Empson and the New Criticism. When Richards said that "Empson's minute examinations . . . raised the standards of ambition and achievement in a difficult and very hazardous art," he was thinking of reading not mountaineering. Blackmur said the effect of Richards' work for Tate and Ransom was to have proved "the enormous difficulty of reading at all." The New Reader was in this sense the New Criticism's unruly child. Reading became writing's partner, a much fuller partner than it used to seem; junior maybe, but only just and not always. The chief, or at least the most attractive effect of the change was that criticism remembered how much it depended on the imagination, and writers became much better readers.

I remember being much upset in school when I was called a bookworm. It wasn't that I didn't like books—I loved them—but I didn't like the idea of being a worm. The suggestion was that I liked only books, and that the very liking was unhealthy; some horribly morbid, indoors, underground activity. Even the friends of such a view of reading, those who like the idea of shelter and calm, might seem like enemies to anyone who wanted to read and also ride. Reading and riding were offered to me not as alternative activities but as opposing destinies. I would not then have been (and am not now entirely) charmed by Wallace Stevens's image of a quiet house and a calm world, figured in the act of reading:

> The house was quiet and the world was calm.
> The reader became the book; and summer night
> Was like the conscious being of the book.
> The house was quiet and the world was calm.

Beautiful; but only for bookworms. It helps if we think of the poem's date—1946—and of an only recently calmed world. Reading is peace, the banishment of violence; and the poem is of course implicitly full of all it holds at bay. Even so, this is the old reading, and the best example I know of the newer vision of the hazardous art is the eerie situation evoked in Julio Cortázar's story, "Continuity of Parks" (1959). Here the house is quiet and the world is calm, but a man is murdered by a character in the novel he is reading. The story is only a page and a half long, and effectively has three moves, or stages:

1. An evocation of reading as escape, a holiday from a busy world—the man sits in his study, his back turned to the door ("even the possibility of an intrusion would have irritated him, had he thought of it"), brushes the green velvet of his favorite armchair, enjoys the sense of cigarettes within reach, of the evening wind in the park seen through his window, and sinks into the story, "word by word, licked up by the sordid dilemma of the hero and heroine, letting himself be absorbed to the point where the images settled down and took on colour and movement."

2. A description of a crucial moment in the novel being read, the lovers' meeting in the cabin ("The woman arrived first"). Their kiss, the man's refusal of her embrace, his mind on their planned business. He has the knife/dagger, reviews their preparations.

3. A movement into the novel being read—imperceptible, the shift between second and third stages—the action related from the man's point of view, in close-up. There is the "yellowish fog" that belongs in this sort of fiction, there is a cliché about the blood thudding in the man's ear. Everything is as the woman—presumably the wife of the man to be killed—has described it: "first a blue chamber, then a hall, then a carpeted stairway. At the top, two doors. No one in the first room, no one in the second. The door of the salon, and then, the knife in hand, the light from the great windows, the high back of an armchair covered in green velvet, the head of the man in the chair reading a novel."

"Moral: it is dangerous to read novels in that way, a kind of mental suicide where fiction will revenge itself on the reader for having believed in it" (Jason Wilson). I'm not sure this brilliant and mischievous little story has a moral. It certainly suggests that reading novels is dangerous—but I would have thought that the suggestion included all novels and whatever way we read them, that it doesn't have any restrictive clauses or exclusions. But there is also pleasure in the story, and a dark triumph of the readerly imagination. The naive reader is a creative reader. If the man had not lost himself in the fiction, the fiction wouldn't have been real enough to murder him. There is surely a grim amusement in such an idea. And then: the sheer spookiness of the story, the Hitchcock effect, doesn't really suggest the danger or triumph of belief so much as the chill of transgression, a confusion of conceptual levels, an impish category mistake. There is a frightening ease in the passage from fictional world to "real" world, from park to park. It's not that we fear for this (after all rather schematic) man, it's that we are made dizzy by Cortázar's refusal to separate the reader from the read, the material from the textual; to allow the man the customary difference between real and imagined harm; to allow us our safe space outside the text. We look over our shoulders as we read, wondering not whether a man has come to kill us but whether we have been invented by Julio Cortázar. We are the victim, I think, not because we are naive novel readers but because we are readers. What is murdered here, or about to be murdered, is not a character but our immunity; the old quiet privilege of reading.

Calvino is a writer who reads, and the imagination for him is a way of thinking possibility, "a repertory of what is potential, what is hypothetical, of what does not exist and has never existed, and perhaps will never exist but might have existed." Literature allows us to change our "image of the world," and for that reason needs spectacular ambitions. "Literature remains alive only if we set ourselves immeasurable goals, far beyond all hope of achievement." This sounds rather grandiose and quite unlike the Calvino we know from his work, until we fully recognize the remoteness of the goals he has in mind, until we remember his quest for the apocryphal, his interest in what lies beyond the human. Like Mr. Palomar, Calvino is drawn to what exceeds or eludes us. We can't get beyond the human, beyond interpretation, and a speaking silence is not silence any more. But as both readers and writers keep learning, there is a silence in words as well as beyond them, and the books hidden in the distance, the children of several silences, may be the books we most need.

Introduction

1. What distinguishes: Walter Benjamin, "The Storyteller," in *Illuminations*, trans. Harry Zohn (New York: Shocken, 1969), p. 87.

2. In every case: *Illuminations*, p. 86.

2. the paradise of reading: Italo Calvino, *If on a Winter's Night a Traveller*, trans. William Weaver (London: Picador, 1982), p. 101.

2. courage, humor: Walter Benjamin, "Theses on the Philosophy of History," in *Illuminations*, p. 255.

2. I'm telling you stories: Jeanette Winterson, *The Passion* (New York: Vintage, 1989), pp. 5, 13, 69, 160.

3. As some secrets: Thomas Pynchon, *Gravity's Rainbow* (New York: Penguin, 1995), pp. 737–738.

4. So long as a man: W. H. Auden, *The Dyer's Hand and Other Essays* (New York: Random House, 1962), p. 6.

4. irregular and complicated: *The Dyer's Hand*, pp. 6–7.

5. Do you know, Quincey: Malcolm Lowry, *Under the Volcano* (New York: Plume, 1971), pp. 133–134.

5. the beauty of the Earthly Paradise: *Under the Volcano*, p. 10.

6. Books: Marcel Proust, *By Way of Sainte-Beuve*, trans. Sylvia Townsend Warner (London: Hogarth, 1984), p. 198.

6. can have nothing: Marcel Proust, *Against Sainte-Beuve and Other Essays*, trans. John Sturrock (London: Penguin, 1988), p. 98.

6. makes nothing happen: W. H. Auden, "In Memory of W. B. Yeats," *Collected Poems* (London: Faber, 1991), p. 248.

6. should not mean/But be: Archibald MacLeish, "Ars poetica," *Collected Poems* (Boston: Houghton Mifflin, 1962), p. 51.

7. What we cannot speak about: Ludwig Wittgenstein, *Tractatus Logico-Philosophicus*, trans. D. F. Pears and B. F. McGuinness (London: Routledge, 1974), p. 74.

7. the gesture of: T. W. Adorno, *Hegel: Three Studies*, trans. Shierry W. Nicholson (Cambridge: MIT Press, 1993), pp. 101–102. Quoted in Marjorie Perloff, *Wittgenstein's Ladder* (Chicago: University of Chicago Press, 1996), p. 12.

7. no more than: *Wittgenstein's Ladder*, p. 12.

7. The expression that there is nothing to express: Samuel Beckett, *Three Dialogues with Georges Duthuit*, quoted in Hugh Kenner, *Samuel Beckett* (New York: Grove, 1961), p. 30. Cf. Samuel Beckett, *Molloy*, trans. Patrick Bowles in collaboration with the author (New York: Grove, 1965), p. 28: "Not to want to say, not to know what you want to say, not to be able to say what you think you want to say, and never to stop saying, or hardly ever, that is the thing to keep in mind, even in the heat of composition."

8. the mind reaching out: Henry James, "The New Novel," in *Literary Criticism: Essays on Literature, American Writers, English Writers* (New York: Library of America, 1984), p. 124.

8. reading books about solemn matters: Gustave Flaubert, *Correspondance*, vol. 3 (Paris: Conard, 1910), p. 508. My translation.

9. a metaphor for the act of reading: Paul de Man, *Blindness and Insight* (Minneapolis: University of Minnesota Press, 1983), p. 107.

9. After all: Walter Benjamin, "The Storyteller," in *Illuminations*, p. 86.

9. knowing how to go on: Ludwig Wittgenstein, *The Blue and Brown Books* (New York: Harper and Row, 1965), p. 40.

9. anyone who claimed: Stéphane Mallarmé, "Quant au livre," in *Oeuvres complètes* (Paris: Bibliothèque de la Pléiade, Gallimard, 1945), p. 372. My translation.

10. What's the difference: Paul de Man, *Allegories of Reading* (New Haven: Yale University Press, 1979), pp. 9–10.

12. a resistance: Roland Barthes, "History or Literature," in *On Racine*, trans. Richard Howard (Berkeley: University of California Press, 1992), p. 155.

12. nostalgic definition: Frank Lentricchia, *After the New Criticism* (Chicago: University of Chicago Press, 1980), p. 310.

13. the music of his music: Edward W. Said, *Musical Elaborations* (London: Chatto and Windus, 1991), p. 93.

1. The Kindness of Novels

17. The novel is the epic of a world; Dostoyevsky did not write novels; a new world: Georg Lukács, *The Theory of the Novel*, trans. Anna Bostock (Cambridge: MIT Press, 1973), pp. 88, 20, 152.

18. conviction and consciousness: Henry James, *Selected Literary Criticism* (Cambridge: Cambridge University Press, 1981), p. 49.

18. Our language can be seen as an ancient city: Ludwig Wittgenstein, *Philosophical Investigations*, trans. G. E. M. Anscombe (Oxford: Basil Blackwell, 1967), p. 8.

18. Only that which has no history can be defined: Friedrich Nietzsche, *The Genealogy of Morals*, in *Werke*, vol. 2 (Munich: Hanser, 1966), p. 820. My translation.

19. the effect of the superimposed image; as if one were winking; the wish . . . is not to have: *Roland Barthes/by Roland Barthes*, trans. Richard Howard (New York: Hill and Wang, 1977), pp. 85, 72, 73. Translation slightly modified.

20. If it is not a novel: T. S. Eliot, "Ulysses, Order and Myth," in *Selected Prose*, ed. Frank Kermode (New York: Harcourt, Brace Jovanovich, 1975), p. 177.

20. form of life: *Philosophical Investigations*, pp. 8, 11, 88, 174, 226.

20. an immense panorama: *Selected Prose*, p. 177.

21. as Geoffrey Hartman and others: Geoffrey Hartman, *Criticism in the Wilderness* (New Haven: Yale University Press, 1980), p. 4; Paul de Man, *Allegories of Reading* (New Haven: Yale University Press, 1979), p. 19.

21. All this must be considered: *Roland Barthes/by Roland Barthes*, p. 119.

21. What to write: *Roland Barthes/by Roland Barthes*, p. 188.

22. *un chateau; du genre romanesque; roman familial*: *Roland Barthes/by Roland Barthes*, pp. 8, 45, 3, 19.

22. The Novel is a Death: Roland Barthes, *Writing Degree Zero and Elements of Semiology*, trans. Annette Lavers and Colin Smith (London: Jonathan Cape, 1984), p. 34.

22. quite different; *simple découpage*: Roland Barthes, *The Pleasure of the Text*, trans. Richard Miller (New York: Noonday, 1989), p. 7.

22. *aucun roman*: Barthes, *A Lover's Discourse*, trans. Richard Howard (New York: Hill and Wang, p. 7.

22–23. *le romanesque sans le roman;* I like the novelistic: Roland Barthes, *S/Z*, trans. Richard Miller (New York: Hill and Wang, 1974), p. 5. See also Roland Barthes, *The Grain of the Voice*, trans. Linda Coverdale (London: Jonathan Cape, 1985), p. 130.

23. any Form which is new to me: Roland Barthes, *"Longtemps je me suis couché de bonne heure,"* in *The Rustle of Language*, trans. Richard Howard (Oxford: Basil Blackwell, 1986), p. 288.

23. because it had been accumulated: Marcel Proust, *Jean Santeuil*, (Paris: Bibliothèque de la Pléiade, Gallimard, 1971), p. 181.

24. a formula whose complete lack of connotation: Vladimir Nabokov, *Ada* (London: Penguin, 1971), pp. 261, 259.

24. are not strangers to one another: Walter Benjamin, "The Task of the Translator," in *Illuminations*, pp. 72–73.

25. the ideal of instrument for every construction: Barthes, *Writing Degree Zero*, p. 27. Translation slightly modified.

25. All happy families are alike: Leo Tolstoy, *Anna Karenin*, trans. Rosemary Edmonds (London: Penguin, 1978), p. 13.

25. Thirty years ago: Charles Dickens, *Little Dorrit* (London: Penguin, 1967), p. 39.

26. There I was: Roland Barthes, *Camera Lucida*, trans. Richard Howard (New York: Hill and Wang, 1981), p. 67.

26. some novel: Frédéric Berthet, in *Prétexte: Roland Barthes* (Paris: Union Générale, 1978), p. 349.

26. *du langage*: Roland Barthes, *The Pleasure of the Text*, p. 31.

26. Barthes is acting: Roland Barthes, *Incidents* (Paris: Editions du Seuil, 1987), p. 94. My translation.

27. A biography is: Roland Barthes, *The Grain of the Voice*, p. 223.

27. a story endowed with characters; purely novelistic: Roland Barthes, *The Grain of the Voice*, p. 176; *The Pleasure of the Text*, p. 7.

27. She added to the final syllable: Roland Barthes, *S/Z*, p. 80.

27. a section called "Impossibilia": Roland Barthes, *Sade, Fourier, Loyola*, trans. Richard Miller (Baltimore: Johns Hopkins University Press, 1997), p. 136.

27. novelistic surface; In daily life: Roland Barthes, *The Grain of the Voice*, pp. 223, 203.

27–28. What Photography reproduces: Roland Barthes, *Camera Lucida*, pp. 4–5.

28. The ethnographical work: *Roland Barthes/by Roland Barthes*, p. 84.

28. as Yeats was: W. B. Yeats, "Reveries over childhood and youth," in *The Autobiography of W. B. Yeats* (London: Collier, 1965), p. 58.

28. He would have liked; theory, critical combat; we submit the objects: *Roland Barthes/by Roland Barthes*, p. 90.

29. theory of pathos; moments of truth; absent from every theory of the novel: Barthes, "*Longtemps je me suis couché*," p. 287.

29–30. something to do with love; and perhaps especially: Barthes, "*Longtemps je me suis couché*," pp. 288, 289.

30. *banalité corrigée*: *Roland Barthes/by Roland Barthes*, p. 137.

30. aesthetic bliss: Vladimir Nabokov, "On a book entitled *Lolita*," in *Lolita* (New York: Vintage, 1989), pp. 314–315.

30. the literary form to which the emotions: Lionel Trilling, *The Liberal Imagination* (Garden City: Anchor, 1953), p. 215.

30. terrible temptation to kindness: Bertolt Brecht, *The Caucasian Chalk Circle*, trans. Ralph Manheim, in*Collected Plays*, vol. 7 (New York: Vintage, 1975), p. 160. Manheim translates "Terrible is the temptation to do good," which makes sense in the dramatic context, but the word is *Güte*, the precise equivalent of Barthes' *bonté*, meaning both goodness and kindness.

2. The Comedy of Ignorance

34. A late evening in the future: Samuel Beckett, *Krapp's Last Tape*, in *Collected Shorter Plays* (London: Faber, 1984), p. 55.

34. imaginary head: Samuel Beckett, *Texts for Nothing*, trans. the author, in *The Complete Short Prose, 1929–1989* (New York: Grove, 1995), p. 120, 132.

34. needless to say in a skull: "The Calmative," trans. the author, in *Complete Short Prose*, p. 70.

34. in the madhouse of the skull: Samuel Beckett, *Ill Seen Ill Said*, in *Nohow On* (New York: Grove, 1996), p. 58.

34. perhaps we're in a head: *Texts for Nothing*, p. 106.

34. How physical all this is: Samuel Beckett, *The Unnameable*, trans. the author, in *Three Novels* (New York: Grove, 1965), p. 357.

34. those nor for God nor for his enemies: Samuel Beckett, *For to End Yet Again*, in *Complete Short Prose*, p. 244.

34. It is in the tranquillity of decomposition: Unable, unable; Perhaps I invented him: Samuel Beckett, *Molloy*, trans. Patrick Bowles in collaboration with the author, in *Three Novels*, pp. 25, 139, 112.

35. No need of a story: Samuel Beckett, *Texts for Nothing*, p. 116.

35. No trace anywhere of life; No way in, go in: Samuel Beckett, *Imagination Dead Imagine*, in *Complete Short Prose* (New York: Grove, 1995), p. 182.

35. eye of prey; Leave them there: *Imagination Dead Imagine*, p. 185.

36. For to end yet again: is this then its last state: Samuel Beckett, *For to End Yet Again*, pp. 243, 246.

36. Imagination dead imagine: Samuel Beckett, *All Strange Away*, in *Complete Short Prose*, p. 169.

36. since sex not seen; Let her lie so from now on; dread of demons; So little by little; proof against enduring tumult: *All Strange Away*, pp. 172, 173, 179, 178; *Imagination Dead Imagine*, p. 184.

37. For in the cylinder alone: Samuel Beckett, *The Lost Ones*, in *Complete Short Prose*, p. 216.

37. its splashing and heaving: Samuel Beckett, "The End," trans. Richard Seaver in collaboration with the author, in *Stories and Texts for Nothing*, p. 89.

37. Closed place: Samuel Beckett, *Fizzles*, in *Complete Shorter Prose*, p. 236.

37. One's own death; the one thing worse than not living: Christopher Ricks, *Beckett's Dying Words* (Oxford: Oxford University Press, 1993), pp. 45, 24.

37. A voice comes to one in the dark: Samuel Beckett, *Company* (New York: Grove Weidenfeld, 1980), p. 7.

37–38. And in another dark; For why or?; Deviser of the voice; figment; standing or sitting or lying; Yet another then; Yet another still: *Company*, pp. 8, 24, 26, 45–46, 26, 46, 59–60.

38–39. And you as you always were; Might not the hearer be improved; The test is company; A dead rat: *Company*, pp. 63, 27, 26–27, 27.

39. A small boy you come out; the bloom of adulthood; You stand at the tip of the high board: *Company*, pp. 10, 38, 18.

40. labour lost and silence: *Company*, p. 63.

40. How need in the end; And every now and then a real creak: Samuel Beckett, *Ill Seen Ill Said*, pp. 56, 68.

40–41. See them again side by side; As had she the misfortune; alive as she alone know how; no shock were she already dead; If only she could be pure figment: *Ill Seen Ill Said*, pp. 75–76, 50, 53, 80, 73, 58.

42. Such the dwelling; Scrapped all the ill seen; On resumption the head is covered: *Ill Seen Ill Said*, pp. 74, 80, 72.

42. They give birth: Samuel Beckett, *Waiting for Godot*, trans. the author (New York: Grove, 1982), pp. 57–58.

42. a long face . . . a lachrymose philosopher: Samuel Beckett, *More Pricks Than Kicks*, (New York: Grove, 1972), p. 163.

42. This is becoming really insignificant: *Waiting for Godot*, p. 44.

43. Personally I have no bone; You can't keep a dead mind down; This is awful, awful; Nothing like breathing your last; When my comfort was at stake: *First Love*, trans. the author, in *Complete Short Prose*, p. 25; *Texts for Nothing*, pp. 124, 78; *Molloy*, p. 83.

43. Do you think he meant human life: *Molloy*, p. 165.

43. The silence is such: Samuel Beckett, *Malone Dies*, trans. the author, in *Three Novels*, p. 253.

43. God is love: *Company*, p. 52.

43. A moor would have better met the case; unchanged for the worse: *Ill Seen Ill Said*, pp. 52, 82.

43. These late masterpieces have not been helped: Colm Tóibín, "The Built-in Reader," *London Review of Books*, April 8, 1993.

44. Beckett's engagement is not with life's little ironies: *Beckett's Dying Words*, p. 85.

44. Imagination at wit's end: *Ill Seen Ill Said*, p. 56.

3. Politics in Paradise

46. with his hands full of Khachaturian: *A Certain Lucas*, trans. Gregory Rabassa (New York: Knopf, 1984), pp. 20–21.

47. on the same plane; kibbutz of desire: Julio Cortázar, *Hopscotch*, trans. Gregory Rabassa (New York: Pantheon, 1966), pp. 216, 209.

47. I suddenly understood better: *Hopscotch*, p. 511.

47–48. The sign of a great short story; It seems to me a form of vanity; spherical: Julio Cortázar, *Ultimo Round*, vol. 1 (Mexico City: Siglo XXI, 1974), pp. 65, 60. My translation.

48. Almost always it was Rema: Julio Cortázar, "Bestiary," in *Blow-Up and Other Stories*, trans. Paul Blackburn (New York: Pantheon, 1967), p. 81.

48. press conference with the usual business; They came out so well: Julio Cortázar, "Apocalypse at Solentiname," in *Change of Light and other stories*, trans. Gregory Rabassa (New York: Knopf, 1980), pp. 119–120, 127.

49. In the years of *Hopscotch*: *Ultimo Round*, vol. 1, pp. 248–249.

49. No one should be surprised: Julio Cortázar, *A Manual for Manuel*, trans. Gregory Rabassa (New York: Pantheon, 1978), pp. 3–4.

49. anyone who knows me: *Ultimo Round*, vol. 1, pp. 249–251.

51. Look at the way we came to meet here: *A Manual for Manuel*, p. 389.

51. We may need: quoted by H. L. A. Hart in the *New York Review of Books*, March 9, 1978.

51–52. So much is done in jest; In this idiotic comedy: *A Manual for Manuel*, pp. 124, 185.

52. man who makes puns: Stendhal, *La Chartreuse de Parme*, (Paris: Garnier, 1960), p. 415.

52. Any resemblance: Guillermo Cabrera Infante, *Tres Tristes Tigres* (Barcelona: Seix Barral, 1968), introductory note. This sentence does not appear in the English translation.

53. Do you believe in writing: *Three Trapped Tigers*, trans. Donald Gardner and Suzanne Jill Levine in collaboration with the author (New York: Harper and Row, 1971), p. 465. The translation renders this exchange as: "Do you believe in words or in the Word?" "I believe in word benders."

53. And she tried: Lewis Carroll, *Alice in Wonderland* (London: Macmillan, 1966), p. 17.

54. this page I am writing; that voice; this is definitely not: *Three Trapped Tigers*, pp. 148, 112, 308.

55. Conrad's rancid prose; Carroll's dream-language; the radiance of the city; the exact moment when; above all, the privilege of memory: Rita Guibert, *Seven Voices* (New York: Vintage, 1973, pp. 435–436).

55. He didn't understand: *Three Trapped Tigers*, p. 472.

56. odor or ardor: *Infante's Inferno*, p. 63

56. The Past: Vladimir Nabokov, *Ada* (London: Penguin, 1971), p. 428.

56. She flew away; It wasn't the last time; It was the first time I climbed: *Infante's Inferno*, p. 50, 118, 1.

56. Only the young have such moments: Joseph Conrad, *The Shadow Line* (New York: Doubleday, 1924), p. 3.

56. eternally: *Seven Voices*, p. 409.

57. The city spoke another language: *Infante's Inferno*, p. 2.

57. The streetlamps were so poor; My finger brushed against the back of her seat: *Infante's Inferno*, pp. 3, 82.

58. sour gropes; Here's where I came in: *Infante's Inferno*, pp. 81, 410.

58. There was an old saw back home; Whatever Zola wants; lecher de main; Daguerre c'est Daguerre; How green was my Valli; aisle of Rite; a coup de data: *Infante's Inferno*, pp. 77, 35, 69, 176, 31, 78, 171.

58. baptism of pale fire; pathetic fellacy; Billy the Kitsch: *Infante's Inferno*, pp. 7, 178, 312.

58. Our works: Carlos Fuentes, *La nueva novela hispanoamericana* (Mexico City: Joaquín Mortiz, 1969), p. 32. My translation.

59. My mind's not right; I myself am Hell: Robert Lowell, "Skunk Hour," in *Selected Poems* (New York: Farrar Straus and Giroux, 1977), p. 96.

59. Another hell, another hell: Reinaldo Arenas, *The Palace of the White Skunks*, trans. Andrew Hurley (New York: Viking, 1990), p. 105.

60. recurrent and musical; long, uninterrupted sentence: Severo Sarduy, "Escrito sobre Arenas," in *Reinaldo Arenas: Alucinaciones, fantasía, y realidad*, ed. J. E. Miyares and Perla Rozencvaig (Glenview: Scott, Foresman, 1990), pp. 14, 16.

60. as it was, as it may have been: Reinaldo Arenas, *El Mundo alucinante* (Caracas: Monte Avila, 1982), p. 11. My translation.

61. been swindled all her life; the dimensions of an immeasurable solitude: Reinaldo Arenas, *Old Rosa*, trans. Ann Tashi Slater and Andrew Hurley (New York: Grove, 1989), p. 41.

61. But you're not the Devil; In the end she went out to the yard: *Old Rosa*, pp. 41, 3.

62. their world; It's easy to fit in anywhere; Arturo did begin to use; they would do anything: *Old Rosa*, pp. 50–51, 58, 68, 71.

62. Leopards break into the temple: Franz Kafka, "Leopards in the Temple," trans. Ernst Kaiser and Eithne Wilkins, in *Parables and Paradoxes*, (New York: Schocken, 1961), p. 93.

63. reality lies not in the terror one feels; aggressive, fixed, unyielding; still convinced that a cluster of signs; reached the monumental row; the only person who had ever loved him: *Old Rosa*, pp. 53, 83, 49, 104, 57.

63. condemned to live in a world: *Old Rosa*, p. 69.

63. a habitable mental space: Juan Goytisolo, "Apuntes sobre *Arturo, la Estrella mas brillante*," in *Reinaldo Arenas: Alucinaciones, fantasía, y realidad*, p. 179.

64. like a lightning rod for terror: *The Palace of the White Skunks*, p. 351.

64. Many times: *The Palace of the White Skunks*, p. 234.

64–65. The moon, soundlessly; Death is out there in the backyard; But what was God for them; screaming "I can't take it any more"; the certainty that nothing, not even something terrible: *The Palace of the White Skunks*, pp. 134, 3, 206, 82, 101.

65. the consolation of some terrible disgrace; the interpreting ceases; And all the games vanish; Everything becomes golden, fleeting: *The Palace of the White Skunks*, pp. 124, 354, 355, 125.

66. The sky and the smell of time; But what I would really like; Somewhere there must be more than this violence; The terrible; Real disaster never comes suddenly; We take advantage of the horrible state of affairs; There are no words: *Farewell to the Sea*, trans. Andrew Hurley (New York: Viking, 1986), pp. 97, 128, 111, 68, 117, 115, 74.

66–67. All she wants: You will live your whole life pleading; for the sea is the memory of some holy thing; unsmirched by legends, curses; all that is not trivial; offensive and offended; Let's go, then; Ah, Whitman, ah, Whitman: *Farewell to the Sea*, pp. 202, 344–345, 303, 333–334, 249, 153, 309, 270–271.

67–68. Writing a book on cutting sugarcane; the era's standard adornments; Man/is of all vermin: *Farewell to the Sea*, pp. 281–282, 202, 252–253.

4. The Motive for Metaphor

69. rarely used in France: Milan Kundera, *The Art of the Novel*, trans. Linda Asher (London: Faber, 1988), p. 132.

69. garden where nightingales sang: Milan Kundera, *The Book of Laughter and Forgetting*, trans. Michael Henry Heim (London: Penguin, 1983), p. 8.

69–70. Raised as we are on the mythology; because only animals were not expelled; The longing for Paradise: Milan Kundera, *The Unbearable Lightness of*

Being, trans. Michael Henry Heim (New York: Harper and Row, 1984), pp. 295, 298, 296.

70. dimensions of existence: *The Art of the Novel*, p. 5.

70. one who is nostalgic for Europe; grounded in the relativity and ambiguity of things human; they fail to participate; The novel's spirit; by definition, the ironic art; no one affirms; Once it is part of a novel; different emotional spaces; fascinating realm where no one owns the truth: *The Art of the Novel*, pp. 128, 12, 14,18, 134, 78, 79, 90, 164.

70–71. Suspending moral judgement; an immense carnival of relativity; Irony means: Milan Kundera, *Testaments Betrayed*, trans. Linda Asher (New York: Harper-Perennial, 1996), pp. 7, 27, 203.

71. The death of the novel; If the novel should really disappear: *The Art of the Novel*, pp. 14, 16.

71. banal, ordinary, quotidian; The present moment does not resemble the memory of it: *Testaments Betrayed*, pp. 130, 128,

71. ontological mission; the prose of life: *Testaments Betrayed*, pp. 132–133.

72. But understand me; Philosophy develops its thought: *The Art of the Novel*, pp. 27, 29.

72. the fear instilled by adulthood; a tiny artificial space: Milan Kundera, *Life is Elsewhere*, trans. Peter Kussi (London: Faber, 1986), p. 112; quoted in *The Art of the Novel*, p. 30.

72. the intoxication of the weak: *The Unbearable Lightness of Being*, p. 76; quoted in *The Art of the Novel*, p. 31.

72. meditative interrogation . . . interrogative meditation; neither sociological nor aesthetic nor psychological; a new art: *The Art of the Novel*, pp. 31, 32, 65.

72. provocative, experimental, or inquiring; there is a great deal of reflection: *The Art of the Novel*, p. 80.

72. Serious is what someone is who believes what he makes others believe; no novel worthy of the name: Milan Kundera, *Jacques and His Master*, trans. Simon Callow (London: Faber, 1986), p. 13.

73. original ideas and an inimitable voice; makes no great issue of his ideas; not to transform the novel into philosophy: *The Art of the Novel*, pp. 143, 144, 16.

73. Their domain lies between religion and knowledge: Robert Musil, *The Man Without Qualities*, vol. 1, trans. Sophie Wilkins (London: Picador, 1995), p. 273.

74. I have been thinking about Tomas: *The Unbearable Lightness of Being*, p. 6.

74. Her arm rose with bewitching ease: Milan Kundera, *Immortality*, trans. Peter Kussi (New York: Grove Weidenfeld, 1991), pp. 3–4.

74. A character is . . . an imaginary being: *The Art of the Novel*, p. 34.

75. I am trying: *Immortality*, p. 237.

75. Imagine me: Vladimir Nabokov, *Lolita*, p. 129.

75–76. Or another image: *Immortality*, p. 252.

76. the imaginative ability to see strange people: Richard Rorty, *Contingency, Irony, and Solidarity* (Cambridge: Cambridge University Press, 1989), p. xvi.

76. *The Unbearable Lightness of Being*: *Immortality*, p. 238.

76. in a famous story by Borges: Jorge Luis Borges, "Funes the Memorious," in *A Personal Anthology*, trans. Anthony Kerrigan (New York: Grove, 1967), pp. 35–43.

77. unknown smile: *Immortality*, p. 270.

77. No, they don't have faces; The gesture revealed nothing of that woman's essence: *Immortality*, pp. 269, 7.

77. All gestures: Milan Kundera, *Slowness*, trans. Linda Asher (New York: Harper-Collins, 1996), p. 126.

78. Napoleon was a true Frenchman: *Immortality*, p. 51.

78. in some fashion withdrawing from the world: *The Art of the Novel*, p. 41.

78. Living: carrying one's painful self; What is unbearable in life is not *being*: *Immortality*, pp. 259, 258.

78. *Homo sentimentalis* cannot be defined: *Immortality*, p. 194.

78. In the realm of kitsch: *The Unbearable Lightness of Being*, p. 250.

78. naively and directly; I think, therefore I am: *Immortality*, pp. 204, 200.

79. trying to apologize to the horse for Descartes: *The Unbearable Lightness of Being*, p. 290.

79. our century of optimism and massacres: *Immortality*, p. 150.

5. The Promised Land

81. one city was depicted by the leap of a fish; you would have said: Italo Calvino, *Invisible Cities*, trans. William Weaver (New York: Harcourt, Brace, Jovanovich, 1978), pp. 21–22, 38–39.

82. the drumming of spoons:Italo Calvino, *The Castle of Crossed Destinies*, trans. William Weaver (New York: Harcourt, Brace, Jovanovich, 1977), p. 5.

82–83. conceal more things than they tell; as soon as a card says more; Each story runs into another; the same cards, presented in a different order: *The Castle of Crossed Destinies*, pp. 71, 41.

83. I'm not familiar with the exact constitution: T. S. Eliot, *The Waste Land and Other Poems* (New York: Harcourt, Brace and World, 1962), pp. 47–48.

83. a machine for constructing stories: *The Castle of Crossed Destinies*, p. 126.

83–84. our eyes seemed suddenly blinded; our fellow guest probably wished; this row of cards . . . surely announced; we could only venture some guesses; might well be that English knight; no longer say which it is; confused it in the dust of the tales: *The Castle of Crossed Destinies*, pp. 29, 7, 8, 12, 35, 41, 46.

84. sets himself the task of sketching the world: Jorge Luis Borges, *El Hacedor* (Buenos Aires: Emecé Editores, 1967), p. 111. My translation.

84. the great shepherd of souls; that story which; the raw material of writing; in writing, what speaks is what is repressed; will I not have been too pontifical; Writing, in short, has a subsoil: *The Castle of Crossed Destinies*, pp. 102, 101, 111, 102, 103–104.

85. the chaotic heart of things: *The Castle of Crossed Destinies*, p. 33.

85–86. emptied from the walls; who has murdered sleep; his only support and mirror; drinking water from the ditches: *The Castle of Crossed Destinies*, pp. 115, 117, 115, 118.

86. If this is neurosis; With daughters, whatever a father does is wrong; they have shared the roles: *The Castle of Crossed Destinies*, pp. 115, 117.

87. to impose, as Stevens said: Wallace Stevens, "Notes toward a Supreme Fiction," in *The Palm at the End of the Mind* (New York: Vintage, 1990), p. 230.

89. more useful than objects or gestures. So, for each city; The pleasure of falling back; sense of emptiness; The foreigner had learned to speak; Marco Polo imagined answering; Kublai Khan interrupted him: Italo Calvino, *Invisible Cities*, pp. 39, 5, 38, 28.

89–90. this garden exists only in the shadow; Tell me another city; the special quality of this city for the man who arrives; knows only departures: *Invisible Cities*, pp. 103–104, 85, 7, 56.

90–91. Perhaps the whole world; a tin can, an old tire; There are twenty-six of us; Nothing exists or happens; It is not so much their copulating or murdering; The two Valdradas lives for each other: *Invisible Cities*, pp. 115, 116, 147, 53, 54.

91. Sophronia is made up of two half-cities; One of the half-cities is permanent; most elevated virtues and sentiments; only moments of generous abandon; invisible thread that binds: *Invisible Cities*, pp. 63, 111, 112, 149.

92. Perinthia's astronomers are faced; Our city and the sky correspond so perfectly; Convinced that every innovation in the city; At first sight nothing seems to resemble Eudoxia: *Invisible Cities*, pp. 145, 151, 96.

92–93. the form the gods gave the starry sky; But you could, similarly; Sphinxes, griffons, chimera; From my words you will have reached the conclusion: *Invisible Cities*, pp. 97, 160, 163.

93. the last landing place; The first is easy for many; Returning from his last mission; Each game ends; By disembodying his conquests: *Invisible Cities*, pp. 165, 122, 123.

95. Your chessboard, sire: *Invisible Cities*, pp. 131–132.

95. the book in which I think I managed: Italo Calvino, *Six Memos for the Next Millennium* (Cambridge: Harvard University Press, 1988), p. 71.

95. When you kill; incapable of killing: *The Castle of Crossed Destinies*, p. 119.

95–96. In fact, silence can also be considered a kind of speech; hopes always that silence contains something more: Italo Calvino, *Mr. Palomar*, trans. William Weaver (London: Secker and Warburg,1985), pp. 94, 24.

96. He would like the duck: *Mr. Palomar*, p. 63.

96. the Promised Land; literature remains alive: as a perpetual pursuit of things: *Six Memos for the Next Millennium*, pp. 56, 112, 26.

97. The sea is barely wrinkled; And so the wave continues to grow; The equal whistle of man and blackbird; the dismay of living: *Mr. Palomar*, pp. 3, 6, 24, 74.

97. sole exemplar in the world; Mr. Palomar feels he understands: *Mr. Palomar*, pp. 73, 74.

97–98. a sample-case of forms; a squandering of forms; perhaps actually the most incredible; the order of the world; Is their a boundless patience: *Mr. Palomar*, pp. 76–77, 77, 78, 79.

98–99. an impassioned and eloquent expert; Mr. Palomar's friend pauses; is fascinated by his friend's wealth; refusal to comprehend; This is the wall of the serpents: *Mr. Palomar*, pp. 86, 87, 87–88, 88.

99. I am accustomed to consider literature: *Six Memos for the Next Millennium*, p. 26.

99. Why is such a person impossible: Paul Valéry, *Monsieur Teste* (Paris: Gallimard, 1984), p. 11. My translation.

6. A Postmodernist Romance

103–104. completely transformed; swatting mosquitoes; I saw in a flash: Gabriel García Márquez, *El Olor de la Guayaba: conversaciones con Plinio Apuleyo Mendoza*, (Bogotá: Oveja Negra, 1982), pp. 50, 51.

104. But there could be no doubt: Virginia Woolf, *Mrs. Dalloway* (London: Penguin, 1973), p. 19; quoted in *El Olor de la Guayaba*, p. 50.

104. The face in the motor car: *Mrs. Dalloway*, p. 19.

104. Quentin had grown up with that: William Faulkner, *Absalom, Absalom!* (New York: Vintage, 1972), p. 12.

105. He was condemned not to know life except from the other side: Gabriel García Márquez, *Autumn of the Patriarch*, trans. Gregory Rabassa (New York: Harper and Row, 1971), p. 268.

105. He do the Police in different voices: Charles Dickens, *Our Mutual Friend* (New York: Oxford University Press, 1989), p. 198; cf. Christopher Ricks, *T. S. Eliot and Prejudice* (London: Faber, 1988), p. 271.

105–106. What did you expect: Gabriel García Márquez, *One Hundred Years of Solitude*, trans. Gregory Rabassa, (New York: HarperPerennial, 1991), pp. 127, 341.

106. A hundred years already: *Autumn of the Patriarch*, p. 215.

106. Make it new: This was the title of a book Ezra Pound published in 1934.

106–107. most important book; like a bolero: *El Olor de la Guayaba*, pp. 65, 73.

107. the first boleros that were just beginning: Gabriel García Márquez, *Love in the Time of Cholera*, trans. Edith Grossman (New York: Penguin, 1989), p. 345.

107. the most authentically Latin American music: *El Olor de la Guayaba*, p. 73.

108. every counted minute: Gabriel García Márquez, *No one Writes to the Colonel and Other Stories*, trans. J. S. Bernstein (New York: Harper and Row, 1979), p. 62.

108. fifty-three years, seven months, and eleven days and nights: *Love in the Time of Cholera*, p. 348.

108. Good stories are best told slowly: Thomas Mann, *Der Zauberberg* (Berlin: Fischer, 1925), p. 10.

108. It was inevitable: *Love in the Time of Cholera*, p. 3.

109. as the date approached he had gradually succumbed: *Love in the Time of Cholera*, p. 15.

109. the only difference: *Love in the Time of Cholera*, p. 35; cf. *One Hundred Years of Solitude*, p. 248.

110. for there were no more wars or epidemics; larval wars that governments were bent on hiding; A decent woman; How noble this city must be: *Love in the Time of Cholera*, pp. 336, 337, 207, 111.

110–111. the entire historic city; fifty-one years, nine months, and four days; so far from their youth; beyond love . . . beyond the pitfalls of passion: *Love in the Time of Cholera*, pp. 132, 53, 305, 345.

111–112. He was a perfect husband: *Love in the Time of Cholera*, p. 222.

112. emergency love; hurried love; loveless love; nothing one does in bed is immoral; My heart has more rooms than a whorehouse: *Love in the Time of Cholera*, pp. 69, 64, 75, 151, 270.

113. the truths about emotional life: Stephen Minta, *Gabriel García Márquez: Writer of Colombia* (London: Jonathan Cape, 1987), p. 126.

113. verses and tearful serialized love stories: *Love in the Time of Cholera*, p. 64.

113. But he made no distinctions: *Love in the Time of Cholera*, p. 75.

113. mists of grief; quicksand; private hell; wasteland of . . . insomnia; night eternal over the dark sea: *Love in the Time of Cholera*, pp. 7, 234, 291, 296, 187.

114. abyss of disenchantment: *Love in the Time of Cholera*, p. 102.

114. revelation . . . correctness: *Love in the Time of Cholera*, pp. 203–204.

114–115. He took the letter: *Love in the Time of Cholera*, p. 61.

115. eternal fidelity and everlasting love: *Love in the Time of Cholera*, pp. 50.

115. He was what he seemed: *Love in the Time of Cholera*, p. 48.

116. even before it's happened . . . I've remained a virgin; the spirited way in which he said it: *Love in the Time of Cholera*, p. 339.

116. She would not have believed it in any event: *Love in the Time of Cholera*, p. 339.

117. Human language: Noam Chomsky, *Language and Mind* (New York: Harcourt Brace Jovanovich, 1972), p. 70.

118. paradise, once lost, is now abandoned: Alan Wilde, *Horizons of Assent* (Baltimore: Johns Hopkins University Press, 1987), p. 10.

7. The Mind Has Mountains

119. Every week: Toni Morrison, *Jazz* (New York: Knopf, 1992), pp. 74–75.

119. something scary: *Jazz*, p. 202.

119. what took place: Toni Morrison, ed., *Race-ing Justice, En-gendering Power* (New York: Pantheon, 1992), p. xii.

120. a crooked kind of mourning: *Jazz*, p. 111.

120. places where the imagination sabotages itself: Toni Morrison, *Playing in the Dark: Whiteness and the Literary Imagination* (Cambridge: Harvard University Press, 1992), p. xi.

120. She shook her head: Toni Morrison, *Beloved* (London: Penguin, 1988), p. 70.

120. It never looked as terrible as it was: *Beloved*, p. 6.

120. They lived there: Toni Morrison, *The Bluest Eye* (London: Picador, 1990), p. 28.

121. loved her enough: *The Bluest Eye*, p. 163.

121. If I hadn't killed her: *Beloved*, p. 200.

121. I was so sure: *Jazz*, p. 220.

122. Joe believed it was it would be perfect; Sth, I know that woman; I'm crazy about this city; I like the way the City makes people think; not so much new as themselves; The City is smart at this: *Jazz*, pp. 107, 3, 7, 8, 33, 64.

122. When I see this sadness: Quoted in Barbara Hill Rigney, *The Voices of Toni Morrison* (Cleveland: Ohio State University Press), 1992, p. 51.

122–123. cracks . . . dark fissures; because nobody actually saw him: *Jazz*, pp. 22–23, 9.

123. Risky, I'd say; I know how she felt; Good luck and let me know; I want to be the language; When he stopped the buggy: *Jazz*, pp. 137, 63, 5, 161, 149.

124. intricate, malleable toy: *Jazz*, p. 33.

124. The very names: Cf. Trudier Harris, *Fiction and Folklore: The Novels of Toni Morrison* (Knoxville: University of Tennessee Press, 1991), p. 104.

124. Names they got from yearnings: *Song of Solomon* (London: Picador, 1989), p. 330.

124. without a trace: *Jazz*, p. 124.

124–125. I lived a long time; Pain; exotic . . . driven; I was sure one would kill the other.; whispering, old-time love: *Jazz*, pp. 9, 119, 221, 220, 228.

125. What's the world for . . . Forgot: *Jazz*, p. 208.

126. If my mother knew me: *Beloved*, p. 140.

126. says she smiled: *Playing In the Dark*, p. vii.

126. Gripped by panic at the idea of dying: Marie Cardinal, *Les Mots pour le dire*, Paris: Grasset et Fasquelle, 1975, p. 53; quoted in *Playing in the Dark*, p. vii.

126. Would an Edith Piaf concert; trope . . . virus; unsettled and unsettling; surrogate selves for meditation; thunderous, theatrical presence; How could one speak of profit: *Playing in the Dark*, pp. viii, 7, 6, 37, 13, 50.

126. Africanism is inextricable: *Playing in the Dark*, p. 65.

127. race music; a complicated anger . . . appetite . . . careless hunger; Come; You would have thought: *Jazz*, pp. 79, 59, 67, 196.

8. Tigers and Mirrors

129. I like anything that flickers: quoted by Susannah Clapp, introduction to Angela Carter, *American Ghosts and Old World Wonders* (New York: Vintage, 1994), p. ix.

129. Henry Glass seemed to flicker; the bar was a mock-up; He could only say he was sorry: Angela Carter, *Shadow Dance* (New York: Penguin, 1996), pp. 109, 1, 119.

129. by the witty irrelevance: Angela Carter, *Love* (New York: Penguin, 1988), p. 67.

130. Gothic tales, cruel tales; The tale does not log everyday experience: Angela Carter, *Fireworks* (New York: Penguin, 1987), pp. 132–133.

130. In 1969: Afterword, *Love*, p. 116.

130. penetrating aroma of unhappiness: *Love*, p. 113.

130–131. Honeybuzzard had the soft; They are all shadows: *Shadow Dance*, pp. 56, 86.

131. It was easier: Angela Carter, *The Magic Toyshop* (London: Virago, 1981), pp. 74–75.

131. He wavered as he walked: Angela Carter, *Several Perceptions* (London: Heinemann, 1968), p. 152.

131. frozen memories of the moment of sight; A kind of expressionist effect; connoisseurs of unreality; Mentally he wandered through his wardrobe; There seemed no connecting logic: *Love*, pp. 25, 55, 95, 19, 26–27.

131–132. suspected that everyday, sensuous human practice: *Love*, p. 4.

132. Surrealist poem for the forlorn daughter: Sue Roe, "The Disorder of *Love*: Angela Carter's Surrealist Collage," in *Flesh and the Mirror* ed. Lorna Sage (London: Virago, 1994), p. 62.

132. When Lee attained the age of reason: *Love*, p. 10.

132–133. ornate formalism; was hardly capable; It is always a dangerous experiment; wander off alone; She left no notes or messages: *Love*, pp. 113, 70, 95, 109–110.

133. Our external symbols must always express: Angela Carter, *The Passion of New Eve* (London: Virago, 1982), p. 6.

133–134. It is impossible for any English writer; built to be happy in; Marvellous, hallucinatory Bath: Angela Carter, *Nothing Sacred* (London: Virago, 1982), pp. 165, 74, 73.

134. A joke need not be funny; So we did not quite fit in; Maybe Yorkshire never really left; At times, Bradford hardly seems an English city; It won't be much *fun*; In the pursuit of magnificence: *Nothing Sacred*, pp. 4, 66, 69, 61, 111, 88.

134. Myths deal in false universals; The notion of the universality of human experience: Angela Carter, *The Sadeian Woman*, (London: Virago, 1979), pp. 5, 12.

134–135. moral pornographer; Sade became a terrorist of the imagination; The pornographer as terrorist; an exercise of the lateral imagination; Sade remains a monstrous and daunting cultural edifice; she cannot envisage a benign sexuality; the persecuted maiden whose virginity; her flesh is sacred because it as good as money: *The Sadeian Woman*, pp. 21, 22, 37, 49, 60, 50.

135. the moral of [her] life; a free woman in an unfree society; will have removed a repressive and authoritarian structure; To be the object of desire; perfect, immaculate terror; It is in this holy terror of love: *The Sadeian Woman*, pp. 99, 27,111, 76–77, 150.

136. Since her fear did her no good; she knew she was nobody's meat; See! sweet and sound she sleeps: Angela Carter, *The Bloody Chamber* (New York: Penguin), 1993, pp. 117, 118

136. The tiger will never lie down: *The Bloody Chamber*, p. 64.

136. The lamb . . . is hampered by the natural ignorance: *The Sadeian Woman*, pp. 138–139.

136. everything it is possible to imagine; the world exists only as a medium: Angela Carter, *The Infernal Desire Machines of Dr. Hoffman* (London: Penguin, 1982), pp. 97, 35.

136–137. It is a northern country; To these upland woodsmen; When they discover a witch: *The Bloody Chamber*, p. 108.

137. a terrified pity; the atrocious loneliness of that monster: *The Bloody Chamber*, p. 35.

137. Bluebeard's castle, it was: *The Magic Toyshop*, p. 80.

137. I found this key: *Shadow Dance*, p. 103.

138. My virgin of the arpeggios; The Marquis stood transfixed: *The Bloody Chamber*, pp. 36, 39.

138. Lor' love you, sir: Angela Carter, *Nights at the Circus*, London: Chatto and Windus, 1984, p. 7.

139. To think I really fooled you; the pure child of the century; And once the old world has turned on its axle; Like any young girl; Nobility of spirit; This is some kind of heretical possibly Manichean version: *Nights at the Circus*, pp. 295, 25, 285, 23, 232, 77.

140. are generously endowed: Lorna Sage, *Angela Carter* (Plymouth: Northcote House, 1994), p. 46.

140. sinuous and ramshackle: *Love*, p. 83.

140. Fevvers' laughter seeped through the gaps: *Nights at the Circus*, pp. 294–295.

140. each with a slate; How irresistibly comic; this first, intimate exchange: *Nights at the Circus*, pp. 107, 108.

141. I didn't know his God: D. H. Lawrence, "Fish," in *Complete Poems* (New York: Viking, 1971), p. 338.

141. Just for that moment, while she knew they wondered: *Nights at the Circus*, p. 149.

141. The cats . . . leapt on to the semi-circle of pedestals: *Nights at the Circus*, p. 148.

142. They had frozen into their own reflections; We saw the house was roofed with tigers: *Nights at the Circus*, pp. 206, 249–250.

9. All the Rage

145. There are apparently: Clive Barker, quoted in Edward Ingebretsen, S.J., *Maps of Heaven, Maps of Hell: Religious Terror as Memory from the Puritans to Stephen King* (New York: Paragon, 1995), p. x.

145. Some of these: Stephen King, in PEN *Newsletter*, 1991.

147. What happens if there are others: Stephen King, *Carrie* (New York: Signet, 1975), p. 206.

147–148. once-religious imperatives; The deflective energies of a largely forgotten metaphysical history; a major comfort; Change the focus slightly: *Maps of Heaven, Maps of Hell*, pp. xv, xiii, 155, 181.

149. You were kids: *Carrie*, pp. 82–83.

149–150. the essential conundrum of time; sort of like beachballs; Reality peeled away: Stephen King, *The Langoliers*, in *Four Past Midnight* (New York: Signet, 1991), pp. xii, 184, 185.

150. An accident: Stephen King, *Dolores Claiborne* (New York: Signet, 1993), p. 189.

150. There was something monstrous and unkillable: *The Langoliers*, p. 159.

151. the awful totality of perfect knowledge: *Carrie*, p. 230.

151–152. Her first thought: The concept of dreaming; quite a bit like a man he had once arrested: Stephen King, *Rose Madder* (New York: Viking, 1995), pp. 4, 9, 187.

152–153. After fourteen years of listening to Norman; not quite a goddess; drunk of the waters of youth: *Rose Madder*, pp. 220, 231, 232.

153. It's a kind of rabies; an almost frantic effort; Rose looks for madness; Her black eyes: *Rose Madder*, pp. 391, 414, 419, 420.

153–154. Her shadow stretched across the stoop; Huge sunflowers; riding through a dream lined with cotton; shards of glass twinkling beside a country road; what she felt like was a tiny fleck of flotsam; This world, all worlds: *Rose Madder*, pp. 20, 212, 335, 5, 33, 378.

10. Lost Paradises

157. just robbery with violence: Joseph Conrad, *Heart of Darkness* (London: Penguin, 1973), p. 10.

158. The conquest of the earth: *Heart of Darkness*, p. 10.

158. he could not see: Cf. Chinua Achebe, *Hopes and Impediments* (London: Heinemann, 1988), pp. 1–13.

158–159. an attempt to do something else; No longer does the logos; cultural energy: It is a misreading: Edward W. Said, *Culture and Imperialism* (New York: Knopf, 1993), pp. xii, 244–245, 274, 275.

159. a phrase Said uses elsewhere: "On Genet's Late Works," *Grand Street* 36 (Winter 1993).

159. for the native: *Culture and Imperialism*, pp. 162, 258.

160. there is such a thing: Edward W. Said, *Orientalism* (New York: Pantheon, 1978), p. 10.

160. the seductive degradation of knowledge: *Orientalism*, p. 328.

160. a structure of attitude and reference: *Culture and Imperialism*, pp. xvii, xxiii, 53, 62, 74–75, 76, 95, 111, 125, 130, 193, 205, 208, 239, 242.

160. "soupy" designations: Edward W. Said, *The World, the Text, and the Critic* (Cambridge: Harvard University Press, 1983), pp. 35, 151.

160. unacceptable vagueness: *Culture and Imperialism*, p. 162.

160–161. Europe held a grand total; primarily imperial; contrapuntal reading; newly engaged interest; a heightened form of historical experience: *Culture and Imperialism*, pp. 8, 57, 66, 68, 185.

161. sense of the human community: *Culture and Imperialism*, p. 32.

161. a compellingly important and interesting configuration: *Culture and Imperialism*, p. 35.

161. noncoercive knowledge produced in the interests of human freedom: *The World, the Text, and the Critic*, p. 29.

161. What is critical consciousness: *The World, the Text, and the Critic*, p. 247.

161. the novel is incompatible with the totalitarian universe: Milan Kundera, *The Art of the Novel*, trans. Linda Asher (London: Faber, 1988), pp. 13–14.

162. there is nothing in *Mansfield Park*: *Culture and Imperialism*, p. 87.

162. right up to the last sentence: *Culture and Imperialism*, p. 92.

162–163. which . . . Fanny had never been able to approach; the happiness of the married cousins: Jane Austen, *Mansfield Park* (Boston: Houghton Mifflin, 1965), pp. 360, 359.

163. recent losses . . . on his West India estate; experience and anxiety; the Antigua estate; Your uncle thinks you very pretty: *Mansfield Park*, pp. 19, 82, 24, 150.

164. But I do talk to him more: *Mansfield Park*, p. 150.

164. since there simply is no common language: *Culture and Imperialism*, p. 96.

165. Narrative itself is the representation of power: *Culture and Imperialism*, p. 273. Cf. "Permission to narrate," *London Review of Books*, February 29, 1984.

165. with no acceptable narrative to rely on: *Culture and Imperialism*, p. 325.

165. lateral, nonnarrative connections: *Culture and Imperialism*, pp. 273, 279, 334.

165. broken narratives: Edward W. Said, *After the Last Sky* (London: Faber, 1986), p. 38.

165–166. And what was your mission in South Lebanon: *After the Last Sky*, p. 65.

166. This story and several others like it: *After the Last Sky*, p. 66.

166. announce the contours of an imagined or ideal community: *Culture and Imperialism*, p. 232.

166–167. Modern music sees absolute oblivion: T. W. Adorno, *Philosophy of Modern Music*, trans. Anne G. Mitchell and Wesley V. Blomster (New York: Seabury, 1973), p. 133; quoted in Edward W. Said, *Musical Elaborations* (London: Chatto and Windus, 1991), p. 14.

167. the expense of greatness; a genuine failure comes hard and slow: R. P. Blackmur, *Henry Adams* (New York: Da Capo, 1984), pp. 18, 4.

167. system of ideas; lives, histories, and customs; real or true Orient; some Oriental essence; liability to be stampeded by a single idea: *Orientalism*, pp. 325, 5, 323, 273, 277.

167. difference is slight; the disparity between texts and reality; the Islamic people; individual Arabs with narratable life histories: *Orientalism*, pp. 286, 109, 87, 229.

168. We are a people of messages and signals; something withheld from an immediate deciphering: *After the Last Sky*, pp. 53, 91.

168. reticence, mystery or allusive silence: *Musical Elaborations*, p. 16.

168. I found myself coming to a sort of unstatable, or inexpressible, aspect: *Musical Elaborations*, p. 93.

169. every soil; Exile is predicated on the existence; to more than one history: *Culture and Imperialism*, pp. 335, 336, xxvii.

11. The Discourse of Others

171. Can you believe it: Kazuo Ishiguro, *The Unconsoled* (New York: Knopf, 1995), p. 444.

172. the crisis I had come to assess: *The Unconsoled*, p. 289.

172. No sooner had I said this: *The Unconsoled*, p. 9.

172–173. Sophie's face; I found myself remembering; The room was by now growing steadily more familiar: *The Unconsoled*, pp. 34–35, 37, 214.

173. My boy, Boris; Leave us; I surveyed the scene around me; I filled my coffee cup: *The Unconsoled*, pp. 155, 532, 524, 535.

173. a vast, dark, empty space: *The Unconsoled*, p. 519.

174. The whole auditorium: *The Unconsoled*, pp. 381–382.

174–175. They've actually brought in; to hear me perform; to perform once more: *The Unconsoled*, p. 444, 386, 420.

175. *Par délicatesse j'ai perdu ma vie*: Arthur Rimbaud, "Chanson de la plus haute tour," *Oeuvres* (Paris: Garnier, 1983), p. 158.

175. in absolute control: *The Unconsoled*, p. 357.

176. I suppose I was perhaps the last: *The Unconsoled*, p. 158.

176. Kafka would say: Franz Kafka, *The Trial*, trans. Willa and Edwin Muir (London: Minerva, 1992), p. 232.

177. I was thinking about someone: Kazuo Ishiguro, *A Pale View of Hills*, New York: Vintage, 1990, p. 10.

178. I knew her when I was living; The worst days: *A Pale View of Hills*, pp. 10; 11.

178–179. Mariko . . . ran down an alleyway: *A Pale View of Hills*, p. 74.

179. As deaths often do in novels: Cf. Margaret Anne Doody, *The True Story of the Novel* (New York: HarperCollins, 1997), pp. 313–316 and elsewhere.

179. I know it was a terrible thing; The English . . . are fond of their idea: *A Pale View of Hills*, pp. 73; 10.

179. the discourse of others: Roland Barthes, *S/Z*, trans. Richard Miller (New York: Hill and Wang, 1974), p. 184.

180. Why have you got that: *A Pale View of Hills*, p. 84.

180. The little girl was watching me closely: *A Pale View of Hills*, p. 173.

180–181. I knew all along; Do you think I imagine for a moment: *A Pale View of Hills*, pp. 176; 171.

12. The Nightmare of Narrative

183. It was not too late: Jeanette Winterson, *Art and Lies* (London: Jonathan Cape, 1994), p. 206.

184. I promised myself: Richard Strauss/Hugo von Hoffmansthal, *Der Rosenkavalier* (London: John Calder, 1981), p. 122.

184. falls for the *very first* little girl: quoted by Michael Kennedy, "Comedy for Music," in *Der Rosenkavalier*, p. 29.

184. The majority of things: *Der Rosenkavalier*, p. 122; quoted in *Art and Lies*, p. 204.

185. I do not write novels; I was in a bookshop recently: Jeanette Winterson, *Art (Objects): Essays on Ecstasy and Effrontery* (New York: Knopf, 1996), pp. 191, 118, 103.

185. There is at present: *Art (Objects)*, p. 129.

186. Ridiculous this waste sad time: Jeanette Winterson, *Written on the Body* (New York: Vintage, 1993), p. 58.

186. unimaginable zero temperature: Jeanette Winterson, *The Passion* (New York: Vintage, 1989), pp. 45, 80.

186. That which is only living: *Art and Lies*, pp. 64, 67, 133.

186. Without past and future: *The Passion*, 62; 74; *Sexing the Cherry* (New York: Vintage, 1991), pp. 100, 152.

186. Then human voices wake us: *The Passion*, p. 74.

186. Through the body, the body is conquered: *Sexing the Cherry*, p. 76.

186. Did the Modernists too far strain the relationship: *Art (Objects)*, pp. 37, 176.

186. the language of shop assistants: *Art (Objects)*, pp. 87, 134, 98.

186–187. I know of no pain; thick with the possibility; Art, all art: *Art (Objects)*, pp. 156, 74, 4.

187. I'm telling you stories: *The Passion*, pp. pp. 5, 13, 69, 160.

187. I am a writer: *Art (Objects)*, p. 189.

188. what I had known dimly: *Art (Objects)*, p. 155.

188. not all dark places need light: *Oranges Are Not the Only Fruit* (London: Pandora, 1985), p. 172; *Art (Objects)*, p. 77.

188–189. Louise in her own right; I had failed Louise; No-one can legislate love; Destiny is a worrying concept; It's the clichés: *Written on the Body*, pp. 153; 157; 77; 91; 163; 10, 71, 155, 189.

189. the nightmare of narrative: Jeanette Winterson, *Gut Symmetries* (London: Granta Books, 1997), pp. 24, 157.

189–190. The separateness of our lives is a sham; I understood that pain; Stella turned towards me; I would have been glad: *Gut Symmetries*, pp. 98; 41; 126, 116.

190. I try to drive together; We mostly understand ourselves: *Art (Objects)*, pp. 173; 59, 175.

190. Oh dear, yes: E. M. Forster, *Aspects of the Novel* (London: Penguin, 1976), p. 53.

190. taken in by someone: *Art (Objects)*, p. 71.

191. What you see: *Gut Symmetries*, p. 115.

191. When we let ourselves respond: *Art (Objects)*, p. 60.

191. He uses winter like a larder; the Bonapartes; we got most of our meat: *The Passion*, pp. 5, 34, 37.

192. gather up their passion for life; somewhere between fear and sex; You can't make sense; You play, you win; we gamble with the hope; It's the gambler's sense: *The Passion*, pp. 28, 55, 62, 68, 82, 43, 66, 73, 133, 89, 137.

192. refuse the passion: *The Passion*, pp. 145–146.

193. other life, the parallel life: *The Passion*, p. 144.

193. Is this the explanation: *The Passion*, p. 144.

193. Every journey: *Sexing the Cherry*, pp. 2, 102.

194. The family who lived in the house: *Sexing the Cherry*, pp. 14–15.

194. it is quite simply *there*: Roland Barthes, *Camera Lucida*, trans. Richard Howard (New York: Hill and Wang, 1981), pp. 38–40.

194. whose inhabitants are so cunning: *Sexing the Cherry*, p. 43.

195. the cherry grew, and we have sexed it: *Sexing the Cherry*, p. 85.

195. He was a man: *Art and Lies*, p. 195.

195. Language always betrays us: *Sexing the Cherry*, p. 100.

195. we cannot move back and forth: *Sexing the Cherry*, p. 100.

195. What a rum thing time is, ain't it, Neddy: Charles Dickens, *The Pickwick Papers* (Oxford: Clarendon, 1986), p. 648; cf. Helen Gardner, *The Composition of Four Quartets* (Oxford: Oxford University Press, 1978), p. 28.

Endings

197. The history of man: Vladimir Nabokov, *Pnin* (London: Penguin, 1997), p. 141.

197. His eyes are staring: Walter Benjamin, "Theses on the Philosophy of History," in *Illuminations* (New York: Schocken, 1969), pp. 257–258.

197–198. In order to exist rationally: *Pnin*, p. 112.

198. to write poetry: Theodor W. Adorno, "Cultural Criticism and Society," in *Prisms*, trans. Samuel and Shierry Weber (Cambridge: MIT Press), 1983, p. 34.

199. the very phrase: *Illuminations*, p. 256.

199. Cultural criticism: *Prisms*, p. 34.

199. The theory . . . was: Vladimir Nabokov, *Bend Sinister* (London: Penguin, 1974), p. 181.

200. spent more time: Italo Calvino, "By Way of an Autobiography," in *The Literature Machine*, trans. Patrick Creagh (London: Secker and Warburg, 1987), p. 341.

200. a little man, shrunken and bent: Italo Calvino, *If on a Winter's Night a Traveller*, trans. William Weaver (London: Picador, 1982), p. 77.

201. he seems to have come from a world where: *If on a Winter's Night a Traveller*, p. 79.

201. as if: *If on a Winter's Night a Traveller*, p. 80.

201. I still have the notion: "By Way of an Autobiography," p. 340.

201. The ideal library: Calvino, "Literature as Projection of Desire," in *The Literature Machine*, pp. 60–61.

201. It is now possible: Frank Kermode, *The Art of Telling* (Cambridge: Harvard University Press, 1983), p. 123.

201. the birth of the reader: Roland Barthes, "The Death of the Author," in *Image-Music-Text*, trans. Stephen Heath (New York: Hill and Wang, 1988), p. 148.

201–202. The author: that anachronistic personage: Calvino, "Cybernetics and Ghosts," in *The Literature Machine*, p. 16.

202. O where are you going: W. H. Auden, "Five Songs," *Collected Poems* (London: Faber, 1991), pp. 59–60.

202. the interests of a writer: Auden, *The Dyer's Hand* (New York: Random House, 1962, p. 3.

203. Empson's minute examinations: I. A. Richards, in *Willam Empson: The Man and His Work*, ed. Roma Gill (London: Routledge and Kegan Paul, 1974), p. 99.

203. the enormous difficulty of reading at all: R. P. Blackmur, *A Primer of Ignorance* (New York: Harcourt, Brace and World, 1967), p. 170.

203. The house was quiet: Wallace Stevens, "The House Was Quiet and the World Was Calm," in *The Palm at the End of the Mind* (New York: Vintage, 1990), p. 279.

204. three moves, or stages: Julio Cortázar, "Continuity of Parks," in *Blow-Up and Other Stories*, trans. Paul Blackburn (New York: Pantheon, 1985), pp. 63–65.

204. Moral: it is dangerous: Jason Wilson, in *Modern Latin American Fiction*, ed. John King (London: Faber, 1987), p. 178.

205. a repertory of what is potential: *Six Memos for the Next Millennium* (Cambridge: Harvard University Press, 1988), p. 91.

205. Literature remains alive: *Six Memos for the Next Millennium*, p. 112.

Index

No kitchen should be without this engaging, carefully researched and practical guide to the carbon in our food.

Prof Mike Berners-Lee
Author of *How Bad are Bananas* and
There is no planet B

Did you know a latte is ten times worse for the climate than a cup of black coffee? Or that each calorie of beef requires 20 calories of feed? Or that an out-of-season tomato can have 80 times the climate impact of an in-season tomato? 'Food and Climate Change Without the Hot Air' provides a levelheaded, clear, and detailed picture of food emissions - a basic literacy we should all have in a time of accelerating climate consequence.

Dr Peter Kalmus
NASA climate scientist and author of
*Being the Change: Live Well and Spark
a Climate Revolution*

This is a wonderful, fact-filled but readable book, full of clear explanations of the emissions associated with everything we eat, identifying what is important and what is negligible. I shall never look at spaghetti bolognese in the same way again.

Prof Sir David Spiegelhalter
Winton Professor of the Public Understanding of
Risk at Faculty of Mathematics,
University of Cambridge

Superb work. In 'Food and Climate Change' Sarah Bridle takes us on an eye-opening journey through the climate costs of our food and drink. From our buttered breakfast toast to teatime tikka masala this book lays bare the carbon footprints of the food choices we make every day. Succinct and well-researched, this book is a great resource for anyone who wants to know how to help tackle climate change with every meal.

Prof Dave Reay
Author of *Climate-Smart Food*

I have already used information and ideas from this book in helping a landowner develop a strategy for climate friendly food production, shaping a research project and deciding on a tasty dinner at my favourite Indian restaurant (approximately 1000g CO^2 equivalent and lower than the 3000g of a typical meal). 'Food and Climate Change without the hot air' will be an essential reference just as David Mackay's companion volume guided many of us through the maze of information about energy.

Prof Sir David Baulcombe
Royal Society Research Professor,
University of Cambridge

I'm rather glad, perhaps, that I hadn't read Sarah Bridle's book before dinner. It allows readers no refuge from the inescapable climatic consequences of their dietary desires because it quantifies them in such orderly and precise terms. It's a marvel of synthesised research, clear explanation, and friendly wit.

Prof Philip Tabor
Former Director of the Bartlett School of
Architecture, University College London

Sarah Bridle leads the reader through the climate impacts of our food, meal by meal. She uses the most up-to-date science and brings it to life in a personal, engaging and non-judgemental way.

Prof Pete Smith
Director of the Scottish Climate Change
Centre of Expertise

Sarah Bridle has turned a page in our understanding of the impacts of our everyday eating habits with this ground-breaking, well-researched and accessible book. It will enable conscious decisions by individuals and industry concerned over the sustainability of our planet.

Prof David J Drewry
Non-Executive Director (Natural Science),
UK Commission for UNESCO

Sarah Bridle provides information about the carbon footprint of foods many of us eat in an attractive, readable, well-researched and nicely-structured volume. I will be dipping into it regularly.

Prof Joanna Haigh
Former co-director of the Grantham Institute on Climate Change and the Environment, Imperial College London

...wonderful book - a fantastic contribution - just what is needed to start the very serious process of getting useful information to people so that they can make informed decisions about the emission associated with what they eat.

Prof Sir Ian Boyd
Former Government Chief Scientific Adviser, DEFRA and Professor of Biology, University of St Andrews

For people who want to eat sustainably Professor Bridle has the answers. The book takes this complicated topic and turns it into something readable, educational and fun.

James Hand
Co-Founder of Giki
(a mobile app that helps you cut your environmental impact)

Bridle has given important information we should all know and understand about emissions and the food we waste, and included tips for how to reduce waste, which adds action to information.

Dr Liz Goodwin
World Resources Institute

This is a terrific book. It unpicks the connections between the food we eat and climate change in an engaging and straightforward manner with numerous notes to help you delve deeper. You will be amazed. Your preconceptions are often wrong.

Prof Sir Martyn Poliakoff
Research Professor in Chemistry, University of Nottingham

Sarah Bridle cuts through much of the confusion and complexity around the climate-change consequences of what we eat to provide a clear guide of how changes to diets can contribute to a more sustainable world.

Prof Sir Charles Godfray
Director of the Oxford Martin School, University of Oxford

Ever wondered whether beef produces over 100 times more carbon emissions than cabbage per gram? Then wonder no more as this book has the answer. An accessible approach to foot printing your meal to help you balance not just your diet but also your planetary impact!

Prof Aled Jones
Director of the Global Sustainability Institute, Anglia Ruskin University

How does the food we eat create climate change? This excellent, accessible handbook tells us; and guides us in personally tackling climate change through changing what we eat.

Prof Tim Benton
Director, Energy, Environment and Resources Programme, Chatham House

Sarah Bridle presents a crystal clear and very readable summary of how our meals through the day affect climate change. This should be an essential addition to all our cookery book shelves!

Dr John Ingram
Food Systems Programme Leader, Environmental Change Institute, University of Oxford

This book provides the information for students to make an educated decision about how to help turn around the climate crisis through food, free of political and personal baggage.

Jennie Hargreaves aka Mrs Physics
Scottish Institute of Physics, Physics Teacher of the year Award (2016)

I've been looking for ages for a guide as useful as this. This book provides a way to think about carbon emissions from food that is both clear and simple as well as providing the details and accuracy needed. The key points at the end of each chapter are really useful and will help many people to know how to make better decisions - without having to be absolutist.

Dr Julian Huppert
Former Member of Parliament for Cambridge and Director of the Intellectual Forum, Jesus College, University of Cambridge

Real food for thought! Sarah Bridle follows up the David MacKay's pioneering approach to sustainability in an absorbing and thought-provoking analysis of cooking's contribution to greenhouse gases. Very easy to follow and make your own judgements.

Prof Malcolm Longair
Emeritus Jacksonian Professor of Natural Philosophy, University of Cambridge

It's all about quality ingredients beautifully prepared. And here you'll be nourished by tasty hard facts and zesty stats, mellowed in a sauce of wit and clarity. A climate friendly kitchen essential.

Tom Heap
Rural Affairs Correspondent of BBC News and presenter of *Costing the Earth, Countryfile* and *Panorama*

Have you ever wondered how you personally can help save the planet? Here are some answers!

Prof Christian Holler
Professor at the Munich University of Applied Sciences and author of *Erneuerbare Energien - ohne heiße Luft*

Engaging and constructive -- this book puts climate facts on food choices into perspective and helps readers make climate-positive changes in the way they eat.

Baroness Jennifer Jones of Moulsecoomb
Green Party Life peer

If you want to understand how our food choices lead to carbon emissions, I thoroughly recommend this book. Using example meals, Bridle explains important but non-trivial issues such as intensive production versus grass fed cattle, the importantance of food waste, the impact of refrigeration and canning, and the nutrition in vegan food substitutes in a straightforward manner. Each chapter has useful tips and a 'key points' summary. Plus, for those of you (like me) who like to know more, there are more detailed notes and references. This book is an accessible overview and a handy reference all in one. It definitely gets a place on my shelf.

Nicola Terry
Energy consultant and Cambridge Sustainable Food volunteer

If you want to do the right thing for the planet but dont know how, this is the book for you. It is evidence-based but never preachy. More importantly it gives you hope and agency- changes to your diet will have a real and meaningful impact on the climate, and this book guides you which ones to choose.

Prof Mark Miodownik
Professor of Materials & Society, University College London

Thinking about what we eat is one of the most important things we can all do to reduce our carbon footprint. This book shows how it's possible to make a big difference and enjoy a nutritious, healthy, balanced diet without having to be an eco-saint every single meal. If you enjoy your food but also care about the planet, as I do, then this book is for you.

Craig Bennett
Leading environmentalist, Chief Executive of The Wildlife Trusts and former Chief Executive of Friends of the Earth

Very accessible guide on how to eat more sustainably. Cuts through all the confusion to give clear figures and diagrams that stay with you.

Dave Darby
Founder of Lowimpact.org

Want to reduce your contributions to climate change? Sarah Bridle's 'Food and Climate Change without the hot air' will help you do so one bite at a time. Her book examines the foods and beverages we eat from breakfast to dinner-- and traces how they affect the climate. If you care about food and climate change, buy this book!

Andrew F Smith
Culinary Historian

'Food and Climate Change without the hot air' is a breath of fresh air! Sarah Bridle provides a clear-eyed and exquisitely readable journey through our food and its impact on climate change and beyond. The book provides exactly the awareness and consciousness that each of us needs in our daily lives to make responsible decisions.

Prof Paul Anastas
Former Head of Research and Development for the US Environmental Protection Agency and the Director of Yale University's Center for Green Chemistry and Green Engineering

This fascinating and important book deserves world-wide success. Sarah Bridle presents, engagingly and clearly, a vast amount of information that's important not just for policymakers but for all of us who want to make a difference in our everyday lives.

Prof Sir Martin Rees
Baron Rees of Ludlow, former Astronomer Royal, Master of Trinity College, University of Cambridge and President of the Royal Society

Climate change is complex. Yet Sarah Bridle's book elegantly illustrates the role that food choices and food waste play in this issue, and how simple steps can greatly reduce our impact.

Dr Tom Quested
Lead Analyst, the Waste & Resources Action Programme

Both astounding and frightening, this book lays out in simple terms that anyone can understand the remarkable environmental impact of our daily food choices.

Prof Ken Albala
Professor of History, University of the Pacific

As an omnivore who loves his food, I loved this book. With a wealth of super-clear, attractive charts Bridle goes through a typical day's meals, ever so gently highlighting the often-small tweaks we can make to produce meals that are as tasty as ever... yet far kinder to our planet.

David Bodanis
Author of $E=mc^2$: A Biography of the World's Most Famous Equation and Einstein's Greatest Mistake

This book is brilliant. Well-presented and understandable information gives both the detail and the big picture to show how our food and climate are linked, and how our dietary choices can make a real difference. The weight-for-weight comparisons are just what are needed. Forget calorie-counting; it is carbon-counting that really matters.

Dr Phil Williamson
Climate Change Scientist, University of East Anglia

Sarah Bridle has written an important book that is full of useful information and is easy to read. I'm already thinking differently about the food I eat.

Prof Jeff Forshaw
Professor of Physics, University of Manchester and author of Why Does $E=mc^2$?

What was once a mystery has now been made crystal clear: the decisions about how we produce and consume food are some of the most impactful humanity can make to solve the climate emergency. This book opens the mind to the realities of the embodied emissions in everything we eat – and waste – from farm to fork to landfill. An essential source for anyone working to save the planet.

Chad Frischmann
Co-author of Drawdown: The most comprehensive plan ever proposed to reverse global warming

FOOD
and
CLIMATE
CHANGE
WITHOUT THE HOT AIR®

Change your diet:
the easiest way
to help save the planet

S L BRIDLE

First published in 2020, in England, by
UIT Cambridge Ltd.
PO Box 145
Cambridge
CB4 1GQ
England

Tel: +44 1223 302 041
Web: www.uit.co.uk

ISBN: 9780857845030 (Paperback)
ISBN: 9780857845054 (EPUB)
ISBN: 9780857845078 (PDF)
Also available for Kindle.

10 9 8 7 6 5 4 3 2 1

In memory of David JC MacKay

"To have constructive conversations ...
one needs to take a calm look at the numbers."
– David JC MacKay

Contents

Preface

In 2015, when my children started school, I wondered about the future: what the world will be like for them in 2050, when they are my age. Around the same time my former mentor and friend David MacKay was diagnosed with terminal cancer. David had brought great clarity to the discussion of greenhouse gas emissions, especially through his brilliant book *Sustainable Energy – Without the hot air*, which greatly influences this book. In his absence, I started to research climate change and to wonder how it might impact the future, and what we can do about it. I now divide my time between food and my other research field of astrophysics, as a Professor at the University of Manchester, UK.

I have immersed myself in the research literature on food and climate change to write the book I'd have liked to read at the beginning of my journey. As a practising physics researcher I bring a balanced synthesis of the academic literature on this topic: asking basic quantitative questions about where foods come from, how much emissions they cause, why, and what can be done about it. As an inquisitive eater I discuss what we citizens can do to reduce greenhouse gas emissions from food. But most of all I want you to benefit from the information in this book to help you figure out for yourself what you're going to do to help the generations to come.

In all this, I am heavily influenced by David MacKay's passion for empowering others to just get started working stuff out.

This book

This book doesn't promote a particular diet or set of food choices. Instead, it sets out clearly the scientific consensus on how individual foods contribute to climate change, and illustrates this with some typical example food combinations. There are no recipes in this book, although it examines some simplified common recipes from the internet and calculates their greenhouse-gas emissions. By the end of the book you will be able to apply what you've learned to your own favourite meals and recipes.

Throughout we visualize greenhouse-gas emissions using **vertical bars** or "**stacks**": the height of a stack indicates the number of grams of emissions. Each stack is drawn to the same scale, so you can use the heights of different stacks to compare the relative amounts of emissions from different foods and activities. This approach draws heavily on the energy stacks in David MacKay's *Sustainable Energy – Without the hot air*. David's motto was "numbers not adjectives": instead of vague descriptions like "huge" or "lots", we need to quantify impacts and compare them numerically to get a useful analysis.

The main body of each chapter presents the information about a specific food as simply as possible. However, the world often isn't as straightforward as we might like, so detailed numbers, calculations, discussions and references are included in the **endnotes** at the end of each chapter. You can use the endnotes to explore topics in depth, and see exactly how each emission figure has been calculated. (Some readers might prefer to skip over the endnotes on first reading.)

This is a **world book**, rather than being specific to any one country. Individual countries may differ in some details – depending on their climate, energy sources, etc. – but the information is valid for the world as a whole.

Errata: the latest list of changes, corrections (and interesting additions) for this book are online, accessed via the book's page at www.uit.co.uk/without-the-hot-air

You can also get details of the free **ebook** version of this book, via the book's page at www.uit.co.uk/without-the-hot-air

Continue the conversation at **#FACCWTHA** on **Twitter**.

Chapter 1 Introduction

How much do you think the last meal you ate contributed to climate change? And which bits of it were the biggest culprits? Diets aimed at reducing environmental impact are becoming more popular, for example vegans avoid all animal products including meat, fish, cheese, milk and eggs. But does this really help, and anyway how much of a big deal is food compared to all the other contributions to climate change?

When I first learned about the impact of food on climate change I went vegan for a while. I put my jacket potato into the oven for two hours and waited around smugly with my can of beans, unpacking my suitcase after a transatlantic flight. I drove to the shop 3 km (1.86 miles) down the road just to buy some plant milk, and also probably picked up a pack of green beans flown in from another continent.

My efforts to help reduce climate change were based on little more than a gut feeling. What I really needed was detailed figures, so I could make informed decisions that would make a big difference, and that's why I wrote this book – to get clear numbers that I could use, and share with everyone else.

Climate change

The overwhelming scientific consensus is that climate change *is* real, it *is* happening, and it needs to be addressed. There is a wealth of information available about climate change, so this book doesn't repeat all that. There is just a short appendix at the end, summarizing the main facts (appendix "Climate change").

However, we will address one issue that often confuses people: what's the difference between climate change and global warming? Yes, greenhouse gases in the Earth's atmosphere are trapping heat and cause the planet to warm up. (There's more detail on greenhouse gases in the next section.) However, some parts of the globe are warming up faster than others. For example the continents warm up faster than the oceans.

However, the world isn't just getting warmer – the changing climate causes extreme weather events such as droughts, floods, and storms, sometimes affecting multiple continents (appendix "Climate change").

So the "global" in "global warming" refers to the temperature change averaged across the whole the surface of the Earth. While it's nice to focus on a single number, this hides a complexity that has serious consequences. Cloud, wind and rainfall patterns have an intricate dependence on variations in temperature from one geographical location to another.

This changing climate also affects food production (appendix "Impacts of climate change on food"); some farmers have already had to change what they grow. Looking ahead, crop yields and the numbers of fish caught at sea are expected to go down.

"The main way that most people will experience climate change is through the impact on food: the food they eat, the price they pay for it, and the availability and choice that they have"
– Tim Gore, Head of Policy, Advocacy and Research of Oxfam's GROW Campaign

Greenhouse gases

We humans release a range of gases into the atmosphere. The most important of these that contribute to global warming are carbon dioxide, methane and nitrous oxide.[1] The best known of these is carbon dioxide (CO_2), which is released by burning fossil fuels – in cars, aeroplanes, heating and to generate electricity.

When plants rot in a damp place they turn into methane, which is how natural gas (which is a "fossil fuel") was made in the first place (appendix "Climate change"). In addition, about one twentieth of all the calories eaten by a cow are burped out again as methane (chapter 4). Because of the amount of food we're producing to feed the world, and because we're producing fossil fuels, the amount of methane in the atmosphere is increasing. When it first enters the atmosphere, 1 gram of methane causes more warming than 80 grams of carbon dioxide, but it only lasts for about 10 years before turning into carbon dioxide, so the total heat-trapping effect is equivalent to about 28 grams of carbon dioxide over a 100-year period.

Have you ever inhaled laughing gas (another name for nitrous oxide)? I had nitrous oxide as a painkiller when I was giving birth – it made the pain seem less important, but I don't remember laughing! One gram of nitrous oxide causes a similar global warming effect to about 270 grams of carbon dioxide.

The amount of nitrous oxide in the atmosphere is increas-

[1] This is the only footnote in the book because we have endnotes instead. For example, you can find an endnote relating to the text "The most important of these that contribute to global warming are carbon dioxide, methane and nitrous oxide." in the notes beginning on page 10.

ing because we're feeding our crops with nitrogen fertilizers (box 2.1), and because nitrous oxide is released from animal manure (chapter 4).

For the rest of this book we will talk about "greenhouse-gas emissions" to refer to the combined effect of all the greenhouse gases. We will describe emissions in grams of carbon dioxide equivalent (written as "gCO_2e" in the scientific literature) which means the amount of carbon dioxide that would cause the same energy input as all the greenhouse gases combined together, averaged over a one hundred year period. Therefore

- 100 grams of carbon dioxide corresponds to 100 grams of greenhouse-gas emissions
- 4 grams of methane corresponds to 100 grams of greenhouse-gas emissions, and
- 0.4 grams of nitrous oxide corresponds to 100 grams of greenhouse-gas emissions.

Box 1.1: Grams, kilos and precise numbers

Throughout this book we will talk about the number of grams of food consumed, as well as the number of grams of emissions. This can be written out the long way e.g. "20 grams" or in a more compact way e.g. "20 g". When the numbers get big we sometimes switch to using kilograms (or "kilos", for short), where one kilogram (1 kg) is the same as 1000 grams (1000 g).

To make this book easier to use and more readable, it has to be specific about the amount of greenhouse-gas emissions from different types of food. To make it easier to use the numbers we have highlighted them throughout, like this:

1 g milk = 2 g emissions

However, the actual values will depend on the specific production systems used. For example, in the case of cows' milk it will depend on what the cow is eating and how much milk it produces. In the case of plants it will depend on the soil type (which affects the amount of fertilizer needed) and weather (which affects yield for a given amount of fertilizer).

So there is no single number, only a range of numbers for different suppliers. But we have to start somewhere. My hope is that you will start to demand the exact information from your food suppliers, so that you can make informed choices and buy from the producers who are making advances in reducing their impact on the climate.

How much emissions?

So where are all these greenhouse gases coming from? Fig. 1.1 shows a map of the world showing total greenhouse-gas emissions (not just food-related) for each country. On average, each world citizen causes about 24 kilos of emissions per day, but this varies greatly from one country (and person) to the next. For example, an average US citizen causes over 50 kilos of emissions per day, whereas an average citizen of most African countries causes less than 2 kilos of emission per day.

Fig. 1.1: A map of the world showing the total greenhouse-gas emissions for each country, per person per day. We are extremely grateful to the Our World In Data project for making this figure. You can find the data for this plot on their website. (URL 2)

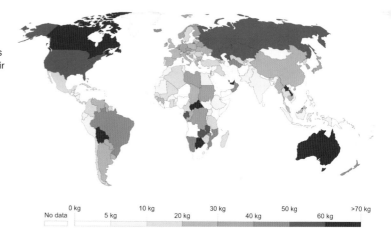

How much do you think food contributes to the total emissions? To work this out we need to add up all the greenhouse-gas emissions from all parts of the food chain. We have to include growing, clearing land, processing, manufacturing, packaging and transportation, as well as cooking the food at home and disposing of any waste. Overall, about a quarter of all global greenhouse-gas emissions come from food (Fig. 1.2). The amount of emissions from food varies from one country to the next, as does the total emissions. Food typically causes about a quarter to one third of the emissions.

The amount of emissions varies greatly depending on which food is being eaten, and on the production method. For example, a steak causes more than 10 times the emissions of a portion of beans. Furthermore, the steak itself can cause 10 times the emissions again if the cow lives for 20 years instead of just 1 year (chapter 24). Fig. 1.3 shows the amount of greenhouse-gas emissions for different food categories, for the amounts of each type of food consumed in the UK. In the rest of this book we

Fig. 1.2: A quarter of all greenhouse-gas emissions come from food.

consider the emissions from producing each of these foods, and investigate some alternatives. But first we need to get a sense of scale.

Box 1.2: Giga/billions tons/tonnes

When we discuss large amounts of CO_2 we use metric tonnes. A metric tonne is 1,000 kg by definition, and an imperial ton is 1,016 kg, so you hardly ever have to worry about the difference – it's less than 2%). One gigatonne (1 Gt) equals one billion tonnes (giga = billion, or one thousand million).

Food emissions in perspective

On average, each person in the world causes 6 kilos of emissions each day because of the food they eat. Just as for total emissions, the emissions from food vary significantly from one country to the next, reaching 13 kilos per person per day in the US (Fig. 1.4), which is 10 times the value for all emissions (including food) in some countries in Africa (Fig. 1.1).

What does 6 kilograms of emissions look like? Most people could pick up something weighing 6 kg, but you probably wouldn't want to carry it around with you all day. Carbon dioxide, methane and nitrous oxide are transparent gases, and so are invisible to our eyes, perhaps making them feel mysterious and hard to imagine. We can visualize the amount of space taken up by 6 kilos of carbon dioxide – it corresponds to the volume of a small car.

Is this a problem? We combine numbers from *IPCC Special Report: Global Warming of 1.5 °C* (IPCC, 2018), chapter 3, to make a crude estimate of the total emissions budget including both CO_2 and non-CO_2 emissions.

1. A CO_2 emissions budget of 420 Gt (i.e. 420 billion tonnes) is given by the latest scientific reports.

2. We subtract 100 Gt to account for Earth system feedbacks, which include melting permafrost and methane emissions from wetlands, that are exacerbated by climate change. Research is ongoing to improve the accuracy of this estimate.

3. We add 320 Gt to allow for non-CO_2 emissions including methane and nitrous oxide. The size of the non-CO_2 budget depends on how much carbon dioxide we emit, and when, because some of the most important non-CO_2 emissions have a much shorter lifetime than CO_2 (especially methane). For

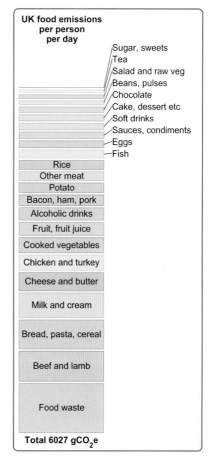

Fig. 1.3: UK average daily greenhouse-gas emissions per person per day from food, showing a breakdown into different types of food.

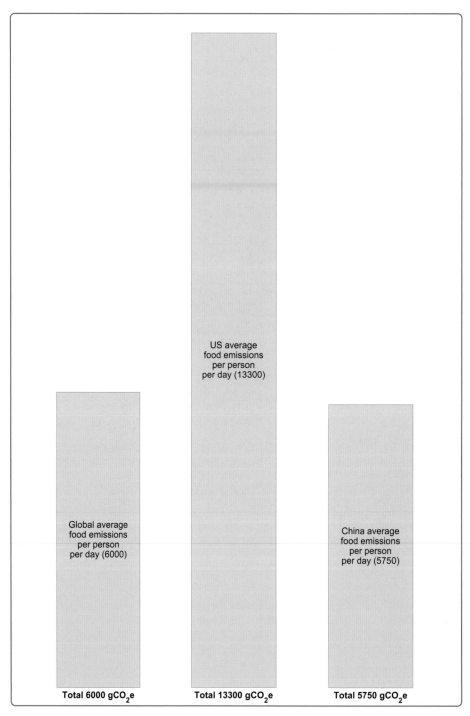

Global average
food emissions
per person
per day (6000)

US average
food emissions
per person
per day (13300)

China average
food emissions
per person
per day (5750)

Total 6000 gCO$_2$e   Total 13300 gCO$_2$e   Total 5750 gCO$_2$e

Fig. 1.4: The total daily greenhouse-gas
emissions from food for the average person for
the world, the US and China.

example, the sooner we reach 1.5°C, the smaller the non-CO_2 budget will be, because over shorter timescales methane has a bigger impact on warming than CO_2.

Adding up these contributions gives 640 GtCO_2e. This might sound like a lot of room for manoeuvre but we will use up the whole 1.5°C budget before 2030 if food continues to make up one quarter of all emissions, even if the average food emissions per year were to remain unchanged and the population didn't rise. Even in the impossible scenario where there are *zero* emissions from everything else, the emissions *from food alone* would exceed this limit in 38 years, i.e. by 2056. (In fact average food emissions per person, total emissions per person, and the world population are all projected to increase – see appendix "Food in the future".)

The world needs to reduce emissions by stopping burning fossil fuels, and switching to using clean energy. But we still have to eat, and food causes greenhouse-gas emissions. So how much is OK? The latest conclusion of world experts is that we can limit global warming to 1.5°C if we can halve all emissions by 2030. Looking beyond 2030, the experts conclude we need to reduce our emissions much more drastically by 2050, by 80% or more.

Throughout this book, we use 3 kg of food emissions (per person per day) as a yardstick, based on halving global average food emissions from changes in which foods we choose to eat. In tandem with this we also need to reduce emissions from the food production process, keep population numbers under control, and ensure that gains arising from spared land are put to work for the purpose of removing greenhouse gases from the atmosphere.

Food emissions yardstick = 3 kg CO_2e per person per day

In short, the answer to the question we asked earlier ("Is this a problem?") is "yes": we need to significantly reduce emissions from food and other activities, especially in countries that are already well above the global average. This book focuses on emissions from food, but to evaluate my post-flight hunch about a vegan jacket potato we need to compare food emissions with those from non-food activities.

Non-food emissions

A single transatlantic round-trip flight causes about 3,000 kilos of emissions per person.

20,000 km as an air passenger = 3,000,000 g emissions

Whether or not this is significant for global warming depends on how often you go, and how typical you are of the world population. If you go once every year, then we can share out the emissions over 365 days to calculate the emissions per day. This works out as about 9 kilos of emissions a day – about 50% more than an average day of food; Figs. 1.5 and 1.6 compare food and non-food emissions.

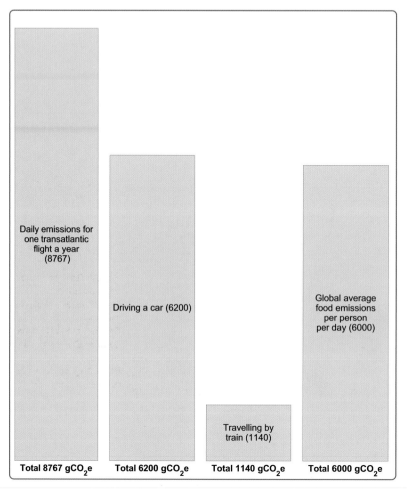

Daily emissions for one transatlantic flight a year (8767)

Driving a car (6200)

Global average food emissions per person per day (6000)

Travelling by train (1140)

Total 8767 gCO$_2$e   **Total 6200 gCO$_2$e**   **Total 1140 gCO$_2$e**   **Total 6000 gCO$_2$e**

Fig. 1.5: Greenhouse-gas emissions showing non-food activities.
Left: A return transatlantic flight (10,000 km [6214 miles]) divided across 365 days (55 km).
Centre left: Driving a car 20 km (12 miles) return (40 km).
Centre right: Travelling by train 20 km (12 miles) return (40 km).
Right: Global average emissions from food per person per day.

Emissions from driving a car depend on the size of the car and whether it burns fossil fuels or uses electricity generated from "clean energy" (carbon-neutral sources including wind and solar). Driving my small fossil-fuelled car for 40 kilometres (24 miles) every day would cause about 6 kilos of emissions a day, which is less than the emissions from one transatlantic flight every year, and similar to the global average daily food emissions.

40 km in a fossil-fuelled car = 6,200 g emissions

How much would it help to travel by train instead? Travelling 40 km by train causes about 1,100 g of emissions, which is

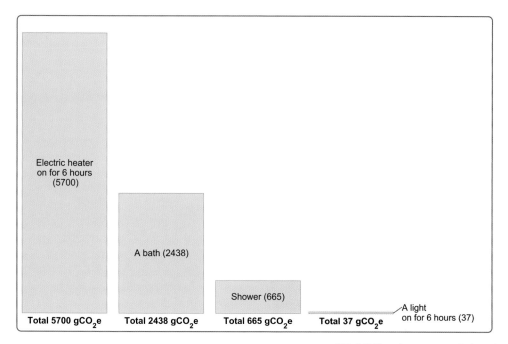

Electric heater
on for 6 hours
(5700)

A bath (2438)

Shower (665)

A light
on for 6 hours (37)

Total 5700 gCO$_2$e   **Total 2438 gCO$_2$e**   **Total 665 gCO$_2$e**   **Total 37 gCO$_2$e**

Fig. 1.6: Greenhouse-gas emissions showing non-food activities.
Left: An electric heater on for 6 hours (360 minutes at 2 kWh).
Centre left: Heating water by 40 ℃ for a bath.
Centre right: Heating water by 40 ℃ for a shower.
Right: A light on for 6 hours, using a 13 W LED bulb (2 minutes at 2 kWh).

about five times better than the value for driving a car the same distance.

40 km by train = 1,100 g emissions

How about emissions from heating or cooking? Again, this all depends on where the energy comes from. Throughout this book we assume a typical global mixture of electricity coming from fossil fuels and from clean energy, of roughly 0.5 kgCO$_2$e / kWh which means that if we put a 2 kW heater (or a 2 kW air conditioner) on for 6 hours a day then it causes about 6 kilos of emissions – similar to the emissions from average food choices.

2 kW of electricity on for 1 minute = 16 g emissions
Depending on your oven, switching it on for two hours causes about 2.5 kilos of emissions (box 12.1).

Recommendations on how to help climate change often include turning off all the lights. It's something we can all do easily, and it feels productive. But how much does it help? Running an old-fashioned (incandescent or halogen 100 W) bulb for 6 hours a day uses 0.6 kWh of electricity and so causes 300 gCO$_2$e, whereas a modern LED bulb (13 W) causes less than 40 gCO$_2$e.

1 LED light on for 6 hours = 40 g emissions
Compared to the heater or the car journey, this is not a big deal. I should lighten up on my light-police duties and focus on the bigger things.

Heating water for an average bath takes about 5 kWh of

energy, which corresponds to about 1.5 kilos of emissions, or for a quick shower the value is around 0.5 kilos of emissions, depending on how long you spend in there, and how much water comes out of your shower head.

1 litre of water warmed by 40°C = 14 g emissions

So we can already start making some informed comments on my jacket-potato-fuelled vegan smugness. I was making more than one transatlantic flight a year, and so this would have been the biggest contributor to my impact on climate change (more than 9 kilos a day). Putting the oven on for two hours caused more than twice the emissions of my trip to the shops, and a lot less than my flight habit. We will find out how the potato, beans, green beans, milk and other individual food emissions add up as we go through the book (chapters 13, 14, 28 and 4).

Key points

- About a quarter of all greenhouse-gas emissions come from food.

- On average each person in the world causes 6 kilos of emissions every day because of the food they eat.

- By 2030 we need to halve our emissions, which would correspond to the average person causing 3 kilos of emissions every day from food.

- One transatlantic round-trip flight every year causes about 9 kilos of emissions per person per day.

- Driving a small family car 40 kilometres (24 miles) causes about 6 kilos of emissions.

- Putting the oven on for two hours causes about 2.5 kilos of emissions.

Notes

Page

1   *What I really needed was detailed figures, so I could make informed decisions that would make a big difference, and that's why I wrote this book – to get clear numbers that I could use, and share with everyone else.* I highly recommend the excellent popular book that discusses the carbon footprints of all sorts of food and non-food emissions by Mike Berners-Lee; *How Bad are Bananas?: The Carbon Footprint of Everything* (Berners-Lee, 2010), and the more recent book by the same author *There Is No Planet B: A Handbook for the Make or Break Years* (Berners-Lee, 2019) which has an extensive discussion of food. For an entertaining and accurate description of the issues I recommend *A Greedy*

Man in a Hungry World: How (almost) everything you thought you knew about food is wrong by Jay Rayner (Rayner, 2013) and for more details on a subset of the foods covered in this book as well as more information about future impacts of climate change, I recommend the well-researched book *Climate-Smart Food* by Dave Reay (Reay, 2019) which is free online. The major feats of political and scientific consensus building from the Intergovernmental Panel on Climate Change (URL 1) are well worth reading. You may also be interested to read the compelling EAT-Lancet report, which summarises the scientific consensus on healthy diets that are good for climate change (Willett, 2019), early influential reports in this area Beddington (2011) and Audsley and Williamson (2010), and a case study based on the UK in P. Allen et al. (2019). The endnotes of this book are full of references to the academic literature, a subset of which is available for free to anyone with an internet connection.

2   *The most important of these for climate change are carbon dioxide, methane and nitrous oxide.* The man-made gases causing the most warming are, in order of impact: carbon dioxide, methane, chlorofluorocarbons / hydrochlorofluorocarbons followed by nitrous oxide. However, because of the restrictions to protect the ozone layer, there is little current injection of chlorofluorocarbons / hydrochlorofluorocarbons so we don't discuss them further (see details in figure 8.6 of Myhre et al. 2013). Water vapour is also an important greenhouse gas, but has its own feedback mechanisms for removal (rain), so I don't discuss it more in this book, except to use the radiative forcing correction for aviation (box 17.4).

2   *When it first enters the atmosphere, 1 gram of methane causes more warming than 80 grams of carbon dioxide, but it only lasts for about 10 years before turning into carbon dioxide, so the total heat-trapping effect is equivalent to about 28 grams of carbon dioxide over a 100-year period.* Averaging over a 20-year period, methane traps more heat than 83 times as much carbon dioxide. However, because methane is destroyed over a 10-year period (and carbon dioxide stays around for more than 100 years) methane is "only" 28 times more potent than carbon dioxide when averaged over 100 years. (Values from table 8.7 of Myhre et al. 2013). These numbers refer to the amount of extra energy trapped under the blanket of the atmosphere ("radiative forcing" in the academic literature), which depends on the amount of each greenhouse gas in the atmosphere, as described in this book. This differs from the amount of global warming for two reasons (i) global warming refers to the mean surface temperature of the Earth, and currently the ocean depths are cooler than the mean surface temperature due to the time it takes for the extra heat to permeate, so some of the extra energy causes deep-sea warming even if emissions are low enough to keep the surface temperature constant (ii) the increased atmospheric temperature causes more heat to be radiated into space. Both of these effects mean that the relationship between the amount of radiative forcing and global (surface temperature) warming depends on both the amount of greenhouse gases in the atmosphere and how these are changing with time. For more details see Cain et al. (2019).

2   *One gram of nitrous oxide causes a similar global warming effect to about 270 grams of carbon dioxide.* The exact value depends on whether feedback is taken into account between the increased temperature causing additional release of the gas in question ("climate-carbon feedback"). Averaging over a 100 year time period nitrous oxide is 265 times more potent than carbon dioxide (for a given weight) if climate-carbon feedbacks are not taken into account (see table 8.7 of Myhre et al. 2013). Taking into account climate-carbon feedbacks this same reference recommends using relative warming effect of 298.

3   *greenhouse-gas emissions from different types of food.* In the main text we talk about grams of emissions, or give the number of grams of emissions for a particular weight of food. In the endnotes we use the same notation as in the scientific literature, so you can more easily find the details in the references given. For example, in the main text we might write "1 g milk = 2 g emissions", and in an endnote we would write that milk causes 2 kgCO$_2$e / kg. We could equally well write that milk causes 2 gCO$_2$e / g, since the grams or kilograms cancel out. Furthermore, in the endnotes we give the exact values from the literature, whereas in the main text these are rounded to avoid giving the impression that these numbers are known to great accuracy – see the discussion about the range of values in the main text.

4   *a map of the world showing total greenhouse-gas emissions (not just food-related) for each country.* This map is the amount of emissions produced in each country (production-based emissions), as opposed to the amount of emissions each country is responsible for (consumption-based emissions). International trade makes these two numbers different, so a country might produce few emissions but be *responsible* for much larger emissions because they import high-emissions products from overseas, thus "exporting" their emissions. For a discussion of the importance of consumption-based emissions accounting see e.g. Larkin et al. (2012). Unfortunately consumption-based emissions values are not available, however you can view consumption-based emissions values for just carbon dioxide here (URL 2).

4   *about a quarter of all global greenhouse-gas emissions come from food* Perhaps surprisingly, this fraction is the about same in countries like the US and China, even though the total amount of emissions is very different in each country. According to Bajželj et al. (2013) (table S19), an average person in the U.S. causes about 65 kilos of emissions each day, whereas an average person in China causes nearly three times less (25 kilos a day), which is similar to the global average of 22 kilos of emissions a day. The exact number depends on how much of the food system is included. For example, Bajželj et al. (2013) (whose results are reproduced in figure 10.1 of Edenhofer et al. 2014) include energy used for cooking, and land clearance for agriculture, as well as emissions on farm and packaging. Springmann, Godfray, et al. (2016) give a value of 1.15 tCO$_2$e per person per year (calculated from their value of 7.6 Gt per year for 2005/7 and a population of 6.6 billion in 2006), which corresponds to 3.2 kg per person per day, i.e. half the value shown in the main text. They use emissions data from Tilman and Clark (2014) which do not include the impacts of land clearance and extend only from "cradle to farm gate" i.e. they do not include transport, processing, packaging or cooking.

4   *the amount of greenhouse-gas emissions for different food categories, for the amounts of each type of food consumed in the UK.* Calculated from the National Diet and Nutrition Survey Year 6 (URL 3) grouping the "FoodCategory" values into broader groupings and matching the "FoodNumber" values with Intake24 (URL 4) greenhouse-gas emissions estimates for each food by the Rowett Institute.

5   *each person in the world causes 6 kilos of emissions each day because of the food they eat.* Dividing the 2.2 tonnes CO$_2$e / person / year from Bajželj et al. (2013) out over 365 days of the year and converting from tonnes to kg gives 6 kg / person / day. Springmann, Godfray, et al. (2016) give a value of 1.15 tCO$_2$e per person per year (calculated from their value of 7.6 Gt per year for 2005/7 and a population of 6.6 billion in 2006), which corresponds to 3.2 kg per person per day, i.e. half the value used in the main text. They

use emissions data from Tilman and Clark (2014) which do not include the impacts of land clearance and extend only from "cradle to farm gate" i.e. they do not include transport, processing, packaging or cooking. Poore and Nemecek (2018) give a value of 13.7 GtCO$_2$e per year for the world in 2010, which converts to a value of 5.4 kgCO$_2$e per person per day. Including food waste adds 2.05 GtCO$_2$e per year for the world in 2010, which brings the total to 6.2 kgCO$_2$e per person per day, in agreement with the number we use in the main text.

5 *the emissions from food vary significantly from one country to the next, reaching 13 kilos per person per day in the US (Fig. 1.4),* See Bajželj et al. (2013).

5 *We can visualize the amount of space taken up by 6 kilos of carbon dioxide – it corresponds to the volume of a small car.* The density of CO$_2$ is 1.98 kg / m^3 at standard temperature and pressure. Therefore 6 kilos of emissions corresponds to 6 kg / (1.98 kg / m^3) = 3 m^3.

5 *A CO$_2$ emissions budget of 420 Gt (i.e. 420 billion tonnes) is given by the latest scientific reports.* See the 67th percentile for 1.5°C warming from table 2.2 of IPCC (2018).

5 *subtract 100 Gt to account for Earth system feedbacks,* From IPCC (2018) - who note that this number has an uncertainty range of about 250 Gt.

7 *Adding up these contributions gives 640 GtCO$_2$e.* This approach is approximate due to a lack of established studies. It would be much better to add up the amount of each greenhouse gas separately and propagate these values into warming, or to calculate separate budgets, as proposed in Rogelj et al. (2019).

7 *we will use up the whole 1.5°C budget before 2030 if food continues to make up one quarter of all emissions, even if the average food emissions per year were to remain unchanged and the population didn't rise.* 6 kg / year / person × 365 days / year × 7.7 billion people / (1000 billion kg / Gt) = 16.8 Gt / year. Sharing out the 640 Gt gives 38 years. 38 years after 2018 is 2056. 38 years × one quarter = 9.5 years. 2018 + 9.5 = 2027.5.

7 *The latest conclusion of world experts is that we can limit global warming to 1.5°C if we can halve all emissions by 2030.* See the table on page 14 of the "Summary for Policy Makers" in IPCC (2018). The line for "Kyoto-GHG emissions in 2030" gives values of -50%, -49% and -35% for scenarios P1, P2 and P3 respectively, and an interquartile range for no/limited overshoot scenarios of -51 to -39%.

7 *Looking beyond 2030, the experts conclude we need to reduce our emissions much more drastically by 2050, by 80% or more.* The table on page 14 of the "Summary for Policy Makers" in IPCC (2018) gives values of -82, -89 and -78 % in 2050 for scenarios P1, P2 and P3 respectively, and an interquartile range for no/limited overshoot scenarios of -93 to -81%.

7 *A single transatlantic round-trip flight causes about 3,000 kilos of emissions per person.* The UK Government greenhouse-gas reporting conversion factors document 2018 (UK Government Department for Business, Energy & Industrial Strategy (DEFRA), 2018) gives 0.16 kgCO$_2$e / passenger / km (i.e. 160 gCO$_2$e / passenger / km) for long-haul flights to/from the UK in economy class (including the radiative forcing factor of 1.9 to account for the higher impact of emissions at altitude, see their paragraph 8.37 – but note that this factor is uncertain). I'm assuming the transatlantic round-trip is 20,000 km, which therefore causes 3,200 kg of emissions, which is rounded to 3,000 kg in the main text. See more discussion of the energy required for transportation in MacKay (2009). Interestingly, the emissions per km are about the same as for driving a car, although note

that short-haul flights will cause more emissions per kilometre than the long-haul flights considered here, because the energy-intensive take off will be a larger fraction of the total energy.

8   *Driving my small fossil-fuelled car for 40 kilometres (24 miles) every day would cause about 6 kilos of emissions a day,* The UK Driver and Vehicle Licensing Agency website (URL 5). says our small family car causes 155 gCO_2e / km.

8   *Travelling 40 km by train causes about 1,100 g of emissions,* We use a value of 6 kWh per 100 person-km from MacKay (2009) for the Japan rail system. For a 40 km trip this corresponds to 2.4 kWh (40 person-km / 100 × 6 kWh per 100 person-km = 2.4 kWh). Converting this into emissions using an electricity conversion factor of 0.475 $kgCO_2e$ / kWh (see next endnote) gives 2.4 kWh × 0.475 $kgCO_2e$ / kWh = 1.14 $kgCO_2e$, which we round to 1.1 kg in the main text.

9   *Throughout this book we assume a typical global mixture of electricity coming from fossil fuels and from clean energy, of roughly 0.5 $kgCO_2e$ / kWh* We use a value for the global energy mix in 2018 from URL 6 of 475 gCO_2e / kWh. We can convert this to gCO_2e per minute if we know the power uptake of our appliance, e.g. 2 kWh corresponds to 15.8 gCO_2e each minute (475 gCO_2e / kWh × 2 kW / 60 minutes/h). This number varies from one country to the next and is decreasing as fossil fuels are replaced by clean energy. The UK electricity mix in 2018 caused 300 gCO_2e / kWh according to the Committee on Climate Change (UK Committee on Climate Change, 2018). For a more detailed discussion of energy from electricity versus chemical heat from fossil fuels see MacKay (2009).

9   *if we put a 2 kW heater (or a 2 kW air conditioner) on for 6 hours a day then it causes about 6 kilos of emissions* 0.475 $kgCO_2e$ / kWh × 2 kW × 6 h = 5.7 $kgCO_2e$.

9   *Depending on your oven, switching it on for two hours causes about 2.5 kilos of emissions (box 12.1).* 15 minutes of warm up time, plus 120 minutes, at an average power of 2.4kW causes 2.4 kW × 135 minutes / (60 minutes / hour) × 0.475 $kgCO_2$ / kWh = 2.56 $kgCO_2e$.

9   *Heating water for an average bath takes about 5 kWh of energy,* See MacKay (2009) for a calculation for a 150 cm × 50 cm × 15 cm depth bath (110 litres), heating the water up by 40°C. Warming 1 litre of water by 40°C causes 4200 Joules / litre / °C × 40°C / 3600000 Joules / kWh × 0.3 $kgCO_2e$ / kWh × 1000 g / kg = 14 gCO_2e. Natural gas causes 190 gCO_2 / kWh if all the energy is captured. For simplicity here we use an inefficiency of 50% in capturing this energy in your bathwater, which gives a conversion factor of 0.3 $kgCO_2$ / kWh, which is the same value as if you had used electricity instead.

10 *for a quick shower the value is around 0.5 kilos of emissions,* We use 30 litres of water, following MacKay (2009), which gives 420 g emissions, which is rounded to 400 in the main text because the exact value depends on your personal circumstances.

Part I: Breakfast

What did you have for breakfast today? A snatched cup of coffee or tea on your way out the door, or a leisurely piece of toast with a boiled egg? Or maybe a quick bowl of cereal?

Where do these foods come from, and why do they contribute to climate change? And are there more climate-friendly alternatives?

Chapter 2 Tea and coffee

Good morning! How about heating some water for a cup of tea or coffee, and maybe stretching out or checking the weather while you wait for the water to boil?

Tea

As you drop the teabag into your cup, think about its journey from tea plants far away, and the hard-working people picking out the top shoots of the tea plant, like in the advertisements.

The good news is that transporting a teaspoon (2 grams) of tea half way across the world by boat causes very little greenhouse-gas emissions compared to most other things you're likely to eat today (we cover transport emissions in chapter 17, but don't worry about that for now).

What about boiling the water? Burning natural gas to heat a pan, or using electricity generated from burning coal or natural gas, unlocks carbon dioxide taken up by plants millions of years ago, and releases it back into the atmosphere, which causes global warming.

Fig. 2.2 shows the amount of greenhouse-gas emissions caused by making one cup of black tea assuming that, like many people, you boil twice as much water as you really need.

Boiling the water causes more emissions than the teabag itself, but even so the total is still small compared to our reference value of 3 kg per day per person (chapter 1).

$$1 \text{ g teabag} = 3 \text{ g emissions}$$

Fig. 2.1: What's the climate impact of your mug of tea? (URL 7)

Fig. 2.2: Emissions for a cup of black tea: a teabag (2 g); boiling half a litre of water (1.5 minutes at 2 kWh).

Coffee

Do you prefer coffee? Coffee is made from the seeds of the coffea plant, which are often referred to as "beans". To grow well, the coffea plants are tended, watered and fertilized (box 2.1). The coffee cherry fruits take most of a year to ripen, and then the seeds have to be extracted from the fruit (Fig. 2.3), then roasted and ground.

Fig. 2.3: A squashed coffee cherry alongside the seed that came out of it. This seed is dried and becomes the coffee "bean". (URL 8)

Box 2.1: Fertilizer emissions

Most nitrogen fertilizer is made from the nitrogen freely available in the air we breathe, so how can it contribute to global warming? Firstly, to produce the fertilizer, nitrogen from the air has to be heated to about 500°C and compressed to a pressure that would crush even a submarine. This takes a lot of energy – usually produced by burning fossil fuels.

The most common fertilizer is ammonium nitrate, a white crystalline powder that looks like salt or sugar. This ammonium nitrate is spread over the soil and much of it is absorbed by the roots of the plants.

Furthermore, about one percent of the applied nitrogen is absorbed by microbes in the soil and turned into nitrous oxide. Nitrous oxide is an extremely potent greenhouse gas (see chapter 1), and so even this tiny amount produces about as much global warming as the fossil fuels used to produce the fertilizer.

For dried coffee, the emissions from the fertilizer cause about one third of the total emissions; processing the bean from plant to cup and packaging contribute most of the remainder.

1 g instant coffee powder = 17 g emissions

For a typical cup of coffee, the instant coffee emissions are similar to those from boiling the water. Even so, the amount of emissions from a single cup (Fig. 2.4), are small compared to our reference value of 3 kg per day per person.

A cup of black coffee
Boiling water (24)
Coffee (33)
Total 57 gCO$_2$e

Fig. 2.4: Emissions for a cup of black coffee: a teaspoon of instant coffee (2 g); boiling half a litre of water (1.5 minutes at 2 kWh).

Take-out drinks

Coffee shops have conveniently sprung up on street corners all over the world, helping us get a quick fix of caffeine on the go. They provide a new social space and often a comfy place to access the internet. However, many of these drinks are taken away in disposable cups. This generates waste that often goes to landfill, but how bad is the cardboard for climate change?

Cardboard is made by processing wood from trees, which remove carbon dioxide from the atmosphere and turn it into wood. So if we're planting extra trees especially to supply the cardboard factory, we are actively removing greenhouse gases from the air. That sounds like good news for the climate, but it depends on two crucial questions: (i) is the cardboard from trees that were planted especially for the purpose, or is its production driving deforestation and (ii) how is the cardboard disposed of at the end of its life?

- If the cardboard is composted with good access to oxygen, it decomposes back into carbon dioxide, thus returns to the air the greenhouse gases absorbed by the tree. In this case the emissions are just those from generating the energy to process the wood into cardboard, which is roughly equal to the weight of the cardboard.

  1 g cardboard, composted = 1 g emissions

- However, if the cardboard is sent to landfill, it is likely to rot into methane, so the total emissions are larger, rising to twice the weight of the cardboard.

  1 g cardboard, landfilled = 2 g emissions

In practice, most disposable coffee cups are lined with a thin layer of plastic, and so need specialist recycling facilities that aren't widely available. Therefore they mostly end up in landfill and rot into methane. The cup emissions are then about the same as those from boiling the water (Fig. 2.5), but still cause lower emissions than their contents.

While it's true that lots of small contributions can add up to a big contribution, we'll see later on there are bigger things to focus on first. So it turns out I'm not making a significant dent in my daily food emissions by whipping out my reusable cup at the coffee shop, especially if I take milk (discussed shortly).

A cup of black coffee in a cardboard cup
Cardboard cup (20)
Boiling water (24)
Coffee (33)
Total 76 gCO$_2$e

Fig. 2.5: Emissions for a cup of black coffee in a cardboard cup: a teaspoon of instant coffee (2 g); boiling half a litre of water (1.5 minutes at 2 kWh); a cardboard cup (10 g).

Key points

- Teabags contribute less to global warming than boiling the water to make the tea.

- Coffee causes more greenhouse-gas emissions than tea because of the fertilizer needed to produce a good crop of coffee cherry fruits and the greater energy needed for processing.

- The greenhouse-gas emissions from making one cup of black tea or coffee are smaller than most other things you're likely to eat today.

Notes

Page

18   *the teabag* Tea causes a total of 12.08 kgCO$_2$e / kg of dry tea, according to Azapagic et al. (2016), which includes 9.20 kgCO$_2$e / kg dry tea from

boiling the water. Since we account for the water heating separately, the value we use here is the difference between these two numbers, i.e. 2.88 kgCO$_2$e / kg dry tea, which covers the raw materials, production, storage and transport, of which packaging is the largest contributor (1.46 kgCO$_2$e / kg dry tea), followed by transport and then production (for which nitrogen fertilizer is the largest contributor). See also Doublet and Jungbluth (2010). and Cichorowski et al. (2015).

19 *the emissions from the fertilizer cause about one third of the total emissions; processing the bean from plant to cup and packaging contribute most of the remainder.* Using 33 grams of emissions per cup of coffee from Humbert et al. (2009) (using their value for spray-dried coffee, and ignoring use phase emissions as these are added separately here), and taking into account that 2 grams of spray-dried coffee is used per cup, gives 17 kgCO$_2$e / kg instant coffee granules. You can read about filtered and capsule coffee in Humbert et al. (2009), which cause higher emissions because they use more coffee beans. 7 grams out of 33 grams of CO$_2$e are caused by cultivation, which is dominated by fertilizer use.

19 *is the cardboard from trees that were planted especially for the purpose, or is its production driving deforestation* The numbers for cardboard emissions assume the trees have been especially planted to produce cardboard, otherwise they would be higher.

20 *If the cardboard is composted with good access to oxygen, it decomposes back into carbon dioxide, thus returns to the air the greenhouse gases absorbed by the tree. In this case the emissions are just those from generating the energy to process the wood into cardboard, which is roughly equal to the weight of the cardboard.* Eriksson et al. (2010) give a value of 0.964 kgCO$_2$e / kg for production and transport of cartons (their table 1). See also the UK Government conversion factors 2019 (UK Government Department for Business, Energy & Industrial Strategy (DEFRA), 2019) which gives a similar value of 0.84 kgCO$_2$e / kg for "Paper and board: board" (842.58 kgCO$_2$e / tonne) for primary material-production plus an additional 0.01 kgCO$_2$e / kg for composting (10.02 kgCO$_2$e / tonne), bringing their total to 0.85 kgCO$_2$e.

20 *if the cardboard is sent to landfill, it is likely to rot into methane, so the total emissions are larger, rising to twice the weight of the cardboard.* In addition to the primary material production emissions, the landfill adds a further 1.0 kgCO$_2$e / kg (1041 kgCO$_2$e / tonne) according to the UK Government conversion factors 2019 (UK Government Department for Business, Energy & Industrial Strategy (DEFRA), 2019), bringing the total to 1.964 kgCO$_2$e / kg cardboard sent to landfill (though note this number depends heavily on the management of the landfill site e.g. see the detailed discussion in Arnold and Yang (2005)). A final (unlikely) disposal option would be to hoard the cardboard at home for decades or, much better, turn the cardboard into something useful, like building materials. This helps to reduce climate change by removing carbon dioxide from the atmosphere for the period of time until it is finally composted. Ultimately it might be disposed of carefully and turned into compost, but in the intervening decades some global cooling would have happened because there was less carbon dioxide in the atmosphere.

20 *cup emissions are then about the same as those from boiling the water* For a cardboard cup weighing 10 grams, we need to multiply the cup weight by the emissions factor of 2 referenced in chapter 2 for cardboard to landfill, which gives 20 gCO$_2$e per cup. See also the detailed discussion of this topic in Harst and Potting (2013), including their figure 2 which compares a range of cup materials and recycling options which span a range from less than 10 gCO$_2$e per cup to 100 gCO$_2$e per cup. There is a nice analysis

in CarbonClear (2012) who compare ceramic (re-usable) cups with paper and polystyrene disposable cups, concluding that if the re-usable cups are used 1000 times then they are better than the disposable paper cups (though note this depends on the amount of hot water used to wash the cups). See also Almeida et al. (2018) and Martin et al. (2018).

Chapter 3 Sugar

Do you take sugar? Most sugar comes from either sugar beet or sugar cane. Either way, sweet juice is extracted from the plant and heated up to concentrate the sugar.

Sugar beet is a small leafy plant with a fat root like a carrot or beetroot (Fig. 3.1). It originated in Europe and grows well in temperate climates. After crushing the root to extract its sugary juices, the water has to be evaporated off to leave the sugar crystals behind; it is this heating that causes most of the greenhouse-gas emissions at the farm.

Sugar cane, by contrast, only grows well in warmer climates, producing a more concentrated sugary liquid in its long stems (Fig. 3.2). Because the juice is more sugary in the first place, it takes less energy to evaporate off the water to turn it into sugar. On the other hand, the sugar has to be transported a longer distance to reach people living in cooler countries. In addition, sugar cane tends to be grown in countries that are expanding their food production by cutting down forests (chapter 7).

Overall the emissions are higher for sugar cane than sugar beet, but for the kind of quantity you're likely to put in your tea, it isn't a big deal either way (Fig. 3.3).

1 g sugar = 3 g emissions

We'll add milk in the next chapter.

Fig. 3.1: A sugar beet plant in a field. You can see the fat root which is crushed to extract its sweet juice. (URL 9)

Fig. 3.2: Some cut sugar canes. If you look closely you can just see white dots on the cut stalk where sugar crystals are starting to form from the leaking sugary sap. (URL 10)

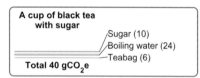

A cup of black tea with sugar
Sugar (10)
Boiling water (24)
Teabag (6)
Total 40 gCO$_2$e

Fig. 3.3: Emissions for a cup of black tea with sugar: a teabag (2 g); boiling half a litre of water (1.5 minutes at 2 kWh); a teaspoon of sugar (4 g).

Key points

- Sugar can be made from either sugar beet or sugar cane.

- The main ways sugar contributes to global warming are (i) heating the sugary juices to crystallize the sugar (ii) transporting the sugar across the world (iii) deforestation to clear land for growing sugar cane.

- Given the kinds of quantities you're likely to be eating, sugar isn't a major contributor to emissions.

Notes

Page

23 *it is this heating that causes most of the greenhouse-gas emissions at the farm.* See Klenk et al. (2012).

23 *it takes less energy to evaporate off the water to turn it into sugar.* However, innovative farmers can reduce these fossil fuel emissions further by capturing the energy made by burning the leftovers from extracting the sugar from the crop.

23 *Overall the emissions are higher for sugar cane than sugar beet, but for the kind of quantity you're likely to put in your tea, it isn't a big deal either way* The average of the global value for sugar cane (3.2 kgCO_2e / kg) and sugar beet (1.8 kgCO_2e / kg) from Poore and Nemecek (2018) gives 2.5 kgCO_2e / kg, used for the figures in this book. See also lower values e.g. 0.32 kgCO_2e / kg in Seabra et al. (2011) and 0.38 kgCO_2e / kg in URL 11. The range in values reflects the different assumptions about transportation, and on whether deforestation has occurred to grow the crop, and whether or not energy is captured from burning the co-products (leftovers from crushing the cane or beet), thus reducing fossil fuel emissions.

Chapter 4 Milk

Most people in the UK drink their tea with milk, typically adding just over one tablespoon (20 ml) to each cup. Consumed in various ways, cows' milk is a major source of nutrients in many countries.

Are you concerned about all the plastic milk cartons? In fact, when it comes to greenhouse-gas emissions, the plastic isn't a big deal compared to the milk itself. Even if we bought all our milk in small plastic bottles, the emissions from producing the plastic would be dwarfed by emissions from the cows themselves.

Fig. 4.1: A glass of milk a day? (URL 12)

Fig. 4.2: A Friesian cow grazing happily. (URL 13)

Rumination

Fig. 4.2 shows a beautiful scene of a cow in a field, munching contentedly on grass. You can almost hear the snuffling, ripping sound as the cow chomps. I'm transported back to childhood walks through the fields near our house, lifting my feet up through the long grass and dodging cow poo.

How do cows contribute to climate change? Tabloid newspaper headlines warn about methane from cow farts, but in fact most methane comes out of their mouths as burps. About one twentieth of all the calories eaten by a cow comes back out of their mouths as methane, a potent greenhouse gas (chapter 1; Fig. 4.3).

Cows have evolved a complicated stomach (Fig. 4.4) to help them digest the most common plant on the planet, grass. Their stomachs have four compartments, the first and biggest of which is called the "rumen". This is home to bacteria which produce methane, in a process called "enteric fermentation". Animals that digest food in this way, including sheep, goats, deer, moose and giraffes, are called "ruminants".

Most animals produce much less methane than ruminants. Horses, rabbits, elephants and other "hindgut fermenters" digest grass differently – in a chamber that comes after the small intestine (although rabbits do eat their own poo in an effort to

5% of calories → methane

Fig. 4.3: About 5% of the calories eaten by a cow are burped out of their mouths as methane, a powerful greenhouse gas. (Adapted from URL 14).

Fig. 4.4: A cow's stomach. (URL 15)

A cup of tea
with milk and sugar
Plastic milk carton (2)
Milk (44)
Sugar (10)
Boiling water (24)
Teabag (6)
Total 85 gCO$_2$e

Fig. 4.5: Emissions for a cup of tea with milk and sugar: a teabag (2 g); boiling half a litre of water (1.5 minutes at 2 kWh); a teaspoon of sugar (4 g); a large tablespoon of milk (20 g); a one litre plastic milk carton weighing 53 g, shared between 50 cups of tea (1 g).

extract even more grassy goodness).

Exactly how much methane are we talking about? A typical dairy cow eats over 70,000 kCal a day – about the same intake as 30 humans (although a cow weighs less than 10 humans). To be fair, the cow is churning out milk at an average rate of 16 litres a day, but at the same time it's burping out over 7 kilos of emissions each day. (But please don't try this at home!)

We can already estimate the emissions from milk by sharing out the 7 kilos of emissions across the 16 litres of milk produced. A more accurate calculation takes into account the methane burped by the cow during the two years before it reached milk-bearing age. Since cows are then slaughtered for beef at around the age of 4, then this roughly doubles the milk emissions, although the emissions can then be shared out between the milk and the beef.

In addition to the cow burps, we have to add in the impact from cow poo. Depending on how it's stored and distributed on the fields as fertilizer, cow manure produces both methane and nitrous oxide and adds about 50% to the total milk emissions. (Cow pats in fields produce less methane than cow slurry stored in a building, because the oxygen in the air allows the cow pats to rot down into carbon dioxide instead of methane. So maybe I shouldn't have been complaining about all the cow poo in the fields on my childhood country walks.)

1 g milk = 2 g emissions

Overall, cows' milk causes about twice its own weight in greenhouse-gas emissions, but this number can vary by more than 50% depending on how the cows are raised. For example, if the cows produce less milk each day then the emissions will be higher.

Milk in tea and coffee

We can now add up the total emissions caused by a cup of tea with milk: we find that half of the emissions come from the milk (Fig. 4.5). For white coffee, the emissions from a splash of milk (20 ml) are slightly more than those from a teaspoon of coffee granules (Fig. 4.6, left). However we can be reassured that our morning brew is still a small fraction of the 3,000 g discussed in chapter 1, assuming we're being reasonably careful with the milk and water.

However, if you're drinking ten cups a day, and being a bit generous with the milk or leaving a lot of water in the kettle, you might want to think more carefully, not least due to the amount of caffeine! (Ten cups of white tea causes over 25% of the reference 3 kg daily food emissions.) However, you can bring the emissions from your drink of choice to relatively insignificant levels by only boiling the water you need, and switching to black tea (Fig. 4.6, centre).

How about a latte or a cappuccino? Popular coffee shops serve half-litre cups of latte, made from a shot of espresso topped up with milk. The emissions from making a latte are more than ten times those from a regular cup of coffee, almost entirely because of the large amount of milk (Fig. 4.6, right). The milk emissions alone are more than 1 kilo, and the total latte emissions are use up nearly half of the 3 kilo food emissions budget for a whole day of food, as discussed in chapter 1.

How can you reduce emissions?

How could milk emissions be reduced? Plant-based milk alternatives have become popular: soya, almond, coconut, rice, oat, cashew, macadamia, hemp... light, no added sugar, organic, fresh, long-life... the range is overwhelming. (We discuss almond milk in more detail in chapter 19.) But, as usual for plants, the emissions mostly depend on the amount of nitrogen fertilizer applied to the growing plant, on the amount of fossil fuels used in processing, and on the transport, packaging and refrigeration. These latter stages are usually as important as the choice of plant. Overall the emissions from producing plant-based milks are usually found to be less than half of those from dairy milk.

1 g plant milk = 0.8 g emissions

The amount of methane produced by a cow is halved if the cow eats higher-quality feed, more like that given to pigs or chickens (mostly wheat and soy) instead of grass (page 25), however the production of soy is currently driving deforestation which tends to cancel out this benefit (chapter 7). There is research into reducing methane emissions from cows by adding special ingredients to their feed and genetically modifying their gut microbes, as well as breeding better cows. One feed additive has been shown to reduce methane emissions by 30% if it is given to the cow regularly. Putting these developments together with improvements in manure handling could potentially halve the climate impact of milk and beef.

In chapter 9, we discuss the feasibility of milking animals other than cows. Alternatively, new products are coming out which use milk proteins produced in a laboratory, using genetically modified cousins of yeast.

Key points

- Cows' milk contributes to climate change mainly because of the cow's emissions.

- Cows burp about 5% of their calories back out into the air as methane, a powerful greenhouse gas.

- Adding a generous tablespoon (20 ml) of milk to your tea or coffee causes more emissions than boiling the water or producing the tea or coffee itself.

- The large amount of milk in a latte pushes the emissions to nearly half a daily food emissions budget of 3 kilos.

- Plant milks cause less than half the emissions of dairy milk.

Fig. 4.6:
Left: Emissions for a cup of coffee with milk and sugar: a teaspoon of instant coffee (2 g); boiling half a litre of water (1.5 minutes at 2 kWh); a teaspoon of sugar (4 g); a large tablespoon of milk (20 g); a one litre plastic milk carton weighing 53 g, shared between 50 cups of coffee (1 g).
Centre: Emissions for a cup of black tea boiling minimal water: teabag (2 g); boiling the right amount (200 ml) of water (0.6 minutes at 2 kWh).
Right: Emissions for a latte: coffee (we assume 4 g of instant coffee for this calculation but the result would be slightly higher if using non-instant, see Humbert et al. (2009)); heating the milk (2.5 minutes at 2 kWh); a teaspoon of sugar (4 g); milk (500 g); a one litre plastic milk carton weighing 53 g, shared between 50 cups of coffee (13 g); cardboard cup (10 g).

Notes

Page

25   *typically adding just over one tablespoon (20 ml) to each cup.* Analyzing the data from the UK National Diet and Nutrition Survey years 5 and 6 (Hemmings, 2016), there is a peak in consumed milk quantity at around 20 grams. I'm guessing this is people putting milk in their tea and coffee. One tablespoon of milk is about 15 grams, so people are using just over one tablespoon of milk in each cup of tea.

25   *Even if we bought all our milk in small plastic bottles, the emissions from producing the plastic would be dwarfed by emissions from the cows themselves.* My plastic carton from a small (1 pint) bottle of milk weighed 20 grams. Using the emissions factor for plastic (box 21.1) of 3.0 kgCO$_2$e / kg plastic, this means 60 grams of CO$_2$e per plastic bottle. The milk is responsible for about 2.2 kgCO$_2$e / kg, therefore about 1,100 gCO$_2$e for 1 pint (~500 g) of milk. The plastic from the bottle is therefore 5% of the emissions. The emissions will be smaller (per pint of milk) if you buy bigger bottles and the packaging becomes even less significant.

25   *About one twentieth of all the calories eaten by a cow comes back out of their mouths as methane, a potent greenhouse gas* This varies with the diet of the cow, from 6.5% for grass-fed to 3% for a more digestible diet e.g. grains and soy (Dong et al., 2017).

26 *A typical dairy cow eats over 70,000 kCal a day* Calculated using the methodology of Dong et al. (2017) using a milk rate of 6,000 litres / year (see their table 10.11; see also 5,380 in O'Brien et al. (2014)) as an input to their equation 10.16, and assuming grass-fed cows to determine the feed digestibility.

26 *but at the same time it's burping out over 7 kilos of emissions each day.* Calculate the number of kCal of methane by multiplying 70,000 kCal by 0.05 to account for the 5% of calories turned into methane. Then we divide by the energy density of methane (13,000 kCal / kg) to turn this into the weight of methane produced by the cow each day (0.26 kg). Since a given weight of methane causes a lot more warming than the same weight of carbon dioxide, we need to multiply by the global-warming potential of methane (chapter 1) of 28 to get the weight of emissions (7.4 kg). We can then convert this into a number of balloons following the method in chapter 1 (292 balloons).

26 *the emissions can then be shared out between the milk and the beef.* This type of allocation is discussed more in box 9.1. See O'Brien et al. (2014) for more allocation details specific to milk.

26 *Overall, cows' milk causes about twice its own weight in greenhouse-gas emissions, but this number can vary by more than 50% depending on how the cows are raised.* Poore and Nemecek (2018) find a value of 2.2 kgCO$_2$e / kg milk for Europe, which is used for the figures in this book. Note that this is lower than the global average (3.2 kgCO$_2$e / kg milk) and slightly lower than the value for the US (2.5 kgCO$_2$e / kg).

27 *on the amount of fossil fuels used in processing, and on the transport, packaging and refrigeration. These latter stages are usually as important as the choice of plant.* For Oatly, the farm stage makes up about half of the plant milk emissions, with the rest coming from processing, transport and packaging (URL 16).

27 *the emissions from producing plant-based milks are usually found to be less than half of those from dairy milk.* Values are given by Poore and Nemecek (2018) for milk alternatives made from soy (1.0 kgCO$_2$e / kg), almond (0.7 kgCO$_2$e / kg), oat (0.8 kgCO$_2$e / kg) and rice (1.2 kgCO$_2$e / kg). See also much earlier studies especially "Tesco Product Carbon Footprint Summary" (2012, accessed 2018). However, these should be superseded by reliable (ideally independent) estimates produced for individual companies. Oatly gives a value of 0.44 kgCO$_2$e / kg on their website (URL 16). For the calculation in chapter 6 we use a value of 0.8 kgCO$_2$e / kg. Note that all these values already include packaging.

27 *reducing methane emissions from cows by adding special ingredients to their feed and genetically modifying their gut microbes, as well as breeding better cows. One feed additive has been shown to reduce methane emissions by 30% if it is given to the cow regularly. Putting these developments together with improvements in manure handling could potentially halve the climate impact of milk and beef.* The 3NOP feed additive (Hristov et al., 2015) blocks the final step of methane production and was found to reduce emissions by 30%. See academic reviews on the topic of reducing cow emissions Grossi et al. (2018) and Haque (2018) or this more accessible overview of the research by the BBC: URL 17.

27 *Alternatively, new products are coming out which use milk proteins produced in a laboratory, using genetically modified cousins of yeast.* For example from the company Perfect Day (URL 18).

Chapter 5 Bread and toast

Fig. 5.1:
Upper: Marmite on toast. Love it or hate it? (URL 19)
Upper middle: Making bread in an orphanage in Tanzania. (URL 20)
Lower middle: A close-up of a head of wheat. (URL 21)
Lower: Rolls fresh from the oven. (URL 22)

Hot buttered toast is a comforting meal on its own, and even better with a simple spread on top. My favourite is Marmite (yeast extract) on toast, served with the butter just starting to melt (Fig. 5.1, upper).

We only really need four ingredients to make bread: flour, water, salt and yeast. Squash them together until the dough becomes smooth and stretchy (Fig. 5.1, upper middle). Leave the dough to rise, i.e. give the yeast time to produce bubbles of carbon dioxide, making the bread lighter and softer. Then bake it in the oven.

So how does bread contribute to climate change? To produce the flour needed for two slices (80 g) of bread, a farmer needs to grow about 20 wheat plants in an area of land about the size of a large dinner plate. So if I eat two slices of bread a day, there is an area about half the size of a small classroom permanently in cultivation to keep me in bread.

Fertilizer is spread on the wheat fields to make sure they yield big, protein-rich grains (Fig. 5.1, lower middle), and about one teaspoon of fertilizer is used to grow the flour for two slices of bread (box 2.1).

$$1 \text{ g flour} = 0.8 \text{ g emissions}$$

Overall, bread causes roughly its own weight in emissions, the biggest single component of which comes from producing and applying fertilizer.

$$1 \text{ g bread} = 0.8 \text{ g emissions}$$

They say you should bake bread when prospective purchasers view your house, because the smell makes people want to buy (it worked the one time I tried it!). Perhaps it's the ultimate sign of domestic bliss, that you have the time and energy to bake a loaf. However, if you put your oven on while the bread proves for one hour, and only use it to bake a single loaf, then you more than triple the emissions of your bread ingredients.

Luckily, most bread is baked in factories (Fig. 5.1, lower), which are about 3 times more efficient as baking one loaf at a time, so the baking only contributes about one fifth of the total bread emissions. People often ask about the emissions from the plastic bag the bread arrives in, but it turns out the plastic bread bag emissions are tiny compared to the other ingredients.

Box 5.1: Shocking statistics: country-sized emissions

In this book we consider emissions per person per day, because that relates directly to the decisions we make every day as individuals. However, some people quote values for a whole country for a whole year, which easily gives a number that sounds shocking.

If everyone in the UK eats two slices of bread every day, the total annual country emissions in tonnes

$$= \text{daily emissions per person in grams} \times$$
$$\text{population} \times \text{number of days in a year}$$
$$\div \text{number of grams in one tonne}$$
$$= 80 \times 66,000,000 \times 365 \div 1,000,000$$
$$\sim 2,000,000.$$

So UK bread is responsible for about two million tonnes of emissions a year, which makes it sound really bad! As well as considering numbers per person per day, it's also helpful to compare with other numbers to work out whether or not we should really feel shocked.

Let's compare the 60 g of emissions for two slices of bread with those for other daily food items and activities. For example, drinking one glass of milk (250 ml) causes nearly 10 times the emissions of the two slices of bread (chapter 4), as does driving a car 4 kilometres (2.5 miles) (chapter 1).

Do you like your bread toasted? One newspaper claims that 3.6 minutes is the perfect toasting time. The required electricity produces about as much global warming as producing the bread (Fig. 5.3).

But who eats dry toast on its own? Making butter results in similar greenhouse-gas emissions to cheese (chapter 9). The milk is concentrated down, raising the emissions by about four times, to around 8 times its own weight in emissions.

1 g butter = 8 g emissions

With one teaspoon (5 g) of butter per slice of toast, you've nearly doubled the carbon footprint of your toast. By contrast, vegetable spread causes about five times lower emissions than butter, so switching to a vegetable spread is the easiest way to reduce emissions (compare Fig. 5.4 left and centre), and is more

Fig. 5.2: Two slices of toast in a toaster. (URL 23)

Fig. 5.3: Emissions for two slices of toast: two slices of bread (80 g); toasting the bread (3.6 minutes at 2 kWh).

important than foregoing the toasting.

1 g vegetable spread = 1.5 g emissions

How about some jam or jelly on that? The emissions depend on whether you're trying to emulate TV chef Mary Berry by making your own, perhaps bubbling up a cauldron on the hob while sweating from the wasted heat (I've been there!). Just as for baking bread, industrially produced jam is more efficient. But unless you like it very thickly spread, the jam emissions are less than those from producing the bread.

1 g jam = 3 g emissions

Perhaps Paddington Bear wasn't as decadent as we thought!

You can more than halve your jam on toast emissions by replacing butter with vegetable spread and foregoing the toasting, or using a clean energy source to run the toaster (Fig. 5.4).

Fig. 5.4:
Left: Emissions for two slices of toast with butter and jam: two slices of bread (80 g); toasting the bread (3.6 minutes at 2 kWh); two teaspoons of butter (10 g); two teaspoons of jam (10 g).
Centre: Emissions for two slices of toast with spread and jam: two slices of bread (80 g); toasting the bread (3.6 minutes at 2 kWh); two teaspoons of vegetable spread (10 g); two teaspoons of jam (10 g).
Right: Emissions for two slices of bread with spread and jam: two slices of bread (80 g); two teaspoons of butter (10 g); two teaspoons of jam (10 g).

Key points

- For a piece of toast with jam, about 40% of the climate-impact comes from the hidden melted ingredient: butter.

- Switching from toast to bread (and butter to vegetable spread) can reduce emissions further, bringing the total emissions down to less than half of the original buttery toast.

Notes

Page

30 *To produce the flour needed for two slices (80 g) of bread, a farmer needs to grow about 20 wheat plants in an area of land about the size of a large dinner plate.* Goucher et al. (2017) state 0.000072 hectares per loaf, which converts to 720 cm^2 for two slices of bread, which corresponds to a circle of diameter 30 cm. This corresponds to 22 wheat plants, assuming a planting density of 300 plants per square metre (which is the middle of the range considered in Li et al. (2016)).

30 *two slices of bread a day, there is an area about half the size of a small classroom permanently in cultivation to keep me in bread.* For an annual harvest we need 720 cm^2 × 365 days / 10000 m^2 / cm^2 = 26 m^2, which corresponds to a square room 5 metres by 5 metres.

30 *flour* Goucher et al. (2017) calculate 0.42 kgCO$_2$e for 0.52 kg of flour (see their figures S5 and S2 respectively), which corresponds to 0.8 kgCO$_2$e / kg flour.

30 *bread causes roughly its own weight in emissions, the biggest single component of which comes from producing and applying fertilizer.* The value used for the figures is 0.75 kgCO$_2$e / kg bread which comes from Goucher et al. (2017) who find 0.6 kgCO$_2$e for an 800 g loaf. This means that two slices (80 g) of bread cause about 60 g of emissions. According to this study, about half of the emissions are caused by producing and applying the fertilizer; the next largest component is baking the bread, which causes about 30% of the emissions. See also Espinoza-Orias et al. (2011) who find 0.97 kgCO$_2$e / kg bread.

30 *if you put your oven on while the bread proves for one hour, and only use it to bake a single loaf, then you more than triple the emissions of your bread ingredients.* In this case the oven would be on for 90 minutes. Using the value in chapter 12.1 this causes 1700 grams of emissions for an 800 gram loaf, so adds 2.1 kgCO$_2$e / kg bread. The emissions from just the ingredients are 80% of 0.75 kgCO$_2$e / kg based on Goucher et al. (2017) i.e. 0.6 kgCO$_2$e / kg. Putting these together means that the home-baked loaf causes 2.7 kgCO$_2$e / kg, which is 3.6 times the emissions of the the mass-produced loaf.

31 *the baking only contributes about one fifth of the total bread emissions.* See Goucher et al. (2017).

31 *the plastic bread bag emissions are tiny compared to the other ingredients.* I weighed a plastic bread bag and it was about 5 grams, which causes 15 grams of greenhouse-gas emissions (gCO$_2$e) (see box 21.1), assuming there is no recycling. Remember that there is one bag for a whole loaf, so per slice the emissions are less than 1 gram from the plastic, which is tiny compared to the fertilizer and baking.

31 *In this book we consider emissions per person per day, because that relates directly to the decisions we make every day as individuals.* This follows the popular approach taken in MacKay (2009) in the context of energy use.

31 *One newspaper claims that 3.6 minutes is the perfect toasting time.* The UK's *Daily Mail* says the perfect toast takes 3.6 minutes (URL 24).

31 *The required electricity produces about as much global warming as producing the bread (Fig. 5.3).* Assuming the toaster draws 2 kW, the toasting time of 3.6 minutes corresponds to 0.12 kWh, which is about 55 g of emissions using 0.3 kgCO$_2$e / kWh (chapter 1).

31 *Making butter results in similar greenhouse-gas emissions to cheese (chapter 9). The milk is concentrated down, raising the emissions by about four times, to around 8 times its own weight in emissions.* The value of 8.3 kgCO$_2$e / kg is an average of values from Vergé et al. (2013) (7.3 kgCO$_2$e / kg), Sheane et al. (2011) (8.9 kgCO$_2$e / kg), Nilsson et al. (2010) (4.8/0.5 kgCO$_2$e / kg for UK butter) and Finnegan et al. (2018) (9.7 kgCO$_2$e / kg).

31 *vegetable spread* The value of 1.4 kgCO$_2$e / kg for vegetable spread (margarine) is an average of the values for the UK (1.1 kgCO$_2$e / kg), Denmark (1.32 kgCO$_2$e / kg) and France (1.66 kgCO$_2$e / kg) from Nilsson et al. (2010).

32 *the jam emissions are less than those from producing the bread.* The emissions value is 3.2 kgCO$_2$e / kg from "The greenhouse gas footprint of Booths" (2012) for jam, marmalade and honey.

Chapter 6 A bowl of cereal

As a child I loved choosing between an array of those tiny individual boxes of cereal (probably because they included the sugary and chocolatey ones I wasn't usually allowed to eat). In the supermarket the range of cereal options stretches out along the shelves with different shapes, sizes, coatings and even fillings.

Despite this huge range of cereals, most are made from corn, rice or wheat. The greenhouse-gas emissions for the cereal itself are about three times the dry weight of cereal, and depend mostly on the type of grain and the amount of processing required to puff, extrude or otherwise create your preferred shape.

1 g cereal = 3 g emissions

However, adding milk usually makes these different options pale into insignificance (see more information on milk in chapter 4). For a typical bowl of cereal the majority of the half kilo of emissions come from the milk (Fig. 6.3).

For a lot of people the simplest way to reduce "cereal" emissions is to pour on less milk, especially if you often find a lot left at the end of the bowl. Or, at the risk of sounding like an annoying parent, please would you at least drink up the leftover milk, instead of pouring it down the sink (for a discussion of food waste, see chapter 33).

We saw in chapter 4 that plant milks cause less than half the emissions of cows' milk. Since most of the cereal emissions come from the milk, then this switch more than halves the cereal breakfast emissions (Fig. 6.2).

Fig. 6.1: A bowl of cereal. (URL 25)

Fig. 6.2: Emissions for a bowl of cereal: cereal (30 g); milk (200 g).

Fig. 6.3: Emissions for cereal with plant milk: cereal (30 g); plant milk (200 g).

Key points

- For a typical bowl of cereal, the greenhouse-gas emissions from the milk are much bigger than the emissions from the cereal itself.

- Make sure not to waste the milk at the end of the bowl!

- Switching to plant milk more than halves your cereal emissions.

Notes

Page

34   *The greenhouse-gas emissions for the cereal itself are about three times the dry weight of cereal, and depend mostly on the type of grain and the amount of processing required to puff, extrude or otherwise create your preferred shape.* Jeswani et al. (2015) figure 7 gives 2.64 kgCO$_2$e / kg, which is used for the figures in this book. See also "Tesco Product Carbon Footprint Summary" (2012, accessed 2018) who give 95 gCO$_2$e for a 30 g serving of cornflakes, which is 3.2 kgCO$_2$e / kg.

Chapter 7 Eggs

Boiled, poached, scrambled or fried: eggs transform from a gloopy liquid into a wobbly solid that tastes satisfying on its own, or even better with a little salt. Or perhaps you like to whisk them up with cream and stir them into soft folds in a buttery scramble?

Packed with all the nutrients needed to make a baby chicken, an egg is a culmination of a hen's hard work pecking for its food. Chickens don't burp significant amounts of methane (do chickens even burp?), but their biggest contribution to global warming is still associated with their front end: the production of chicken feed is the most important source of egg greenhouse-gas emissions at the farm.

Fig. 7.1: A soft boiled egg. (URL 26)

Chicken feed

An average egg-laying chicken is fed mostly on wheat, with some soy added for extra protein. As discussed in the bread chapter (chapter 5), the main climate impact of wheat comes from making and applying fertilizer.

However, growing soy raises an important additional issue. Most soy varieties need a long hot summer to produce a good crop. Global soy production has been doubling approximately every 10 years, driven by its use in animal feed. The biggest producers of soy are Brazil and Argentina, where agricultural expansion is mostly into rainforest, often to grow soy.

Even though most of the chicken feed is wheat, soy contributes similar emissions to the wheat because forest is cut down to grow soy, and cutting down forest is bad news for the climate.

There are many problems with cutting down forest, not least the destruction of the habitat of endangered animals and plants. However, this book is about climate change so we'll focus exclusively on how deforestation affects greenhouse gases.

When forest is converted into agricultural land, the carbon stored in the trees and shrubs is mostly returned to the air as carbon dioxide (along with some carbon from the soil). This happens quickly if the forest is burnt, or over several years if the plants are left to rot. The amount of emissions released depends on how much vegetation there is in the deforested area.

To produce each egg, a chicken must eat about three times the weight of an egg. We also have to add in other contributions to global warming including feed production for the young chicken before it starts to lay eggs, and emissions from chicken manure, as well as transport and storage. Overall each egg is responsible for about 5 times its own weight in greenhouse-gas emissions.

$$1 \text{ g egg} = 5 \text{ g emissions}$$

Cooking eggs

Cookery writer Delia Smith recommends boiling an egg for 6 minutes. Even for a single boiled egg the cooking emissions are small compared to the emissions from producing the egg (Fig. 7.2, left).

There is much debate about whether or not to add milk when scrambling an egg. Jamie Oliver recommends adding only a knob of butter, the size of which is also a matter of debate. Using 25 grams of butter increases the emissions from a two-egg scramble by 30%. Some recipes recommend adding a few tablespoons of cream as well, which can push the total emissions over 1 kilo – three times as much as the emissions from a single boiled egg (Fig. 7.2, centre).

Fig. 7.2:
Left: Emissions for one boiled egg: one egg (60 g); boiling the egg (6 minutes at 2 kWh).
Centre: Emissions for scrambled eggs: two eggs (120 g); cooking the eggs (10 minutes at 2 kWh); a knob of butter (25 g); cream (50 g).
Right: Emissions for two fried eggs: two eggs (120 g); frying the eggs (10 minutes at 2 kWh); two teaspoons of vegetable oil (10 g).

How can you reduce emissions?

Combining a smaller number of eggs with a lower-emissions food like toast reduces the total carbon footprint of your breakfast. Alternatively, skipping the dairy and replacing with vegetable oil reduces emissions by one third, compared to the dairy-heavy scramble (compare Fig. 7.2 centre and right).

The chicken feed can be sourced from land that has not been recently deforested. This helps if the total demand for soy is no longer increasing, otherwise it just pushes the problem elsewhere. Alternative chicken feeds can also be used: for example, duckweed is a highly nutritious food that can even be grown in deserts, given the right enclosed conditions.

Some companies are researching their holy grail of plant-based low-carbon egg substitutes, and several options are on the market. Few if any of these plant-based alternatives are going to give you the perfect omelette yet, let alone a soft-boiled egg. But they can work well as a substitute in baking or in a pancake.

Meanwhile the bizarre discovery of aquafaba has spread around the world, making it into the dictionary in 2018. This liquid leftover from cooking chickpeas can act like egg whites by trapping small air bubbles and solidifying around them during cooking. Aquafaba meringues and mayonnaise can taste great, if combined with other ingredients (though probably not when combined with each other!). Maybe the recently-found properties of chickpea liquid points to other discoveries yet to be made for lower-carbon food alternatives.

Key points

- The most significant way eggs contribute to climate change is through production of chicken feed.

- The biggest reason chicken feed contributes to climate change is through the destruction of forest to produce soy.

- A dairy-heavy scrambled egg causes 40% of a 3 kilo daily food emissions budget, and three times the emissions of a single boiled egg.

Notes

Page

36 *An average egg-laying chicken is fed mostly on wheat, with some soy added for extra protein.* See Leinonen et al. (2011b).

36 *Global soy production has been doubling approximately every 10 years, driven by its use in animal feed. The biggest producers of soy are Brazil and Argentina, where agricultural expansion is mostly into rainforest, often to grow soy.* See figures C1 and C2 and surrounding discussion in MacLeod et al. (2013) and T. C. Ponsioen and T. J. Blonk (2012).

36 *soy contributes similar emissions to the wheat because forest is cut down to grow soy,* Table 5 of Leinonen et al. (2013) states that 41.9 % of emissions are due to wheat and 34.1 % of emissions are due to soy, even though 60 to 70 % of the feed is wheat (depending on life stage, see their table A1) and 10 to 15 % is soy.

37 *The amount of emissions released depends on how much vegetation there is in the deforested area.* Numbers have been estimated for different types of forest in

different countries e.g. table 4.7 of Aalde et al. (2006), based on exploration and counting the number of trees of different sizes (Malhi et al., 2004). See the bottom two rows of table 3 of T. C. Ponsioen and T. J. Blonk (2012), which give about 10 tonnes of CO_2e per hectare from land-use change.

37 *To produce each egg, a chicken must eat about three times the weight of an egg.* Chickens eat 0.130 kilograms of feed per bird per day (free range value from Table 1 of Leinonen et al. 2011a). During the laying phase they lay 0.75 eggs a day (calculated from 293 eggs in 56 weeks given in table 1 of Leinonen et al. 2011b) i.e. 0.75×0.057 kg egg / bird / day so 0.130 / (0.75×0.057) kg feed / kg egg = 3.04 kg feed / kg egg.

37 *Overall each egg is responsible for about 5 times its own weight in greenhouse-gas emissions.* The world average for eggs from Poore and Nemecek (2018) is 4.7 kgCO_2e / kg, which is in between the value for Europe (5.1 kgCO_2e / kg) and North America (3.7 kgCO_2e / kg).

38 *Alternative chicken feeds can also be used: for example, duckweed is a highly nutritious food that can even be grown in deserts, given the right enclosed conditions.* For more information see Leinonen and Kyriazakis (2016).

38 *Few if any of these plant-based alternatives are going to give you the perfect omelette yet, let alone a soft-boiled egg.* Amazingly, fake eggs are a problem for food fraud, because it is possible to make cheap realistic-looking egg shells (see the fascinating popular book *Sorting the beef from the bull* (Evershed and Temple, 2016)).

Chapter 8 Breakfast summary

Having looked at all these breakfast options, let's see how they compare with each other in terms of greenhouse-gas emissions, and how a typical breakfast compares with more decadent or frugal options.

Typical-emissions breakfast

To make a typical breakfast, let's add up the emissions from a cup of coffee and a bowl of cereal. This comes to just over half a kilo of greenhouse-gas emissions in total, about 20% of a 3 kilo daily food emissions budget (Fig. 8.1, left). Most of this is caused by the bowl of cereal, most of which comes from the milk (chapter 6).

Higher-emissions breakfast

If you're eating out you might be tempted by a latte or a hot chocolate, some toast and some creamy scrambled eggs. (We've deliberately picked some of the higher-emissions options here, to see how much difference it makes.) This really starts to add up, to nearly 4 times the emissions of the more typical breakfast (compare Fig. 8.1 centre and left). It blows most of a daily budget of 3 kilos of emissions, even though we've only had breakfast so far. Most of the emissions are from the dairy products, even though the egg is the most prominent item on the menu.

Is this a fair comparison? Maybe not, because you get so much more nutrition from the higher-emissions breakfast than the typical-emissions breakfast. If you're planning a big healthy lunch and dinner then the typical-emissions breakfast will be fine. On the other hand, if the rest of the day is going to be hectic and low on nutrients then the higher-emissions breakfast might be just the ticket to keep you healthy.

At the end of the book we'll add up the emissions from a typical-emissions breakfast, a typical-emissions lunch, some typical-emissions snacks and a typical-emissions dinner (chapter 32). We'll try to pick out some options that complement each other and meet our daily nutritional requirements. It will be a fairer comparison when the whole day of food is considered.

Fig. 8.1: Comparison of breakfast options.
Left: Emissions for a typical-emissions breakfast: a white coffee; bowl of cereal.
Centre: Emissions for a higher-emissions breakfast: a latte; scrambled eggs.
Right: Emissions for a lower-emissions breakfast: a cup of black tea, boiling minimal water; bread (4 slices).

Lower-emissions breakfast

Could you make a lower-emissions breakfast from the options on the menu? How about going really frugal by having black tea with bread and jam? You could be careful to only boil just enough water for the tea, and use vegetable spread instead of butter. This would reduce the emissions by over five times, compared to the typical-emissions breakfast. To avoid being hungry at the end of the day, let's double up the amount of bread in this lower-emissions option from two to four slices (and correspondingly increase the amount of spreads). This still keeps emissions down at nearly one third those the typical breakfast, and one tenth those of the higher-emissions breakfast (Fig. 8.1, right).

Key points

- For a typical breakfast of coffee and cereal, the milk causes most of the emissions.

- A higher-emissions option with a latte, scrambled eggs and buttered toast causes nearly four times more emissions, more than half of which comes from the dairy products.

- Going frugal with bread and black tea reduces emissions by nearly 3 times compared to the typical breakfast, or 10 times compared to the higher-emissions breakfast.

Part II: Lunch

What do you normally do for lunch? Head to a canteen, eat a sandwich at your desk, or whip up a fresh meal at home? In this part, we're going to consider a few standard western lunch options.

A cheese and ham sandwich seems simple enough, but involves turning milk into cheese, and raising animals to eat. Salads can contain a huge range of ingredients, but for simplicity we'll focus on the challenges of growing tomatoes and lettuce. We then put the tomatoes together with bread, cheese and a few toppings to make a pizza.

Next on the menu is a baked potato, with beans and cheese. As well as being a popular baked potato topping, beans are a type of legume – a highly nutritious plant-based option and an important component of animal feed. We round off our lunch with a milk-based dessert.

Chapter 9 A cheese sandwich

We can take the bread and butter discussed in the breakfast section, and just add some slices of cheese to make a tasty sandwich.

Making cheese

To make cheese, warm some milk to body temperature (or you could freshly milk a cow), add rennet and leave it to solidify. The result wobbles like a fragile jelly. Cheese makers cut these curds to release the liquid whey, keeping just the semi-solid curds to turn into cheese (Fig. 9.1).

I put in a photo of some curds in one bowl, and the whey in another, to emphasize the big difference in quantity. There is about 10 times as much watery whey as there is cheese curds, so it takes approximately 10 kilos of milk to make 1 kilo of cheese.

The whey contains milk proteins, along with many vitamins and minerals. It's used in various products including baby formula milk, and is also fed to calves. Recently, whey proteins have become popular in body-building drinks.

Fig. 9.1: Cutting the curds to release the whey. (URL 27)

Milk storage

The curds can be eaten straight away as a soft cheese. Or to make a tangy hard cheese extra ingredients are needed – for example yogurt cultures, acid and salt. The curds are pressed, dried and matured at carefully controlled temperature and humidity – sometimes for years for the strongest cheeses.

It's more difficult to produce milk in the winter than in the summer. By the time autumn comes around, a calf would be getting most of its nutrition from solid food and the mother cow would stop producing milk, unless milked regularly. Even in modern dairies it's usual to give the cows a break from producing milk before they give birth again in spring. The gaps can be

Fig. 9.2: In cheese-making, milk is separated into plentiful whey (large bowl) and meagre curds (small bowl). The curds are then pressed to make cheese. It takes about 10 kilograms of milk to make 1 kilogram of cheese. (URL 28)

staggered to provide a continuous supply of milk, but cheese is an important way to store up many of the nutritional benefits of a milk supply that doesn't match up with demand.

Cheesy emissions

Most of the climate impact of cheese production comes from the burps of the dairy cow. We should share out the emissions between the end products (cheese and whey, see box 9.1), and add in the contribution from processing the cheese.

Fig. 9.3: Cheeses being matured in carefully controlled conditions. (URL 29)

Box 9.1: Emissions from co-products

When calculating the emissions from a process that produces more than one product, we have to share out the emissions between the outputs to avoid double counting. How should we divide the emissions up? The most common approach is to use the economic value, or cost, of each product. This means that the most sought-after products are allocated the largest share of the emissions.

It also means that when we have an unwanted by-product, such as the liquid left over from draining chickpeas (aquafaba, see chapter 7), we would assign this item zero emissions. This is also relevant for some by-products of the meat industry, for example the pigs' blood used to make black pudding. More generally, we can reduce greenhouse-gas emissions if we use every edible part of the food production process, and therefore help to avoid food waste (chapter 33).

Taking everything into consideration, cheese turns out to be responsible for producing about 16 times its own weight in greenhouse-gas emissions.

1 g cheese = 16 g emissions

We can now build up our cheese sandwich from two slices of bread (80 g), a smear (10 g) of butter and two slices (50 g) of cheese (Fig. 9.4, left). Most of the greenhouse-gas emissions come from the cheese. Only a small fraction comes from the bread, even though it provides about half the calories, and a slightly larger amount comes from the butter. The total emissions add up to nearly a kilo of greenhouse gases, or one third of a daily food emissions budget of 3 kilos.

Fig. 9.4:
Left: Emissions for a cheese sandwich: two slices of bread (80 g); two teaspoons of butter (10 g); two medium slices of cheese (50 g).
Centre: Emissions for a cheese sandwich (1 thin cheese slice): two slices of bread (80 g); two teaspoons of vegetable spread (10 g); one thin slice of cheese (20 g); two teaspoons of relish (20 g).
Right: Emissions for a peanut butter and jam sandwich: two slices of bread (80 g); two teaspoons of peanut butter (20 g); one teaspoon of jam (10 g).

How can you reduce emissions?

Can you reduce the cheese sandwich emissions? The simplest option is to use less cheese, for example by using one thin 20 g slice of cheese instead of two standard 25 g slices. Maybe some relish or mustard could fill the gap? Even a generous 25 g portion of relish is unlikely to have a big impact on emissions.

1 g relish = 3 g emissions

By reducing the amount of cheese and replacing the butter with vegetable spread, the emissions are halved (Fig. 9.4, centre). You lose out on some of the nutrition from the cheese and butter, but much of this can be restored by using wholemeal instead of white bread. As an added bonus, switching to wholemeal bread doubles your fibre intake, which will keep you feeling fuller for longer and, for most people, it will also improve gut health (see chapter 34).

Cheese from other animals

How about making cheese from the milk of animals other than cows? The most common alternatives are sheep, goats and buffalo. Unfortunately, from the point of view of greenhouse-gas emissions, these are similar to cows: they are all ruminants, with the same methane-producing rumen compartment in their stomachs.

It is said that Cleopatra bathed in the milk of over 700 donkeys every day, and its health benefits are widely claimed. Horses and donkeys have both been farmed for their milk and, because they are not ruminants, the greenhouse-gas emissions could be lower than those for cows (depending on how much milk they can produce). However, I'm not going to place my bets on a future rise in the popularity of horse cheese.

Vegan "cheese"

"It is important to combat false claims. Our products must be designated correctly: the terms of #cheese or #steak will be reserved for products of animal origin" – **tweeted by French MP Jean-Baptiste Moreau**

Some people say cheese made from anything other than animals' milk should not be called cheese. Nevertheless there are a number of plant-based cheese alternatives you can make or buy, and this chapter would not be complete without considering them. To avoid being sued, we refer to them as vegan "cheese".

I'd be more enthusiastic about the vegan "cheese" option if I hadn't been disappointed by the taste and texture so many times. But maybe this is just a problem with the brands I've tried so far. I am an optimist and I want to know how this switch would affect emissions.

Standard shop-bought vegan "cheese" is usually made from oil, starch and water. Putting together these ingredients brings the emissions of a standard vegan "cheese" down to around one tenth of that of cows' cheese, allowing for processing and refrigeration.

1 g oil-based vegan cheese = 1.4 g emissions

If, in addition, you replace the butter with vegetable spread then the "cheese" sandwich stack now looks quite different: the total emissions are six times lower than the standard cheese sandwich (compare Fig. 9.5 with Fig. 9.4, left).

The main ingredients of the majority of vegan "cheeses" (oil and starch) are derived from plants using processes which remove most of the vitamins and minerals. This means that standard vegan "cheeses" lack many of the nutritional benefits of regular cheese. Part of this can be made up by switching to wholemeal bread, and some vegan "cheeses" are fortified with nutrients that can't easily be made up by the bread, including calcium and vitamins A, B12 and D. Some people eat cheese to get their protein fix, but standard vegan "cheese" usually contains little or no protein, unless protein has been specifically added to the formulation.

Search for vegan "cheese" recipes on the internet and you will find bold claims of tastiness, yet almost none are made from the starch and oil used in most shop-bought vegan "cheese". Some are based on tofu, but most are made from nuts (chapter 19). The total emissions will be slightly higher than those of standard oil- and starch-based vegan "cheese" (and the price is much higher), but as a food it is much more nutritious, and causes about 6 times lower emissions than regular cheese, depending on the processing and water content.

Vegan "cheese" sandwich
Vegan "cheese" (72)
Vegetable spread (14)
Bread (60)
Total 145 gCO$_2$e

Fig. 9.5: Emissions for a vegan "cheese" sandwich: two slices of bread (80 g); two teaspoons of vegetable spread (10 g); two slices of vegan "cheese" (50 g).

Other alternatives

If you don't feel like whipping up a batch of vegan nut "cheese" at home, you can have a similar emissions footprint and nutritional profile by using nut or seed butter (chapter 19). Readily available options include peanut butter and almond butter (but watch out for added salt and sugar, and nut allergies).

My favourite is peanut butter with orange marmalade for a bit of tang to cut through the thick nut butter. Jam is also popular. The peanut butter (chapter 19) and jam (chapter 5) emissions come to about the same as the low values for the vegan "cheese" sandwich (Fig. 9.4, right).

Alternatively, any improvements in emissions from milk production (discussed in chapter 6) will translate into lower cheese emissions.

Of course, many other sandwich fillings exist, and that's without even considering the non-sandwich lunchbox options. In the next chapter we consider replacing a slice of cheese with some ham.

Key points

- It takes about 10 kilos of milk to make 1 kilo of cheese, so cheese is a relatively high-impact food.

- A cheese sandwich causes nearly 1 kilo of emissions, which is one third of a daily food emissions budget of 3 kilos.

- This means that switching out some cheese for a low-impact alternative, like relish, halves the total sandwich emissions, particularly if butter is also replaced by vegetable spread.

- Cheese alternatives are usually much more climate-friendly than cheese, but often lack nutrition.

- Switching a cheese sandwich for a nut butter sandwich reduces emissions by five times.

Notes

Page

44 *add rennet* Rennet occurs naturally in the stomachs of cows and other ruminants. This cheese-making combination of warm milk and rennet is not as surprising as it might seem at first sight, because cows' stomachs were historically used as handy waterproof containers. Fill up an empty cow stomach with warm milk straight from a cow and leave it until the morning, and you've got curds and whey. Even more fascinating is that

the rennet exists in the young cow's stomach precisely because it curdles the mother's milk. This slows down the passage of milk through the calf's digestive system and allows more nutrients to be extracted. These days most cheese in the US and UK is vegetarian, because it's made using artificial rennet. The artificial rennet is made using a black mould found on onions; this has been genetically modified to produce the rennet enzyme in carefully controlled laboratory conditions. The result is then purified to remove all traces of the mould, so the final rennet doesn't contain any GM material.

45 *The most common approach is to use the economic value, or cost, of each product. This means that the most sought-after products are allocated the largest share of the emissions.* Alternative approaches include sharing the emissions out according to the weight of the product, or the weight of the solids in the product. For example, to share the emissions between cream and skimmed milk (chapter 15), the weight of dried milk is used, rather than the weight of the milk, because most of the milk is water.

45 *cheese turns out to be responsible for producing about 16 times its own weight in greenhouse-gas emissions.* The value used here is for European cheese of 16 kgCO$_2$e / kg cheese from Poore and Nemecek (2018), which is similar to the value for the US (15 kgCO$_2$e / kg), although note that this is much lower than the global average (24 kgCO$_2$e / kg) due to varying milk production practices.

46 *Even a generous 25 g portion of relish is unlikely to have a big impact on emissions.* Due to a lack of available information on emissions from relishes, the value here is an average of the value of Frankowska et al. (2019a) for UK pickled onions (2.4 kgCO$_2$e / kg) and the value for jam (see chapter 5), which gives 2.8 kgCO$_2$e / kg.

47 *"It is important to combat false claims. Our products must be designated correctly: the terms of #cheese or #steak will be reserved for products of animal origin"* Tweeted by French MP Jean-Baptiste Moreau, as reported in the Guardian (URL 30).

47 *emissions of a standard vegan "cheese" down to around one tenth of that of cows' cheese, allowing for processing and refrigeration.* This uses the estimate of 1.43 kgCO$_2$e / kg for vegan "cheese" by Frankowska (private communication) based on retailer information on ingredients, and adding a margin for processing using the cheese processing figure from Frankowska (2019) (0.79 kgCO$_2$e / kg), and adding 0.3 kgCO$_2$e / kg for retail following Poore and Nemecek (2018) for cheese.

47 *The total emissions will be slightly higher than those of standard oil- and starch-based vegan "cheese" (and the price is much higher), but as a food it is much more nutritious, and causes about 6 times lower emissions than regular cheese, depending on the processing and water content.* Later, in our afternoon snack (chapter 19) we will find that nuts are responsible for about 3.2 grams of emissions per gram of nut, although this varies widely depending mostly on how the land was used before it came into nut production (since nut production is on the increase). The recipes mostly call for the nuts to be pre-soaked in water, before being blitzed and combined with other ingredients, typically including salt, garlic and lemon juice. For a nut "cheese" made of 50% nuts, the nuts contribute about 1.6 grams of emissions per gram of nut "cheese". To this add 1.1 gram of emissions for processing and retail combined (see previous endnote), giving total emissions for nut "cheese" of less than three times its own weight. Replacing the dairy cheese with a nut-based vegan "cheese" still reduces the sandwich emissions by more than four times.

Chapter 10 Ham, pork and bacon

How about replacing some, or all, of the cheese in your sandwich with ham? Ham is such an easy sandwich filling – you don't even have to get out a knife!

Where does ham come from anyway? Wikipedia says it comes from the leg of a pig, but in Fig. 10.2 it's more like the pig's bottom, which sounds less appetizing, although it still tastes great to me.

Fig. 10.1: Sliced ham. (URL 31)

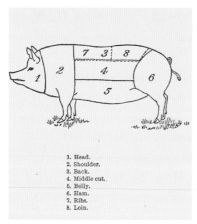

1. Head.
2. Shoulder.
3. Back.
4. Middle cut.
5. Belly.
6. Ham.
7. Ribs.
8. Loin.

Fig. 10.2: Map of a pig showing where different cuts of meat are taken from. (URL 32)

Piglets

A one-year-old female pig usually has about 11 piglets at once, and may give birth to 11 more just 5 months later. She typically gives birth to about 50 piglets in total before being slaughtered for bacon herself at 2 or 3 years of age.

A piglet eats nearly twice as many calories as an average human each day, so there is some justification to the phrase "to pig out". And pigs do put on weight fast: a piglet is born weighing less than a human baby, and grows to weigh more than the average adult human in just 5 months, when it is slaughtered for about 70 kilos of pork meat.

On western commercial farms the piglets mostly eat grains like wheat, beans like soy, and some leftovers from human food production. This includes "seed cake", which sounds like it would be tasty with a cup of tea, but in fact is the squashed remains of seeds after pressing out vegetable oil. For every 7 calories eaten by the pigs, about 1 goes into pork and the other 6 end up in manure.

Animal wee and poo

We do need to talk about all that manure. An archetypal cow lives outside in pasture doing their business all over the field (chapter 4). At first glance this sounds bad for climate change, but the alternative is worse...

Fig. 10.3: Piglets. (URL 33)

Farmed pigs typically live indoors and their manure is collected and stored in a big "slurry pit", to be spread on the fields at a later date. When I used to walk to school as a kid, there was one day of the year when there was an awful smell – the day the winter pig manure got spread on the fields to feed the crops. I don't think I would have liked it much if the muck spreading had happened more frequently, but that would actually have been better for the environment.

Manure is a combination of both wee and poo – the wee is important because it contains much of the valuable nitrogen. Because wet pig manure can't rot down using oxygen from the air, it instead makes methane, a powerful greenhouse gas (chapter 1). The amount of methane released by manure depends on the temperature and the length of time it is kept for – the longer it is kept in wet and warm conditions, the more methane is produced.

Fig. 10.4: Some pigs looking content. (URL 34)

Box 10.1: Animal efficiency / inefficiency

Many animals eat several times as many calories as they provide to us in the form of meat.

- For every calorie we get from chicken, 3 have to be eaten by the animal (chapter 25).

- For every calorie we get from ham or pork, 7 have to be eaten by the pig (see above).

- For every calorie we get from beef, 20 have to be eaten by the cow (chapter 24).

One nutritional benefit of this apparent inefficiency is that the animals concentrate the nutrients from the plants, so meat has a higher concentration of some nutrients than plants. In fact the nutrient profile of meat is extremely well matched to what we need to grow strong muscles. (This is neither a coincidence or grand design – it's simply because we too are animals and are mostly made of meat!)

However, with a large population on a limited planet demanding increasing amounts of animal products, this inefficiency is now driving deforestation which is bad news for the climate (see chapters 7 and 37).

As a result of this inefficiency, you will notice a trend emerging, that the even the lowest-emissions animal products generally cause more climate change than plant-based products.

Fig. 10.5: A high-quality ham sandwich, which is a lot more photogenic than the plain white bread ham and cheese sandwich we're mainly discussing here. (URL 35)

A piece of ham causes about 11 times its own weight in emissions, depending mostly on how the farm is managed.

1 g ham = 11 g emissions

Growing food for pigs causes about half of this total, manure is responsible for about a quarter, and the other quarter is mostly energy, including the processing from pig into ham.

The more the pork is processed (for example dry-cured ham or bacon) the higher the emissions. However, if the pork product uses less popular parts of the animal that would otherwise be unused (e.g. black pudding or sausages) then the emissions are lower (see box 9.1).

Cheese and ham toastie emissions

Ham emissions are therefore usually lower than those caused by cheese (which is typically responsible for 16 times its own weight in emissions – see chapter 9). In a ham sandwich containing two slices of ham (50 g), most of the emissions are caused by the ham (Fig. 10.6, left). If you replace the ham with cheese, the greenhouse-gas emissions will increase by about 40% (compare Fig. 10.6 left and centre). We'll settle on one slice of each for now (Fig. 10.6, right).

Fig. 10.6:
Left: Emissions for a ham sandwich: two slices of bread (80 g); two teaspoons of butter (10 g); two slices of ham (50 g).
Centre: Cheese sandwich (duplicated from chapter 9 for ease of comparison).
Right: Emissions for a cheese and ham sandwich: two slices of bread (80 g); two teaspoons of butter (10 g); one slice of cheese (25 g); one slice of ham (25 g).

Would you like the sandwich toasted? With melting cheese in the middle and crunchy cheese bits oozing out of the sides? Go on... put the grill on for 10 minutes, so it heats up and gets the cheese really gooey. This adds about 20 per cent to the emissions, so it's better to focus on reducing the amount of cheese and ham in the sandwich, rather than feeling too virtuous by forsaking the toasting.

How can you reduce emissions?

What about ham alternatives? Switching from ham to beef steak more than triples the total sandwich emissions (Fig. 10.7, centre; see steak details in chapter 24). A single steak sandwich containing 50 grams of beef blows most of a 3 kg daily food emissions budget. On the other hand, switching from ham to chicken *reduces* the climate-impact by about a third, if you're also prepared to use vegetable spread instead of butter (compare Fig. 10.7 left and right; see chicken details in chapter 25).

Ham emissions can be reduced further by feeding pigs on more leftovers from processing human food, or other novel feed sources (chapter 7), and their manure can be spread on the fields more frequently, or the methane collected to use as fuel. However, it would be hard to make ham that has lower emissions than chicken, because pigs are less efficient at converting feed calories into meat calories (box 10.1).

Steak sandwich
Steak (2310)

Ham sandwich
Ham (535)
Butter (83)
Bread (60)
Total 678 gCO$_2$e

Butter (83)
Bread (60)
Total 2453 gCO$_2$e

Chicken sandwich
Chicken (435)
Vegetable spread (14)
Bread (60)
Total 509 gCO$_2$e

Fig. 10.7:
Left: Greenhouse-gas emissions for a ham sandwich (duplicated from Fig. 10.6 for ease of comparison.
Centre: Emissions for a steak sandwich: two slices of bread (80 g); two teaspoons of butter (10 g); two slices of steak (50 g).
Right: Emissions for a chicken sandwich: two slices of bread (80 g); two teaspoons of vegetable spread (10 g); two slices of chicken (50 g).

Lab protein

For medical purposes, animal cells are routinely grown in small petri dishes in laboratories. The dish is kept warm and nutrients are added to keep the cells happy and growing. So why not grow our food that way too? Less energy wasted on being an animal is good news for the climate, and there may be welfare benefits.

As an innovation enthusiast I'm excited at the idea of producing meat without the need to grow a whole animal, but I realize not everyone is going to be so enthusiastic. And for all my technophilia, how would I really feel when it came time to put the lab burger into my mouth? Is it safe? What are the ethics here? Would you eat it?

Academic studies of consumer reactions to the concept have recorded disgust, and concern about the impact on farming and eating traditions, with less than half of consumers prepared even to try lab meat.

However, the idea of growing protein in a laboratory is not new. Mycoprotein is a naturally occurring close relative of mushrooms and is sold commercially in Quorn. The greenhouse-

Fig. 10.8: Emissions for a Quorn sandwich: two slices of bread (80 g); two teaspoons of vegetable spread (10 g); two Quorn slices (50 g).

gas missions of making mycoprotein arise mostly from growing it in a warm nutrient bath. On top of that, for the sliced Quorn used in sandwiches, we have to add on the processing from mycoprotein into Quorn slices, which triples the emissions.

$$1 \text{ g Quorn pieces} = 1 \text{ g emissions}$$
$$1 \text{ g Quorn slices} = 3 \text{ g emissions}$$

Overall the fresh sliced Quorn emissions are still less than half those for ham or chicken – so this provides another low-carbon option for our sandwich, without waiting around for tasty lab meat to become widely available (Fig. 10.8).

Of course you can just eat plants directly! In the next chapter we consider a bowl of salad, which can also be used as a sandwich filling.

Key points

• Ham and pork contribute to climate change mostly because of emissions from pig feed and manure.

• Ham and cheese cause similarly large amounts of emissions, so the exact proportions of ham and cheese in the sandwich aren't as important as reducing the total amount.

• A steak sandwich causes triple the emissions of a ham sandwich, and uses up most of a daily food emissions budget of 3 kilos.

• Switching to mycoprotein can more than halve the sandwich emissions, to one tenth of a daily food emissions budget of 3 kilos.

Notes

Page

50 *She typically gives birth to about 50 piglets in total before being slaughtered for bacon herself at 2 or 3 years of age.* The number of litters per sow per year is 2.3 and the number of piglets is 11.2 pigs weaned per litter, taken from the UK 2018 AHDB Pig Pocketbook (AHDB, 2018a). From the same source, the average pig replacement rate is 51.6%, so the sow phase is nearly 2 years – which allows time for 4 or 5 litters (44 to 55 piglets in total). A single sow gives birth to so many piglets that she contributes just under 10% of the total pig emissions (assuming the emissions are proportional to the number of pig years) since she is alive for 2.5 years and the 50 piglets are alive for 0.5 years (2.5 / (2.5 + 50*0.5) * 100 = 9%). There is typically 1 male pig for 20 or more female pigs (Roese and Taylor, 2006) so the emissions from the boar are less than 1% of the total (approximately 9%/20). This means that when we calculate the greenhouse-gas emissions of ham the thing we need to consider most carefully is the emissions from the piglets as they grow up.

50 *grows to weigh more than the average adult human in just 5 months, when it is slaughtered for about 70 kilos of pork meat.* According to the UK 2018 AHDB Pig Pocketbook (AHDB, 2018a) the average number of days in the herd was 146 in the UK in 2017, which is 4.8 months. The average weight of pigs produced is 109.9 kg. To convert this into the weight of pork meat we use the lean meat percentage of 61.1 from the AHDB Pork Yearbook 2017 (AHDB, 2017), which gives 67 kg of lean meat per pig (rounded up to 70 kg in the main text for simplicity).

50 *piglets mostly eat grains like wheat, beans like soy, and some leftovers from human food production.* e.g. see Table 3.1 of Kool et al. (2009).

50 *For every 7 calories eaten by the pigs, about 1 goes into pork and the other 6 end up in manure.* Growing pigs eat 3872 kCal a day, calculated from 16.2 MJ/day given in Table A1.10 of Kool et al. (2009). The pigs are fed for 146 days, and so consume 3872 kCal/day $\times$ 146 days = 565,312 kCal in total. 67 kilograms of lean meat is produced from one pig. Pork has about 120 kCal per 100 g (1200 kCal / kg), so a whole pig provides 67 $\times$ 1200 kCal = 80,400 kCal for human consumption. Therefore we eat 80,400 / 565,312 $\times$ 100 = 14% of the calories consumed by the pig, or one in seven.

51 *the wee is important because it contains much of the valuable nitrogen.* In humans most of the valuable nitrogen is in the urine rather than the faeces (Rose et al., 2015). It's a running joke on my favourite gardening show that panellist Bob Flowerdew pees on his compost heap – urine is a great fertilizer once diluted or composted. In pigs the fraction is lower, but still usually more than 50% (Jørgensen et al., 2013).

51 *The amount of methane released by manure depends on the temperature and the length of time it is kept for – the longer it is kept in wet and warm conditions, the more methane is produced.* Because the UK doesn't get very hot, an annual manure spread leads to only about one fifth of the maximum methane being released. Kool et al. (2009) use a methane conversion factor (MCF) of 20% for England).

52 *ham causes about 11 times its own weight in emissions, depending mostly on how the farm is managed.* This is based on the value of 10.7 kgCO$_2$e / kg from Noya et al. (2016) which specifically studied ham, though see also values in Poore and Nemecek (2018) of 10 kgCO$_2$e / kg for pork from Europe and 12 kgCO$_2$e / kg for the global average.

52 *The more the pork is processed (for example dry-cured ham or bacon) the higher the emissions.* Noya et al. (2016) calculate emissions of 12.7 kgCO$_2$e / kg for dry-cured ham.

53 *Less energy wasted on being an animal is good news for the climate, and there may be welfare benefits.* The main contributions to lab meat emissions are from the nutrients provided to the growing cells, and the heat required to warm the system up to body temperature. The feed conversion ratio is thought to be better than two, which is better even than for chicken meat, which is good news for fertilizer-related emissions and use of land (Tuomisto and Mattos, 2010).

53 *less than half of consumers prepared even to try lab meat.* According to Siegrist et al. (2018).

54 *the fresh sliced Quorn emissions are still less than half those for ham or chicken* The comprehensive book *Sustainable Protein Sources* (Nadathur et al., 2016) contains a chapter contributed by employees of Quorn Foods which describes the process and emissions. The Quorn webpage (URL 116) gives carbon footprints from a 2019 study accredited by the Carbon Trust: the mycoprotein itself causes 0.8 kgCO$_2$e / kg, whereas Quorn Pieces cause

1.3 kgCO$_2$e / kg up to the point of sale and Quorn Vegan Ham-free Slices cause 3.2 kgCO$_2$e / kg. The Quorn sandwich calculation uses the Quorn Slices value and the Quorn tikka masala (chapter 25) uses the Quorn Pieces value.

Chapter 11 Salad

How about some refreshing salad to go with all that melty cheese and ham? Perhaps some tomatoes or lettuce mixed with a little oil and vinegar?

Tomatoes

Most tomatoes grow in open fields and are given fertilizer and water to produce a heavy crop. We eat some of those fresh, and preserve the rest to use later, for example in sauces.

Fertilizer dominates the greenhouse-gas emissions on the farm, just as for most vegetables (box 2.1). Depending on the weather, they may also need water pumped to the fields to keep the plants happy, which contributes to the emissions if the pumps are powered by fossil fuels. However, even adding this in, the total tomato emissions are still small for in-season field-grown tomato emissions, at one sixth of their own weight (although out-of-season tomatoes are a different matter, as we shall see next).

1 g local, in season, field-grown tomatoes = 0.16 g emissions

How about chopping up your tomatoes and taking them to another level by drizzling on some oil and vinegar, and maybe a pinch of salt (Fig. 11.1)? (Salt causes negligible emissions, so is not shown in the stacks.) The salad dressing causes more emissions than the tomatoes themselves, but the total is still less than 2% of a daily food emissions budget of 3 kilos (Fig. 11.3, left).

Fig. 11.1: Tomato salad. (URL 36)

You prefer cherry tomatoes (Fig. 11.2)? I do, and my kids can finish off a bumper pack in one sitting! What a great way to eat more veg! So I was disappointed to learn that most cherry tomatoes are grown in heated greenhouses or plastic constructions called polytunnels. Natural gas (fossil fuel) is burned to keep the plants warm and to produce carbon dioxide for the plants to breathe. Electricity is used to circulate water, nutrients and air.

Fig. 11.2: Tomatoes growing on their vines. (URL 37)

The emissions from a heated greenhouse totally depend on the

Tomato salad
(in season)
Vinegar (5)
Oil (37)
Tomato (8)
Total 50 gCO₂e

Tomato salad
grown in a heated
greenhouse
Vinegar (5)
Oil (37)
Tomato (626)
Total 668 gCO₂e

Lettuce salad
(by truck 400km)
Vinegar (5)
Oil (37)
Truck (3)
Lettuce (73)
Total 117 gCO₂e

Fig. 11.3:
Left: Emissions for a tomato salad (in season): a local in-season tomato (50 g); two teaspoons of vegetable oil (10 g); a teaspoon of vinegar (5 g).
Centre: The same salad but using tomatoes grown in a heated greenhouse, without any additional measures such as combined heat and power.
Right: Emissions for a lettuce salad (by truck 400 km [250 miles]): a portion of lettuce (50 g); transport 400 km [250 miles] by truck; two teaspoons of vegetable oil (10 g); a teaspoon of vinegar (5 g).

outside temperature and on how well insulated the greenhouse is (i.e. the thickness of the glass or plastic, and the quality of the draught exclusion). Commercial heated-greenhouse tomato farms can produce over 10 kilos of carbon dioxide for every kilo of tomatoes (Fig. 11.3, centre), which is right up there with the ham (chapter 10) and chicken (chapter 25).

1 g tomatoes grown in a heated greenhouse = 13 g emissions
The small tomato salad now causes over 20% of a 3 kilo budget for total daily food emissions.

A number of improvements have been made by the most advanced growers, most significantly by using waste heat and carbon dioxide from fossil-fuelled power stations instead of burning fossil fuels just for the tomatoes. In this case we have to share out the greenhouse-gas emissions between the electricity produced by the power station and the fresh produce (box 9.1). This can reduce the out-of-season tomato emissions significantly. Savvy growers also store the excess daytime warmth from the sun and pump sun-warmed water back through the greenhouses at night time to even out the temperature.

Lettuce

Lettuce, spinach and herbs are increasingly grown using a new technology called vertical farming: plants are illuminated by artificial lights, which means they can be grown indoors and stacked up high, layer after layer. This might sound extremely inefficient, but the colour of the lights can be tuned to match the needs of the plants, thereby saving electricity and giving the grow rooms an eerie pink glow (Fig. 11.4).

The indoor vertical farms can be kept warm more easily than greenhouses and polytunnels, thus reducing the need for heating. Vertical farms usually avoid using soil, which means that fertilizers cannot escape or be turned into nitrous oxide by soil microbes. Finally, vertical farms can produce a lot of food in a very limited land area, and can be situated close to the consumer,

Fig. 11.4: Vertical farming. Image thanks to LettUsGrow (URL 39).

for example in basements of city buildings. Vertical farming is currently only economically viable for high-value crops such as salads and herbs, and isn't expected to produce anywhere near enough food to replace soil-based farming, but it is (literally) a growing industry and may be coming soon to a building near you.

Salads like lettuce, peppers (capsicum) and cucumbers have to be kept in refrigerators or else they rot quickly, whereas tomatoes taste best if they aren't chilled. This is partly why the emissions from lettuce are higher than those for seasonal tomatoes (compare Fig. 11.3 left and right).

1 g lettuce = 1.5 g emissions

Other than that, the emissions of lettuce depend crucially on how it is grown: whether it is grown outdoors, in a heated greenhouse (leading to emissions like the tomato in Fig. 11.3, centre) or in a vertical farm powered by clean energy.

Box 11.1: Supermarket fridges

I get excited about the quality of a supermarket when I walk through an array of tasty-looking fresh fruit and vegetables, perhaps while subconsciously inhaling the smell of fresh bread piped over from the bakery. But unfortunately there is a cost to the climate of having the most fragile foods out on display. Refrigerators use a significant fraction of the electricity used by the whole supermarket and the refrigerant fluid used to cool the fridge has historically been a powerful greenhouse gas.

The greenhouse-gas emissions of an item of food therefore depend on whether it is kept refrigerated, or frozen, for how long, and how much room it takes up (which determines how many can fit in the fridge or freezer). It has been calculated that supermarket fridges can add around 1 kilo of emissions for every kilo of product, with roughly equal contributions from electricity consumption and refrigerant leakage.

Winter salad

We're being told to eat more fruit and vegetables, so what are the most climate-friendly options? You can enjoy local tomatoes in season without worrying about emissions. In the middle of winter you can still get plenty of tomatoey goodness by eating them preserved (e.g. tinned tomatoes, passata or tomato puree), which can be made from field-grown tomatoes picked in season.

Many winter vegetables can also be eaten raw in salads, including carrot, parsnip, turnip and cabbage. These have much lower emissions than a winter tomato. We'll come back to these at dinner (chapter 28).

Key points

- Local, in-season, field grown tomatoes are a very low-emissions food.

- Salad grown in heated greenhouses can cause emissions comparable with chicken and ham, but this can be significantly reduced with heating technology.

- Keeping salad items (e.g. lettuce) in supermarket chiller cabinets can add roughly their own weight in emissions compared with those that don't (e.g. tomatoes).

Notes

Page

57   *the total tomato emissions are still small for in-season field-grown tomato emissions, at one sixth of their own weight (although out-of-season tomatoes are a different matter, as we shall see next).* Field-grown tomatoes in Italy cause 0.16 kgCO$_2$e / kg according to Frankowska et al. (2019a). Note that this is 78 times lower than the UK value (which includes heating greenhouses). See also Payen et al. (2015).

57   *oil* Assuming a 50% mix of sunflower and rapeseed oil gives a global average of 3.7 kgCO$_2$e / kg from Poore and Nemecek (2018).

57   *vinegar,* Due to a lack of studies, this uses the wine value (chapter 29).

57   *Salt causes negligible emissions, so is not shown in the stacks.* Salt causes about 0.2 kgCO$_2$e / kg salt accordingly to "CCaLC PVC Manual (V2.0)" (2011). Half a teaspoon of salt weighs about 3 grams, so it causes less than 1 gram of emissions, which is tiny compared to all the other items.

58   *Commercial heated-greenhouse tomato farms can produce over 10 kilos of carbon dioxide for every kilo of tomatoes* Frankowska et al. (2019a) find 12.52 kgCO$_2$e / kg tomatoes for the UK taking into account heating greenhouses.

58   *Savvy growers also store the excess daytime warmth from the sun and pump sun-warmed water back through the greenhouses at night time to even out the temperature.* These ideas are taken from the webpage of the tomato growers APS Group (URL 38). See chapter 21 of MacKay (2009) for comments on combined heat and power, and some ways smart heat storage can be taken to another level using heat pumps.

59   *tomatoes taste best if they aren't chilled.* See Zhang et al. (2016).

59   *emissions from lettuce* Figure S44 of Frankowska et al. (2019a) gives a value of 1.45 kgCO$_2$e / kg lettuce for UK production.

59 *Refrigerators use a significant fraction of the electricity used by the whole supermarket* "In UK supermarkets, more than 70% of the energy consumed is electricity of which between 30% and 60% is used to drive the refrigeration equipment in the store." – *Greenhouse Gas Impacts of Food Retailing: Report for Defra* (2008).

59 *It has been calculated that supermarket fridges can add around 1 kilo of emissions for every kilo of product, with roughly equal contributions from electricity consumption and refrigerant leakage.* This was calculated for strawberries in Table 5.2 of *Greenhouse Gas Impacts of Food Retailing: Report for Defra* (2008). This assumes the supermarket is using electricity almost entirely from fossil fuels (0.537 kgCO$_2$e / kWh) and the refrigerant (R-404A) is 3860 times more potent than carbon dioxide as a greenhouse gas. This number would be reduced depending on the fraction of clean energy in the electricity mix, and using modern refrigerants such as carbon dioxide. However, the lower density of lettuce (compared to strawberries) would significantly increase emissions (e.g. see Table 11 of Frankowska et al. 2019a).

59 *preserved (e.g. tinned tomatoes,* A value of 1.8 kgCO$_2$e / kg comes from figure S26 of Frankowska et al. (2019a) for canned tomato, using 92% of 1.95 (to exclude the cooking and waste emissions which are covered separately in chapter 33).

59 *passata* Figure S26 of Frankowska et al. (2019a) gives a value of 2.04 kgCO$_2$e / kg for bottled tomato, using 88% of 2.32 (to exclude the household cooking and waste emissions).

59 *tomato puree* Figure S26 of Frankowska et al. (2019a) shows a value of 4.6 kgCO$_2$e / kg, after excluding waste emissions.

Chapter 12 Pizza

Who doesn't like pizza (Fig. 12.1)? It's the safest bet to serve at a kids' play date these days. In terms of ingredients though, it isn't very different from the cheese sandwich we already discussed (chapter 9). The main difference in ingredients is the tomato sauce which, as we just saw, is not going to contribute much to greenhouse-gas emissions because it can be made from in-season field-grown tomatoes and stored at room temperature. The total emissions for a pizza can approach 1.5 kilos, or half of a budget of 3 kilos for daily food emissions (Fig. 12.2, left). Of this 1.5 kilos, nearly 1 kilo comes from the cheese.

Fig. 12.1: A pepperoni pizza with plenty of cheese. (URL 113)

Meaty feast?

What about a ham or pepperoni pizza, or a meat feast with several meat and sausage toppings? Pepperoni can be made from pork or beef, or some combination. As we discovered in chapter 10, meats from pigs have comparable emissions to cheese, weight-for-weight. So it doesn't make much difference if you swap out some cheese for ham (compare Fig. 12.2 centre and left).

Other meaty options include beef pepperoni or ground beef, for which the emissions depend significantly on the quality of the beef (chapter 24). In the extreme case of using high quality steak as a pizza topping, the pizza emissions are increased to nearly 2 kilos – about 30% more than the ham pizza (Fig. 12.2, right).

Oven use

Unlike a sandwich, a pizza is best served crispy and hot. The oven is pre-heated to a high temperature, and the pizza goes on the top shelf until the cheese just starts to bubble. Depending on your oven and energy supplier, the cooking may be the next biggest contributor to emissions after the toppings (Fig. 12.2).

Fig. 12.2: Emissions from different choices of pizza topping, assuming the pizza is cooked for 10 minutes for one person.
Left: Emissions for a cheese and tomato pizza: a pizza base (210 g); tomato puree (30 g); cheese (60 g); putting the oven on for 10 minutes, plus warm-up time (25 minutes at 2.4 kWh).
Centre: The same as the cheese and tomato pizza, but replacing half the cheese with ham.
Right: The same as the cheese and tomato pizza, but replacing the 60 g cheese with 20 g cheese, 20 g ham and 20 g steak.

Box 12.1: Oven emissions

The emissions from cooking depend mostly on how long you have the appliance on for. Which do you think impacts the climate more i) putting the oven on for one hour or ii) putting the grill on for 10 minutes? Just by comparing the two durations you can already correctly guess that the oven is going to use more electricity.

For appliances that stay on for a long time, we also have to factor in leakage of the heat. I don't know how efficient your own oven is, but you can find out if you watch the little temperature indicator light: when the light is on, the oven is using electricity to heat itself up, but when the light is off the oven is at the right temperature and not using electricity.

A really well-insulated oven would heat up to the required temperature and then stay there without needing extra power (so long as you don't go opening the door to check on the pizza...) but realistically some heat is going to escape into your kitchen, which means that the power will have to switch on again.

If you needed the kitchen to be warmed up anyway, and if you turn the heating down to compensate for the heat generated by the oven, then the energy used to heat the oven has been compensated for. Also, if you're cooking for several people at once, then the cooking emissions per person reduce proportionately.

How can you reduce emissions?

How can you still enjoy the crunchy tastiness of a pizza without blowing half a daily food emissions budget of 3 kilos in one go?

- Halving the amount of cheese reduces the emissions by 30%. Or, if you cook for two people at once, and if you can cope with using just a sprinkling of cheese, you halve your pizza emissions (Fig. 12.3, centre).

- Switching to vegan cheese makes the biggest single difference.

- Or you might want to switch in some vegetables – I like sweetcorn because it adds back in a lighter colour to compensate for the missing cheese, and a sprinkling of ground almonds feels a bit like Parmesan (for more details on nuts see chapter 19).

  1 g sweetcorn = 2 g emissions

  If you're also cooking for a family of four then you've just reduced your pizza emissions by 70% (Fig. 12.3, right), down to less than half a kilo per pizza.

I'll be honest though that, in my experience, without any of the gooeyness of melted cows' cheese, the toppings do tend to fall off. You might want to warn people to keep that pizza slice level – or maybe those artificial lab milk proteins will come to the rescue (chapter 6)?

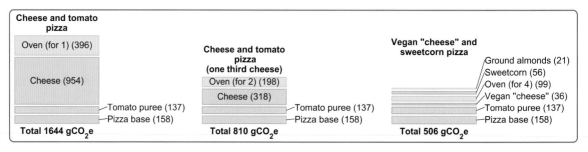

Fig. 12.3:
Left: The cheese and tomato pizza from Fig. 12.2 (left), reproduced for ease of comparison.
Centre: Emissions for a cheese and tomato pizza (one third cheese): a pizza base (210 g); tomato puree (30 g); cheese (20 g); putting the oven on for 10 minutes, plus warm-up time, shared between two people (13 minutes at 2.4 kWh).
Right: Emissions for a vegan "cheese" and sweetcorn pizza: a pizza base (210 g); tomato puree (30 g); vegan "cheese" (25 g); putting the oven on for 10 minutes, plus warm-up time, shared between four people (6 minutes at 2.4 kWh); sweetcorn (30 g); ground almonds (10 g).

Key points

- For a typical cheesy and/or meaty pizza, the topping is responsible for most of the emissions, so reducing the amount of cheese and meat on the top is the single most effective way to reduce the climate impact.

- Using alternative toppings, such as vegetables, and cooking for four people at once, can make the pizza a low-emissions meal, and three times better for the climate than a traditional pizza.

Notes

Page

63   *but realistically some heat is going to escape into your kitchen, which means that the power will have to switch on again.* The calculations here assume your oven draws 2.4 kW of power while it warms up for 15 minutes, and is then on at an average of 2.4 kW for the rest of the cooking time too. In practice the emissions will depend not only on your oven but also on the temperature you're cooking at: the hotter the cooking temperature, the more heat will flow into your kitchen.

64   *sweetcorn* An emissions value of 1.9 $kgCO_2e$ / kg comes from figure S58 of Frankowska et al. (2019a) for frozen UK sweetcorn, taking the first 82% of 2.27 $kgCO_2e$ / kg to avoid double-counting cooking (household) and waste.

Chapter 13 A baked potato, or fries

I do like a baked potato, with baked beans and cheese and lots of butter. Fig. 13.1 shows a really greasy-looking serving in a polystyrene tray – a classic British lunch – as yummy as it is squeaky (Fig. 13.1).

Growing potatoes

Have you ever grown your own potatoes? I couldn't see what the excitement was about until I gave in last year and bought a special potato bag for the patio. The potatoes sprouted, I didn't get around to earthing them up, they dried out and wilted between the rains and got mostly eaten by enormous black slugs. Eventually the leaves looked so yellow I thought I should move them at least out of view. I have to admit to a great sense of satisfaction and amazement – and excitement from the kids – at searching through the compost and finding all the small potatoes that grew, despite my neglect.

Commercial potatoes grow in the ground with fertilizers, but even a large potato isn't going to make much of an impact on your daily food emissions, until you start factoring in the cooking and accompaniments.

1 g potato = 0.6 g emissions

Cooking potatoes

What could be an easier meal than sticking a potato in the oven and forgetting about it for an hour or two? My oven has usually been on for at least 2 hours by the time I've pre-heated it, remembered to put the potatoes in, and remembered to take them out. If you're cooking for one, then the oven alone causes over 2 kilos of emissions (see also chapter 1 and box 12.1). A generous helping of cheese and some butter brings the total emissions up to over 3 kilos per portion (Fig. 13.4, left), using up a daily food emissions budget of 3 kilos.

Fig. 13.1: Baked potato with beans and cheese. (URL 40)

Fig. 13.2: Potato plants in a field. (URL 41)

Fig. 13.3: Potatoes as they are dug up. (URL 42)

But this is lunchtime – perhaps you're at a work canteen where there are lots of potatoes and other food in the oven, so the cooking emissions per potato would be very small. Or, if you're cooking for two and prepared to halve the amount of cheese, and replace butter with vegetable spread, you can halve the emissions (Fig. 13.4, centre).

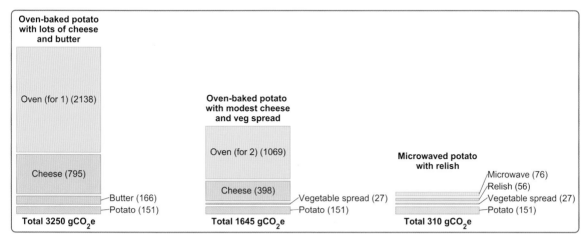

Fig. 13.4: Comparison of some different baked potato choices.
Left: Emissions for an oven-baked potato with generous cheese and butter: one potato (250 g); a large tablespoon of butter (20 g); two slices of cheese (50 g); putting the oven on for 2 hours, plus warm-up time (135 minutes at 2.4 kWh).
Centre: Emissions for an oven-baked potato with modest cheese and veg spread: one potato (250 g); a large tablespoon of vegetable spread (20 g); one slice of cheese (25 g); putting the oven on for 2 hours, plus warm-up time, divided between 2 people (67.5 minutes at 2.4 kWh).
Right: Emissions for a microwaved potato with relish: a potato (250 g); a large tablespoon of vegetable spread (20 g); two teaspoons of relish (20 g); microwave oven (8 minutes at 1.2 kWh).

Maybe you're being quick at home and cooking your potato in the microwave oven? I'm not a big fan of this method, but the internet says it takes about 8 minutes per potato. Assuming the microwave is on full power for that time, the cooking produces nearly 30 times less greenhouse-gas emissions per potato than baking in the oven for two hours (see box 12.1).

If you want to go ultra-low-emissions then you can also replace the cheese with a lower-emissions alternative, like chutney or relish (Fig. 13.4, right; see also chapter 9). This produces the lowest-emissions hot meal in the book, at less than 400 grams of emissions.

Chips or french fries

Chopping up the potato before putting it in the oven, for example to make small roast potatoes, potato wedges or chips, reduces the cooking time, but the climate impact depends a lot on how they are processed and cooked.

The lowest-emissions chip or potato wedge would be made from hand-chopped potatoes, cooked in a modest amount of oil on a large scale. When cooking for one person for 30 minutes, the oven causes most of the emissions (Fig. 13.5, left). On the other hand, if cooking for four people at once then the oven emissions are nearly as small as those from the potato (Fig. 13.5, centre) – this is even lower than the microwaved jacket potato emissions.

However, taking into account the processing of potatoes all the way to frozen oven chips can increase emissions to 3 times the weight of the chips (Fig. 13.5, right).

1 g chips = 3 g emissions

Potato wedges (homemade)	Potato wedges (homemade) (cooking for four)	Chips
Oven (for 1) (713)	Oven (for 4) (178)	Oven (for 2) (356)
Oil (19)	Oil (19)	Oven chips (405)
Potato (91)	Potato (91)	
Total 822 gCO₂e	Total 287 gCO₂e	Total 761 gCO₂e

Fig. 13.5: Emissions for potato wedges and chips.
Left: Emissions for potato wedges (homemade): potato (150 g); vegetable oil (5 g); putting the oven on for 30 minutes, plus warm-up time (45 minutes at 2.4 kWh)..
Centre: Same as left but cooking for four people at once so the oven emissions are divided by four.
Right: Emissions for chips: oven chips (150 g); putting the oven on for 30 minutes, plus warm-up time, shared between 2 people (22.5 minutes at 2.4 kWh).

Fig. 13.6: I love potatoes! (URL 43)

Key points

- The emissions from a simple potato are small compared to those from dairy toppings or heating an oven using fossil fuels.

- Adding in cheese and butter, and cooking for one, brings the baked potato emissions to over 3.2 kilos, which is greater than our daily food emissions budget of 3 kilos.

- You can halve the emissions by going easy on the cheese, replacing butter with vegetable spread, and cooking two potatoes at once.

- Cooking in the microwave oven and replacing cheese with relish turns the baked potato into a very low-emissions meal, causing nearly 0.3 kilos per portion, which is one tenth of a 3 kilo food emissions budget per day.

- Chopping up potatoes before putting them in the oven re-duces the cooking time, and therefore the emissions. Using home-chopped potatoes instead of processed shaped potatoes saves energy.

Notes

Page

66   *but even a large potato isn't going to make much of an impact on your daily food emissions*, 0.6 kgCO₂e / kg of raw potato is taken from Frankowska et al. (2019a) (figure S.52) who give a value of 1.2 kgCO₂e / kg of which household/cooking and waste contribute 50% so are subtracted to avoid

double counting. See also 0.5 kgCO$_2$e / kg from Poore and Nemecek (2018).

67   *hand-chopped potatoes, cooked in a modest amount of oil on a large scale.* **This** doesn't mention peeling the potatoes, because keeping the skin on helps reduce emissions because there is less waste (chapter 33). Eating the skin is also healthier because it contains more of some nutrients (including fibre) than the potato flesh.

68   *taking into account the processing of potatoes all the way to frozen oven chips can increase emissions to 3 times the weight of the chips* Frankowska et al. (2019a) find a value of 3.9 kgCO$_2$e / kg for frozen chips prepared in the oven at home of which 14% is household/cooking and waste, which we discuss separately, giving 3.4 kgCO$_2$e / kg. Alternatively T. Ponsioen and H. Blonk (2011) find a value of 2.0 kgCO$_2$e / kg. The figures in this book use an average of these two numbers. Ultimately the value will depend greatly on the type of energy (fossil or clean) used in the manufacturing).

Chapter 14 Beans and other legumes

Reach for a tin of beans from the store cupboard or pantry and you have a nutritious meal in your hand – if you're desperate the beans can even be eaten cold, straight from the can. (I have done this.) The beans have been transformed from their green beginnings, when they grew like peas in a pod (Fig. 14.1).

In this chapter we focus on mature beans and other legumes that have been left on the plant to grow fat and ready to sprout into a new generation of plants whenever they get enough water to start swelling and growing. These include soya beans, the beans used to make baked beans, haricot beans (Fig. 14.2), and their close relatives lentils and chick peas.

Fig. 14.1: Soya bean pods on the plant. (URL 44)

Legumes and nitrogen

In terms of greenhouse gases, beans and other legumes are almost magical: they work with bacteria in their roots to take nitrogen from the air and convert it into a form that the bean plant can use. This reduces the amount of fertilizer needed by the plants and, if the roots are left in the ground, they even reduce the amount of fertilizer needed by the next crop. This means that alternating or mixing other crops with legumes helps to cut greenhouse-gas emissions.

Fig. 14.2: Haricot beans (also known as navy beans, so-called not because of their colour, but because they are so nutritious they are fed to the US Navy). (URL 45)

Cooked beans

The beans themselves cause less than their own cooked weight in emissions,

1 g beans, cooked weight (excluding cooking) = 0.63 g emissions

so the big question is how much energy is used to cook them. Dried beans need a lot of cooking, and the boiling time varies significantly between different types. The amount of energy required also depends on whether you cook the beans in a sealed pressure cooker or in ordinary saucepan that allows lots of water to evaporate.

Two different bean-cooking calculations illustrate the wide variation in energy use. On the one hand, cooking for one person using an open pan for 40 minutes is very inefficient, and causes higher than half a kilo of emissions (Fig. 14.3, left): the cooking causes much more emissions than the beans themselves. On the other hand, you can be much more efficient by cooking four portions at once using a pressure cooker for 20 minutes (Fig. 14.3, centre). Now the cooking emissions are similar to those from the beans, and the total is only one quarter of the emissions of the inefficiently cooked beans.

Fig. 14.3: Comparison of some different ways of cooking beans.
Left: An extremely inefficient example of boiling up an open pan for 40 minutes to cook 45 g of dried beans into 125 g of cooked beans.
Centre: A much more efficient case in which the same quantity of beans are cooked for 20 minutes (for example in a pressure cooker) and the cooking emissions are shared between four people (5 minutes of 2 kWh electricity per person).
Right: Emissions for canned beans re-heated: the same quantity of beans (125 g cooked beans, or half a drained can); a 50 g steel can, shared between 2 people (25 g); cooking in a microwave oven (3 minutes at 1.2 kWh).

How do home home-cooked beans compare with ready cooked beans in a tin can? I put in a diagram showing the emissions from canned beans, showing separately the contribution from the steel packaging, and reheating the beans in a microwave for three minutes (Fig. 14.3, right).

$$\text{1 g beans, tinned} = 1.8 \text{ g emissions}$$

The total emissions are nearly double those of the efficiently cooked beans, but less than half those of the inefficiently cooked beans.

Box 14.1: Tin cans

A typical 400 g-capacity tin can is made from about 50 g of steel. For typical recycling rates and energy mix, steel causes about twice its own weight in emissions.

$$\text{1 g steel} = 2 \text{ g emissions}$$

If we don't recycle then this number increases, but if we eat communally then it goes down – since caterers use bigger containers, the relative contribution from the steel tin becomes smaller.

Most of the tin-can emissions are caused by energy to run the steel plant, which can be reduced if sufficient renewable energy is used. The canning process itself also uses energy, mostly to heat the food.

The calculations here assume 100% fossil fuels are used to run the steel-processing plant and the canning process.

Fig. 14.4: Emissions for beans on toast: two slices of bread (80 g); toasting (3.6 minutes at 2 kWh); two teaspoons of vegetable spread (10 g); a 400 g can of baked beans, shared between 4 people (100 g); a 50 g steel can, shared between 4 people (12.5 g); microwave oven (3 minutes at 1.2 kWh).

Canned beans often come with a tomato sauce, which makes little difference to the emissions.

$$1 \text{ g baked beans} = 2 \text{ g emissions}$$

We can serve the baked beans on toast with vegetable spread to make one of my favourite dinners (Fig. 14.4). This is the second-lowest hot meal, after the baked potato with relish (chapter 13).

Alternatively, we can add the beans on to our baked-potato lunch. Adding beans to the cheesy oven-baked potato makes little difference to the total (Fig. 14.5, left), whereas the plain microwaved potato had such low emissions in the first place that the beans nearly double the emissions, but the result is still a low climate impact meal (Fig. 14.5, right), and packs in a good deal of nutrition from both the beans and potato.

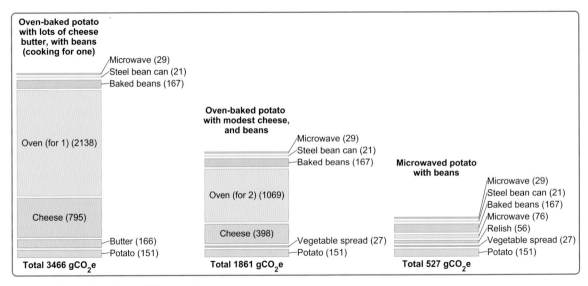

Fig. 14.5: Comparison of some different choices for potato and beans.
Left: Rich, oven-baked: a potato (250 g); tbsp butter (20 g); two slices of cheese (50 g); oven 15 mins warm-up + 2 hours (at 2.4 kWh).
Centre: Microwaved, with relish: a potato (250 g); tbsp vegetable spread (20 g); two tsp relish (20 g); microwave oven (8 mins at 1.2 kWh).
Right: Microwaved, with beans: a potato (250 g); tbsp vegetable spread (20 g); two tsp relish (20 g); microwave oven (8 minutes at 1.2 kWh); 400 g can of baked beans, shared between 4 people (100 g); 50 g steel can, shared between 4 people (12.5 g); microwave (3 mins at 1.2 kWh).

Key points

- A portion of beans cooked efficiently at home causes very low greenhouse-gas emissions.

- Beans from a tin can cause about twice their own weight in emissions, if fossil fuels are used to do the canning.

- Adding beans makes very little difference to the large emissions from an oven-baked potato cooked for one person with added butter and cheese.

- Adding a portion of tinned beans more than doubles the tiny emissions of a microwaved potato, but it still makes a very low-emissions healthy meal, causing just over half a kilo of emissions.

Box 14.2: Personal emissions

When I give public talks about emissions from beans, there's usually someone bold enough to ask about the greenhouse-gas emissions from farts. Here I'm going to refer to human flatulence as "personal emissions" to spare readers' blushes. Often the questioner is concerned that switching from beef to beans is simply moving the cow methane problem elsewhere, i.e. into personal emissions.

Some personal emissions do contain methane, but academic research finds that this is not connected with the amount of beans or other legumes in the diet. Even for the people who do produce methane, the daily output is still a tiny fraction (1%) of the amount of methane produced by cows to make a large steak. However, an increase in the amount of dietary fibre (e.g. from beans) is linked to increased amounts of personal emissions, and improved health (chapter 34).

Notes

Page

70 *The beans have been transformed from their green beginnings, when they grew like peas in a pod (Fig. 14.1).* Young soya beans can be eaten lightly steamed with salt, and are better known as edamame beans – they are more like the green beans discussed in chapter 28.

70 *if the roots are left in the ground, they even reduce the amount of fertilizer needed by the next crop.* For example see fertilizer application recommendations in Kissel and Harris (n.d.).

70 *The beans themselves cause less than their own cooked weight in emissions,* The global average for beans and pulses from Poore and Nemecek (2018) is 1.8 kgCO$_2$e / kg dry beans. To convert this into the cooked weight of beans (described in the text) we use a value of 100 g of cooked pulses from 35 g dry pulses (from table 4.21 of Durlinger et al. (2017), which gives 0.63 kgCO$_2$e / kg rehydrated beans (1.8 kgCO$_2$e / kg × 35 g / 100 g).

71 *emissions from canned beans, showing separately the contribution from the steel packaging, and reheating the beans in a microwave for three minutes* Taking an average of UK (1.6 kgCO$_2$e / kg after subtracting the can) and imported (1.7 kgCO$_2$e / kg) beans, values from Frankowska et al. (2019a) for beans in a can. To subtract the can we use the emissions for steel of 1.68 kgCO$_2$e / kg, a steel weight of 50 g for 250 g of beans from a 400 g can after draining: 1.68 kgCO$_2$e / kg steel × 50 g steel / 250 g beans = 0.3 kgCO$_2$e / kg for the can.

71   *steel causes about twice its own weight in emissions.* The value from "CCaLC PVC Manual (V2.0)" (2011) for recycled tinplate (steel) is 1.68 kgCO$_2$e / kg (62% recycled) and 2.7 kgCO$_2$e / kg for virgin (not recycled) tinplate. To learn more about the energy needed to make materials, see *Sustainable Materials – Without the Hot Air: Making Buildings, Vehicles and Products Efficiently and with Less New Material* (Allwood and Cullen, 2015).

71   *Canned beans often come with a tomato sauce, which makes little difference to the emissions.* The value of 2.0 kgCO$_2$e / kg is taken from Frankowska et al. (2019a) for baked beans in a can (including canning and tomato sauce), averaging the values for UK (1.6 kgCO$_2$e / kg after subtracting 0.2 kgCO$_2$e / kg for the can) and imported beans (2.3 kgCO$_2$e / kg after subtracting the can).

73   *Some personal emissions do contain methane, but academic research finds that this is not connected with the amount of beans or other legumes in the diet. Even for the people who do produce methane, the daily output is still a tiny fraction (1%) of the amount of methane produced by cows to make a large steak.* For the sake of science, 16 people agreed to have a tube inserted into their rectums (bottoms) to collect gas (Suarez et al., 1997). They had to eat 200 grams of beans the previous day, to make sure there would be enough material to study. They each passed gas between 3 and 9 times in the 4-hour hour period of the study, producing between 100 ml and 1000 ml of gas. Most of the gas was hydrogen, carbon dioxide and nitrogen, and only 5 of these people produced any significant amount of methane, on average about 100 ml each. By contrast, a cow and calf produce 0.4 kg or 400 litres of methane a day for 700 g of steak (chapter 24). This means that production of a large (8 oz or 226g) steak causes 130 litres of methane to be released into the atmosphere, which is 1000 times the daily amount for people who produce a lot of methane in their personal emissions.

Chapter 15 Yogurt and cream

To round off lunch, how about a yogurt (Fig. 15.1)? In this chapter we also consider cream, which you might like as a topping on fruit (chapter 17) or dessert (chapter 30), or as a cookery ingredient (chapters 7, 22 and 25).

Yogurt

A mesmerizing array of yogurt options stretches along the supermarket aisles – from light to extra creamy, to fruit layers and crunchy corners. By definition though, they are all mostly made of milk. Special bacteria feed off the lactose (milk sugar) and produce lactic acid, which changes the shape of the milk proteins and causes the milk to get thicker.

Unlike cheese, nothing is strained off when making most types of yogurt, so the emissions from yogurt are similar to those from milk, causing twice their own weight in emissions.

1 g yogurt = 2 g emissions

What about the plastic pot? For research purposes I've just eaten a large (150 g) yogurt and weighed the pot – 10 g – which means the pot causes only about one tenth of the total emissions (Fig. 15.2; see box 21.1 for more details on plastic emissions).

Cream

Nowadays, most western milk is processed (homogenized) to mix together the cream and the milk, but in the olden days (well, when I was growing up!), the milk gradually separated into cream at the top of the bottle, and milk at the bottom. These days, whole milk is separated commercially into skimmed milk and cream, and turned into a full spectrum of products from double cream and single cream at one end, through to whole milk, semi-skimmed milk and skimmed (nonfat) milk at the other extreme.

Fig. 15.1: A pot of yogurt. (URL 46)

A pot of yogurt
Plastic pot (30)
Yogurt (270)
Total 300 gCO$_2$e

Fig. 15.2: Emissions for a pot of yogurt: yogurt (150 g); plastic pot (10 g).

**Cream
(two tablespoons)**
Cream (147)
Total 147 gCO$_2$e

Fig. 15.3: Emissions for cream (two tablespoons): cream (30 g).

This means that the greenhouse-gas emissions for cream depend on the emissions of the original full-fat milk, and on how you share out the full-fat milk emissions between the cream and the skimmed milk. If cream were unpopular and considered a by-product of the skimmed milk industry then we could treat it like a free by-product (box 9.1). But in reality both cream and skimmed milk are popular, and cream has been attributed about five times its own weight in emissions.

1 g cream = 5 g emissions

It's unusual to eat cream as a stand-alone dessert, but cream can appear in ingredients lists in larger quantities and ends up making a significant difference to the emissions of some foods, despite being relatively hidden from view; for example, in this book we consider scrambled egg (chapter 7), a black forest cake (chapter 22) and chicken tikka masala (chapter 25). At the end of the evening meal we will drizzle two tablespoons of cream (Fig. 15.3) over a slice of apple pie (chapter 30), which adds about 150 g of emissions.

Alternative puddings include super-healthy fruit, or less-than-healthy cake (with added cream), both discussed in the next Part on snacks.

Key points

- Yogurt emissions come mostly from the production of the milk.

- Since yogurt is simply milk thickened by the action of good bacteria, it has lower emissions than products that are concentrated down from milk, such as cheese, cream and butter.

- Cream emissions are a few times higher than those for milk, depending on how they are shared with its skimmed-milk co-product.

Notes

Page

75 *the emissions from yogurt are similar to those from milk, causing twice their own weight in emissions.* A value of 1.8 kgCO_2e / kg is from Frankowska (2019) for packaged yogurt in cold storage at the retailer and consumer, after subtracting packaging.

76 *cream has been attributed about five times its own weight in emissions.* 4.9 kgCO_2e / kg cream is an average of values from Finnegan et al. (2018) (5.06 kgCO_2e / kg), Djekic et al. (2014) (4 kgCO_2e / kg) and Sheane et al. (2011) (5.6 kgCO_2e / kg).

Chapter 16 Lunch summary

At the risk of comparing apples and oranges (though we will literally do that in the next Part!), we now compare the greenhouse-gas emissions of the various lunch options.

Lunch has illustrated that there is often a big range of emissions for a single type of food, depending on the ingredients, their seasonality and the method of preparation. For example, the simple sandwich emissions vary by more than ten times depending on whether it contains beef or peanut butter (compare Figs. 10.7 centre and 9.4 right). Emissions also change by more than ten times depending on whether salad is grown locally and seasonally, or in a heated greenhouse (chapter 11). And baked potato emissions are significantly reduced by using the microwave instead of the main oven, and reducing the amount of cheese. In Fig. 16.1 we compare typical-, high-, and low-emissions lunches.

Typical-emissions lunch

A ham sandwich with a lettuce salad and a yogurt comes to about a kilo of emissions (Fig. 16.1, left), which is one third of a 3 kilo daily food emissions budget. The biggest single ingredient is the ham, followed closely by the yogurt.

Higher-emissions lunch

For a higher-emissions alternative, we'll take the oven-baked potato dripping with butter and generous cheese (cooking for one), and add to this a tomato salad, produced from a dedicated heated greenhouse, plus the same yogurt we had for the typical-emissions lunch. This quadruples the total lunch emissions to 3 kilos, more than half of which come from the cheesy baked potato, cooked for one person, followed by the hothouse tomatoes (Fig. 16.1, center). In this one meal, we've already blown a daily emissions budget of 3 kilos.

Fig. 16.1: Comparison of some different lunch choices.
Left: Emissions for a typical-emissions lunch: ham sandwich; lettuce salad; a pot of yogurt.
Centre: Emissions for a higher-emissions lunch: an oven baked potato with butter and cheese; a tomato salad, from tomatoes grown in a heated greenhouse; a yogurt.
Right: Emissions for a lower-emissions lunch: a microwaved potato with relish and beans; a local seasonal salad.

Lower-emissions lunch

You can reduce the typical lunch emissions by 40% by eating a microwaved baked potato with beans, eating an in-season salad (Fig. 16.1, right), and postponing a treat until snack time, discussed next.

Key points

- The typical-emissions lunch options cause about one kilo of emissions, which makes up one third of a daily 3 kilo food emissions budget.

- The higher-emissions option is four times as bad (for the climate) as the typical-emissions lunch, mostly due to the energy to power the oven, the cheese, and heating a greenhouse to grow tomatoes out-of-season.

- You can halve lunch emissions by skipping dessert, eating a microwaved potato with beans and eating a seasonal salad.

Part III: Snacks

Lets face it, snacks are a temptation at any time of day. They're usually ready to eat, and provide pleasant sensations such as crunchiness, saltiness or sweetness.

In this Part we'll consider fruit first, and compare the impact of different transport options. Will the emissions story of chocolate leave a bitter taste, or are there simple fixes that can keep it as a daily not-so-guilty pleasure? Nuts are sometimes hailed as great substitutes for animal products, increasingly in some milk alternatives, but are they really better for climate change? Crisps (potato chips) are my favourite snack, but what level of emissions am I causing? Soft drinks raise the topic of emissions from different sorts of packaging. Finally, baking a cake allows us to play with combining some of the ingredients discussed so far.

Chapter 17 A piece of fruit

Fruit, the archetypal healthy snack, has evolved especially to be attractive to animals like ourselves (Fig. 17.1). Here we focus on the widely eaten fruits: apples, oranges, bananas and strawberries.

Apples

Fig. 17.1: Which fruit do you think is responsible for the most greenhouse-gas emissions? (URL 47)

Fig. 17.2: Apples on a tree. (URL 48)

I was brought up on the mantra "an apple a day keeps the doctor away". This was partly fuelled by visits to the local fruit farm where I would be encouraged by the owner to take a fresh, new-season apple from the big crate, and eat it right there in the shop. I was thrilled when the first house we bought had a garden complete with apple trees (Fig. 17.2). By autumn we had a lot more than one apple a day, and tens of blackbirds would fly in to eat the fallen fruit that still lay on the ground as the snow arrived.

In contrast to our back garden, commercial apple orchards do a lot of pruning, thinning and picking. Hydraulic ladders make the work less precarious but this and other mechanization make up about half of the greenhouse-gas emissions at the farm. To get the best apple crop, extra nitrogen is applied as fertilizer, which causes most of the rest of the emissions from the farming stage. Cold storage of the apples to eat out of season doubles their emissions, but the impact of an apple is still relatively low.

1 g local seasonal apples = 0.4 g emissions

Even if you eat two apples a day, you still only spend 3% of a daily food emissions budget of 3 kg.

A typical (100 g) apple racks up a minuscule 5 grams of emissions when transported across a small country – just one thousandth of a typical day of food emissions (Fig. 17.3, left). This is not something to worry about! But how can you keep the doctor away in the spring, when apples are out of season? UK shops are full of apples from New Zealand, on the other side of the world – the highest possible food miles away.

Box 17.1: Transporting food by truck

Within a country, usually food is transported by road in a big truck. As an example, consider a journey of 400 km across the UK, from the 'garden of England' in Kent to my local supermarket in Manchester. If the truck is powered by fossil fuels, and has a typical packing density of food, the trucking emissions are about one twentieth of the weight of the product being transported.

1 g transported 400 km by truck = 0.05 g emissions

Box 17.2: Shipping food by sea

Emissions from ships vary significantly depending on the ship size and type of fuel. As a rule of thumb, transporting food by boat to the other side of the world (20,000 km, e.g. from New Zealand to the UK) causes about one quarter of its own weight in emissions.

1 g transported 20,000 km by boat = 0.3 g emissions

For a shorter journey, for example around a continent, the emissions are correspondingly lower. For example, for a typical distance (3,000 km, e.g. from Spain to the UK), the sea-freight emissions are about one twentieth of the weight of the food being transported, which is the same as trucking across a small country.

1 g transported 3,000 km by boat = 0.04 g emissions

Fig. 17.3:
Left: Emissions for an apple, trucked across the UK (400 km): an apple (100 g); transport 400 km by truck.
Centre: Emissions for an apple, shipped across the world (20,000 km): an apple (100 g); transport 20,000 km by boat.
Right: Emissions for an apple, from the local farm shop: an apple (100 g); transport 30 km by car, shared between 60 apples (0.5 km).

An apple on a journey from one side of the world to the other is responsible for 26 grams of emissions due to transportation (Fig. 17.3, centre). Perhaps surprisingly, shipping apples from the other side of the world turns out to be only five times worse than driving the fruit across a small country. An alternative to shipping from overseas is storing locally grown fruit: apples can keep for months in properly controlled conditions (this is already factored into the apple emissions used here).

How about driving to the local fruit farm? My last drive there and back took at least 30 minutes. Maybe we bought a crate of apples to keep us going for a couple of weeks. But even if we bought 50 apples, this trip caused 3 times the emissions per apple compared with shipping from New Zealand. Local isn't always better. They were the best apples I ever tasted though. And maybe it was the merry banter with the owners of the farm that sparked my curiosity about food production and led me to write this book?

Visiting local farms and talking to local farmers at markets are fantastic when they help us to appreciate where our food comes from. However, making a dedicated extra excursion every week in a fossil-fuelled car would do more harm than good to the climate. In contrast, vegetable and fruit box deliveries can be a great way to reduce transport emissions and support your local farm, because the delivery trip emissions are shared out across many customers.

Oranges

Like apples, oranges grow on trees, but orange are sensitive to cold temperatures and need a lot of sunshine. Despite not being well suited to the UK, oranges have become associated with the British, because the Navy fed them to sailors on long sea journeys to avoid scurvy. And it turns out that the ability of oranges to keep well on a long journey is critical to their relatively low impact on the climate.

Emissions from growing the oranges are similar to those for growing apples, but they do not need to be kept so cold to store them between seasons.

Fig. 17.4: Oranges growing in an orange grove. (URL 49)

$$1 \text{ g oranges} = 0.3 \text{ g emissions}$$

The emissions are still extremely low, though, and the same transportation issues apply as for apples: oranges are fine sitting on a ship for a couple of months, which is enough time to ship them across the world. Shipping across a single continent causes about 4 grams of emissions, which is smaller than the emissions from growing the fruit (Fig. 17.5, left).

Bananas

Bananas come in their own easily removable skin as packaging, and don't even need much chewing (they would be a very lazy healthy snack if I didn't end up with a forgotten squashed brown banana at the bottom of my bag most of the times I'm organized enough to take one to work). To transport bananas across the world they need to be carried in protective boxes to stop them getting squashed, which adds to their total emissions, and is a much bigger issue than the thin plastic bag we often see as a consumer.

An orange, shipped across a continent (3000 km)
— Boat (4)
— Orange (31)
Total 35 gCO$_2$e

A banana, shipped across the world (20,000km)
— Boat (26)
— Banana (43)
Total 69 gCO$_2$e

Strawberries (by air)
Air freight (608)
— Strawberries (168)
Total 776 gCO$_2$e

Fig. 17.5:
Left: Emissions for an orange, shipped across a continent (3000 km): an orange (100 g); transport 3,000 km by boat.
Centre: Emissions for a banana, shipped across the world (20,000 km): a banana (100 g); transport 20,000 km by boat.
Right: Emissions for strawberries (by air): a bowl of strawberries (80 g); transport 5,000 km by air.

Bananas are usually grown in even hotter countries than oranges, so often require longer voyages to reach us. Overall the emissions caused by a banana are 70% of their own weight, of which less than half comes from transport by sea (Fig. 17.5, right).

1 g banana, transported by boat = 0.7 g emissions

This is about twice the emissions caused by an orange or a local apple, but one banana (100 g) still causes only about 2% of a daily food emissions budget of 3,000 g.

Soft fruits

For me, summer isn't complete without gorging on a bowl of strawberries (Fig. 17.6). Ideally I would also fit in a trip to a pick-your-own fruit farm, bringing back childhood memories of hunching over and searching for the perfectly ripe fruits among the straw, and hiding the evidence from "testing" a few sample fruits to make sure they were OK.

Nowadays commercial strawberries are grown more like cherry tomatoes (chapter 11): away from the soil, watered with fertilizer and usually protected by glass or plastic; they cause about twice their own weight in emissions if grown locally and in-season. The emissions for raspberries are similar.

1 g strawberries = 2 g emissions

1 g raspberries = 2 g emissions

We can enjoy eating plenty when the fruit is in-season in our hemisphere, but what about the food miles travelled by a strawberry in the winter?

The wonders of world trade mean that in our winter we can eat strawberries grown in the summer of the opposite hemisphere, which makes a kind of sense, until you factor in the transportation by air. Bringing food by air causes 100 times the emissions of bringing the food the same distance by ship, and flying over a portion (80 g) of strawberries adds more than 0.5 kilos of emissions to the serving, using up one sixth of a 3 kg daily food emissions budget.

Fig. 17.6: A delicious bowl of strawberries – but did they fly over to you? (URL 50)

Box 17.3: Perishable produce

"Perishable" food deteriorates quickly after being harvested, if not preserved somehow, for example by freezing or canning. Examples of perishable fruits and vegetables include strawberries, raspberries, blueberries, green beans, lettuce and cucumber. By contrast, "non-perishable" foods like oranges and bananas can be shipped across the world and stay fresh in the hold of a temperature-controlled container ship. Perishable foods need to be consumed shortly after they have been harvested and must be air-freighted if they are to remain fresh over a long journey.

Box 17.4: Flying food

A lot of fresh produce is carried in the hold of passenger planes (one reason why budget airlines charge us a fortune for hold luggage, especially when we bring it along at the last minute). Transporting food 5,000 km from another continent (e.g. Africa to the UK) causes 8 times the weight of the food in emissions, once we factor in the extra impact of burning fossil fuels at altitude where they cause more warming.

1 g transported 5,000 km by air = 8 g emissions

This puts air-freighted fruit and veg in the same climate-impact category as lower impact animal products like chicken.

Key points

- Enjoy local fruits when in season.

- Enjoy seaworthy (non-perishable) fruits, like apples, oranges and bananas, at any time of the year.

- Cut back on soft (perishable) fruits, like strawberries, when they are out of season.

Notes

Page

82 *Hydraulic ladders make the work less precarious but this and other mechanization make up about half of the greenhouse-gas emissions at the farm.* See Fig 5 and 7 of Milà i Canals et al. (2006).

82 *the impact of an apple is still relatively low.* Commercial apples cause about 0.35 kgCO$_2$e / kg apple, based on Frankowska et al., 2019b, figure S15

which gives 0.5 kgCO$_2$e / kg apple including 18% waste (subtracted for now but discussed in chapter 33) and 13% for transport (subtracted for now and added back in later). Most of the remainder is divided equally between on-farm emissions and storage.

83 *trucking emissions are about one twentieth of the weight of the product being transported.* Based on values for transportation from the UK government transport reporting factors document (UK Government Department for Business, Energy & Industrial Strategy (DEFRA), 2018) For a diesel refrigerated heavy goods vehicle (HGV) with an average load, this gives 0.13 kgCO$_2$e / tonne / km. Therefore for a load of 1 kilo travelling 400 km, the emissions are 0.13 kgCO$_2$e / tonne / km × 1 kg × 400 km / (1,000 kg / tonne) = 0.05 kgCO$_2$e.

83 *transporting food by boat to the other side of the world (20,000 km, e.g. from New Zealand to the UK) causes about one quarter of its own weight in emissions.* The value for refrigerated boat cargo used for UK government reporting (UK Government Department for Business, Energy & Industrial Strategy (DEFRA), 2018) is 0.01308 kgCO$_2$e / tonne / km. Converting this into kgCO$_2$e for a 20,000 km trip for 1 kilo of food means multiplying by 20,000 km and dividing by 1000 kg / tonne, which gives 0.26 kgCO$_2$e / kg.

83 *for a typical distance (3,000 km, e.g. from Spain to the UK), the sea-freight emissions are about one twentieth of the weight of the food being transported,* Modifying the previous calculation from 20,000 km to 3,000 km gives 0.04 kgCO$_2$e / kg of produce.

84 *even if we bought 50 apples, this trip caused 3 times the emissions per apple compared with shipping from New Zealand.* A 30 kilometre round trip in a typical small family car causes nearly 5 kilos of emissions (30 × 155 gCO$_2$e / km; see chapter 1). Sharing this out between 50 apples works out to be nearly 100 grams of emissions per apple.

84 *Emissions from growing the oranges are similar to those for growing apples, but they do not need to be kept so cold to store them between seasons.* Poore and Nemecek (2018) give a value of 0.4 kgCO$_2$e / kg. Subtract the value of 0.09 kgCO$_2$e / kg which they added to account for the transport, as this is added back on in the calculations in this book for consistency across different types of food, giving a value of 0.31 kgCO$_2$e / kg for the figures. This is similar to the value of 0.27 from Frankowska et al. (2019b) without transport, retail and waste (although note that Frankowska et al. 2019b have a value of 1.27 kgCO$_2$e / kg including retail, which would be most relevant for oranges sold in chiller cabinets).

84 *To transport bananas across the world they need to be carried in protective boxes to stop them getting squashed, which adds to their total emissions, and is a much bigger issue than the thin plastic bag we often see as a consumer.* See Iriarte et al. (2014).

85 *the emissions caused by a banana* This uses 0.43 kgCO$_2$e / kg banana, taking the value from Frankowska et al. (2019b) which gives 1.3 kgCO$_2$e / kg of which 67% is transport and waste, which is discussed later. See also Svanes et al. (2011) and Iriarte et al. (2014) which give similar values.

85 *strawberries are grown more like cherry tomatoes (chapter 11): away from the soil, watered with fertilizer and usually protected by glass or plastic; they cause about twice their own weight in emissions if grown locally and in-season.* 2.1 kgCO$_2$e / kg comes from Frankowska et al. (2019b), which gives 2.23 kgCO$_2$e / kg for fresh UK strawberries, of which 94% is before the household/waste stage (which we discuss separately in this book).

85 *raspberries* Fresh UK raspberries from figure S34 of Frankowska et al. (2019b) cause 2.2 kgCO$_2$e / kg. Subtract off 6% to remove the household

and waste components which gives 2.1 kgCO$_2$e / kg. Note that more than one third of this is "retail" mostly due to fridges (box 11.1).

86   *Transporting food 5,000 km from another continent (e.g. Africa to the UK) causes 8 times the weight of the food in emissions, once we factor in the extra impact of burning fossil fuels at altitude where they cause more warming.* The UK Government reporting factors document (UK Government Department for Business, Energy & Industrial Strategy (DEFRA), 2018) gives 0.8 kgCO$_2$e / tonne / km for long-haul dedicated-cargo flights (table 34), to which we apply the radiative forcing factor of 1.9 to account for the higher impact of emissions at altitude (see paragraph 8.37 – but note that this factor is uncertain – previous advice was to use a factor of 2.7 (UK Government Department for Business, Energy & Industrial Strategy (DEFRA), 2016)) To get the number for 1 kilogram of food transported 5,000 km we have to multiply by 5,000 and divide by 1,000 kg / tonne, which gives 7.6 kgCO$_2$e / kg.

Chapter 18 Chocolate and sweets

These days it's often hard to get out of a shop without being tempted by rows and rows of sweets and chocolates. These are popular snacks: on average in the UK we each eat the equivalent of about one small chocolate bar every day.

Chocolate comes from cocoa trees, grown in tropical climates and producing large pods directly on their branches (Fig. 18.1). Each tree makes about 20 of these fruits, which contain the cocoa seeds (Fig. 18.2), which have to be removed from their pods and dried to produce cocoa "beans" (Fig. 18.3), ready for roasting, milling and pressing into cocoa butter, liquor and powder.

The emissions from cocoa products depend greatly on whether forests have been cut down to grow the trees (chapter 7). Considering a stable cocoa plantation, the emissions are about 3 times the weight of the cocoa, mostly due to fertilizing and watering the cocoa trees, their relatively low yields, and the energy needed to process the beans.

Fig. 18.1: Cocoa pods growing on a cacao tree. (URL 51)

$$1 \text{ g cocoa} = 3 \text{ g emissions}$$

How does this stack up when we consider a realistic portion size and include the other ingredients in chocolate? Dark chocolate is often made with 70% cocoa carefully mixed with sugar. A small (25 g) bar of this chocolate causes about 100 grams of emissions (Fig. 18.4, left), which is just 3% of a daily food emissions budget of 3,000 g.

Chocolate often contains less than half this amount of cocoa, with added milk and sugar. Does this reduce the carbon footprint? As highlighted on some chocolate bars, the weight of milk in a bar of chocolate can actually be greater than the weight of the chocolate bar (which is possible because the milk is concentrated into powder before being added to the cocoa).

Fig. 18.2: A cocoa pod showing the beans in white pulp. (URL 52)

$$1 \text{ g milk powder} = 9 \text{ g emissions}$$

Reducing the amount of cocoa reduces the emissions, but this is more than made up by the addition of the milk powder, which pushes the chocolate bar emissions up by 30% relative to the dark chocolate (compare Fig. 18.4 centre and left).

Fig. 18.3: Cocoa beans alongside cocoa pods. (URL 53)

Fig. 18.4:
Left: Emissions for dark chocolate (25 g bar): cocoa (17.5 g); sugar (7.5 g); processing.
Centre: Emissions for milk chocolate (25 g bar): cocoa (6 g); sugar (12.5 g); processing; powdered milk (6 g).
Right: Emissions for sweets (25 g bag): sugar (25 g); processing.

Finally we consider sweets (candies), which are basically all sugar. Just as for cocoa, the emissions depend mostly on whether forest has been cut down to clear land for agriculture, but are lower than those for the dark chocolate (Fig. 18.4, right).

I would enjoy the challenge of eating enough chocolate to make a significant impact on my daily food emissions. However, a large (100 g) bar of milk chocolate contains one quarter of my daily calorie intake, and causes half a kilo of emissions, or one sixth of a daily budget of 3 kilos of emissions caused by food. Furthermore, by increasing demand for products that grow in equatorial regions we drive deforestation. In any case, I think if I ate this much chocolate every day I would have bigger concerns about my health than about the environment.

Key points

- A small bag or bar of chocolate causes about 3% of a budget of 3 kilos of emissions from food, so probably isn't the main thing for most people to cut back on when trying to reduce emissions.

- Sweets (candies) usually cause less emissions than chocolate but don't provide any nutrients.

- Switching from dark to milk chocolate increases emissions by 30%.

Notes

Page

89   *one small chocolate bar every day.* In the UK we eat 7.9 kg / person / year (Konstantas et al., 2018), which is 7900 grams / 365 days a year = 21.6 grams per day. A small chocolate bar usually weighs 25 grams.

89   *roasting, milling and pressing into cocoa butter, liquor and powder.* For details of all the processes and how they contribute to emissions, see Recanati et al. (2018) and Myhre et al. (2013).

89   *The emissions from cocoa products depend greatly on whether forests have been cut down to grow the trees (chapter 7). Considering a stable cocoa plantation, the emissions are about 3 times the weight of the cocoa, mostly due to fertilizing*

and watering the cocoa trees, their relatively low yields, and the energy needed to process the beans. An average of values from (i) Recanati et al. (2018) who give 2.63 kgCO$_2$e / kg (ii) Ntiamoah and Afrane (2009) who give 3.56 kgCO$_2$e / kg. See also Konstantas et al. (2018) whose values for manufactured chocolate we use for manufacturing emissions. However, note the extremely wide range for different cocoa production estimates in Poore and Nemecek (2018), which range from negative values where cacao trees have been newly planted thus capturing carbon dioxide, through to values of around 200 kgCO$_2$e / kg where deforestation has occurred to plant cacao.

89   *A small (25 g) bar of this chocolate causes about 100 grams of emissions* Each of the examples in this chapter, allows 1 kgCO$_2$e / kg of final product for processing emissions, based on figure 2 of Miah et al. (2018).

89   *the weight of milk in a bar of chocolate can actually be greater than the weight of the chocolate bar* It takes 7.69 kilograms of milk to produce 1 kilogram of milk powder, and a typical milk chocolate recipe is 24.5% milk powder, according to Konstantas et al. (2018). The emissions of 8.7 kgCO$_2$e / kg for milk powder are taken from Frankowska (2019) though note that this does not include the additional emissions from drying the milk, so is an underestimate.

Chapter 19 Nuts

Most plants create their offspring by making seeds. The seeds can often stay alive outside the plant until conditions are right to spring into life, perhaps as the weather starts to warm up, or when enough rain falls. Just like a chicken's egg, the seed contains all the nutrients needed for the first stages of growth of the next generation, making them very nutritious for us to eat. Some types of seed have a hard outer shell and are referred to as nuts.

How many different types of nut have you tried? Peanuts are a popular snack, often salted and roasted. Classier alternatives includes almonds, cashews or Brazil nuts. Peanut butter is a popular sandwich filling, especially when paired with jam or jelly (chapter 9). Nowadays nut milk alternatives, particularly almond and cashew, are gaining popularity as an alternative to cows' milk. In this chapter we focus on emissions from almonds and peanuts because they are the two most popular and best studied nuts.

Almonds

Have you ever eaten a juicy ripe peach or apricot, and then fiddled with the stone at the centre, wondering what lies inside the intricate lacy carpentry of the stone? On prizing it apart you might find a small almond-like seed inside. Peach and apricot seeds are bitter and poisonous because they contain cyanide.

Almond trees are closely related to peaches and apricots, and we call their seeds almonds. (Wild or "bitter" almonds are also poisonous, but you can enjoy regular sweet almonds without worrying.)

As with most crops, the greenhouse-gas emissions are mostly from fertilizer (box 2.1). The amount of almonds harvested from a tree can vary significantly (by 5 times) depending on the amount of fertilizer available, as well as other factors including the weather and the soil quality. Also, depending on where

Fig. 19.1: Almonds as they grow on trees, inside their hulls. (URL 54).

Fig. 19.2: Almond kernels after being taken out of their hulls and shells. (URL 55).

the almonds are grown, they may need to be watered – if fossil fuels are used to power pumps to bring the water up from under the ground then this can contribute about one third of all the almond greenhouse-gas emissions (and cause other environmental problems). Overall, typical commercial almonds cause about twice their own weight in emissions.

1 g almonds = 2 g emissions

Almond milk

How does the climate impact of almond milk compare with that of cows' milk? We have to take into account the emissions from producing almonds, as well as processing them into almond milk, and the packaging, transportation and refrigeration.

To be really be climate-friendly, should we make our own almond milk at home, to keep the transport emissions as low as possible? Just soak some almonds overnight in water, then whizz them up in a blender and strain the result. Anyone who makes their own almond milk sees the large amount of leftovers in the strainer. It takes about 50 grams of almonds to make one (250 ml) cup of almond milk at home, of which more than two thirds gets left over as pulp.

Apparently you can use the pulp for smoothies, or dry it out and use it as a handy gluten-free flour for baking. But how many people really do this, and how much mush goes into the bin and causes methane at the landfill site (chapter 33)? Industrial production lines can get a lot more milk out of their almonds than I can from squeezing my tea towel full of almond mush. And if the factories aren't already turning the residue into cakes and puddings, they will at least be using it as animal feed.

In terms of reducing greenhouse-gas emissions, it makes sense to make your own almond milk only if you use the pulp as well. If you put the oven on especially to dry out the pulp then this might blow all the emissions you've saved from avoiding dairy milk. And, if you're making almond milk to put into a smoothie, then you can reduce emissions and get some extra fibre by instead adding ground almonds and water and skipping the straining (if you don't mind a slightly grainy texture).

Returning to the commercial almond milk calculation, and assuming only 25 grams of nuts are needed to make one cup, the almond milk raw ingredient (almonds) cause 10 times less emissions than dairy milk. Transportation, packaging and storage in supermarket fridges (box 11.1) adds to both the almond and cows' milk total emissions. However because the almond emissions are so small, the other contributions are likely to make up most of the total almond-milk emissions, which often makes estimates of non-dairy milk emissions "only" two times better than cows' milk (chapter 6).

Peanuts

Fig. 19.3: Peanuts in their shells. (URL 56)

Did you know that peanuts are more closely related to peas and beans than to almonds? As a type of legume, they can extract nitrogen from the air via microbes, and therefore don't need so much fertilizer (chapter 14). Unlike peas and beans, they push their seed pods under the ground, leading to their other name, "groundnuts". The pods are pulled up and dried, giving the brittle outer shell of the peanuts, inside which live about two peanuts inside their papery brown coats (Fig. 19.3).

Just like almonds, the amount of peanuts produced in a field can vary greatly (by about 10 times) depending on the ground type, climate, crop variety, cultivation methods, irrigation and the crop rotation scheme. As with other legumes, even though peanuts can get some nitrogen fertilizer from the air, they usually have nitrogen fertilizer applied to the soil to increase the yield further (chapter 14). On average, peanut emissions come out slightly higher than those for almonds, causing about 3 times their own weight in emissions.

1 g peanuts = 3 g emissions

Peanut butter is essentially just blended roasted peanuts. Some health food shops whizz them while you wait, putting in peanuts at the top and squirting out peanut butter at the bottom. You can even do it yourself in a food processor, if you don't mind some messy washing up. Being turned into butter increases the peanut emissions to about four times the weight of the spread.

1 g peanut butter = 4 g emissions

Fig. 19.4: Emissions for mixed nuts: peanuts (15 g); almonds (15 g).

Mixed nuts

To conclude this chapter, consider a tasty and nutritious snack of mixed nuts: a handful (30 g) containing equal quantities of almonds and peanuts. This portion causes 80 grams of emissions (Fig. 19.4), which is less than 3% of a budget of 3,000 g of emissions from food per day, but packs a punch in terms of nutrition.

Key points

- Nuts and seeds are literally the plant-based alternative to eggs and as a result they are very nutritious.

- On average, nuts cause 2-3 times their weight in greenhouse-gas emissions, although there is a wide variation in the values depending on the type and growing conditions.

- The almond raw ingredient in almond milk causes very little emissions compared to dairy milk, but taking everything else into consideration nut milks cause less than half the climate-impact of dairy milk (chapter 4).

Notes

Page

92 *you can enjoy regular sweet almonds without worrying.* The wild bitter almond contains cyanide and can be fatal. Bitter almonds yield about 6.2 mg of cyanide per almond, whereas the standard sweet almond contains 100 times less, bringing it well below toxic levels. For more information see Chaouali et al. (2013).

92 *amount of almonds harvested from a tree can vary significantly (by 5 times) depending on the amount of fertilizer available, as well as other factors including the weather and the soil quality.* Almond yields vary from 1 to 5 tonnes per hectare, see Nemecek et al. (2012).

93 *typical commercial almonds cause about twice their own weight in emissions.* The value of 2.1 $kgCO_2e$ / kg is based on Bartzas et al. (2017) who give a value for shelled almonds. This is consistent with the individual numbers for almonds calculated by Poore and Nemecek (2018) but note there is a very large range, from negative numbers (where almond trees are reducing greenhouse-gas emissions relative to the previous use of the land) to larger numbers.

93 *the almond milk raw ingredient (almonds) cause 10 times less emissions than dairy milk.* Depending on the brand, a glass (250 ml) of almond milk alternative can contain 5% almonds, which is 12.5 grams of almonds (1 ml weighs about 1 g). Here we assume that half the almonds are wasted as pulp, so 25 grams of almonds will be needed to make the drink. (If the "milking" process were less efficient then more almonds would be needed, which would reduce the difference between the almond milk ingredients and cows' milk.) For almonds that cause 2.1 times their own weight in emissions, 25 grams of nuts will cause 53 grams of emissions. Compare this to 250 grams of dairy milk, which causes about 550 grams of emissions (chapter 4). On the other hand, many brands contain more like 2.5% almonds, which increases the difference between almond milk and cows' milk.

94 *amount of peanuts produced in a field can vary greatly (by about 10 times)* Peanut yields vary between 0.5 and 4 tonnes per hectare, according to Nemecek et al. (2012)

94 *On average, peanut emissions come out slightly higher than those for almonds, causing about 3 times their own weight in emissions.* Value of 3.2 $kgCO_2e$ / kg taken from Poore and Nemecek (2018) for groundnuts (peanuts) global average.

94   *Being turned into butter increases the peanut emissions to about four times the weight of the spread.* The value for processing of the peanut butter is 0.238 kgCO_2e / kg from McCarty et al. (2014). We add this to the value for peanuts from earlier to get 4.2 kgCO_2e / kg for peanut butter.

Chapter 20 Potato crisps / chips

In this chapter we focus on thin slices of potato, fried in oil and sprinkled with salt and maybe some other flavourings (Fig. 20.1), known as potato chips in the US, and as crisps in the UK. Crunchy, salty and very moreish, I felt compelled to precede writing this chapter by munching though a packet. I will refer to them as "crisps" to avoid confusion, because in the UK "chips" means thick-cut fried potatoes.

We already covered the carbon footprint of potatoes in chapter 13 and used oil and salt in the context of salad (chapter 11). Overall, crisps cause about twice their own weight in emissions (Fig. 20.2).

Fig. 20.1: Some crunchy crisps. (URL 57)

$$1 \text{ g crisps} = 2 \text{ g emissions}$$

The potato and oil cause about half of the total; the remainder comes from processing, cooking and packaging.

Since crisps are very light, even if I eat two small (25 g) packets a day, they still cause less than 5% of a 3 kg daily food emissions budget. Anyone eating significantly more than two packets a day probably has bigger health issues to consider from all the salt and oil.

> **Crisps**
> Total 54 gCO$_2$e ——Crisps (54)

Fig. 20.2: Emissions for a packet of crisps (25 g).

What about flavoured crisps, particularly the meaty ones? Many meaty crisps are suitable for vegetarians, because they often contain the classic seasonings used on meat, but without any actual meat, which is likely to be good for their carbon footprint.

But what about crisps containing meat, cheese or even (new to me) egg? We learned at lunchtime that ham and cheese have a comparable carbon footprint, so we'll focus on cheese. Cheesy crisps contain up to about 10% cheese, which less than doubles the crisp emissions. In other words, crisps still make up only a small fraction of the average daily food emissions, even for a relatively cheesy crisp.

Key points

- A packet of crisps causes about twice its own weight in emissions.

- A small packet of crisps causes less than 5% of a daily food emissions budget of 3 kg.

- For most people, cutting down on crisps isn't going to be the best place to start reducing their food emissions.

- Meaty and cheesy crisps don't usually contain enough meat or cheese to change these conclusions.

Notes

Page

97 *crisps cause about twice their own weight in emissions* We use a value of 2.15 kgCO$_2$e / kg from Nilsson et al. (2011) which is consistent with the Carbon Trust Walkers Crisps analysis in 2009 (no longer available) and roughly consistent with Frankowska et al. (2019a) if a the current clean energy mix (chapter 1) is used for the processing and storage (which dominate the emissions in this calculation which assumes 100% fossil fuels for electricity generation and finds a value of 4.4 kgCO$_2$e / kg).

97 *Cheesy crisps contain up to about 10% cheese, which less than doubles the crisp emissions.* Since cheese causes about 16 times its weight in emissions, 10% cheese adds 1.6 kgCO$_2$e / kg to the crisps, taking their total emissions factor to 3.6 kgCO$_2$e / kg, which is less than twice the original value of 2 kgCO$_2$e / kg.

Chapter 21 Soft drinks and juices

The hiss of a can of fizzy drink opened on a hot summer's day might evoke a Pavlovian dribble – will we be tempted to drink more of these refreshing beverages in a warmer world (Fig. 21.1)? And, if so, will we accelerate climate change further with the release of lots of little bubbles of carbon dioxide?!

Fizzy drinks

Each small (0.5 litre) bottle of soft drink causes less than half its own weight in emissions. However, only a tiny part of that is caused by the gas that makes it sparkle.

Fig. 21.1: Fizzy drink. (URL 58)

The other ingredients cause few emissions, since the main ingredient is water, followed by sugar (chapter 3). Refrigerators in shops cause about a quarter of the total climate impact of a store-bought cold drink (box 11.1). It turns out that nearly half of the greenhouse-gas emissions come from the plastic bottle (Fig. 21.2, left).

> **1 g fizzy drink on tap = 0.2 g emissions**

From a climate change perspective, would it be better to instead buy a drink in a glass bottle, or in a can?

Soft drink in a plastic bottle
Plastic bottle (81)
Soft drink (107)
Total 188 gCO₂e

Water in a 500ml plastic bottle
Plastic bottle (81)
Water (0)
Total 81 gCO₂e

Orange juice in a small plastic bottle
Plastic bottle (32)
Orange juice (360)
Total 392 gCO₂e

Fig. 21.2:
Left: Emissions for a soft drink in a plastic bottle: a soft drink (500 g); a plastic bottle (27 g).
Right: Emissions for water in a 500 ml plastic bottle: bottled water, including manufacturing and transport (500 g); a plastic bottle (27 g).
Centre: Emissions for orange juice in a plastic bottle: orange juice (200 g); a plastic bottle (10.8 g).

Box 21.1: Plastic and glass bottles, and drinks cans

Plastic is usually made from fossil fuels. This association might automatically suggest it is therefore bad for the climate, but in this case the fossil fuels are converted into plastic, not into greenhouse gases. The main cause of plastic-bottle emissions is the energy needed to turn the fossil fuels into plastic, including separating out the important components of the fossil fuel and joining these pieces together into long molecular chains.

The manufacturing processes cause emissions of about 3 times the weight of the final plastic container, so you can weigh any plastic food packaging and multiply by 3 to get the emissions likely to be caused by the packaging.

$$1 \text{ g plastic} = 3 \text{ g emissions}$$

However, if the bottle is made entirely from recycled material then the emissions are significantly reduced, to less than the weight of the container.

$$1 \text{ g recycled plastic} = 0.8 \text{ g emissions}$$

Glass causes about half its own weight in emissions, which is much lower than for plastic. But the fragile nature of glass means that the bottles have to be much thicker and heavier than very light and thin plastic bottles.

$$1 \text{ g glass} = 0.6 \text{ g emissions}$$

This more than cancels out the benefits of the lower emissions factor, making glass bottles have almost twice the climate impact of plastic.

What is your **drinks can** made of? If you have a magnet handy (maybe stuck to the fridge?) you can tell whether it is made of steel or aluminium. If the magnet sticks to the can, then it's made of steel (box 14.1), and you can also rest assured that the magnetic properties of the steel will allow your drinks can to be automatically picked out of the rubbish from the recycling bin, to be used again.

If your magnet doesn't stick, the can is made of aluminium, which causes 6 times its weight in emissions, for typical recycling rates.

$$1 \text{ g aluminium} = 6 \text{ g emissions}$$

This is nearly four times the value for steel (box 14.1), and twice the value for the same weight of plastic.

However, aluminium cans weigh less than plastic bottles, so which wins? The higher emissions factor for aluminium cancels out the difference in weight, making the can packaging emissions about the same as for the slightly bigger plastic bottle.

So, overall, plastic is usually the lowest-emissions choice, followed closely by aluminium cans, and glass bottles cause the most emissions. However, this depends a lot on the mix of fossil fuels used for manufacturing, as well as the fraction of recycled materials used. And there are other environmental issues you may want to consider beyond the climate, such as microplastics pollution, and the future journey of your packaging after it leaves your house: will it be recycled into new packaging, burned in place of fossil fuels, or go to landfill?

Bottled water

Because of the health impact of these sugary drinks, you might choose bottled water instead. However, from an emissions perspective, switching to bottled water from a supermarket chiller cabinet doesn't help as much as you might think, because the packaging, refrigeration, manufacture and waste disposal still have to be accounted for (Fig. 21.2, centre). For maximum climate brownie points, carry a refillable water bottle and top it up at public water fountains or by asking for a refill in drinking establishments. (Tap water causes negligible emissions once the infrastructure is in place.)

1 g tap water = 0.001 g emissions

Orange juice

Fruit juice (Fig. 21.3) provides a healthy dose of vitamins and minerals, but it isn't as healthy as eating the fruit itself because the chewy part of the fruit has been removed, depriving you of dietary fibre. Juice is so easy to drink that we can consume the juice of several fruits in a single glass: for example, it takes nearly three oranges to make a 200 ml serving of pure juice. This can provide a significant fraction of our recommended daily maximum intake of sugar, and the fruit emissions also start to add up.

Fig. 21.3: Fresh orange juice. (URL 59).

To calculate the total greenhouse-gas emissions, we have to include the emissions from growing the fruit (chapter 17), as well as the processing, packaging, transport and refrigeration, which brings the orange juice emissions to approximately twice its own weight (Fig. 21.2, right).

1 g orange juice = 2 g emissions

The emissions from a single packaged drink are around 10% of a daily food emissions budget of 3 kilos but, although it might not look much in your home recycling bin, it is estimated that nearly half of all food packaging in the UK is drinks packaging, and the numbers can add up if you have several packaged drinks each day.

Key points

- The carbon dioxide in drinks isn't a major contributor to climate change.

- For a small drinks bottle, the packaging causes nearly half the emissions.

- The ultra-low-emissions option is to carry around your own cup or bottle and refill it from water fountains and catering outlets.

Notes

Page

99 *Each small (0.5 litre) bottle of soft drink causes less than half its own weight in emissions. However, only a tiny part of that is caused by the gas that makes it sparkle.* This uses the values from Amienyo et al. (2013), see in particular their Figure 5, which shows the contributions from the separate processes. Subtract their number for the packaging (174 gCO_2e / litre) and group all the other contributions together (388-174 gCO_2e / litre), for the 0.5 litre PET bottle. Regarding the bubbles in the drink, the amount of carbon dioxide fizz is 0.6% the weight of the drink (Amienyo et al. 2013 Table 1), so a 0.5 litre bottle contains 3 grams of carbon dioxide, which is less than 2% of the total emissions caused by the drink and its packaging (388 gCO_2e / litre * 0.5 litres = 194 gCO_2e).

99 *Refrigerators in shops cause about a quarter of the total climate impact of a store-bought cold drink* From Amienyo et al. (2013) Fig. 5, 95 / 388 = 0.25.

99 *nearly half of the greenhouse-gas emissions come from the plastic bottle (Fig. 21.2, left).* In the figures, the packaging emissions are shown as the upper boxes, and the lower boxes include all the other contributions to emissions, such as refrigeration, ingredients, manufacturing and transport.

100 *emissions of about 3 times the weight of the final plastic container,* This means that we can estimate the emissions of any container just by weighing it and multiplying up the number of grams by 3. The value 3.0 $kgCO_2e$ / kg plastic comes from v3.1 of Ecoinvent (Frischknecht and Jungbluth, 2007) for virgin (i.e. non-recycled) polyethylene terephthalate. See also Boustead (2005) who give a value of 3.4 $kgCO_2e$ / kg.

100 *However, if the bottle is made entirely from recycled material then the emissions are significantly reduced, to less than the weight of the container.* From the written evidence submitted by the British Plastics Federation and PlasticsEurope to the UK House of Commons Environmental Audit Committee "it takes 75% less energy to make a plastic bottle from recycled material than when using virgin materials" (British Plastics Federation and PlasticsEurope, 2017). Doing the calculation (1-0.75)×3.0 gives 0.75 $kgCO_2e$ / kg for recycled plastic.

100 *Glass causes about half its own weight in emissions,* For 85% recycled glass CCalc2 ("CCaLC PVC Manual (V2.0)" 2011) gives 0.62 $kgCO_2e$ / kg glass.

100 *aluminium, which causes 6 times its weight in emissions, for typical recycling rates.* The value from CCalc2 ("CCaLC PVC Manual (V2.0)" 2011) for aluminium is 5.94 $kgCO_2e$ / kg aluminium for 48% recycled aluminium. For virgin (not recycled) aluminium the value is 10.5 $kgCO_2e$ / kg aluminium.

100 *The higher emissions factor for aluminium cancels out the difference in weight, making the can packaging emissions about the same as for the slightly bigger plastic bottle.* A typical empty 330 ml-capacity aluminium drinks can weighs about 14 grams, which is about half the weight of an empty 500 ml plastic bottle. The emissions factor of plastic is half that of aluminium so the two effects cancel out. Though note that you get a bit more to drink in a 500 ml plastic bottle than a 330 ml drinks can.

101 *from an emissions perspective, switching to bottled water from a supermarket chiller cabinet doesn't help as much as you might think, because the packaging, refrigeration, manufacture and waste disposal still have to be accounted for* This assumes the manufacturing, transport and retail (refrigeration) stages are the same for the fizzy drink and bottled water, and then uses the values from Amienyo et al. (2013) for the fizzy drink, minus the packaging (listed separately) and the ingredients (i.e. 388 - 174 - 40 = 174 gCO_2e / litre), which gives 0.17 $kgCO_2e$ / kg for water in a bottle. (Packaging emissions are added separately later.)

101 *carry a refillable water bottle and top it up at public water fountains or by asking for a refill in drinking establishments.* It took me a while to figure out, but carrying an empty water bottle is still useful, and much lighter than carrying a full one – you can fill it up next to a tap and then drink it straight away!

101 *(Tap water causes negligible emissions once the infrastructure is in place.)* Tap water from conventional drinking water treatments (scenario 1 of Garfi et al. 2016) causes emissions of about 0.5 $kgCO_2e$ / m^3 of water. 1 m^3 of water weighs 1,000 kg, so this corresponds to 0.0005 $kgCO_2e$ / kg of water, the lowest emissions ratio in this book by a large margin. We round this to 0.001 $kgCO_2e$ / kg in the main text due to a lack of studies.

101 *it takes nearly three oranges to make a 200 ml serving of pure juice.* Based on numbers from Dwivedi et al. (2012).

101 *orange juice emissions to approximately twice its own weight* From Frankowska et al. (2019b) for orange juice, which gives 2.0 $kgCO_2e$ / kg including complete lifecycle (which includes 10% from packaging). Since packaging is shown separately in this book, the value used for the juice alone is 1.8 $kgCO_2e$ / kg.

101 *nearly half of all food packaging in the UK is drinks packaging,* Amienyo et al. (2013) state that 40% of all food packaging comes from drinks in the UK.

Chapter 22 A piece of cake

Fig. 22.1: A Victoria sponge cake. (URL 60)

A piece of cake is the ultimate snack-time indulgence, perfect with tea or coffee (chapter 2). We've worked hard to understand the carbon footprints of enough different ingredients so we can now get baking!

We start with a classic sponge cake containing just four ingredients: eggs, flour, sugar and butter. While it's baking, let's make a batch of butter icing, by mixing together butter and icing sugar; when the cake is cooled we slice it in half, and slather on the icing and some jam.

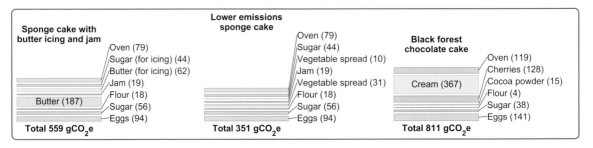

Fig. 22.2:
Left: Emissions for sponge cake with butter icing and jam: 4 eggs, shared between 10 slices (20 g); sugar (22.5 g); flour (22.5 g); butter (22.5 g); jam (6 g); butter (for icing) (7.5 g); sugar (for icing) (17.5 g); putting the oven on for 35 minutes, plus warm-up time, shared between 10 slices (5 minutes at 2.4 kWh).
Centre: The same ingredients as the left panel replacing butter with vegetable spread in both the cake and the icing.
Right: Emissions for Black Forest chocolate cake: 6 eggs, shared between 10 slices (30 g); sugar (15 g); flour (5 g); cocoa powder (5 g); cherries (40 g); cream (75 g); putting the oven on for 1 hour, plus warm-up time, shared between 10 slices (7.5 minutes at 2.4 kWh).

How big is a slice of cake? (How long is a piece of string?) We'll divide our cakes into ten pieces, as recommended in standard recipes. We will also restrain ourselves from eating more than one slice, because this already provides about 500 kCal – one fifth of the recommended daily calorie intake. We can now add up the emissions from all the individual ingredients. Each slice clocks up about half a kilo of emissions, about half of which comes from the butter (Fig. 22.2, left).

Many recipes specify vegetable spread, or margarine, instead of butter, so we can safely make this switch – as long as the tub says the dairy-free spread is suitable for baking. This one change reduces the cake impact by 40% (Fig. 22.2, middle).

Alternatively you could go large on your waistline and your emissions by making a really creamy cake. For example, a whole

Black Forest chocolate cake contains about 750 ml of cream (Fig. 22.3), as well as jammy stewed fruit. One slice has more than twice the emissions of the dairy-free sponge (compare Fig. 22.2, right and centre).

How climate-friendly could you make the cake? Most of the main ingredients are low-impact foods: flour, sugar and vegetable spread. With care you can make an entirely vegan cake by replacing egg with one of the growing number of alternatives such as aquafaba (chapter 7). The oven emissions can also be reduced by cooking several cakes at once, or by buying from someone else who made a batch.

Fig. 22.3: A slice of melt-in-the-mouth creamy Black Forest cake? (URL 61)

Key points

- A piece of cake causes 0.6 kilos of emissions, which is one fifth of a daily food emissions budget of 3 kilos.

- The climate impact can be reduced to 10% of a 3 kilo daily food emissions budget by switching to a dairy-free butter alternative, or having a smaller piece of cake!

- A very creamy cake (e.g. Black Forest cake) causes 0.8 kilos of emissions per slice, which is one quarter of a budget of 3 kilos from food per day.

- You can reduce cake emissions further by batch cooking, and replacing the eggs to make an entirely vegan cake.

Notes

Page

104 *a classic sponge cake containing just four ingredients: eggs, flour, sugar and butter.* This calculation uses 4 eggs, 225 g sugar, 225 g flour and 225 g butter for the cake ...

104 *slather on the icing and some jam.* ... with 75 g of butter and 175 g of sugar for the icing, plus 60 g of jam.

104 *because this already provides about 500 kCal* Using standard values of 143, 394, 352, 748 and 238 kCal per 100 g for egg, sugar, flour, butter and jam respectively, and eggs weighing 50 g each. Note that cooking doesn't affect the total calories, unless you leave a lot in the mixing bowl and on the mixing spoon (and, let's face it, this can happen because licking it off while no-one's looking is the best bit of baking!). So we can divide approximately 4000 kCal between the 10 pieces to get the total kCal per slice.

105 *jammy stewed fruit.* Using the emissions value for jam due to a lack of literature on stewed cherries (see chapter 5).

Chapter 23 | Snacks summary

We've considered a range of popular snacks that can be enjoyed as part of a meal, or scattered throughout the day.

Typical-emissions snacks

Fig. 23.1 (left) shows a typical day's collection of snacks: an apple, a banana, some milk chocolate and a packet of crisps. The emissions are relatively modest at about 300 grams, which corresponds to 10% of a 3,000 g daily food emissions budget (chapter 1).

Fig. 23.1:
Left: Emissions for typical-emissions snacks: an apple; a banana; milk chocolate; crisps.
Centre: Emissions for higher-emissions snacks: black forest chocolate cake; strawberries (by air); a soft drink.
Right: Emissions for lower-emissions snacks: mixed nuts; two oranges; dark chocolate.

Higher-emissions snacks

Air-freighted fruit and creamy cakes are in a different (high-emissions) league to the other snacks. Totting up the totals from a handful of air-freighted berries, a creamy cake and a bottle of juice comes to over 1.5 kilos of greenhouse gases (Fig. 23.1, centre) which is more than half of a daily food emissions budget of 3 kg.

Lower-emissions snacks

Sticking to healthy wholefood options like nuts and non-perishable fruit (box 17.3) works out well for the climate. Fig. 23.1 (right) shows a stack for mixed nuts, two oranges and a small bar of dark chocolate. The result is a little lower than for the typical-emissions snacks, but also healthier for replacing crisps with nuts.

Key points

- Fruit is both a healthy and low-impact snack, if it is non-perishable, or in season . . .

- . . . but air-freighted fruit adds a quarter of a daily food emissions budget of 3 kg.

- Snacks containing cream or butter can have relatively large emissions too.

- Nuts and seeds are both healthy and low-emissions.

Part IV: Evening Meal

This is the last Part of the book devoted to the climate change impact of individual foods, before we take stock and consider some broader issues later on.

Our dinner menu includes some of the biggest emissions contributions, getting our teeth into beef and chicken. We recall some issues from breakfast when we add milk and eggs. Then we consider one of the most widely eaten foods, which also makes a surprise appearance on the list of higher-emissions plant-based foods – rice.

We dive into two very different ways to bring fish to the table, before comparing different vegetables and their preparation methods. Wine and beer round out the main course, followed by a session in the kitchen combining ingredients from earlier, to make apple pie and chocolate mousse.

Chapter 24 Spaghetti bolognese

Fig. 24.1: A bowl of spaghetti bolognese, with a generous sprinkling of cheese. (URL 63)

Spaghetti bolognese can be a student staple containing just pasta, beef and tomato sauce, or it can be taken to sophisticated heights by using fresh pasta with homemade sauce including sun-dried tomatoes and red wine (Fig. 24). We already discussed tomato sauce over lunch (chapters 11, 12), and most pasta is just a processed form of wheat, so it's time to address the elephant (or cow) in the room: beef.

Just as for the milk emissions (chapter 4), beef contributes to global warming mostly because cows burp methane and their manure decomposes into methane and releases nitrous oxide. This means that the climate impact of a piece of beef depends on how many days the cow has lived, how much it eats, and how much meat it can be slaughtered for.

We first consider "prime" beef herds, in which cows are raised for producing beef and do not produce milk for human consumption. This differs from a dairy herd (discussed later in this chapter), where the cow is milked and is then slaughtered for beef; we can share out the cow emissions between the beef and the milk.

Prime beef

A mother cow usually has a new calf every year, and that calf is fattened for about one year itself before being slaughtered for about 250 kilograms of beef meat (about four times the weight of a human). On average a calf eats over 40,000 kCal each day to grow big and strong, and we have to also take into account a similar number of calories eaten each day by the mother cow. In total the calf and mother cow eat about thirty times the average calorie intake of one human each day.

As discussed at breakfast (chapter 4), about 5% of the calories consumed by a cow are turned into methane. In the case of the beef cow and calf, this would create about half their own body volume of methane each day. However, the greater potency of methane as a greenhouse gas means that this amount of methane causes the same warming effect as a weight of 10 kg of carbon dioxide (chapter 4).

Each day the calf grows nearly 700 grams (24 oz) of extra flesh that can become beef meat, which would be enough for three large (8 oz) steaks. This means that just from the methane burps alone, beef causes 14 times its own weight in emissions. It also means that only about 2% of the calories eaten by the cow make it through to our stomachs; this is the least efficient of all the animal products considered in this book (box 10.1). However, we should note that pasture-fed cows are creating a nutritious food that we can eat from the most abundant yet effectively inedible-to-humans food source on the planet (grass).

Where do all the other calories go, if not into the beef? Most of the calories come out of the other end of the cow, as manure. This is a good fertilizer for crops, if transported to the right place. Unfortunately it can also decompose into methane, if left without sufficient oxygen to help it decompose into carbon dioxide. While the manure is an excellent fertilizer because it contains a lot of nitrogen, this nitrogen causes nitrous oxide emissions whether or not the manure is being used to grow crops. The exact emissions depend on how dry the manure pile is, and how it is spread, but manure helps bring the total emissions for beef to around 46 times the weight of the portion.

Fig. 24.2: A juicy steak. (URL 64)

1 g steak = 46 g emissions

However, there is a huge range in the way beef is produced across the world. To take an extreme example, a calf can live for 20 years instead of just the 1 year we assumed in the above calculation. If the only purpose of keeping that calf was to produce beef, then the steak emissions from that animal would be 10 times higher than for the calf that lived to the age of 1, i.e. the emissions will be 200 times the weight of the beef!

Cows are sometimes fed a more protein-rich diet including soy. This reduces the amount of methane burped by the cow (chapter 4), but requires more land to grow the soy, which can cause deforestation (chapter 7). If forest is cleared to create grassland then this is even worse.

Given all the variability it seems rash to provide a single number for beef in this book. However, for the sake of comparison with other foods, I use one number (beef causes 46 times its own weight in emissions) which corresponds to a relatively efficient beef production system, bearing in mind that this is at the low (better) end of the range for beef.

Fried steak

Frying (79)

Vegetable oil (19)

8oz steak (10487)

Total 10585 gCO$_2$e

Fig. 24.3: Emissions for a fried steak: 8 ounces of steak (227 g); a teaspoon of vegetable oil (5 g); frying (5 minutes at 2 kWh).

A meaty digression: steak

We can now calculate the global warming impact of the highest-emissions regularly eaten meal: a large steak (Fig. 24.2). A 225 g (8 oz) steak causes about 10 kilos of greenhouse-gas emissions (Fig. 24.3), which is three times larger than a budget of 3 kg of emissions for a whole day. If everyone in the world ate such a large steak every day then the steaks alone would use up the remaining 1.5°C carbon budget before 2040 (chapter 1).

Here are some other comparisons. Eating one large steak is equivalent to driving a fossil-fuelled car about 70 kilometres (40 miles), which is a relatively short daily commute to work in many countries. Alternatively, taking one transatlantic flight every year is equivalent to eating one large steak a day. So we should think twice about ordering a steak on a regular basis, but at the same time look at our non-food emissions.

Spaghetti bolognese emissions

Now we're ready to make spaghetti bolognese. Every cook has their own special recipe, but the details are unlikely to make a big difference to global warming because almost all the greenhouse-gas emissions come from the beef (Fig. 24.4, left). The main issue is how much beef each person eats; a moderately sized portion causes over 6 kilos of emissions, which is twice a daily food emissions budget of 3 kg, just from this one dish. This is more than twice the emissions of all the non-ruminant meals considered in this book, is exceeded only by the steak and is similar to the lamb tikka masala (in the next chapter).

Lower impact beef

The climate impact of efficiently produced prime beef has roughly equal contributions from the calf and the mother. But what if the mother cow were also producing milk during most of her one year gap between calving, and if we slaughtered the mother for beef at the end of her milk-producing life?

Furthermore, male dairy calves aren't needed for milk production and so are often killed young (producing a negligible amount of meat). Fattening them up for meat instead would produce a lower-emissions piece of beef, which can be as much as 2 times better for the climate than prime beef.

In fact, about half of all beef already comes from dairy cows. This can significantly reduce the environmental footprint of beef, by 2 or more times, depending on whether the male calves are fattened and how the emissions are allocated between the milk and beef (box 9.1).

Based on the current quantities of meat from dairy herds, we would have to roughly halve our beef consumption to remove the demand for dedicated prime-beef herds. To support dairy beef and encourage the most efficient practices, we also need more information on the meat we are buying, at very least we need the packet to tell us what kind of herd the meat comes from!

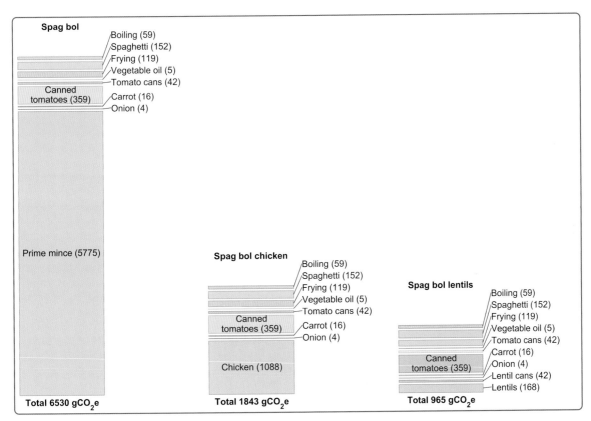

Fig. 24.4:
Left: Emissions for spag bol: prime mince (125 g); a small onion, shared between 4 people (25 g); carrot (25 g); two cans of tomatoes, shared between 4 people (200 g); two steel cans, shared between 4 people (25 g); vegetable oil (1 g); frying for 30 minutes, shared between 4 people (7.5 minutes at 2 kWh); spaghetti (230 g); boiling the spaghetti for 15 minutes, shared between 4 people (4 minutes at 2 kWh).
Centre: Switching the beef for the same weight of chicken.
Right: Switching the beef for the same weight of cooked lentils.

Beef alternatives

How about using a different meat in the spaghetti bolognese? Lamb is delicious but it has about the same emissions as beef, because sheep have similar stomachs to cows (chapters 4 and 6).

1 g lamb = 43 g emissions

Pork causes fewer emissions than beef (chapter 10), but chicken is lower still (chapter 25). A chicken spaghetti bolognese causes three times lower emissions than a prime beef spaghetti bolognese (compare Fig. 24.4 centre with Fig. 24.4 left). Switching to beans or lentils (chapter 14) halves the emissions again, to 1 kilo per person, (Fig. 24.4, right).

Key points

- A piece of efficiently produced beef causes 15 times its own weight in emissions from cow burps alone, which is already higher than the values for pork and chicken. The longer the cow lives, the higher this number is.

- Prime beef (even when efficiently produced) causes the highest emissions of any commonly consumed food at over 40 times its own weight in emissions; for example it causes 5 times the emissions of the same weight of chicken.

- An 8 oz steak causes 10 kilos of emissions, which alone is three times over budget compared to the value of 3 kilos of food emissions discussed in chapter 1.

- A portion of prime-beef spaghetti bolognese causes 6 kilos of emissions, depending on the amount of beef used.

- Eating beef from dairy cows instead of prime beef reduces the climate impact by 2 or more times, because the emissions are shared between the meat and milk.

- Replacing beef mince with chicken reduces the spaghetti bolognese emissions by more than 3 times, to below 2 kilos of emissions for each portion.

- Replacing the beef with lentils reduces emissions by 7 times, to 1 kilo of emissions per portion.

Notes

Page

110 *most pasta is just a processed form of wheat,* An average of values from Recchia et al. (2019) (1.71 and 1.76 kgCO$_2$e / kg dry spaghetti) modified to account for hydration during cooking (62% of cooked spaghetti is water according to (URL 62), which brings the value to 0.66 kgCO$_2$e / kg hydrated spaghetti. Note that this number does not include cooking, which is added separately.

110 *calf is fattened for about one year itself before being slaughtered for about 250 kilograms of beef meat (about four times the weight of a human).* Steer average dressed carcass weight (after removing gut, skin, etc.) was 372.4 kg for August 2019 in the UK, from Defra (2019) which can be converted into a bone-free meat content of 260 kg, using the ratio of carcass weight to bone free meat from Clune et al. (2017). This number will vary from one farm and country to another so it is rounded to 250 kg in the main text.

110 *a calf eats over 40,000 kCal each day to grow big and strong, and we have to also take into account a similar number of calories eaten each day by the mother cow.* This is calculated using the equations in chapter 10 of Dong et al. (2017, hereafter IPCC2006), in particular their equation 10.16 and preceding equations, using default values from GLEAM (*GLEAM Global Livestock Environmental Assessment Model* 2017) of 34 kg birth weight and 511 kg for the mother cow, and a final weight of 511 kg for the calf when it is slaughtered at 1 year old. The feed is assumed to be grass, with a digestibility of 60% taken from table 10.2 of IPCC06 for "Pasture fed animals" and a crude protein percentage of 12 from Beauchemin et al. (2010) for pasture. Energy requirements are taken from table 10.4 of IPCC06 for Cattle/Buffalo (cows), from Table 10.5 of IPCC06 for activity levels in a feeding situation for Pasture, and the mother cow is assumed to be pregnant for 9 months of the year, causing an increase in feed requirement of 10% (Table 10.7 IPCC06).

110 *In total the calf and mother cow eat about thirty times the average calorie intake of one human each day.* Note that the mother cow and calf consume fewer calories per day than a dairy cow because they are not producing as much milk.

110 *In the case of the beef cow and calf, this would create about half their own body volume of methane each day.* 5% of calories being turned into methane means that 80,000 kCal (total eaten by the calf and cow each day) produces 4000 kCal of methane, which weighs 300 grams (given the energy content of methane of 13,300 kCal / kg). The density of methane is 0.717 kg m^{-3}, so this corresponds to a volume of 300 g / 1000 g/ kg / 0.717 kg m^{-3} = 0.4 m^{-3}, which is the volume of a small cow.

111 *Each day the calf grows nearly 700 grams (24 oz) of extra flesh that can become beef meat,* 250 kilograms of meat produced during 365 days corresponds to 684 grams of meat a day.

111 *just from the methane burps alone, beef causes 14 times its own weight in emissions.* 10 kg of emissions / 700 g beef = 10 kgCO$_2$e / 0.7 kg beef = 14 kgCO$_2$e / kg.

111 *only about 2% of the calories eaten by the cow make it through to our stomachs;* Compare the number of calories eaten by cows with the number of calories we get from beef. Beef typically provides about 200 kCal per 100 grams (check the supermarket label of your favourite cut of meat). So the calf provides us with an extra 1,400 kCal each day it grows a bit fatter. This is about 2% of the 80,000 kCal of food required by the cow and calf.

111 *total emissions for beef to around 46 times the weight of the portion.* Using a value of 46 kgCO$_2$e / kg beef for Europe prime beef from Poore and Nemecek (2018), which is lower than the value for the US of 54 kgCO$_2$e / kg beef from the same reference. However, the global average (mean) is 100 kgCO$_2$e / kg beef, because some countries have much higher emissions. For more explanation of the details of the calculation see *GLEAM Global Livestock Environmental Assessment Model* (2017) and Beauchemin et al. (2010), as well as examining the range of values compiled in the open access full spreadsheet of details from Poore and Nemecek (2018).

111 *the steak emissions from that animal would be 10 times higher than for the calf that lived to the age of 1, i.e. the emissions will be 200 times the weight of the beef!* Our calculation accounted for a calf and a cow being alive for one year, i.e. 2 years of burping. For the calf that lives to age 20, we need to account for 21 years of burping (20 years for the calf, and 1 year for the original mother cow). For simplicity we round 21 divided by 2 down to 10.

112   *If everyone in the world ate such a large steak every day then the steaks alone would use up the remaining 1.5°C carbon budget before 2040 (chapter 1).* 10 kg / person / day corresponds to 7.7 people * 365 days / year * 10 kg / person / day / 1,000,000,000,000 Gt / kg = 28 Gt / year. Therefore sharing out 640 Gt over the years gives 640 Gt / (28 Gt / year) = 23 years from the 2018 report date i.e. 2041, which is rounded to 2040 in the main text to avoid giving the impression this number is known to an accuracy of 1 year (the number 640 Gt depends on our understanding of warming triggered by warming (Earth system feedbacks) and depends on the time profile of future emissions see chapter 1).

112   *The main issue is how much beef each person eats;* This calculation assumes a 500 g packet of mince shared between four people.

112   *slaughtered the mother for beef at the end of her milk-producing life?* Prime-beef cows have been bred for the quality and quantity of their meat, and the beef from dairy cows isn't usually considered to be as delicious. Whether this is really true depends on the breed of cow and the quality of life of the dairy cow. But note that if the dairy cow has a luxury retirement after milking has ended, then she is also burping out methane which will increase the emissions of the dairy beef.

112   *male dairy calves aren't needed for milk production and so are often killed young (producing a negligible amount of meat). Fattening them up for meat instead would produce a lower-emissions piece of beef, which can be as much as 2 times better for the climate than prime beef.* If the male dairy calves live for 1 year and if they grow at the same rate and burp the same amount of methane as the prime beef calves, then their beef emissions are about half those of the prime beef. This is because we no longer have to account for the emissions of the mother cow, assuming these are attributed to the milk and the beef from the old dairy cow.

112   *about half of all beef already comes from dairy cows. This can significantly reduce the environmental footprint of beef, by 2 or more times,* The average dairy beef value for the US from Poore and Nemecek (2018) is just 10 kgCO$_2$e / kg beef because of the way emissions are allocated across the beef and milk, whereas the value for Europe is close to that for non-dairy beef at 38 kgCO$_2$e / kg. This makes putting a single number on dairy beef very difficult – it all depends on the farming practice, as discussed in the text. Globally just under half of all beef comes from dairy herds (26.8 million tonnes of beef come from dairy herds and 34.6 from beef herds), but in Europe the figure rises to 80% of all beef coming from dairy herds (Gerber et al., 2013).

113   *Lamb is delicious but it has about the same emissions as beef,* Poore and Nemecek (2018) find a value of 43 kgCO$_2$e / kg lamb for Europe, which is similar to the global value of 40 kgCO$_2$e / kg (using the value for mutton and goat meat). Note that transportation by ship across from the other side of the world causes far fewer emissions than the sheep themselves (see especially figure 2 of Ledgard et al. 2011). See chapter 17 for more information on transport emissions.

Chapter 25 Chicken curry tikka masala

Chicken is the most popular meat in both the US and the UK, and consumption is rising steadily. In this chapter we focus on chicken tikka masala, which is now described as a British national dish (allegedly invented in Scotland when a customer demanded sauce in their chicken curry).

However, a wide range of sauces are available to turn pieces of chicken into a quick and nutritious meal, and most of this chapter is relevant to any chicken dish. We consider the emissions from chicken farming and then get cooking.

Fig. 25.1: A bowl of chicken tikka masala with rice. (URL 65).

Raising chickens

Whereas egg-laying chickens live for about one year, "broiler" chickens grown especially for their meat typically live for just a few weeks. Standard broilers grow from about 40 grams at birth, to around 2 kg in just six weeks. Over the festive season I think I could probably eat enough to put on this much weight (2 kilos, or 4 lb), but these chicks are increasing their body weight by 50 times! Most incredible is that they do this while only eating less than twice their final body weight in food.

What are these chickens eating? Typically, more than half of their food is a grain such as wheat, a quarter is soya beans, and the rest includes seeds, oil and fish. These are the same foods eaten by the egg-laying chickens (chapter 7), but the amount of protein-rich soy is nearly doubled for the broilers, to build them up big and meaty.

Most of the on-farm greenhouse-gas emissions from chicken meat comes from producing food for them to eat – more than half of which comes from producing soya beans, because the increasing global demand for soy leads to deforestation (chapter 7). There are also some smaller emissions from heating the sheds and from the chicken manure. Additionally taking into account packaging, transport and refrigeration, chicken meat causes about 9 times its own weight in greenhouse-gas emissions.

Chickens are relatively efficient at turning animal feed into meat: about 3 grams of chicken feed are eaten by the chicken for every gram of chicken meat (this takes into account that the final body weight contains inedible parts like bones and intestines). This makes chickens over 10 times as effective as cows at turning food into meat. Even so, our appetite for poultry means that more than 3 chickens need to be fattening all the time to keep one Brit in chicken, and more than 4 per US citizen.

1 g chicken = 9 g emissions

Added ingredients

Chicken tikka masala recipes vary wildly, but many people fry chicken in butter with onions, garlic and spices and then simmer with tomatoes and cream. The environmental impact comes mostly from the chicken (Fig. 25.2, left). The cream and butter cause about a quarter of the emissions, followed by the tomatoes. Even though the spices are the most important sensory ingredient, they hardly make any difference to the total emissions because we add only a few grams at most.

1 g spices = 1 g emissions

Fig. 25.2: Greenhouse-gas emissions estimates for chicken-tikka masala options:
Left: Emissions for chicken tikka masala: two tablespoons of butter, shared between 4 people (7.5 g); an onion, shared between 4 (42.5 g); two cloves of garlic, between 4 (5 g); spices (5 g); passata (100 g); cream (50 g); chicken (125 g); frying for 10 minutes, shared between 4 (2.5 minutes at 2 kWh); simmering for 1 hour, shared between 4 people (15 minutes at 2 kWh).
Centre: The same as the left panel, but using half the amount of chicken (62.5 g).
Right: The same as the centre panel, but switching butter to vegetable oil (7.5 g) and switching cream to 12.5 g of nut butter.

Can you tweak the recipe to reduce the emissions? Would your guests notice if you halved the amount of chicken from 125 grams per portion to 63 grams (Fig. 25.2, centre)? This reduces the emissions by 30%, from approaching 2 kilos to less than 1.5 kilos per portion. Using yogurt (chapter 15) instead of double cream reduces the total emissions further. Alternatively replace the cream with nuts (chapter 19) and the butter with vegetable oil, reducing the halved chicken tikka masala emissions by nearly a further 20% (compare Fig. 25.2 centre and right).

Organic chicken

Does switching to organic chicken reduce the emissions even further? Organic chickens are raised more slowly than standard chickens and so consume more food, which *increases* their emissions. However if the organic feed comes from mature agricultural land instead of deforested land, this helps to *reduce* emissions attributed to the organic chicken (although it doesn't help reduce the global demand for soy, which is causing defor-estation). Overall, in the limited number of studies done so far, the emissions of organic chicken are higher those for standard chicken.

> **Box 25.1: Organic food**
>
> People often ask whether going organic helps reduce the impact of food on climate change. It turns out that the answer depends on the specific food being considered.
>
> Organic food is grown according to strict sets of rules. These include tight restriction on the use of chemicals, which can increase the amount of wildlife on the farm (i.e. increase biodiversity) and increase the amount of micronutrients in the food.
>
> In organic crop agriculture, synthetic fertilizers are re-placed by animal manures, which reduces the amount of energy needed to make the fertilizers (box 2.1). However, manure is less finely matched to the needs of the plants, so more fertilizer is needed, which releases more nitrous oxide. Furthermore, for some crops, yields are lower, so organic agriculture generally requires more land, which can contribute to deforestation and thus decreasing biodi-versity.
>
> Overall, the various effects tend to cancel each other out, and on average there isn't a big difference in greenhouse-gas emissions between organic and non-organic foods.

Chicken-less tikka masala

Let's replace the chicken with something else and see how that changes things. My favourite curry meat is lamb, slow-cooked and infusing its delicious flavour through the sauce. Unfortunately this is bad news for emissions, and it causes 6 kilos of emissions per portion, which is double a 3 kg food emissions budget for a whole day. Even halving the quantity of lamb causes nearly twice the emissions of the original chicken tikka dish. I'll keep that for special occasions then!

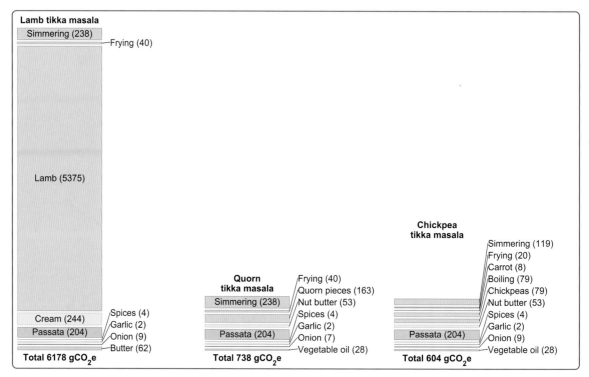

Fig. 25.3: Greenhouse-gas emissions estimates for chicken alternatives:
Left: The same ingredients as in Fig. 25.2 (left) but replacing the chicken with the same weight of lamb.
Centre: The same ingredients as in Fig. 25.2 (right) but replacing the lamb with the same weight of Quorn pieces.
Right: The same ingredients as the centre panel above, but replacing the Quorn with the same weight of rehydrated chickpeas.

You can reduce the emissions further by switching to Quorn (chapter 10), or even chickpeas (chapter 14). Efficient cooking of the chickpeas and using the dairy-free sauce keeps the emissions below 0.6 kilos – three times lower than the original chicken dish (compare Fig. 25.3 right and Fig. 25.2 left), and one fifth of a daily food emissions budget of 3 kg. Chickpea tikka masala anyone? Go on, it's only three letters different from chicken tikka masala! Could it become the next British national dish?

Key points

- About half the chicken emissions come from growing crops to feed to chickens, much of which is from deforestation to produce soy.

- Chicken causes about 9 times its weight in emissions, which is the lowest of the commonly consumed land-animal meats.

- A chicken tikka masala portion causes nearly 2 kilos of emissions, with more than half of the emissions coming from the chicken.

- Replacing chicken with lamb increases the tikka masala emissions by three times, to 6 kilos, which is twice the 3 kg food emissions budget for a whole day discussed in chapter 1.

- Replacing chicken with chickpeas, and dairy with plant products in the sauce, reduces emissions to less than 0.6 kilos per portion.

Notes

Page

117 *Chicken is the most popular meat in both the US and the UK, and consumption is rising steadily.* The word "popular" here refers to the amount eaten. In 1960 Americans ate about 35 pounds per capita per year. By 2017 they ate about 85 pounds. Furthermore, in the 1960s in the US, chicken was half as popular as beef or pork, but by 2017 it was twice as popular as either. This information comes from URL 66; UK statistics can be found in the UK Poultry Pocketbook 2018 (AHDB, 2018b).

117 *chicken tikka masala, which is now described as a British national dish (allegedly invented in Scotland when a customer demanded sauce in their chicken curry).* "Chicken Tikka Masala is now a true British national dish" declared the British Foreign Secretary Robin Cook in 2001.

117 *Standard broilers grow from about 40 grams at birth, to around 2 kg in just six weeks.* See Table 1 of Leinonen et al. (2011a).

117 *while only eating less than twice their final body weight in food.* 3.36 kilograms of food for a final bodyweight of 1.95 kilograms from Table 1 of Leinonen et al.'s broilers paper (Leinonen et al., 2011a).

117 *more than half of their food is a grain such as wheat, a quarter is soya beans, and the rest includes seeds, oil and fish.* See Leinonen et al. (2011a) Table A3. Chicken feed also contains limestone rock, which is needed for making eggshells. Chickens are also given vitamins, minerals and artificial proteins, which helps to reduce the need for more emissions-intensive foods such as more fish and soya beans.

117 *Additionally taking into account packaging, transport and refrigeration, chicken meat causes about 9 times its own weight in greenhouse-gas emissions.* This number (8.7 kgCO$_2$e / kg chicken) is the Europe value from Poore and Nemecek (2018). This number is similar to their world average value (9.9 kgCO$_2$e / kg chicken), but nearly double their value for the US (4.9 kgCO$_2$e / kg). For details of how the calculation is done, see Leinonen et al. (2011a) and *GLEAM Global Livestock Environmental Assessment Model* (2017).

118 *about 3 grams of chicken feed are eaten by the chicken for every gram of chicken meat (this takes into account that the final body weight contains inedible parts like bones and intestines). This makes chickens over 10 times as effective as cows at turning food into meat.* This takes into account that the amount of chicken meat is less than the final weight of a chicken, because the bones and other inedible parts have to be removed. Using a live-weight to bone-free meat ratio of 0.54, taken from Clune et al. (2017) Table 1. The amount of meat

from one standard chicken is therefore 1.95 kg × 0.54 = 1.05 kg. The ratio of feed weight to meat weight is then 3.36 kg / 1.05 kg = 3.19. (Clune et al., 2017) Compare this with beef (chapter 24) where about 2% of calories eaten by the cow are turned into beef i.e. 50 grams of food is eaten by the cow for each gram of beef.

118   *more than 3 chickens need to be fattening all the time to keep one Brit in chicken, and more than 4 per US citizen.* First let's work out the amount of chicken eaten per person per day in each country. According to the UK Poultry Pocketbook 2018 (table 6.1 of AHDB 2018b for 2017), the average Brit eats 36.3 kilograms of poultry per year, which is 99.4 grams per person per day. Only 90% of poultry is chicken though (see table 3.2 of the same reference, which assumes that the UK consumption fraction of chicken is the same as the UK production fraction), therefore the average person in the UK eats 88 grams of chicken meat a day. The average US person eats 92.2 lb of chicken per year (URL 66), which corresponds to 115 g per day. To work out the number of fattening chickens per person, we need to know the lifetime of a chicken and the amount of meat each chicken produces. The standard chicken lifetime is 39 days from Leinonen et al. (2011a), and the amount of meat per chicken is 1.05 kg, so the number of chickens per person is 88 g / day / person × 39 days / (1.05 kg / chicken × 1000 g / kg) = 3.27 chickens per person. The US calculation gives 4.3 chickens per person.

118   *onions,* Taking the pre-household stages for UK fresh onions from Frankowska et al. (2019a) (their figure S46) gives 0.18 kgCO$_2$e / kg.

118   *garlic* A value of 0.36 kgCO$_2$e / kg garlic is used for the figures in this book, based on values of 0.39 kgCO$_2$e / kg, 0.248 kgCO$_2$e / kg and 0.43 kgCO$_2$e / kg taken from Moudrý jr. et al. (2015) and Khoshnevisan and Rafiee (2013).

118   *The environmental impact comes mostly from the chicken* See also the detailed studies by the World Wide Fund for Nature Schreiber (2018) and the Defra (2012) which analysed chicken tikka masala with a slightly different recipe and numbers, but with a lot of similarities.

118   *Even though the spices are the most important sensory ingredient, they hardly make any difference to the total emissions because we add only a few grams at most.* Audsley and Williamson (2010) table 13 state 0.87 kgCO$_2$e / kg for spices. This is rounded to 1 in the main text because there are very few studies.

119   *Organic chickens are raised more slowly than standard chickens and so consume more food, which* increases *their emissions.* Table 1 of Leinonen et al. (2011a) has standard chickens living to 39 days and organic chickens living to 73 days, so nearly twice as long. The total feed is 5.75 kg compared to 3.36 kg i.e. 70% more feed. The final weight is slightly higher, at 2.17 kg, but the feed conversion ratio is still worse, at 5.75 / (0.54×2.17) = 4.9, compared to 3.2 for standard chicken farming.

119   *the emissions of organic chicken are higher those for standard chicken.* 19% higher in Leinonen et al. (2011a) and 33% higher in Williams et al. (2006), which are the two studies cited for poultry in the Clarke and Tilman (2017) comparative study of organic vs non-organic.

119   *organic agriculture generally requires more land,* See figure 1 of Clarke and Tilman (2017).

119   *Overall, the various effects tend to cancel each other out, and on average there isn't a big difference in greenhouse-gas emissions between organic and non-organic foods.* For more details, read Clarke and Tilman (2017).

Chapter 26 Rice

A curry is traditionally served with rice, the staple food of over half the people in the world (Fig. 26.1, top). Fig. 26.1 (upper middle) shows the seed heads on the rice plant, with the grains developing. It looks a bit like wheat, with the long grassy leaves and slightly drooping elongated seed heads, and with many seeds on each stalk. The ripened seeds must be thrashed off the stalk, and hulled to remove the outer husk.

But, unlike wheat, most rice is grown submerged in 5-10 centimetres of water (Fig. 26.1, lower middle), sometimes on lush green hillsides terraced to create submerged paddy fields (Fig. 26.1, bottom). Why go to all this trouble? Most crops can't thrive with their roots in stationary water, but rice is different. Rice growers can save themselves a lot of work by growing the rice in conditions where the usual weeds will die off.

Unfortunately this waterlogging is bad news for the climate, because fertile soil usually contains the remains of living things, such as decaying plants or manure. The complex carbon molecules that make up living things decompose into either carbon dioxide or methane; underwater there is little oxygen and so bacteria turn the organic matter into methane.

Taking this and other factors into account, dry rice causes over 4 times its own weight in emissions, but if we take into account the absorbed water, this reduces to 2 times its own weight in emissions for cooked rice, so a (200 g) bowl causes nearly half a kilo of greenhouse gases, once we include the energy used in cooking (Fig. 26.2).

1 g cooked weight of rice = 2 g emissions

And humans eat a lot of rice – averaged across the world, we all eat two portions of rice a day. Growing rice causes about 10% of global methane emissions, and 2% of all global warming.

However, in a personal context, eating one (200 g) portion of rice causes one sixth of a daily food emissions budget of 3 kg, and the same emissions as driving a fossil-fuelled car for 3 kilometres (2 miles).

Fig. 26.1:
Upper: A bowl of rice. (URL 67)
Upper middle: Rice grains forming on the plant. (URL 68)
Lower middle: Rice seedlings emerging in a flooded field. (URL 69)
Lower: Traditional paddy fields, with tiers of flooded fields down the side of a slope. (URL 70)

Fig. 26.2: Emissions for rice: rice, plus enough water (200 g); boiling the rice for 20 minutes, shared between 4 people (5 minutes at 2 kWh).

Adding a portion of rice to your chicken tikka masala from the previous chapter adds about 25% to the total greenhouse-gas emissions (Fig. 26.3, left), whereas for the ultra-low-emissions chickpea tikka masala, the rice portion nearly doubles the emissions (Fig. 26.3, centre).

How can you reduce emissions?

Given rice is so integral to many food cultures, is there a way to grow rice that causes lower emissions? The amount of methane depends on the length of time the paddy fields are flooded, and the amount of organic matter in the soil. These can both be reduced. In fact, rice can be grown on dry land just like wheat and other grains, and this is common practice in some countries; the main disadvantage is the increased burden of weeding or applying herbicides and pesticides.

Fig. 26.3: Emissions stacks comparing alternatives to chicken tikka masala with rice.
Left: Emissions for chicken tikka masala with rice: chicken tikka masala; a portion of rice.
Centre: Emissions for chickpea tikka masala with rice: chickpea tikka masala; a portion of rice.
Right: Emissions for chickpea tikka masala with bread: chickpea tikka masala; bread.

Growing rice without flooding might be practical on commercial farms with suitable land, but what about the many small farms where growing rice is a way of life? Emissions can be more than halved if the fields are kept flooded for the minimum time outside the growing season and by allowing the fields to dry out multiple times while the rice is growing. The way fertilizer is applied can also make a big difference; for example, applying fertilizer significantly before the waterlogging further reduces emissions.

Furthermore, new varieties of rice are being developed that produce higher yields for a given area, and that exude less nutrients into the soil to feed the microbes. The bottom line is that rice emissions can be reduced significantly by suitable growing.

What alternatives are there to rice? Wheat-based alternatives include bread, and a naan bread goes nicely with curry. Or couscous (usually made from wheat) brings a similar grainy comfort.

Switching from conventional rice to bread reduces the emissions of the chickpea tikka masala meal by nearly one third (compare Fig. 26.3 centre and right). Switching to low-emissions rice reduces emissions by a similar amount, but at the moment this is not an option for most people because the emissions information is not available.

Key points

- Rice is traditionally grown in flooded fields, which cause about 2% of all greenhouse-gas emissions.

- A portion of rice still causes less emissions than lower-impact animal products.

- Switching from rice to bread or low-impact rice reduces the emissions by nearly four times.

Notes

Page

123 *dry rice causes over 4 times its own weight in emissions, but if we take into account the absorbed water, this reduces to 2 times its own weight in emissions for cooked rice,* The global average is 4.5 $kgCO_2e$ / kg of dry rice. This is divided by a hydration factor of 2.25 to account for the change in weight on cooking, to give 2.0 $kgCO_2e$ / kg of cooked rice. Note that the cooking emissions are not included in this number as they are added separately.

123 *Growing rice causes about 10% of global methane emissions, and 2% of all global warming.* Rice paddies cause 0.9 $GtCO_2e$ compared to a total of 9.3 $GtCO_2e$ for methane and 50.6 $GtCO_2e$ in total in 2010 from Bajželj et al. (2013) figure 2.

124 *The amount of methane depends on the length of time the paddy fields are flooded, and the amount of organic matter in the soil.* See chapter 5 of Lasco et al. (2006) especially section 5.5, equation 5.2 and related equations.

124 *Emissions can be more than halved if the fields are kept flooded for the minimum time outside the growing season and by allowing the fields to dry out multiple times while the rice is growing.* Lasco et al. (2006) Table 5.12 gives scaling factors for intermittent flooding of 0.52 and 0.60 compared to continuous flooding during the growing season. Table 5.13 of the same reference gives scaling factors of 0.68 to 1.9 depending on whether the fields are flooded in the non-growing season. Taking these two factors together can produce a greater than 50% reduction in emissions (0.52 * 0.68 = 0.35).

124 *new varieties of rice are being developed that produce higher yields for a given area, and that exude less nutrients into the soil to feed the microbes.* Adding a gene to rice was found to produce more rice and less methane in Su et al. (2015).

Chapter 27 Fish and chips

It was a childhood treat to visit the fish 'n' chip shop and come out with steaming bundles of food, ripping through the paper to pull out fat, greasy vinegar-soaked chips. Then shovelling in crunchy pieces of fish and biting through to the soft flakes inside. Shouldn't eating fish be low on emissions – the fish were already there in the sea after all?

Fig. 27.1: Fish and chips. (URL 71)

Wild food

In fact, more generally, might eating from the wild be a good route to reducing food emissions? Eating wild ruminants like deer or moose would cut their large methane emissions. Some people in Australia advocate eating kangaroo that have been culled for other reasons.

Leaving aside ethical issues with killing wild animals, and taking a human-centric view for now, it turns out that the amount of wild food just doesn't come close to the quantity of food demanded for the current human population. While our ancestors may have lived by rivers and the sea, happily eating fish without depleting their annual numbers, over-fishing has been a problem in recent decades. For fishing to be sustainable into the long-term future, the amount of fish being caught has to be balanced by enough new fish being born and surviving long enough to reproduce.

Fishing emissions

So, if we take only a little fish from the sea, what emissions is your fish and chips responsible for? A ship has to go to sea, haul in the fish and refrigerate or freeze the catch to keep it fresh. The fuel burnt to power these activities, and the leakage of refrigerant (box 11.1), causes the greenhouse-gas emissions of deep-sea-caught fish (e.g. cod) to be about 5 times the weight of the fish.

$$1 \text{ g cod} = 5 \text{ g emissions}$$

This is lower than chicken, and only slightly higher than eggs, which are the lowest nutritionally-dense animal-based food considered so far (excluding milk, cream and yogurt). However, it is higher than all the plant-based ingredients considered in this book (with the exception of hothoused tomatoes, air-freighted fruit and vegetables and coffee granules, the latter of which isn't likely to become a staple foodstuff).

For both the fish and the chips, portion sizes vary wildly from one chip shop to the next, but using a typical portion size, the total fish 'n' chip emissions is over 1.5 kilos, mostly from the fish (Fig. 27.4 left), and has the largest climate-impact of any of the non-ruminant dishes in this book (closely followed by chicken tikka masala and a steak pizza).

Why is it so high, when the fish causes relatively low emissions per kilo? Simply because we've used a large portion of fish, weighing 250 grams: this is twice the weight of meat used in the chicken tikka masala, and the fish itself causes most of the battered fish emissions (Fig. 27.2). Adding the emissions from a portion of chips takes the large fish 'n' chips emissions over 2 kilos, using up most of a 3 kg emissions budget for a whole day (Fig. 27.4, left).

How can this be reduced? I think the anticipation of the vinegar and salt makes me greedy to have a large portion, whereas often I'd be equally happy with half the quantity of fish, which would reduce emissions for the whole meal by about half a kilo (Fig. 27.4, centre). I might want to add some lower-impact foods to compensate though, maybe some extra chips, or some old-fashioned protein from classic mushy peas (produced in a similar way to beans, discussed in chapter 14).

Fish farming

An increasing proportion of the fish we eat is from fish farms. These fish farms can be entirely inland, for example in an artificial pond, or they can be in a caged part of the sea or river (Fig. 27.3). Most salmon is now farmed.

The emissions per gram of farmed fish are higher than for wild fish, and more similar to chicken (which is a relatively low-impact meat).

1 g salmon = 8 g emissions

Just as for chicken, about half of the carbon footprint comes from producing the fish food, which is mostly fishmeal and fish oil, as well as seed cake (chapter 10), soy and wheat (chapter 25).

Fig. 27.2: Emissions for battered cod: cod (250 g); flour (30 g); milk (60 g); egg (12.5 g); vegetable oil (20 g); putting the fryer on for 30 minutes, shared between 4 people (7.5 minutes at 2 kWh).

The figure shows, for Battered cod: Fryer (119), Oil (74), Egg (59), Milk (132), Flour (24), Cod (1325). Total 1733 gCO$_2$e.

Fig. 27.3: Salmon farming in Norway, using floating cages. (URL 73)

Fig. 27.4:

Left: Emissions for fish 'n' chips: battered cod; fried chips.

Centre: The same ingredients as the left panel but using 125 g of cod instead of 250 g.

Right: Emissions for fish pie: salmon (100 g); butter (15 g); potato (100 g); milk (100 g); boiling the potatoes for 15 minutes, shared between two people (7.5 minutes at 2 kWh); putting the oven on for 40 minutes, plus warm-up time, shared between 2 people (28 minutes at 2.4 kWh).

Fish pie

Fig. 27.4 (right) shows the emissions for a fish pie. The total emissions are about one quarter less than for the large fish and chips (Fig. 27.4 left), mostly because we used much less fish. Even so, nearly half the total emissions come from the fish, with the cooking causing a quarter of the emissions, and the dairy products making up most of the rest.

Reducing the amount of salmon and replacing it with some vegetables or beans is therefore the easiest way to reduce emissions. The fishy footprint also depends on the type of fish, since some fish are easier to catch than others. For example, small fish such as herring cause about half the emissions of the more commonly eaten large fish like cod, mostly because the nets do not need to be cast as deeply, which reduces the fuel needed to run the ship.

If we could lower the emissions of the farmed fish food, then this could significantly reduce the salmon emissions. Developments in new animal feeds have the potential to significantly decrease this, as discussed at breakfast in the context of eggs (chapter 7).

Given most of the sea-caught fishing emissions come from fuel on boats, how about a nice family fishing trip to the local lake or river? If the only purpose of your trip is to catch dinner for two, then your fossil-fuelled car emissions will be worse than those of the fishing vessels if you drive more than 15 kilometres (10 miles) each way.

Key points

- Caught-fish emissions are between chicken and eggs, in terms of emissions per kilo of fish, which puts them at the low end of animal-based foods and higher than all the plant-based foods (other than out-of-season perishable fruit and veg).

- Just as for chicken, farmed-fish emissions arise largely from producing the fish food, and the emissions per kilo are similar to those for chicken.

- The easiest way to reduce emissions is to reduce the quantity of fish, and perhaps bulk out with vegetables or pulses.

Notes

Page

126   *the greenhouse-gas emissions of deep-sea-caught fish (e.g. cod) to be about 5 times the weight of the fish.* The most recent review and calculations for sea-caught fish was done by Buchspies et al. (2011), who find 5.3 kgCO$_2$e / kg cod (their figure 4.3). See also the earlier review by Winther et al. (2009) which gives more details on the shipping emissions.

127   *portion sizes vary wildly from one chip shop to the next, but using a typical portion size,* A newspaper report (URL 72) says "Currently a medium portion of cod varies from 93 g to 562 g and a medium portion of chips varies from 100 g to 797 g." so the calculation assumes 250 g of fish.

127   *the total fish 'n' chip emissions is over 1.5 kilos, mostly from the fish (Fig. 27.4 left),* Per portion using 250 g cod, 30 g flour, 60 g milk, $\frac{1}{4}$ of an egg, and 20 g oil. See also Schreiber (2018) who examine a fish and chips meal, among others.

127   *The emissions per gram of farmed fish are higher than for wild fish, and more similar to chicken (which is a relatively low-impact meat).* Averaging the values for salmon from Poore and Nemecek (2018) (which is all for farmed fish), which gives 8 kgCO$_2$e / kg salmon. See also Buchspies et al. (2011); Ziegler et al. (2012), who find 6.6 kgCO$_2$e / kg salmon.

127   *Just as for chicken, about half of the carbon footprint comes from producing the fish food, which is mostly fishmeal and fish oil, as well as seed cake (chapter 10), soy and wheat (chapter 25).* Figure 4.3 of Buchspies et al. (2011) shows that nearly 4 kgCO$_2$e / kg salmon is due to the fish feed. Table 4.11 of the same reference shows the non-fish components of fish feed used in that study.

128   *small fish such as herring cause about half the emissions of the more commonly eaten large fish like cod, mostly because the nets do not need to be cast as deeply, which reduces the fuel needed to run the ship.* Buchspies et al. (2011) calculated a value for tinned herring (their figure 4.3), but removing the tin can (packaging emission) and replacing it with the fresh fish overheads (packaging, storage and distribution) from as cod (and using no oil) would give a value of 2 kgCO$_2$e / kg herring. See also figure 2 of Winther et al. (2009).

128   *If the only purpose of your trip is to catch dinner for two, then your fossil-fuelled car emissions will be worse than those of the fishing vessels if you drive more than 15 kilometres (10 miles) each way.* Emissions from 500 g of fish (to make a large fish and chips for two people) are about 8 × 500 g = 4 kg. Driving 30 kilometres causes 155 gCO$_2$e / km × 30 km = 4,650 g for a medium-sized family car. If the fishing location is 15 kilometres away, you drive 30 kilometres for the round trip.

Chapter 28 Veg

We're told to eat more vegetables to improve our health, but will this also be better for the climate? The answer is affected mostly by the method of transportation, the cooking time and the additional ingredients.

Carrots

Fig. 28.1: Some tasty-looking carrots, including a cute couple that wouldn't normally make it to the supermarket shelves. (URL 74)

You can watch carrots growing on your own windowsill by putting a seed down the side of a clear plastic cup of soil. The orange root is visible through the side of the container, but it takes a frustratingly long time to grow into a sizeable snack! Alternatively, cut the top off a carrot from the shop and put it in a saucer of water on the windowsill and wait for edible green shoots to sprout out of the top. (Clean your windowsill first though, and make sure there is plenty of ventilation to avoid mould.)

Carrots need fertilizer to grow well, although they don't need much because they are good at extracting the nitrogen from the soil and can produce a heavy crop in a small area. Carrots are doing a beefed-up version of what nature intended: storing up energy in the roots to tide the plant through the winter and allow strong growth in the spring, ahead of producing seeds in the second year. Because the fertilizer emissions are so low, the storage, sorting, packing and transportation cause most of the carrot climate impact, but the total is still small.

1 g carrots = 0.6 g emissions

Carrots are a common ingredient in many soups and stews, along with onions and celery, and are also served boiled on their own, with or without melting butter. Depending on how big the carrots are (which affects the cooking time) and on the amount of butter added, the carrot itself is only one third of the total climate impact of cooked, buttered carrots (Fig. 28.2, left). This can be reduced by using vegetable spread instead of butter, or reduced to a tiny amount (less than 1% of average daily emissions) by eating the carrot raw (Fig. 28.2, centre).

Buttered carrots
Boiling (119)
Butter (42)
Carrot (50)
Total 211 gCO$_2$e

Raw carrot
Carrot (50)
Total 50 gCO$_2$e

Oven roast root veg (cooking for 2)
Oven (for 2) (475)
Oil (19)
Root veg (50)
Total 544 gCO$_2$e

Oven baking is a popular way to make vegetables taste great with very little effort. Other root vegetables have similar impacts to carrots, and also taste good roasted in the oven. Try beetroot, turnip, parsnip, sweet potato or swede (rutabaga). These have low emissions when raw, but if you cook for two people, and cook nothing else at the same time, the oven baking is the biggest contribution to the emissions (Fig. 28.2, right).

However, if you only cook the veg as an extra when cooking something else, then you can attribute the oven emissions to the other food and you get the veg roasted "for free". Root vegetables can be washed and chopped a couple of days in advance and left in the fridge until the oven is on for something else, and then when cooked they can be put back in the fridge ready to be added to any meal, or as a fridge-raid snack.

Green-vegetable emissions

Would you like some green vegetables with your meal? Green beans are popular and easy to cook. Opinions are divided on whether to steam them lightly (retaining their vibrant green colour and crunch) or whether to cook them for longer (leading to a softer, greyer texture).

Like carrots, green beans are strong growers, and fix nitrogen on their roots like the other beans in their family (chapter 14). More than half their contribution to climate change comes from being stored at the supermarket in open-fronted fridges that chill the aisle as well as the produce (box 11.1).

1 g french/green beans = 0.8 g emissions

However, even with supermarket refrigeration, seasonal green beans have very little impact on climate change, especially if cooked al dente in the microwave (Fig. 28.4, left). The total emissions are less than 5% of a daily emissions budget of 3 kg.

However, do you know when green beans are in season in your area? (I had to look it up.) The rest of the year they are imported, often from another continent by air, which causes similar emissions per kilo to the lowest-impact animal products (Fig. 28.4, centre).

Fig. 28.2: Carrots three ways:
Left: Emissions for buttered carrots: carrots (80 g); a teaspoon of butter (5 g); boiling the carrots, shared between two people (7.5 minutes at 2 kWh).
Centre: Emissions for a raw carrot: a raw carrot (80 g).
Right: Emissions for oven roast root veg (cooking for 2): root vegetables (80 g); a teaspoon of oil (5 g); putting the oven on for 45 minutes, plus warm-up time, shared between two people (30 minutes at 2.4 kWh).

Fig. 28.3: A bowl of green beans. (URL 75)

Even if you add a teaspoon of butter and boil them for 10 minutes, the air transport still dominates the climate impact, and a single portion of beans causes nearly 0.8 kilos of emissions, or a quarter of a daily food emissions budget of 3 kg.

1 g beans, french/green, by air = 8 g emissions

Fig. 28.4:
Left: Emissions for green beans with spread: green beans (80 g); a teaspoon of vegetable spread (5 g); microwave oven (3 minutes at 1.2 kWh).
Centre: Emissions for green beans (by air) with butter: green beans (80 g); transport 5,000 km by air; a teaspoon of butter (5 g); boiling for 10 minutes, shared between two people (5 minutes at 2 kWh).
Right: Emissions for fried cabbage: cabbage (80 g); a teaspoon of vegetable oil (5 g); frying for 10 minutes, shared between two people (5 minutes at 2 kWh).

So what can you eat when green beans are out of season? Unfortunately it turns out that a lot of other vegetables are also out of season at the same time!

Cabbage is the archetypal go-to year-round vegetable of our grandparents.

1 g cabbage = 0.4 g emissions

I remember many school dinners of cabbage boiled to a mushy grey. Nowadays I love cabbage fried in oil with cumin seeds. It tastes so good, it could be a different vegetable. Frying makes up half the emissions, but the numbers are still low – you could eat 6 portions before you match the climate impact of air-freighted green beans (Fig. 28.4, right).

Before the days of global food transportation, the over-abundance of food at harvest-time had to be turned into supplies that would last the winter, using a range of preservation methods. We still benefit from the commercial versions of many of these preservation methods today, including drying, pickling, canning/bottling and cool or cold storage. Freezing works really well for a lot of vegetables, especially if they are to be used in a soup or stew.

To get even lower emissions, how about eating the green leaves of root vegetables? Baby beetroot greens are a popular addition in posh salad mixes (look out for the red stems and earthy taste). Mature beetroot leaves, turnip leaves, and even the leaves of carrots are extremely nutritious. They can be eaten raw, or quickly fried up with garlic and oil, and maybe some mustard or cumin seeds.

> **Box 28.1: Frozen food**
>
> Emissions from frozen food add up because the produce has to be prepared, is often blanched (which heats it up) and then cooled down again to the freezer temperature. It's often transported at this cold temperature, then kept in supermarket freezers, and then kept in your freezer at home. Finally, unless it's ice-cream, you have to heat the food up from frozen before you eat it.
>
> How do the emissions from frozen food compare with their refrigerated counterparts? To work this out we have to compare with the emissions from running a refrigerated chiller cabinet, and the increased amount of food waste that arises because of the shorter shelf life and fluctuating demand for refrigerated products. Taking all this into account, frozen vegetables cause more emissions than fresh, adding roughly the weight of the vegetables again in emissions.
>
> Frozen food emissions can be reduced further by using clean energy to freeze and transport the food, and to run the freezers in the supermarkets and in your house, as well as using the latest refrigerants (box 11.1).

Key points

- Seasonal vegetables have a very low impact on the environment.

- Emissions from cooking are often the same or greater than those from the vegetables themselves.

- If the vegetables are air-freighted then this contributes 8 times the weight of the food in extra emissions, putting air-freighted veg into the same emissions category as animal products.

Notes

Page

130 *the storage, sorting, packing and transportation cause most of the carrot climate impact, but the total is still small.* **Figure S34** of Frankowska et al. (2019a) gives 1.12 $kgCO_2e$ / kg for carrots, of which about 56% is the stages before household/cooking and waste. Including only these stages gives 0.63 $kgCO_2e$ / kg. Note that about half of this value is for storage, so will depend on the length of time the carrots are stored for. See also the value of 0.4 $kgCO_2e$ / kg from Poore and Nemecek (2018) for root vegetables.

131 *Other root vegetables have similar impacts to carrots, and also taste good roasted in the oven.* See the "Root Vegetables" references in Poore and Nemecek (2018) which include parsnip, celeriac and swede.

131 *More than half their contribution to climate change comes from being stored at the supermarket* Information is from figure S24 of Frankowska et al. (2019a) who find a value of 1.1 kgCO$_2$e / kg. The figures in this book use a value of 0.84 kgCO$_2$e / kg to avoid double-counting of cooking (household) and waste. Of this value, 0.64 kgCO$_2$e / kg comes from retail (e.g. open-fronted refrigerators).

132 *Cabbage is the archetypal go-to year-round vegetable of our grandparents.* Emissions are about half the weight of the raw cabbage. The figures use a value of 0.44 kgCO$_2$e / kg taken from figure S32 of Frankowska et al. (2019a) which gives 0.61 kgCO$_2$e / kg for UK fresh cabbage, of which 72% is pre-household.

132 *drying, pickling, canning/bottling and cool or cold storage.* See Frankowska et al. (2019a) for a wide range of storage methods for different vegetables.

133 *Taking all this into account, frozen vegetables cause more emissions than fresh, adding roughly the weight of the vegetables again in emissions.* The average difference between fresh and frozen emissions is 0.85 kgCO$_2$e / kg, calculated from Frankowska et al. (2019a) for all UK vegetables with both fresh and frozen values. However, there is a wide range from 0.2 to 1.3 kgCO$_2$e / kg depending on whether the item is stored at ambient temperature when fresh (e.g. onions) and how much processing is needed in freezing.

Chapter 29 Beer or wine?

How about a drink with dinner? Do you prefer beer or wine, or maybe a bottle of water? Which do you think has the biggest impact on climate change?

For beer and wine we need to take into account the nitrogen fertilizer used to grow the barley or grapes. These main ingredients are fermented with much smaller quantities of other ingredients (such as hops, for beer).

Transportation varies hugely depending on your preferred tipple, but can be a major contributor.

Cans and bottles

Just as for soft drinks (chapter 21), packaging is an important contribution to the total impact. Fig. 29.3 shows the total emissions from a can of beer, a bottle of beer and a medium (175 ml) glass of wine poured from a regular wine bottle.

Fig. 29.1: Red wine or white? (URL 76)

$$1 \text{ g beer on tap} = 1 \text{ g emissions}$$

$$1 \text{ g wine on tap} = 1 \text{ g emissions}$$

The results are surprisingly similar for the canned and bottled beer, given that the serving sizes are different. The reduced emissions from the lower amount of beer in the bottle are cancelled out by the increased emissions from the bottle itself: the beer bottle causes over a quarter of the emissions.

The emissions for the glass of wine are about half those for the can or bottle of beer, but again this depends greatly on where the wine has been transported from (and note that the quantity of wine in a glass is less than half the quantity of beer in a can).

One way to reduce the climate impact is to make sure we recycle cans and bottles, and to drink from bigger containers. Drinking beer on tap saves greatly on packaging emissions, but should we then add in the electricity necessary to run the pub? One study did this and found that heating and lighting the pub doubled the beer emissions.

Fig. 29.2: A cold beer to stave off global warming? (URL 77)

Beer (in a can)		Beer (in a bottle)		Glass of wine	
	─Aluminium can (54)		─Glass bottle (131)		─Glass bottle (61)
Beer (440)		Beer (330)			─Wine (175)
Total 494 gCO$_2$e		**Total 461 gCO$_2$e**		**Total 236 gCO$_2$e**	

Fig. 29.3:
Left: Emissions for beer (in a can): beer (440 g); an aluminium can (9 g).
Centre: Emissions for beer (in a bottle): beer (330 g); a glass bottle (210 g).
Right: Emissions for a glass of wine: wine (175 g); a 750 ml-capacity glass bottle shared between 4.3 servings (98 g).

Fancy glass-bottled water is commonly provided by restaurants. If you're thirsty and drink a whole bottle of water, then it causes emissions similar to those for a single glass of wine. This because the emissions saved by drinking water instead of wine are cancelled out by drinking a larger quantity of water.

Potable tap water is better than other drinks, as far as climate change is concerned, because its production causes very little greenhouse-gas emissions and it requires no packaging or transportation, since the pipe network is already in place (chapter 21). Restaurants can increase their green credentials (if not directly increasing their profits) by refilling carafes with tap water instead.

At what price luxuries?

Do drinks other than tap water offer enough psychological benefits to justify their consequences for the climate? Or perhaps we should ask ourselves how these drinks compare with other luxuries? One can of beer causes emissions similar to those from 30 cups of black tea (chapter 2), four cups of white coffee (chapter 4), a piece of cake (chapter 22) or driving one mile in a fossil-fuelled car (chapter 1).

Most of us can cut our emissions significantly before we need to give up all our luxuries. However, these numbers can help you to weigh up the benefits against the climate impact, and to really appreciate the luxuries you choose to keep.

Key points

- The impact on climate change is similar for a can of beer, a bottle of beer, or two glasses of wine, so pick your favourite!

- One beer causes half a kilo of emissions, which is one sixth of a 3 kg budget for daily food emissions.

- For wine in a glass bottle, the packaging causes about a quarter of the emissions, so it helps to drink (the same size serving!) from a large container or, even better, from a tap.

Notes

Page

135 *Transportation varies hugely depending on your preferred tipple, but can be a major contributor.* See Garnett (2007) where Figs 21, 24, 25 show transport at 10-20% of emissions.

135 *beer* A value of 1.0 kgCO$_2$e / kg of beer is from the global average for beer from Poore and Nemecek (2018) of 1.2 kgCO$_2$e / kg, subtracting a rough average of 0.2 kgCO$_2$e / kg for packaging. See also figure 3 of Amienyo and Azapagic (2016) which have a value of 0.34 kgCO$_2$e / kg for beer not including packaging.

135 *wine* Using a value of 1.0 kgCO$_2$e / kg, taken from the global average from Poore and Nemecek (2018) of 1.8, after subtracting their value of 0.8 for the packaging which we add on separately. See also the references cited in Garnett (2007) including only growing/viticulture and wine making contributions. Aranda et al. (2005) gives (205 + 189) / 750 = 0.525 kgCO$_2$e / kg of wine, and Fullana et al. (2005) gives (491.51 + 20.87) / 750 = 0.683 kgCO$_2$e / kg wine, so a value of (0.525 + 0.683) / 2 = 0.604 on average.

135 *given that the serving sizes are different.* Typical can and bottle sizes mean that the amount of beer in the bottle (330 ml) is a bit smaller than the amount in the can (440 ml).

135 *heating and lighting the pub doubled the beer emissions.* See figure 21 of Garnett (2007).

136 *a whole bottle of water, then it causes emissions similar to those for a single glass of wine. This because the emissions saved by drinking water instead of wine are cancelled out by drinking a larger quantity of water.* A medium glass of wine is about a quarter of a 750 ml bottle. For a glass of wine, the glass bottle causes about a quarter of the emissions. Obviously drinking a whole bottle of wine causes other problems.

Chapter 30 Dessert

Do you have a dessert after dinner? Perhaps it's time for a treat at the end of a long day, or a bribe to convince children to eat their main course? In this chapter we'll get creative with some of the ingredients already covered in other chapters, focusing on two popular desserts: apple pie and chocolate mousse.

Apple pie

Apple pie is a classic pudding, at its best made by a kindly grandparent and decorated with pastry shapes of leaves and fruit (Fig. 30.1). It's an American staple, and has similar ingredients to the traditional British crumble and the US cobbler. Apples are baked under a crust of buttery pastry, and the finished pie is often topped with cream or ice cream.

Which ingredient do you think causes the most greenhouse-gas emissions? Fig. 30.2 (left) shows the total emissions for a classic apple pie recipe shared between four people, baked in the oven for an hour, and drizzled with a teaspoon of cream. The result for one portion is over half a kilo, and one fifth of a 3 kg daily food emissions budget.

Of all the ingredients, butter causes the highest emissions: the butter and cream cause 40% of the total. The apple itself isn't a big deal, causing about 10% of the total. (We could ask whether the apple was a windfall from the back garden, or transported by ship from another hemisphere, but this turns out to be a minor issue – see chapter 17.)

What if you bake an apple pie for one person? It's unlikely that anyone would make an apple pie at home for one person, but shops sell individual pies, for reheating at home. If you use the oven just for reheating this dessert, and add a generous helping of cream, you nearly triple the emissions.

From TV baking shows I understand that the type of fat, and how it is handled, can make a big difference to the quality of pastry. I'm not going to give an opinion on that here, but

Fig. 30.1: Apple pie. (URL 114)

Fig. 30.2:

Left: Emissions for apple pie and cream: apple (125 g); sugar (19 g); flour (37.5 g); butter (19 g); putting the oven on for 1 hour, plus warm-up time, shared between 4 people (19 minutes at 2.4 kWh); a teaspoon of cream (5 g).

Centre: The same ingredients as the left panel, but all the cooking emissions are attributed to one portion (75 minutes at 2.4 kWh), and more cream is added (two tablespoons of cream, 30 g).

Right: The same ingredients as the left panel but replacing butter with the same weight of vegetable spread, and sharing the cooking emissions between 8 people instead of 4 people (9 minutes at 2.4 kWh, per portion).

note that switching from butter to vegetable spread can make a significant difference to the greenhouse gases caused by an apple pie. Making this substitution and cooking for 8 instead of 4 nearly halves emissions from the standard apple pie recipe we first considered. Many people have been cooking with margarine or other vegetable spreads for years, illustrating nicely that it's not always necessary to switch to novel ingredients to make a significant difference to emissions. The single teaspoon of cream makes very little difference to the total, so it isn't necessary to go completely vegan either (assuming you're going to put the rest of the tub of cream to good use...).

Chocolate mousse

Let's have some decadent chocolate mousse to end the day: creamy yet airy, with the bitter chocolate flavour coming through the sugar (Fig. 30.3). The simplest chocolate mousse recipes contain no cream at all, just eggs, with their whites whisked up until light and smooth before folding in the chocolate and sugar.

The result is quite rich, so the mousse is often served in small pots. And, since a lot of it is air, the environmental impact is nowhere near as bad as you might think considering how decadent it seems (Fig. 30.4, left), dialling up about 0.25 kg of emissions. Most of the impact comes from the egg.

However, the toppings can really add up. How about some raspberries air-freighted from another continent (chapter 17), and whipped cream? You more than quadruple the emissions this way, to over 1 kilo per person (compare Fig. 30.4 centre)!

We discussed egg alternatives in chapter 7: if you have some leftover chickpea water (aquafaba) from boiling chickpeas, or draining a can, you can whisk this up just like egg white. I tried this and it does take quite a lot longer than whisking egg whites, so I've taken care to add on the electricity for the whisking (although it actually makes little difference to the total).

Fig. 30.3: Chocolate mousse. (URL 115)

Fig. 30.4: A trio of chocolate mousse options:
Left: Emissions for a chocolate mousse: cocoa powder (15 g); sugar (15 g); three eggs, shared between 4 people (37.5 g); whisking for 5 minutes, shared between 4 people (1 minute at 2 kWh).
Centre: Emissions for a chocolate mousse with cream and raspberries (by air): a chocolate mousse; cream; raspberries by air.
Right: The same ingredients as the left panel, but replacing the egg white with aquafaba and whisking for 10 minutes instead of 5 minutes.

If you were otherwise going to throw out the aquafaba, then you can count it as zero emissions (box 9.1). It will be quite a while before the production of chickpeas is driven by the demand for aquafaba so it's shown as zero in the stack for now. With this substitution, the standard chocolate mousse emissions are halved (compare Fig. 30.4 right and left) to less than 5% of a daily food emissions budget of 3 kilos. Now most of the emissions come from the cocoa (without which it wouldn't really be a chocolate mousse!).

Key points

- The most important ingredients, e.g. apples, are not always the biggest contributors to climate change.

- Hidden butter can have two or three times the impact of the main ingredient, but is easily replaced with vegetable spread.

- Putting the oven on to reheat one portion of apple pie causes more emissions than the butter- and cream-laden pie itself.

- Watch out for adding toppings of perishable out-of-season fruit.

Notes

Page

138 *a classic apple pie recipe shared between four people,* 500 g apple, 75 g sugar, 150 g flour and 75 g butter.

139 *The simplest chocolate mousse recipes contain no cream at all,* Just three ingredients, serving four people: 60 g cocoa, 60 g icing sugar and 3 eggs.

Chapter 31 Evening meal summary

How do these different dinner options compare side by side? We'll combine them to make three different meals – typical-emissions, then high- and then low-emissions evening meals, which are compared in Fig. 31.1.

Typical-emissions dinner

One possible typical-emissions dinner includes chicken tikka masala with rice, with a beer, followed by apple pie and cream (Fig. 31.1, left). This comes to over 3 kilos of emissions, of which 1 kilo is caused by the chicken. This uses up the entirety of a 3 kg budget for food greenhouse emissions for a whole day, in one meal.

Higher-emissions dinner

Of all the single food items considered in this book, the highest emissions item is the 8 oz steak, which causes 10 kilos of emissions from just the one item. If everyone in the world ate a steak every day, and caused no other emissions from other food or any other activities including transport or heating, the steaks alone would blow the 1.5°C carbon budget by 2040 (chapter 24).

For a higher-emissions dinner, to a steak add fries, air-freighted green beans, a glass of wine and the chocolate mousse topped with cream and air-freighted raspberries (Fig. 31.1, centre). It does sound delicious.

Even in this extravagant pile, the steak still causes most of the damage, with the air-freighting coming in second, although quite far behind. Overall this is 4 times worse for climate change than the typical-emissions dinner, and this one meal causes 4 times a daily food emissions budget of 3 kg.

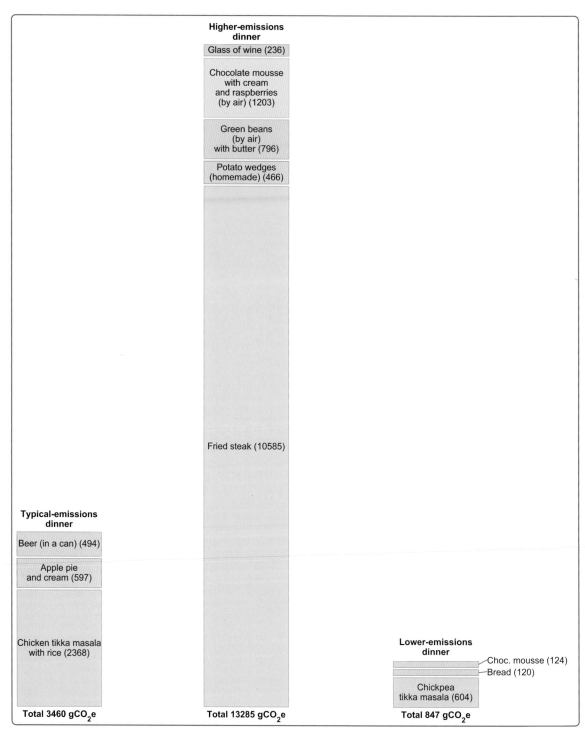

Fig. 31.1: Stacking up the emissions from
different dinner options discussed in this Part.

Lower-emissions dinner

What happens if you choose the lowest-emissions options from the chicken and dessert chapters (chapters 25 and 30) and get frugal by drinking only tap water? Chickpea tikka masala with bread, followed by aquafaba chocolate mousse, comes in at less than 1 kilo of emissions (Fig. 31.1, right). This is more than three times lower than the typical-emissions dinner, mostly due to cutting back on the chicken, rice and beer, and replacing with chickpeas, bread and tap water. Unlike the typical- and higher-emissions dinner options, the lower-emissions dinner allows room for other meals in a daily food emissions budget of 3 kilos.

The next chapter combines these dinner choices together with those from the other meals to see how they contribute to a whole day of food.

Key points

- The typical-emissions dinner causes about 3 kilos of emissions, more than half of which comes from the chicken tikka masala.

- An 8oz steak dominates all other menu items in the higher-emissions dinner, which causes more than 4 times the emissions of the typical-emissions dinner.

- The lower-emissions dinner replaces chicken with chickpeas and makes use of the chickpea cooking liquid to make a chocolate mousse. The emissions are 4 times lower than those for the typical-emissions dinner, and 16 times lower than those for the higher-emissions dinner.

Part V: Looking ahead

In this final Part of the book, we bring everything together, and look at the bigger picture from several different perspectives. We combine all our food choices, to work out the total emissions from a whole day of food, and consider the emissions impact of food waste.

The main point of this book is comparing the emissions of different foods rather than pitting different diets against each other (e.g. veganism versus vegetarianism). We look at the health implications of making long-term major changes to your diet, and consider the relative green credentials of different popular diets.

Most of this book has been about changes that you as an individual can make. However, suppliers and governments also have a role to play.

Finally, we discuss whether food in all its aspects could be an important part of the solution to climate change, and the options that changing our food habits could open up.

Chapter 32 Food emissions for a whole day

So far we have stacked up the emissions for three different choices for each meal. Now we can add up all the "typical-emissions" choices for all the meals and see the total for a whole day. We will compare it to the totals from the "higher-emissions" and "lower-emissions" choices.

Typical-emissions day

The total of all the "typical-emissions" choices for breakfast, lunch, snacks and dinner comes to more than 5 kilos of greenhouse gases (Fig. 32.1, left). This is about the same as the global average for a day of food (chapter 1) once waste is taken into account (chapter 33), and is significantly above a daily food emissions budget of 3 kg (chapter 1).

The biggest single items within this stack are the chicken used in the chicken tikka masala, and the ham in the lunchtime sandwich. Between them they cause over one fifth of the total. Dairy products appear throughout the day: especially milk in cereal at breakfast, yogurt at lunch, and cream in the sauce of the chicken tikka masala; taken together they add up to over 1 kilo of emissions, or about 20% of the total. The other biggest items are the rice and beer, which cause about 10% each.

From a nutritional perspective, the typical-emissions food choices meet most of the standard daily health requirements, with the exception of fibre and vitamin D, which are often deficient in average western diets (see discussion in chapter 34).

Higher-emissions day

The total for the "higher-emissions" choices is 20 kilos, which is 4 times the "typical-emissions" total (Fig. 32.1, centre). Half of this comes from one single food item: the 8 oz steak for dinner. There are also more dairy products than in the "typical-emissions" day – the milk-based latte at breakfast, and cheese in

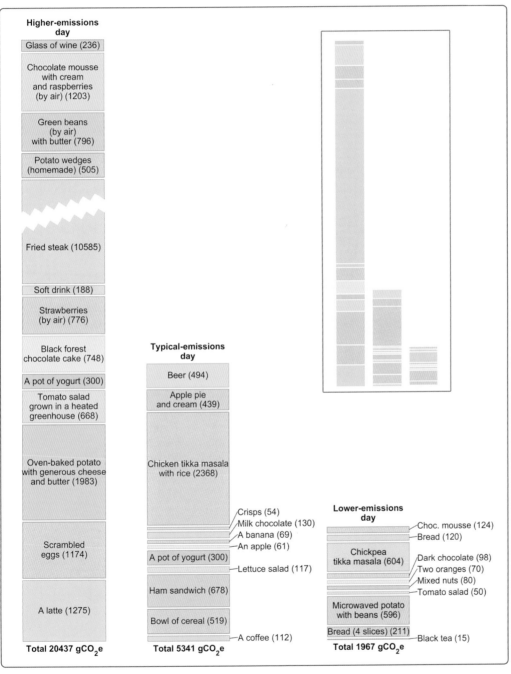

Fig. 32.1: Whole-day emissions. (The steak contribution is so high we've had to truncate it; the inset shows the true ratio of the options.)

the lunch sandwich. Taken together the dairy items alone cause over 3 kilos of emissions, with the largest contributions from milk in the latte and cheese on the potato. And air-freighted fruit and vegetables added about 1.5 kilos of emissions.

The higher-emissions food choices provide more than we need of most of the nutritional requirements, including nearly 3 times the recommended daily intake of protein. The only exception is that the higher-emissions choices provide less than half the recommended daily intake of fibre, which is a common feature of western diets. This decadent option also provides 50% more calories than we need.

Lower-emissions day

With our "lower-emissions" choices (Fig. 32.1, right), we've reduced emissions by 10 times compared to the "higher-emissions" day, and more than halved the climate impact compared to the "typical-emissions" day. The total comes to under 2 kilos of emissions, which fits comfortably within the 3 kg daily food emissions budget discussed in chapter 1.

But are these lower-emissions food choices good for our bodies? The whole day of food provides 20% more protein than our bodies require and, unlike the typical and higher-emissions choices, meets the recommended daily intake of fibre. Just as for the typical-emissions choices, and a typical western diet, the lower-emissions options do not provide enough vitamin D. Vitamin B12 can only be found in animal products, or in plant-based products that have extra vitamin B12 added, so the lower-emissions options need to be complemented with a vitamin B12 supplement (see chapter 34). The lower-emissions options are a little low on selenium and vitamin B2, which could be fixed by eating a Brazil nut and consuming B2-fortified dairy alternatives.

Key points

- Meat products are the single largest emissions food items in the typical and higher-emissions days of food.

- Meat is closely followed by dairy items.

- Air-freight of perishable fruits and vegetables can cause similar emissions to a whole lower-emissions day of food on its own.

- It is possible to reduce food emissions to fit comfortably within a 3 kg daily budget without resorting to novel foods, and you can probably use the information in this book to be much more creative than I have been!

Notes

Page

146 *the typical-emissions food choices meet most of the standard daily health requirements, with the exception of fibre and vitamin D,* The typical-emissions day of food contains 10.5 grams of fibre, which is 35% of the recommended daily intake (calculated using nutrition information from the National Diet and Nutrition Survey (NDNS) year 6 Hemmings 2016). It contains 2.3 micrograms of vitamin D, which is 23% of the recommended daily amount.

148 *the higher-emissions choices provide less than half the recommended daily intake of fibre, which is a common feature of western diets.* The higher-emissions day of food contains 12 grams of fibre, which is 40% of the recommended daily intake of 30 grams. The UK average is about 60% of the recommended daily intake (URL 78).

148 *meets the recommended daily intake of fibre.* The lower-emissions day of food provides 95% of the recommended daily intake of fibre if you eat white bread, or 130% if white bread is replaced by wholemeal bread.

148 *The lower-emissions options are a little low on selenium and vitamin B2, which could be fixed by eating a Brazil nut and consuming B2-fortified dairy alternatives.* This option meets the other dietary requirements of vitamins and minerals, with the exception of selenium and vitamin B2, only providing about half the recommended daily levels, using the nutrition data from the National Diet and Nutrition Survey UK Year 6. However, note that there is considerable variation in selenium levels even for a single type of food depending on the soil it is grown in. According to the standard nutrition information, a single Brazil nut provides the recommended daily intake of selenium, but no emissions data was available for Brazil nuts so they are not included in chapter 19. Since the lower-emissions day of food is supposed to be an example rather than a prescription for healthy living, and selenium deficiency is rare, we don't discuss this further here. The daily requirement of Vitamin B2 is provided by dairy products in the average UK diet (NDNS year 6 Hemmings 2016, own calculation) but is also provided by fortified breakfast cereals and rice. Again vitamin B2 deficiency is rare, and can be addressed with vitamin supplements.

Chapter 33 Leftovers and food waste

Do you often have leftovers as a snack, raiding the fridge when you get home, or on the way up to bed? To me, leftovers rarely look as attractive as a new crunchy packet of crisps, but maybe that says a lot about my cooking, or my addiction to crisps! It turns out that reducing food waste can be as important as switching foods when it comes to combating climate change, but not for the reason most people expect.

Binning food

Globally, about one third of food is lost or wasted. Our first thought might be to sigh at the supermarkets or lawmakers for setting their standards too high and throwing away perfectly edible (and sometimes amusingly) wonky veg (Figs. 33.2 and 33.2). But the embarrassing fact is that in western countries, more than half of wasted food is caused by us, the citizens.

Fig. 33.1: Happily, misshapen fruit and veg are not the biggest food waste problem. (URL 80)

We might expect catering outlets, for example canteens and restaurants, to contribute to food waste because they have to over-cater in case of unexpected high demand yet, of all the wasted food, only 10% occurs here. By contrast about 70% of the wasted food is discarded in people's homes, when we scrape food off our plates into the bin, or throw out unopened packets. On average, each UK citizen wastes over 200 grams of food each day, almost literally throwing 60 pennies in the bin.

What sorts of food are we throwing away? Researchers were so keen to find out that they went through people's rubbish bins to find and identify rotting leftovers. (Don't worry, they got permission from the residents first and the bins were all anonymized, so they aren't out there right now tutting over your most recent guilty food oversight.) They found that the most wasted foods are vegetables and salads, followed by drinks and bread.

Fig. 33.2: The most wasted foods are vegetables and salads, but not because they are misshapen. (URL 81)

Isn't this just stuff like orange peel or teabags? Actually no. So far this chapter included only food that was intended to be eaten.

If we were to include those other sorts of inedible food waste then all the numbers would be about 50% larger.

Needless to say, the exact definition of "edible" and "inedible" food waste depends on culture and personality. We all know of *someone* who eats the whole apple – peel, core and all. It turns out they are going above (and perhaps beyond) the call of duty when it comes to reducing greenhouse-gas emissions.

Fig. 33.3: What to do with all that stalk? (URL 82)

I'm not advocating everyone starts eating apple cores. However, the statistics on "inedible" food waste do mean that buying pre-prepared vegetables is not as extravagant as it might seem. I love my veg box, but it's surprising how much waste is produced as I carve off the outer leaves of a cauliflower and snap off the Brussels sprouts from their thick stalk. While I sometimes find this therapeutic, it is actually wasteful, because when these operations are carried out at scale, the waste can often be put to better use than compost: often "inedible" food waste is fed directly to animals. Some of the less digestible foods can be fed to insects, which are then fed to animals as a high protein food. This is important because it can help reduce the amount of crops grown for animal feed.

With an increasing awareness of the importance of reducing food waste, there are some exciting new projects to re-purpose the less popular parts of fresh foods into new food. For example, fashionable and healthy cauliflower rice can be made from cauliflower stalks (Fig. 33.3), ugly and undersized fruit and veg are made into juices, and the bread-ends left by the sandwich industry are being made into beer.

Emissions from wasted food

Why is it so important to reduce food waste? When I was growing up I was told to finish the food on my plate because there were starving children who would have been glad to eat my leftovers. For climate change, we are clearly wasting resources by producing food that is then wasted. But there is another problem that can be an even bigger contributor to emissions, depending on the type of food.

Most wasted food goes into the bin, which goes to rubbish dumps, or landfill as they are now more correctly known. Landfill sites smell of rotting food – I've learned to close my car window when I see lots of seagulls circling overhead because I'm probably approaching a rubbish dump. Because all the rubbish is piled up, not much air can reach the buried food waste. As discussed in the rice chapter (chapter 26), rotting stuff without enough oxygen makes methane, which is a powerful greenhouse gas.

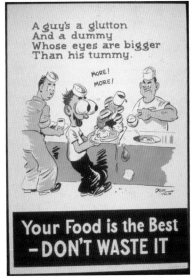

Fig. 33.4: A poster attempting to shame people into not wasting food, from the US government in World War II. Image credit: the United States National Archives and Records Administration. (URL 83)

Fig. 33.5: If food waste ends up in landfill it adds about one kilo of emissions per person, per day.

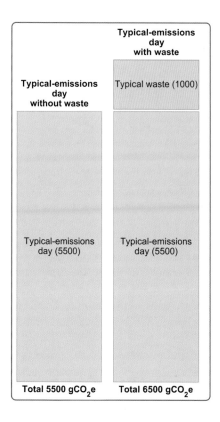

Including the waste in our homes, and in catering outlets, and the "inedible" food waste, as well as processing and manufacturing that happens after food leaves the farm, each of us is responsible for about one kilo per day of greenhouse-gas emissions from food waste.

$$1 \text{ g food waste} = 3 \text{ g emissions}$$

This is about the same as one extra cheese and ham toastie! Fig. 33.5 includes this in the emissions stack for a typical day of food, to illustrate that it adds about 20% to the total food emissions for the "typical-emissions" day of food , bringing the total close to the 6 kilo global average daily food emissions discussed in chapter 1.

Tips for reducing food waste at home

Are you now wondering how you can reduce your food waste, or are you like a lot of people who think they don't waste food when they actually do? It's just not a big part of our day like, say, eating. We don't think "OK, what food am I going to waste today?". It happens when we're tired and looking for something to eat and have to move something mouldy out of the way to find something tasty, or when we're hastily clearing up after the kids at the end of a meal.

It also turns out that we can't exclusively blame it all on a different generation. A UK survey found that all ages wasted a significant amount of food, although millennials wasted 50% more than people over retirement age. It's a long time since the World Wars, when it was socially unacceptable to waste food in the UK.

I'm sure you have lots of thoughts about how other people waste food – I do! So probably the first painful step towards reducing food waste is to try to spot when we're the ones doing it. We can try to notice what sorts of food we regularly throw away. Milk at the bottom of bowls of cereal? Bread crusts? Unopened liquified bags of salad discovered too late at the bottom of the fridge? Meals that are past their use-by-date?

Box 33.1: Top tips for reducing food waste

- Make a habit of storing leftovers and reheating them as a bonus snack the next day.

- Check whether old food is still safe to eat or simply of a lower quality which can be eaten in a different way (for example by toasting old bread).

- Plan your food before going shopping, so you only buy food you expect to use.

- Measure out the amount of products like rice or pasta before cooking, so you don't make too much.

- If you buy extra of a product on special offer, remember to buy less of something else to compensate.

Governments have big incentives to cut food waste, not least because it contributes to their greenhouse-gas emissions quotas. Several governments provide helpful guidelines on how to cut food waste, so you can find more ideas on their websites.

Key points

- Globally, about one third of food is wasted. In western cultures more than half of that food waste is caused by individuals at home.

- Wasted food that goes into rubbish bins turns into methane at landfill sites. Because methane is a much more potent gas than carbon dioxide, this typically causes over 1 kilo of emissions per person per day.

- Most people think they don't waste food even though they do. Try to spot yourself wasting food over the coming days.

- Check out some tips for reducing waste (box 33.1).

Notes

Page

150 *Globally, about one third of food is lost or wasted. Our first thought might be to sigh at the supermarkets or lawmakers for setting their standards too high and throwing away perfectly edible (and sometimes amusingly) wonky veg (Figs. 33.2 and 33.2). But the embarrassing fact is that in western countries, more than half of wasted food is caused by us, the citizens.* Take a look at the graphic in the following reference, which shows the food waste from different parts of the food chain, for each continent separately (URL 79). In North America and Oceana, and in Europe, the fraction lost in the "consumption" phase is over 50%.

150 *We might expect catering outlets, for example canteens and restaurants, to contribute to food waste because they have to over-cater in case of unexpected high demand yet, of all the wasted food, only 10% occurs here. By contrast about 70% of the wasted food is discarded in people's homes, when we scrape food off our plates into the bin, or throw out unopened packets.* These figures are for the UK, from section 1 of the UK Waste and Resources Action Programme report (Waste Resources Action Plan (WRAP) UK 2019b, especially their figure 2).

150 *On average, each UK citizen wastes over 200 grams of food each day, almost literally throwing 60 pennies in the bin.* See section 2.2.1 of Waste Resources Action Plan (WRAP) UK (2019a), which says the amount of wasted food that could have been eaten was 5 million tonnes, worth approximately 15 billion for the whole UK in 2015. Sharing this out across people and days gives 209 grams per person per day and 63 pence per person per day.

150 *the most wasted foods are vegetables and salads, followed by drinks and bread.* See Waste Resources Action Plan (WRAP) UK (2019b) who state 28% of fresh vegetables and salad are wasted, followed by 15% of drinks, followed by 11% of bakery items.

151 *If we were to include those other sorts of inedible food waste then all the numbers would be about 50% larger.* See Table 3 of Waste Resources Action Plan (WRAP) UK (2019b), which shows 427 g per person per day (156 kg per person per year) of post-farm food waste (food plus inedible parts) versus 293 g per person per day (107 kg per person per year) of post farm-gate food waste (food only).

151 *the exact definition of "edible" and "inedible" food waste depends on culture and personality.* There is no worldwide agreement on the definition of "inedible" food waste. Inedible food waste includes skin, bones, meat or fish carcasses, inedible peelings, banana skins, other fruit peels, fruit pits, teabags and eggshells.

151 *With an increasing awareness of the importance of reducing food waste, there are some exciting new projects* Did you ever search through the packets on a supermarket shelf, to find one that has a later sell-by date? I certainly

have. This "date-picking" is a significant cause of waste at the supermarket. It has been suggested that packets could gradually change price as their sell-by date approaches, depending on demand. Some airlines already use this tactic with plane ticket pricing to maximise their profit and reduce the "waste" of flying under-filled aircraft. This is probably a fair way to price foods and reduce waste, although I'm a little in trepidation of adding any *more* things to consider when choosing which packet to put in my basket.

151   *Including the waste in our homes, and in catering outlets, and the "inedible" food waste, as well as processing and manufacturing that happens after food leaves the farm, each of us is responsible for about one kilo per day of greenhouse-gas emissions from food waste.* WRAP reports that 10 million tonnes of food caused 25 million tonnes of emissions (Waste Resources Action Plan (WRAP) UK, 2019b).

153   *A UK survey found that all ages wasted a significant amount of food, although millennials wasted 50% more than people over retirement age.* See figure 10 of Quested and Luzecka (2014) which found 1950 grams of food waste per week when survey respondents were aged 18-34, and 1250 grams of food waste per week when respondents were over 65 (these numbers are controlled for household size).

153   *Check whether old food is still safe to eat or simply of a lower quality which can be eaten in a different way (for example by toasting old bread).* The UK rules are that food past its "use-by" date is not safe to eat, but food past its "best-before" date is safe but of a lower quality so you can taste it to see if you think it's OK or not. For example see the UK guidance to food producers here: URL 84

153   *If you buy extra of a product on special offer, remember to buy less of something else to compensate.* This list was compiled based on the WRAP report quantifying how different behaviours correlate with reduced food waste (see table 3 of Quested and Luzecka 2014).

153   *Several governments provide helpful guidelines on how to cut food waste, so you can find more ideas on their websites.* For lots more great ideas check out these lists: URL 85 and URL 86.

Chapter 34 Health

Changing what you eat might be easy compared to insulating our house, or changing how you get to work. But it's also close to your heart, both metaphorically and literally. What you eat directly affects your health, and making a major change needs to be done with care. Do seek medical advice before making a big long-term change to your diet.

Cutting back versus switching

You don't need me to tell you that continuing to eat as normal, but abstaining from high-emissions foods, would leave you hungry at the end of the day. If you just eat more sugar to make up the calories then you're likely to be short on the vitamins and minerals which are plentiful in some of the highest emissions foods, such as meat.

Many people find abstaining completely from particular types of food to be challenging and undesirable. It may also be unnecessary if we can make enough changes to the majority of our food intake. As a result, most official advice recommends significantly reducing your intake of red meat (rather than needing to cut it out completely) while significantly increasing your intake of fruit and vegetables.

Many people worry about getting enough protein when cutting back on meat. Fig. 34.1 shows the emissions for a range of different protein-rich foods, per gram of protein. There are four clusters in the chart:

- "Very high-emissions proteins" ruminant meat (lamb and beef) is at the top, causing over 10 times the emissions of the "low-emissions protein" at the bottom of the chart.

- Milk, cheese and pig meat form a "high-emissions protein" group, each causing less than half the emissions of the "very high-emissions proteins".

- The "medium-emissions protein" group, which includes eggs, farmed fish (salmon), chicken, and tinned beans, halves emissions yet again.

- At the bottom the two "low-emissions proteins" each cause half the emissions of the "medium-emissions proteins". The "low-emissions protein" group contains beans and nuts.

Caught fish (cod) is intermediate between the "medium-emissions protein" and the "low-emissions protein" groups. However, note that in practice all these values depend on decisions made throughout the food production process, particularly around deforestation for feed (especially for eggs, chicken and salmon) and the amount of fossil versus clean energy used for processing and cooking (especially for beans and Quorn).

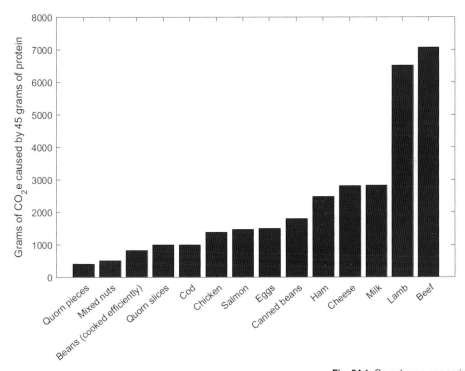

Fig. 34.1: Greenhouse-gas emissions for a quantity of food that provides the same amount of protein as a 150 g chicken breast (45 grams of protein), for some high-protein foods.

Many governments issue dietary guidelines, indicating the vitamins and minerals, and how much of them, that you need to get from your food. (In the US these are published by the Department of Health & Human Services, in the UK by the National Health Service.) For example, UK guidelines state that children under the age of 4 should take vitamin D tablets during the winter, when our bodies can't naturally synthesize vitamin

D from the weak sunlight – and that's before making any climate-motivated diet changes. If you eat no animal products at all, you will likely need to take a vitamin B12 supplement to stay healthy. Normal quantities of vitamin tablets cause less than 1% of the average daily emissions from food.

1 g vitamin tablets = 10 g emissions

Dietary guidelines

Have you ever looked at your government's dietary guidelines? And if so, did you try to work out whether you are following them? I hadn't until I started researching this book. But they are there, and a lot of research goes into them. In practice we eat twice as much red meat as in the guidelines and eat 25% less fruit and vegetables.

What would happen to greenhouse-gas emissions if everyone followed the guidelines? It turns out that emissions would be reduced by 25%. So one quarter of our emissions from food come about just because we aren't eating the healthy government-recommended diet. Why are the emissions so different? The 25% reduction in emissions comes almost entirely from the reduced red-meat consumption in the healthy diet.

We need to change our diets anyway

Would following the dietary guidelines improve our health? The government guidelines limit red-meat consumption because there's an increased risk of bowel cancer when people eat more than the recommendation. The recommended daily limit corresponds to about two sausages, three rashers of bacon, three slices of ham, or one third of an 8 oz steak.

Another major result of not following the guidelines is that western diets contain a lot less fibre than would be healthy. This is largely because the healthiest, most fibrous part of grains is removed when making white bread or white rice. But it's also because we don't eat nearly enough fruit and vegetables. Eating more fibre can reduce our risk of heart disease, stroke and type II diabetes, as well as bowel cancer.

Health-wise, the most dangerous single way in which we are flouting the recommendations is in the amount of sugar we consume. This is causing a massive rise in obesity. In 2015/16 nearly 4 out of every 10 people in the US were obese, and the rates of obesity are rising at an alarming rate across the globe. Obesity causes a range of problems including heart disease, stroke, type II diabetes and some cancers.

Not only is this bad news for the people involved, but it is also hugely problematic for governments who need to find money for treatment. Estimates suggest that obesity costs economies billions of pounds a year, which includes the health-care costs and missed working days. Even though obesity is not a problem for climate change, it is relevant because it means that governments are extremely motivated to change our diets.

Key points

- We are what we eat, so making changes to our diet needs serious consideration and medical advice.

- Following government dietary guidelines would make a significant reduction to food greenhouse-gas emissions, mostly because they recommend a lot less red meat than people actually eat on average.

- Worldwide our diets are becoming increasingly unhealthy. Dietary change is needed irrespective of climate change.

Notes

Page

156 *most official advice recommends significantly reducing your intake of red meat (rather than needing to cut it out completely) while significantly increasing your intake of fruit and vegetables.* For example Willett (2019).

157 *beans* Using the "efficient" cooking time for 4 people, from chapter 14, to try to make a fair comparison with low-emissions foods that can be eaten raw.

157 *UK guidelines state that children under the age of 4 should take vitamin D tablets during the winter,* For more information see URL 87.

158 *vitamin tablets cause less than 1% of the average daily emissions from food.* Audsley and Williamson (2010) set the emissions for vitamin supplements to the value for lysine production, which we take as 7.7 $kgCO_2e$ / kg from CCalC2 ("CCaLC PVC Manual (V2.0)" 2011) (from their "sugar cane 1"). We round this to 10 $kgCO_2e$ / kg in the main text due to a lack of studies.

158 *we eat twice as much red meat as in the guidelines and eat 25% less fruit and vegetables.* See Springmann, Godfray, et al. (2016).

158 *It turns out that emissions would be reduced by 25%.* Springmann, Godfray, et al. (2016) table S9 gives a value of 0.89 tCO_2e per person per year, which we compare to their 2005/7 value of 1.15 tCO_2e per person per year (calculated from their value of 7.6 Gt per year for 2005/7 and a population of 6.6 billion in 2006); the ratio is 0.89 / 1.15 = 0.77 i.e. their healthy global diet causes 77% of the emissions of the global average diet in 2006.

158 *The 25% reduction in emissions comes almost entirely from the reduced red-meat consumption in the healthy diet.* See the HDG bars in Fig 1B of Springmann, Godfray, et al. (2016).

158 *there's an increased risk of bowel cancer when people eat more than the recommendation.* For example see the UK National Health Service website (URL 88).

158 *But it's also because we don't eat nearly enough fruit and vegetables. Eating more fibre can reduce our risk of heart disease, stroke and type II diabetes, as well as bowel cancer.* For more information see (URL 89). See also the fantastic popular book by James Wong (*10-a-Day the Easy Way: Fuss-free Recipes & Simple Science to Transform your Health*, Wong 2019) for links to the scientific studies and loads of great ideas about how to sneak more fruit and veg into your diet

158 *In 2015/16 nearly 4 out of every 10 people in the US were obese,* See Hales et al. (2017).

158 *the rates of obesity are rising at an alarming rate across the globe.* NCD Risk Factor Collaboration (NCD-RisC) (2016).

159 *obesity costs economies billions of pounds a year, which includes the health-care costs and missed working days.* For example the cost to the UK National Health Service is estimated at £6.1 billion, and the cost to wider society is estimated at £27 billion for 2014/15 (URL 90).

Chapter 35 Vegan and other climate-motivated diets

It's convenient to have a name for a set of dietary choices, for example "vegetarianism". It makes it easier to communicate preferences, or spot suitable dishes when ordering food, or when choosing what to buy or cook. In this chapter we discuss a few popular diet choices, and then speculate on how low our food emissions could be if we designed a diet especially for the climate.

In every chapter where we found a high-emissions food, we found simple lower-emissions alternatives which are already available in most shops. Not all of these might be to your taste, or be convenient for your lifestyle at the present time, but they do show you can eat in a climate-friendly way without switching to a strict or specialist diet.

However, because detailed emissions information about each food hasn't been readily available, people concerned about food and climate change often think specific strict diets are necessary, so let's look at the evidence.

Mediterranean diet

There are many definitions of the Mediterranean diet, but most are high in plant-based foods and low on red meat. The Mediterranean diet has been investigated in many research studies and is linked with better health, including heart health. Research has shown that the Mediterranean diet has similar emissions to the global average diet and so would cause a significant reduction for countries with the highest emissions. For example, the US diet causes over twice the emissions of the global average diet (chapter 1), so switching to the Mediterranean diet would more than halve emissions.

Vegetarianism

Vegetarians usually exclude all parts of formerly-living creatures from their diets and don't eat meat, fish or other sea creatures. Their impact on emissions depends on what they eat instead of meat. For example, cheese has higher emissions than chicken or fish so a chicken-eater who otherwise eats a vegetarian diet would actually make their emissions worse by replacing chicken with cheese. However, estimates suggest that vegetarian diets produce only 60% of the emissions of a global average diet.

Veganism

How about cutting out *all* animal products, and going vegan? Being vegan usually involves avoiding any food that comes from animals, so it excludes eggs, milk, cheese and other dairy products, on top of the restrictions of a vegetarian diet.

We might expect a vegan diet to be good for reducing greenhouse-gas emissions because dairy products are some of the highest impact protein sources (Fig. 34.1). Research has found that existing vegan diets cause only 50% of the emissions of the global average diet, and therefore less than 25% of the average US diet.

However, just as for the vegetarian diet, vegans can cause *more* emissions than omnivores, depending on their food choices e.g. by eating air-freighted fruit and vegetables, cooking single portions in the oven, and sending food waste to landfill (including the inedible waste from preparing vegetables at home).

Fig. 35.1: Fried crickets for lunch anyone? (URL 91)

Insectivore

Insects have been touted as a possible animal-based food of the future because they are very effective at turning crops into edible protein. This might not be the future you've been dreaming of, but some cultures already eat plenty of insects as a delicacy. Fig. 35.1 shows some particularly tasty-looking crickets at a marketplace.

You might already be eating insects without realizing it. Have you ever eaten a pink marshmallow? A popular natural pink food colouring comes from grinding up cochineal insects (Fig. 35.2). And, unless you're washing your fruit and vegetables extremely carefully, you're probably getting a bit of extra nutrition from tiny creatures living in their nooks and crannies.

Fig. 35.2: Some cochineal insects on a cactus plant. You've probably already eaten an extract made from them. (URL 92)

Some farmers now grow insects on a commercial scale – you might have seen some on sale in the shops. Popular choices include meal worms, crickets and locusts. People often describe the freeze-dried versions as nutty, or like crisped rice or popcorn. Before you rush in, if you have a seafood allergy you might also be allergic to insects, since they have the same substance in their hard shells. In case you don't fancy eating insects whole, you can also buy insect flour for baking, or buy them ready-made into cricket pasta, or a high protein energy bar.

Some exciting new enterprises are farming insects, feeding them on food that would otherwise go to waste, or on by-products of food production, such as leftovers from brewing beer. The insect meal is then fed to animals such as farmed fish or chicken, to reduce the need to grow crops which currently make up about half of their climate-impact.

Designing a climate-friendly diet

Could we design an ultra-low-emissions diet, and if so, what would it look like? Some researchers have devised the lowest pos-sible emissions diet that still meets our nutritional requirements. It involves a lot of high fibre breakfast cereal with no milk, and a lot of seeds, peas and onions. It reduces emissions to 10% of the original value! However, the researchers note that this diet is unrealistic, and go on to investigate less extreme diets.

Some companies are already producing meal-replacement shakes they claim contain all the nutrition you need. By picking the ingredients from the lowest-emissions foods out there, and supplementing with vitamins and minerals produced for vitamin tablets, it should be possible to design very low-emissions foods.

What if an ultra-low-emissions diet looks like grey goop, as suggested by some science fiction stories? Will we one day consider it a luxury, or even a socially shameful act, to eat anything else? I'd rather figure out how to reduce emissions in some less drastic way before we reach that stage.

Key points

- For most of us, there is no need to follow a rigorous new diet to significantly reduce the impact our food on climate change. Just substitutions wid Mediterranean diets have been found to have similar emissions to the global average diet. (In contrast, the diets of some countries, e.g. the US, cause more than twice the emissions of the global average diet (see chapter 1).)

- On average, vegetarianism roughly reduces emissions to 50% of the emissions of the global average diet.

- Average vegan diets reduce emissions to 30% of the global average diet.

- The lowest-emissions diets can cause up to 10 times less emissions than an average diet, but might not be acceptable to our tastes.

Notes

Page

161 *Mediterranean diet has similar emissions to the global average diet* Tilman and Clark (2014) calculate emissions from a global average diet (in 2009) and compare it with a Mediterranean diet and find that the Mediterranean diet causes about 5% less emissions than the global average diet.

162 *vegetarian diets produce only 60% of the emissions of a global average diet.* Tilman and Clark (2014) find a vegetarian diet causes 57% of the emissions of the global average diet in 2009 (using the left panel of their figure 4 which shows 189 $kgCO_2e$-C_{eq} per person per year for the vegetarian diet compared to 332 $kgCO_2e$-C_{eq} per person per year for the 2009 average diet; 189 / 332 = 0.57). Springmann, Godfray, et al. (2016) table S9 gives a value of 0.46 tCO_2e per person per year for a vegetarian diet, which we compare to their 2005/7 value of 1.15 tCO_2e per person per year for a global average diet (calculated from their value of 7.6 Gt per year for 2005/7 and a population of 6.6 billion in 2006); this is (0.89 - 0.46)/(0.89 - 0.37)*100% = 83% of the way towards their value for a vegan diet of 0.37 tCO_2e per person per year. In the following footnote, we conclude that a vegan diet causes a 50% reduction compared to the global average diet. Combining these two results we estimate that the vegetarian diet causes about 59% of the emissions relative to the global average diet (100 - 50 * 83 / 100). Springmann, Godfray, et al. (2016) attribute the biggest reduction to red meat (in the context of a change from the projected 2050 diet and the vegetarian diet). These are rounded to a value of 60% in the main text.

162 *Research has found that existing vegan diets cause only 50% of the emissions of the global average diet, and therefore less than 25% of the average US diet.* For their "No Animal Products" scenario, Poore and Nemecek (2018) give a value of 7.04 $GtCO_2e$ per year for the world, which converts to a value of 2.78 $kgCO_2e$ per person per day. This is a reduction of (5.41 - 2.78) = 3.56 $kgCO_2e$ per person per day. They find that the amount of food waste was almost unchanged from the current (∼2010) diet, so their value including food waste is $(7.04 + 2.05)/6.993/365 \times 1000 = 3.56$ $kgCO_2e$ per person per day i.e. the emissions are halved in their "No Animal Products" scenario, relative to their value of 6.2 $kgCO_2e$ per person per day in their "Current (∼2010) Diet". See their Fig S14 for more details. This is similar to the value found in Blake (2014), who state a 43% reduction in food emissions on eliminating animal products. For comparison, Springmann, Godfray, et al. (2016) table S9 gives a value of 0.34 tCO_2e per person per year for the vegan diet, which we compare to their 2005/7 value of 1.15 tCO_2e per person per year. The ratio is 0.34 / 1.15 = 0.32, i.e. their vegan diet causes only 32% of the emissions of the global average diet in 2006. For consistency with the other numbers in this book, we use the Poore and Nemecek (2018) value in the main text, which includes land use change and post-farmgate emissions (see chapter 1).

162 *Insects have been touted as a possible animal-based food of the future because they are very effective at turning crops into edible protein.* Table 6 of Oonincx

et al. (2011) presents values as low as 0.001 kgCO$_2$e / kg for the farming part of the insect production phase, however, this does not include the rest of the supply chain which will depend particularly on the feed source and energy used for processing.

162 *some cultures already eat plenty of insects as a delicacy.* If you're intrigued then take a look at the book *Insects: An Edible Field Guide* by Stefan Gates (Gates, 2017) which devises imaginative recipes for common insects, including woodlouse cocktail (replace prawns with cleaned-up woodlice in a prawn cocktail recipe) and stir-fried earthworms. (I haven't tried them yet...!)

163 *leftovers from brewing beer.* From the Entocycle website (URL 93).

163 *Some researchers have devised the lowest possible emissions diet that still meets our nutritional requirements. It involves a lot of high fibre breakfast cereal with no milk, and a lot of seeds, peas and onions. It reduces emissions to 10% of the original value! However, the researchers note that this diet is unrealistic, and go on to investigate less extreme diets.* See Macdiarmid et al. (2012). See also Reynolds et al. (2019) which more than halves emissions and takes affordability into account.

Chapter 36 How can governments help?

So far we've discussed changes that we as individual consumers can make to reduce the impact of food on climate change. This chapter asks whether we need some more coordinated effort, for example by governments. What can governments do to help, and how can we as citizens help governments to help us?

Consumers and producers need incentives

There are lots of different types of change that food producers can make to reduce emissions. Some changes will improve profits, for example by using less fertilizer or energy. Others don't; for example spreading muck more often costs more money. Reducing the amount of water used in rice production might be risky for the farmer unless supported by good technical advice. Improving the welfare of animals to reduce disease and losses might cost more initially, but can save money and reduce emissions in the longer term.

Can we expect food producers to reduce emissions on their own? Is it even reasonable to expect the majority of farmers, growers and businesses to know which changes would help? Even if they do know, then how can they be appropriately rewarded for making improvements?

As citizens we might want to have a meat-free day, and try a new plant-based meal. But it takes time to investigate the options, and we take a risk by trying something new; Maybe at first we don't like the taste of the new foods, and it might take weeks to find good options, or for our preferences to change. We're going to some personal effort to try to reduce climate change for future generations, but what if our neighbour is still tucking into their daily steak? Most people are going to need more than a warm fuzzy feeling to reward their efforts to help.

We and future generations will pay a price for actions that degrade the environment – for eating foods that cause the largest greenhouse-gas emissions. It's unrealistic to expect the majority of people, including food producers and individuals, to change their choices at the scale and speed needed, without incentives and help. Governments have a role to play here.

Food labelling

I hope that soon there will be no need for this book. If food producers and suppliers label their products with accurate emissions data you'll be able to create your own emissions stacks yourself.

This book uses typical or average numbers for each type of food, but in reality there is a huge variation in climate impact depending on many decisions made by farmers, growers, manufacturers and suppliers. (If this book showed every value for all possible circumstances it would not only be huge, but unreadably over-complex too.)

As a consumer we can't often tell whether a piece of beef is from a dairy herd or a prime beef herd (chapter 24), or whether a piece of fruit came by boat or by plane (chapter 17). We also don't usually know whether a tomato was produced in a heated greenhouse (chapter 11) or whether the chickens were fed on soy from sustainable sources (chapter 25). Only if we have accurate and comprehensive labelling can we make properly informed choices about which food to buy.

Around 2008 some companies worked out the emissions from their products and put them on their packets. One major UK supermarket made a plan to provide emissions estimates across their product range. Some hoped that this would become the norm. In practice though, it took a lot of work to do these calculations at that time, and it wasn't clear that the public really wanted the information enough to make the effort worthwhile.

I confess that if in 2008 I had noticed that my bag of crisps caused 85 grams of emissions then I wouldn't have had a clue what to make of it. Is that number good or bad? And compared to what? This book addresses this carbon literacy problem, and shows why emissions labelling would be very useful.

Emissions calculations have moved on a long way in the past decade, with many software packages available to help. Is now the time for emissions labelling to become mainstream? Would you be more likely to buy a product that has a carbon footprint figure printed on the packet?

We need mandatory standardized emissions-labelling to give consumers the data they need, and ensure that responsible producers who label are not at a commercial disadvantage to those who would otherwise not label. Then food producers have a good reason to examine where their emissions are coming from, and reap some benefit for making improvements, even if it's just a lower number on a packet. And producers who have already gone to great lengths to do the right thing will be easier to recognize. Look out for certified emissions calculation schemes in your country, because this will help improve the quality of the numbers that get provided.

Would a number on a packet realistically influence your shopping habits, even with your new-found carbon literacy? There is already plenty of information on the packet that it is too easy to ignore, although researchers have demonstrated that traffic light systems *can* influence behaviour. What's surprising is that even if we as consumers don't look at the labels it can still make a difference. For example, although there is some debate about whether people really understand what the traffic light nutrition labels mean, they can still have a big effect, because food producers don't want a red label on their packets, and make the recipes healthier to avoid getting a red traffic light.

How do we get to the point where we have mandatory labelling? We citizens have a big role to play in showing our support for environmental labelling by choosing foods that state their emissions values, and also by campaigning. That shows the food suppliers and governments how much we want it. It might take a while to standardize the labelling calculations, but at the moment any labelling is a step in the right direction.

Changing diets is difficult

Unfortunately, the ongoing struggle to address obesity also illustrates a major problem. It's very difficult for governments to change what we eat. We get through our busy lives relying on habits developed over a lifetime and, for many people, choosing what to eat is just one of those ingrained habits. However, switching one or two of the most emissions-expensive ingredients you eat each day to more climate-friendly alternatives is probably easier than avoiding your favourite sweet treat.

At the time of writing, most government dietary guidelines do not take into account planetary as well as human health, and this requires a concerted collaboration between environment and nutrition experts.

There is a burgeoning market in vegan recipes and products, as well as an increased awareness of the need to reduce the quantity of meat in dishes, but more remains to be done. Most well-meaning climate-friendly food products and recipes are not yet based on facts about emissions, and the foods most easily available are usually not the climate-friendly options. While individual actions can work well for a subset of dedicated people, most of us could use some help.

Taxes

"I don't think we should be in the business of prescribing to people how they should run their diets... Who would I be to sit there advising people in the country coming home after a hard day of work to not have steak and chips?"
– Claire Perry, UK Minister of State for Energy and Clean Growth in 2018

No-one wants to be told they must (or must not) do something, especially when we're told it's for our own good. Compulsory car seat belt laws were initially opposed, for libertarian and other reasons. However, with time the public has accepted that wearing seatbelts saves injuries and lives, and the laws are no longer so controversial. Restrictions on smoking and taxes on cigarettes were extremely unpopular when they were first introduced, but people now realize the dangers of smoking People seem to accept that smoking doesn't affect just the smoker: passive smoking is harmful to others. It is argued that if someone makes a lifestyle choice that costs other people money, then that person should have to contribute to the cost of dealing with the consequences.

So what about taxing food that's bad for our health?

In 2016 the UK announced a "sugar tax" on drinks with very high sugar content, in spite of industry opposition. However, by 2018 when the tax came into effect, many manufacturers had already reduced the sugar content to avoid the taxes. Consumers don't seem to mind the change, which almost certainly helped reduce obesity.

Plastic bags used to be given out for free at shop checkouts so people could carry their shopping home, and advertise the store around town. So many were thrown away that seeing a disused shopping bag blowing down the street or floating in a river was commonplace. Many countries have now banned or imposed a charge on plastic bags. In the UK a charge was brought in in 2014, which led to an 80% reduction in the number of plastic bags over the following four years.

So while we don't want the government restricting our liberties unnecessarily, initially unpopular "nanny" legislation can become widely accepted and make a significant difference.

Taxes on meat have been proposed to account for the environmental and health burdens of high meat consumption. Should meat be taxed for environmental reasons? Is this fair on the producers of low-emissions meat? What about non-meat high-emissions products? For example, we saw that cheese typically has higher emissions than chicken (chapter 25). A tax based on the emissions of each food item would reward producers for reducing emissions, because the cost of their product would decrease, making it more likely to be bought.

One possible problem with emissions labelling is that it neglects other problems, and so could make some of them worse – for example water use, air pollution or animal and human welfare. Ideally we would have labels for the other impacts too, and have a way to combine them into a single tax which might vary from one country to the next.

Implementing this comprehensive solution will take several years but we can't wait that long. Some impacts, such as land or water use, involve a lot of the same numbers and calculations as the greenhouse-gas emissions, so it might make sense to include them at the same time. Other more complex environmental risks, such as biodiversity, may be overshadowed by climate change anyway if we don't do something about emissions soon. So this shouldn't hold us back from trying to sort out emissions taxes on food.

Changing subsidies

Many countries give money to farmers to help them produce the food their country needs. These subsidies can help protect farmers from changes in weather from one year to the next, as well as changes in demand. In addition to government payments in many countries, supermarkets also subsidize the price of milk in their stores to tempt people into their shop.

Reducing the subsidies for the most emissions-intensive foods is an alternative to taxes. This increases the price of these foods, encouraging consumers to make more climate-friendly choices.

However, such changes have to be done very carefully to help farmers through a difficult transition phase. For example, it just isn't realistic for a beef or dairy farmer to suddenly switch to farming vegetables. We also need a transition plan that respects the dedication of farmers over many decades during which we, and governments, asked for more and more of their products.

Food fairness

An increase in the price of your weekly shop might not be a big issue for you if you have enough money to buy a book like this one. But a new food tax can end up taking money away from people who are already struggling to feed their families.

The success or failure of new taxes often depends on how the government uses the extra money, and on whether the benefits are seen to outweigh the economic disruption. The UK sugary drinks tax has been used to support extra sports in schools, thereby addressing the childhood obesity problem from two different directions at the same time. However, Denmark's tax on saturated fat was scrapped after a year because it was considered bad for the economy.

The money from a food-emissions tax could be used to subsidize healthy lower-emissions foods including vegetables, or used to help provide healthy food to people with less money.

How can we get governments to change?

In a democracy, governments have to listen to the voters or they won't win the next election. Unfortunately, climate change is happening over a longer timescale than the gap between elections. In the run-up to the election, voters are often swayed by promises on short-term issues like extra money in their pockets.

It might seem unrealistic to expect governments to prioritize climate change until it's too late. I'm optimistic citizens can make governments make a difference on food. We vote every time we make a choice about which food to buy. Retailers, food producers and governments can see the statistics.

I am writing this book because I believe ordinary citizens have the greatest power to change the food system. A number of individual choices by a small number of people will make a small difference in the short term. But we can make these choices *now* – without waiting for government legislation or producer changes, and our actions now will be amplified by the reactions of supermarkets and governments when they see that enough people want them to make changes that affect everyone.

Beyond this, individual governments also need to work with each other to help incentivize uncooperative countries or manage the truly international nature of the food system. For example, cutting down forest to make way for agricultural land is a major problem for climate change (chapter 7). Satellite images can help with monitoring, but international agreements have to be made and acted upon too, in a way that takes into account the historical deforestation of now-wealthy nations.

Key points

- Buying foods labelled with their emissions encourages food producers to calculate and share information about the emissions caused by their foods.

- The rise in obesity shows that it is incredibly difficult for individuals and governments to change what we eat, even with excellent dietary guidelines.

- We need to demand the changes we want from producers and government, for example mandatory emissions labelling, reduced subsidies for the highest-impact foods, or emissions taxes on food.

- Without waiting for anyone, we can vote with our stomachs every meal time, choosing low-emissions options based on the emissions information already available.

Notes

Page

167   *in reality there is a huge variation in climate impact depending on many decisions made by farmers, growers, manufacturers and suppliers.* See the ranges in figure 1 of Poore and Nemecek (2018). For example, the range for prime steak spans from 25 kgCO$_2$e to 75 kgCO$_2$e for 100 g of steak protein steak.

167   *Only if we have accurate and comprehensive labelling can we make properly informed choices about which food to buy.* Joseph Poore makes a very readable and coherent case for labelling foods with their environmental impact in The Guardian (URL 94), pointing out the significant impact of mandatory labelling on the efficiencies of fridges and freezers, and the freedom of choice provided to producers and consumers in a metric-based system.

167   *One major UK supermarket made a plan to provide emissions estimates across their product range.* Tesco supermarket produced a landmark document providing emissions estimates for over 500 food items ("Tesco Product Carbon Footprint Summary" 2012, accessed 2018).

167   *bag of crisps caused 85 grams of emissions* For more details see URL 95.

168   *Look out for certified emissions calculation schemes in your country,* For example the Carbon Trust in the UK (URL 96).

168   *researchers have demonstrated that traffic light systems can influence behaviour.* Study participants were found to be more influenced by avoiding red traffic lights than being attracted to green lights (Scarborough et al., 2015).

168   *food producers don't want a red label on their packets, and make the recipes healthier to avoid getting a red traffic light.* The Canadian Health Check programme was examined to assess its impact on levels of salt, and found that manufacturers reformulated their products to meet the criteria (Dummer, 2012).

169   *many manufacturers had already reduced the sugar content to avoid the taxes.* HM Treasury report "Soft Drinks Industry Levy comes into effect". (URL 97)

169   *In the UK a charge was brought in in 2014, which led to an 80% reduction in the number of plastic bags over the following four years.* Defra (2018).

169   *Taxes on meat have been proposed to account for the environmental and health burdens of high meat consumption.* Wellesley and Froggatt (2015) considered the potential of meat taxes, among other interventions, and Springmann, Mason-D'Croz, et al. (2016) looked at the economic impact of meat taxes based on the potential health benefits.

170   *Ideally we would have labels for the other impacts too, and have a way to combine them into a single tax which might vary from one country to the next.* As suggested by Joseph Poore, Cambridge Climate Lecture Series 2019 (URL 98).

171   *Denmark's tax on saturated fat was scrapped after a year because it was considered bad for the economy.* "The fat tax and the extension of the chocolate tax – the so called sugar tax – has been criticised for increasing prices for consumers, increasing companies' administrative costs, and putting Danish jobs at risk." – Danish health ministry, as reported in Stafford (2012).

Chapter 37 Food as part of the solution

What if everyone changed what they ate, to reduce their greenhouse-gas emissions from food? If everyone managed to halve their food emissions, it would reduce global greenhouse-gas emissions by over 10%. Somehow though, we need to make total emissions zero by 2050. Are we ever going to get there?

Emissions from heating, cars, planes and other non-food activities are not the subject of this book – often they require much bigger lifestyle changes than switching which shelf to pick food from, or they require governments to change in an internationally coordinated way. But the good news is that a major shift in diets can actually reduce climate change by *much more than 10%*, depending on what is done with the land that would otherwise have been used for farming. Since over one third of the Earth's land area is currently used for food production, repurposing farmland is a big deal (Fig. 37.1).

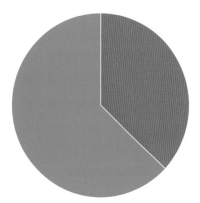

Fig. 37.1: 37% of Earth's ice- and desert-free land is used for food production.

Freeing up land by moving towards plant-based foods

Animal products cause more emissions than most plant-based products, and animals also use more land. This is not a coincidence – it's due to the inefficiencies of producing food via animals. For example, even the relatively efficient chicken has to eat three calories for every one calorie we get from eating the meat (chapter 25). Globally, over 4 in every 5 farmed fields are used to grow food for animals. Despite this, less than one in every five calories we eat comes from animal products.

> **Animal products: 80% of land → 20% of calories.**
>
> **Plant products: 20% of land → 80% of calories**

Therefore plant products are 16 times more land-efficient. This means that if we reduce the amount of animal products in our diets, then we free up a lot of land that can be used for other things.

If we were to stop eating animal products entirely then we would reduce the amount of land needed for food production by 75%, thus freeing up three quarters of the agricultural land on the planet. Such a radical shift would dramatically change the landscape and countryside; the rolling green hillsides I grew up with in the UK would become a thing of the past. We would have to confront not only our cultural attachments to meat and the livelihoods of farmers, but also our national identities, as defined by our landscapes. If we shift to lower emissions foods we can then use this freed-up land to help reduce global warming further. Currently several of the potential solutions to climate change are limited by the amount of land available. However, with the land freed up by shifting towards plant-based foods, we can implement three very different types of large-scale climate-change projects:

1. forests
2. solar power
3. bioenergy with carbon capture and storage.

1. Forests

There is one tried and tested solution to climate change, that has been tested at scale many times over, even before humans came into existence – trees! Trees take in carbon dioxide and store it both in their wood and underground in their roots and in the soil. Forests already remove about a quarter of all the greenhouse-gas emissions produced by humans. Forests also protect against some of the impacts of climate change: they reduce air pollution and absorb rainwater thus reducing flooding.

If we spare land from food production and turn it into forest, we can help to suck carbon dioxide out of the atmosphere. If we stopped eating animal products entirely and let the land change into natural forest, shrub or grassland, this would remove about 3 kilos of emissions per person per day. This number can then be equal to, or ideally greater than, the total emissions caused by the food production itself.

2. Solar power

Solar panels are now a common sight on the roofs of buildings, but to produce a significant fraction of the world's power requirements would also need solar farms, in which large areas of land are covered in panels or mirrors to harness the energy from the sun.

Unlike forests, solar farms can be situated in areas not

currently suited to plants, such as deserts. However, for countries with a large fraction of arable land (e.g. the UK), solar energy collection competes with food production. In these cases, a shift towards plant-based diets would provide land that could be used to provide renewable energy such as solar power.

3. Bioenergy with carbon capture and storage

If we grow plants ("biofuels") and then burn them in cars and power stations, we can burn less of the fossil fuels which cause global warming. The plants take in carbon dioxide as they grow, and mostly turn back into carbon dioxide when they are burned to make energy. Therefore the biofuels temporarily help reduce greenhouse gas levels by taking in carbon dioxide, and can be used in place of fossil fuels to reduce emissions. However, since the plants don't live for very long, they don't actively reduce the total amount of greenhouse gases. Also, if nitrogen fertilizer is used to increase the growth of the biofuel crops then they will contribute to global warming (box 2.1).

Most climate projections which meet the 1.5°C target assume that someone will invent and deploy new ways to suck carbon dioxide out of the atmosphere in the second half of this century. The most discussed of these is called Bioenergy with Carbon Capture and Storage, or BECCS for short. In BECCS, we grow biofuels, that are then burnt in power stations, and the carbon dioxide they produce is captured. This captured carbon dioxide is then trapped underground, for example in old fossil-fuel mines. If we could carry out BECCS on a large area of land, for example the size of Europe, over 50 years, we could reduce global warming by more than 1°C.

Unfortunately, we have never tested the full BECCS process on anything like this scale so whether or not this would really work remains uncertain, and it is very risky to rely on it.

We need to find a way to reward regions and countries that preserve – and especially increase – their forest cover, and that implement emissions-reduction technologies at the scale needed. In 1987 we banned the production of chemicals that were causing the hole in the ozone layer, and the hole is on course to close up again this century. What if we were to implement emissions-reductions at unprecedented speed and scale? We might keep the temperature rise below 1.5°C, or ideally reduce it back down towards pre-industrial temperatures. We could find ourselves with the luxury problem of needing international agreement on exactly what temperature the planet should be. I don't envy future politicians that job though, given that it's hard enough for two humans to agree on the temperature for a bedroom!

Key points

- The foods that produce the most greenhouse-gas emissions also often require the most land.

- Therefore, switching to lower-emissions foods frees up land that we can put to good use in helping to reduce climate change.

- Forests are extremely good at taking carbon dioxide out of the air and locking it up in trunks, branches, roots and the soil.

- By switching agricultural land to climate-improving uses such as forest, we can turn our current food system into a part of the solution to climate change.

Notes

Page

174   *If everyone managed to halve their food emissions, it would reduce global greenhouse-gas emissions by over 10%.* This is simply because food causes about a quarter of all greenhouse-gas emissions (chapter 1), so halving this reduces total emissions by 12.5%.

174   *Fig. 37.1* 43% of the ice- and desert-free land is used for agriculture, of which 87% is used for food and the rest is used or allocated for other purposes including biofuels, textiles, wool and leather (Poore and Nemecek, 2018).

174   *Globally, over 4 in every 5 farmed fields are used to grow food for animals.* Producing food for animals including fish and grazing uses 83% of global farmland (Poore and Nemecek, 2018). See also Ruiter et al. (2017).

174   *less than one in every five calories we eat comes from animal products.* Poore and Nemecek (2018) find that 18% of global calories (and 37% of protein) come from animal products. Therefore, 83% of farmland produces 18% of calories (and 37% of protein) from animal products. Reversing the numbers (and assuming farmland is used only for growing food) means that 17% of the land produces 82% of calories (and 63% of protein). We round these numbers to 80 and 20% for simplicity but note that the statements would be even more striking by using the exact numbers.) If instead, we were to use the animal-products land to grow plant products, it could produce much more than 20% of the calories (because just 20% of land is currently used to produce 80% of plant-based calories). Specifically, it could provide 80% of calories × 80% of land / 20% of land = 320% of calories i.e. plants can provide 320% / 20% = 16 times as many calories from the same quantity (80%) of land.

174   *If we were to stop eating animal products entirely then we would reduce the amount of land needed for food production by 75%, thus freeing up three quarters of the agricultural land on the planet.* We would continue to need 20% of the land to produce 80% of calories from plant foods. We would need

to make up the calorie shortfall from stopping eating animal products by increasing the amount of plant products grown by 25% i.e. to 25% of the land. This would therefore free up 75% of the land. (Redoing the calculation using calories and exact numbers gives 17 + 17 * 18 / 82 = 21% of land required to grow all required calories from plants i.e. 79% of farmland is freed up; redoing the calculation using protein and exact numbers instead gives 17 + 17 * 37 / 63 = 27% of land required to grow plant protein i.e. 73% of farmland is freed up.) Note that this is a crude calculation because it does not consider other nutrients. A more detailed protein-based calculation in Poore and Nemecek (2018) gives a reduction of 76% in land use for food, corresponding to 3.1 billion hectares, or about 4,000 square metres per person (2019 population), or about half a football pitch. A UK study (Harwatt and Hayek, 2019) that found that if the UK stops farming animals, it can feed the entire population from the current cropland (including the land currently used to produce animal feed), i.e. freeing up all the existing *pasture* land (their scenario 2). This pasture freed up for other things amounts to about one third of the entire land area of the UK, or the area of one Olympic-sized swimming pool per person (1290 m^2) (calculated by dividing current pastureland area 84,000 km^2 by the total land area of the UK 243,000 km^2, which gives 34% or roughly one third). Note that we do not currently feed the whole UK from UK land, therefore in addition there is land freed up in other countries as well as in the UK.

175. *Forests already remove about a quarter of all the greenhouse-gas emissions produced by humans.* Pan et al. (2011) via the excellent and accessible resource (URL 99).

175 *If we stopped eating animal products entirely and let the land change into natural forest, shrub or grassland, this would remove about 3 kilos of emissions per person per day.* The IMAGE integrated assessment model (URL 100) has been used to calculate that "the land no longer required for food production under the "no animal products" scenario could remove… 8.1 GtCO$_2$ on average each year, with continued but lower uptake after 100 years … as it naturally succeeds to forest, shrubland, or grassland" by Poore and Nemecek (2018). Converting this into kgCO$_2$e per person per day: (8.1 billion tonnes CO$_2$ / year) / (7.7 billion people) / (365 days / year) * (1000 kg / tonne) = 2.88 kg / person / day. A UK study found that if all the pastureland of the UK were turned into forest, this would pull about 4.5 kg of carbon dioxide out of the atmosphere per day, per person in the UK (Harwatt and Hayek 2019 scenario 2 finds 108 MtCO$_2$ per year).

175 *This number can then be equal to, or ideally greater than, the total emissions caused by the food production itself.* "6.6 Gt / year of avoided agricultural CO$_2$e emissions… (which is a 49% reduction in the annual emissions of the food sector)." – Poore and Nemecek (2018).

175 *to produce a significant fraction of the world's power requirements would also need solar farms, in which large areas of land are covered in panels or mirrors to harness the energy from the sun.* See MacKay (2009).

176 *Most climate projections which meet the 1.5°C target assume that someone will invent and deploy new ways to suck carbon dioxide out of the atmosphere in the second half of this century.* See for example chapter 3 of IPCC (2018).

176 *If we could carry out BECCS on a large area of land, for example the size of Europe, over 50 years, we could reduce global warming by more than 1°C.* IPCC (2018) cites Kriegler et al. (2018) who assume 8 GtCO$_2$ / year from 375 million ha for their "limited CDR scenarios".

176 *we have never tested the full BECCS process on anything like this scale so whether or not this would really work remains uncertain, and it is very risky to rely on it.* Larkin et al. (2018).

Chapter 38 Making the change

Small things

"If everyone does a little, we'll achieve only a little"
– **David JC MacKay**

"Let the small bad things happen and make the big good things happen."
– **Tim Ferriss**

It can be overwhelming to think about the importance of the climate challenge and the complexity of the issues. This book demystifies the main causes of emissions from food and gives some ideas about how to start reducing them.

Some people (myself included) exhaust themselves by trying to do everything they can think of to reduce their emissions. But doing "everything you can think of" isn't a sustainable way to live – you're likely to burn out or give up.

Here are examples of things that that don't help much but can exhaust you, compared with other activities that do help a lot:

- Switching to plant milk in tea, while continuing to eat an 8 oz steak once a week.

- Switching the kettle off every time just before it boils, to save on electricity, but using a fossil-fuelled oven for an hour a day (box 12.1).

- Reading every last detail of the ingredients of every food packet to avoid small amounts of milk derivatives or eggs, but then only having time to buy food for today, so that you have to go to the shops again tomorrow (driving 15 minutes in a fossil-fuelled car), as I found I was doing (see chapter 1).

This list emphasizes that you need to keep food decisions in context: consider your other activities that may have much greater impact. Check out the emissions from driving, flying and heating buildings (chapter 1). Once you address the big issues, you can be lenient on yourself in small things – especially the small things that bring you pleasure.

Big things

The most important message from this book is that different foods cause very different emissions. This is good news because it means that most of us can make a big difference to our food climate impact by focusing on a relatively small number of things that we do on most days. To recap the highest emissions foods:

- Beef and lamb are the most emissions-intensive of all the common foods (chapter 24).

- Cheese, butter and pork are the runners-up, causing less than half the emissions of beef and lamb (chapters 9, 5 and 10).

- Chicken, eggs and fish are the lowest-emissions animal products, about half the emissions of cheese (e.g. Fig. 34.1). However, they still cause more emissions than most plant products (e.g. chapter 34).

Psychology research suggests that it's not very helpful to focus on what to avoid; instead it's better to focus on what to *include*. So, to help the climate, look for ways to add more of these foods to your diet:

- Pulses like beans, lentils and peas are full of protein and other nutrients.

- Plant-based substitutes for animal products are improving rapidly (but make sure you're getting the nutrients you need).

- Nuts and seeds are the plant equivalent of eggs, and are similarly nutritious (chapter 19).

- Eating yesterday's leftovers saves time and wasted emissions, as well as reducing emissions from landfill.

We're particularly encouraged to eat more fruit and vegetables for their health benefits. How can we do this?

- Transporting food long distances by boat is not particularly bad for climate change, so tuck in to foods that can last for a long time in the hold of a ship, including apples, oranges and pulses (see chapter 17).

- Steel tin cans and other packaging aren't as bad for the climate as many people think. As well as being convenient, they also reduce the home cooking time needed (see chapter 14).

- Frozen fruit and vegetables cause much lower emissions than their air-freighted counterparts (chapter 28), as well as preserving a lot of the nutrition.

- And continue to enjoy lots of local, seasonal fruit and vegetables.

Influencing others

Governments and food producers need pressure from citizens to be able to change. They need to know if people want more help to switch to electric cars, or international agreements on aviation, or more money to be invested in producing renewable energy.

Do you want governments to subsidize production of animal products, or of fruit and vegetables? And how much incentive should be given to food producers to change to lower-emissions products and practices? Only governments can create laws that require emissions of foods to be measured and tracked through the food chain, enabling the consumer to make truly informed decisions.

Most importantly for food, governments need to know how we feel about the land around us: whether we want take advantage of land freed up from animal production to plant forests (which can double the climate change benefits), or whether we want to keep the landscape as it is and hope we can fix climate change some other way.

People sometimes ask me how they can reduce the emissions from their diets even further. Often the questioner is already doing all the good big things described above, and has already reduced their emissions down to half or even one third of the average. Can they go down even further?

Suppose such a person works hard to reduce their food emissions by one third again. A bit of maths tells us that this has the same impact on the climate as convincing one friend to reduce their emissions by 10%, down to 90% of the average. Which is easier? Which has the more potential to make a difference later on? That friend might then reduce their emissions further, and then influence *their* friends. I think the best thing we can all do is to spread the word, and work together to find a comfortable and efficient way to live a low-emissions life, that everyone wants to share!

Being a human

"We don't need a handful of people doing zero waste perfectly. We need millions of people doing it imperfectly"
– **Anne-Marie Bonneau**

Several times a day we make a choice about what to eat, so there's lots of scope for making changes. But there are lot of opportunities to be imperfect. I'm pretty sure it's not possible to always choose the most climate-friendly foods and still stay sane.

I try to focus on the emissions of something I do regularly, and then experiment with a few different options when I have time, rather than trying to get everything "right" all the time. I realize some people prefer to make one big decision, like never eating a particular food again, rather than make a more complicated mixture of changes. But eating the more climate-friendly options most of the time is a huge step forward for the majority of people. Since all food causes emissions, the additional benefit of *always* choosing the absolutely most climate-friendly option is both exhausting and subject to the law of diminishing returns.

Movements like Veganuary and Meat-free Mondays mark out a time to be focused on trying new foods, while leaving you time to recover your energy for the rest of the year or week. At first glance, changing to a more climate-friendly diet on one day out of seven could sound like an ineffectual "little thing". Surely the maximum climate impact is one seventh, or 14%? But we humans are creatures of habit, and it takes effort to create a new habit, especially if the change requires creativity when we're tired and hungry. By carving out dedicated time to try out new climate-friendly ideas, you start to develop a repertoire of new dishes that you might enjoy so much that you start to eat them at other times too.

Sharing food with others is important, socially and culturally. By changing our diets we might affect our relationships with others, perhaps by offending them with our new choices, or by removing a shared meal. Feastarians are vegetarian all year, except for treats or feasts, which allows them to join in the big occasions when others think meat is essential – e.g. turkey at Christmas or Thanksgiving. Emissions are only one aspect of choosing food – we need to enjoy life as well!

Notes

Page

180   *"If everyone does a little, we'll achieve only a little."* Taken from *Sustainable Energy – Without the Hot Air* by David JC MacKay (MacKay, 2009).

180   *"Let the small bad things happen and make the big good things happen."* Taken from the Tim Ferriss blog (URL 101) and discussed more in *The 4-Hour Work Week: Escape the 9-5, Live Anywhere and Join the New Rich* (Ferriss, 2011).

180   *Switching to plant milk in tea, while continuing to eat an 8 oz steak once a week.* If you drink 100 grams of cows' milk a day in tea, it causes about 200 grams of emissions a day (chapter 4). One 8 oz steak causes 9 kilos of emissions. Sharing the 9 kilos out over 7 days is more than 1 kilo a day, so is greater than the 200 grams of emissions a day from the cows' milk. The contrast is even greater if you allow for the emissions of making the plant milk.

181   *Steel tin cans and other packaging aren't as bad for the climate as many people think.* Some people think of canned food as being expensive or unhealthy but, although some vitamins are reduced, they can be an easy source of extra plants that make a quick addition to a meal. As demonstrated in Jack Monroe's "Tin can cook" you can even make a surprisingly wide range of delicious and cheap meals from canned food.

183   *Sharing food with others is important, socially and culturally.* Thanks to Rosemary Randall for stimulating insights on this topic. See *In Time for Tomorrow? the International Carbon Conversations Handbook* for more information www.carbonconversations.co.uk/p/materials.html.

Appendixes

Appendix A Climate change

The effects of climate change are well documented. For example, we've already had an increase of nearly 1°C between the late 1850s and the early 2000s (chapter 1), and we have already seen:

- melting of the Greenland ice sheet, the Antarctic ice sheet, and sea-ice in the Arctic

- rising sea levels and coastal erosion

- land changing to a different type of habitat, which reduces the range of species

- changes in migration and reproduction patterns of birds and fish

As well as impacts on food and water availability. We discuss climate change impacts on food in the next chapter.

Looking ahead, these problems are set to worsen as the temperature rises, with increasing numbers of extreme weather events. In addition to impacts on food production (see the next chapter), there will be adverse effects on human health from diseases such as malaria spreading more widely. Furthermore, climate change is expected to impact the rate of climate change itself. For example, warming causes melting of permafrost, which releases methane – a potent greenhouse gas – which causes more warming. While the poorest people will be the most affected, everyone will be affected to some extent.

The above list summarises why it's important to reduce greenhouse-gas emissions – the topic of this book's main chapters. In this chapter we discuss some of the basic terminology. The Appendix after this discusses the specific impacts of climate change of most relevance to food production.

The greenhouse effect

Fig. A.1 shows a diagram to illustrate the greenhouse effect. First, consider an actual greenhouse, or a window in your house. Sunlight comes in through the glass – mostly this is visible light, that your eyes can see. The sunlight warms up the things inside the greenhouse, or inside your house. Warm things make infrared light. Our eyes can't see this infrared light, but it is extremely important for the greenhouse effect, and so for understanding climate change.

Although the glass is transparent to visible light, it is not transparent to infrared light. If you were wearing infrared goggles, then you wouldn't be able to see out of the window! Infrared light gets trapped inside the greenhouse, and so the greenhouse warms up as more and more visible light comes in, and the energy is turned into warmer things and infrared light. That's why gardeners use greenhouses!

The Earth's atmosphere is like a greenhouse

The Earth's atmosphere acts like a greenhouse. Most of the air we breathe is nitrogen and oxygen, both of which let the sunlight and infrared light pass straight through them. This means that nitrogen and oxygen don't cause a greenhouse effect.

The next biggest component of Earth's atmosphere is carbon dioxide. Just like glass, carbon dioxide is transparent to visible light, but isn't transparent to infrared light. This means that carbon dioxide in our atmosphere warms up the surface of the Earth, just like glass warms up a greenhouse – hence the name "greenhouse gas" (see Fig. A.1), top.

Our atmosphere is changing

You may have learned about carbon dioxide and oxygen at school: animals (including humans) breathe in oxygen, and breathe out carbon dioxide. On the other hand, plants use carbon dioxide and give off oxygen as waste. In essence the plants take the carbon atom out of the carbon dioxide, leaving just the two oxygen atoms behind. They use this carbon to build up their stem, leaves and roots, adding in small amounts of other nutrients usually taken from the soil.

Over a period of about 60 million years, around 300 million years ago, dead plants were compressed into coal, oil and gas. Since the Industrial Revolution we have been digging up and burning more and more of these fossil fuels, turning them back into carbon dioxide. Figure A.3 shows that over the last 800,000 years the concentration of carbon dioxide has gone up and down between 200 and 300 parts per million. However, in just the past 200 years it increased by over 30%, to more than 400 parts

Fig. A.1: The greenhouse effect
Upper: in a greenhouse
Lower: at the Earth's surface.

Fig. A.2: About 5% of the air we breathe out is carbon dioxide.

Fig. A.3: Carbon dioxide variations in our atmosphere over the last 800,000 years. Inspired by (URL 103) and updated thanks to numbers provided via Our World in Data.

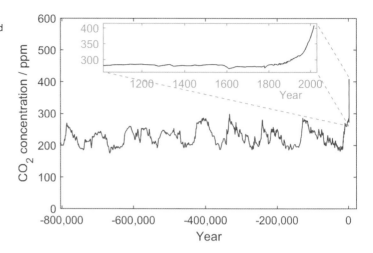

per million. The world has changed unimaginably over that time, from the invention of the light bulb to the rollout of gas and electricity to individual homes. Nowadays fossil fuels are routinely burned by many people without thinking, to heat a radiator or to generate the electricity used to power a light.

Global warming

The world is getting warmer. Fig. A.4 shows a visualisation of the average temperature each year from 1850 to 2018: bluer colours indicate lower temperatures and redder colours show warmer temperatures. The left side of the box is mostly blue, corresponding to the late 1800s and early 1900s, whereas the far right side of the box contains most of the red colours, corresponding to about the year 2000 onwards.

Fig. A.4: The average annual temperature each year from 1850 (left side of the box) until 2018 (right side of the box), displaying blue for low temperatures and red/brown for higher temperatures. Taken from the beautiful Climate Stripes project (URL 104) from which you can also download stripes graphics for other years and parts of the world. Reproduced with permission from Ed Hawkins.

By analyzing these numbers and more, going back thousands

of years, the international scientific consensus is that:

- "Warming of the climate system is unequivocal, and since the 1950s, many of the observed changes are unprecedented over decades to millennia."

- The world has warmed up by 0.97°C between the late 1850s and the early 2000s.

Using the laws of physics it's possible to predict the warming effect of all the ingredients of Earth's atmosphere. Using chemistry we can forecast how long each ingredient is likely to remain in the atmosphere unaltered, or when it will react with other ingredients to produce new molecules. We can also calculate the warming and cooling effects of snow, aeroplane condensation trails, volcanoes, and even changes in the amount of radiation from the sun.

Adding up the effects of all these ingredients over time shows that most of the warming comes from greenhouse gases. More than half of the warming is caused by carbon dioxide. The next most significant greenhouse gases are methane, chlorofluorocarbons (CFCs) and nitrous oxide (laughing gas; see chapter 1).

Sunspots and other changes in solar radiation average out and are unimportant on timescales of more than a decade, over the past two centuries at least. Volcanoes can have a big effect in the year of the eruption but, when added up over time, they have a very small impact. Taking into account all the effects, almost all of the warming over the last two hundred years can be explained by human activities.

Scientists have compiled a wide range of possible scenarios for future human activity. These have been combined with the available science to forecast the amount of global warming expected. The details are complicated; for example they depend on how much the greenhouse gases mix with other gases in the atmosphere. However, one conclusion is clear: if we increase the total of all human greenhouse-gas emissions, then we increase the global temperature at the end of this century. More precisely, if we double the amount of greenhouse gases released, we double the amount of global warming.

In the best-case scenarios we will turn things around and produce less and less greenhouse gases every year until, by 2050, we reach zero emissions, and then start removing greenhouse gases from the atmosphere, using new technologies that are still being investigated. In most of these optimistic scenarios the total human-induced global warming peaks at around 1.5 degrees Celsius. Alternative scenarios that simply extend the emissions of the 2010s take us above 5 degrees Celsius of warming, which could trigger irreversible changes that increase the temperature yet further.

Regional warming

The word "global" in "global warming" hides a complexity that can have serious impacts on humans. When we look in more detail at the temperature of the Earth it turns out that the global average temperature rise of 0.97°C since 1850 is very unevenly distributed across the Earth's surface.

Have you ever gone to the seaside to cool down on a hot day, or marvelled at the exotic plants that can survive winter near the coast, away from the coldest weather? In both cases, the reason is because water warms up much more slowly than the land. The vast oceans are slow to cool down in winter, and barely heat up in summer.

Some patches of ocean have hardly warmed at all in the past century. On the other hand, some land on most continents has already warmed by more than 1.5°C. The greatest warming is happening at the Arctic, which has now warmed by nearly 3°C.

Looking ahead, the same basic patterns are expected to continue. If greenhouse-gas emissions continue rising at their current rate, warming is expected to increase by more than 10 additional degrees in the Arctic.

Nearly half of all the Arctic sea ice has melted since the 1980s (Fig. A.5). Looking ahead, scientists expect the whole Arctic ice sheet to completely melt in some years. This would seriously threaten the survival of wildlife including the polar bear. If global average warming is limited to 2°C, then we expect the Arctic will be ice-free one summer in every decade. If the warming can be curbed to 1.5°C then this is only expected to happen once a century.

Global average annual rainfall is also expected to change as global warming increases. However, just like the temperature, the local change in rainfall depends on where you are in the world, and on the season.

Over the course of this century, some places like Scandinavia and parts of China are expected to have over 20% more rain each year – other areas like Spain and South Africa are expected to have over 20% less. The timing of rainfall during the year will also be affected. For example the UK will probably have more rain in the winter, and less rain in the summer. Science can't say whether a particular storm or drought was due to climate change. However, science can say that storms or droughts of a particular severity are 5 times (or 10, or 100 times) more likely. So if we

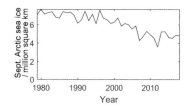

Fig. A.5: Average September area of Arctic sea ice, showing how it has nearly halved in the last decades. (URL 105)

get far more storms than we did before, we can say that most of them are because of climate change – because only a few would have been expected otherwise.

The fact that the temperature changes are different in different places also affects weather patterns, causing much more complicated effects. For example, the relatively fast warming of the North Pole is speculated to cause changes in air currents, which in turn cause longer periods of extreme weather (e.g. heatwaves), which spread across large areas of the Northern hemisphere including the United States and western Europe.

Notes

Page

186   *a diagram to illustrate the greenhouse effect.* NASA give a really clear description of this process at the following link: URL 102.

187   *This means that nitrogen and oxygen don't cause a greenhouse effect.* An oxygen molecule is made up of two oxygen atoms, which can jiggle around, moving closer together and further apart from each other. Because the two atoms are exactly the same, it turns out that there is no change in the electric or magnetic field when they move around, which means that oxygen molecules do not emit or absorb visible or infrared light. The same is true for nitrogen molecules, and also for the single-atom noble gases that make up the next most common components of the air.

However, a carbon dioxide molecule is made up of one carbon atom and two oxygen atoms. Imagine your body is a carbon atom and your hands are oxygen atoms. If you stand with your arms outstretched, one on each side, then the three atoms are in a straight line. These atoms can move around if they gain energy from absorbing infrared light. For example you can flap your arms up and down or move your body from side to side.

Unlike in the oxygen molecule, the atoms in a carbon dioxide molecule are of different types. When the atoms in the carbon dioxide molecule jiggle around they cause a changing electric and magnetic field. Just as a ball bobbing on a pond produces ripples on the pond surface, so a changing electric and magnetic fields causes electromagnetic waves, commonly known as radiation or light. Conversely, light can be absorbed by the molecule and make it jiggle. The amount of energy required to make the molecule jiggle corresponds to the light in the infrared part of the electromagnetic spectrum.

Infrared radiation gets absorbed by carbon dioxide and makes it jiggle around. And from time to time the carbon dioxide will emit infrared light and take a break from jiggling for a while. Most of the time this heat travels back down to Earth. These dancing carbon dioxide molecules act like a blanket and keep us from freezing.

189   *"Warming of the climate system is unequivocal, and since the 1950s, many of the observed changes are unprecedented over decades to millennia."* Taken from the Intergovernmental Panel on Climate Change (IPCC) 2014 Synthesis Report (IPCC, 2014).

189   *The world has warmed up by 0.97°C between the late 1850s and the early 2000s.* Specifically, the average near-surface air temperature increase between pre-industrial times (1850-1900) and the recent decade (2006-2015) is 0.97°C (IPCC, 2018). The surface temperature increase is 0.87°C over the

same period, however we state the near-surface air temperature in the main text since this is the value used in IPCC (2018) chapter 2 for the carbon budget calculations.

189 *We can also calculate the warming and cooling effects of snow, aeroplane condensation trails, volcanoes, and even changes in the amount of radiation from the sun.* You can read a detailed account of all these effects in Myhre et al. (2013).

189 *almost all of the warming over the last two hundred years can be explained by human activities.* In 2014 the IPCC wrote "Anthropogenic greenhouse-gas emissions... together with... other anthropogenic drivers... are extremely likely to have been the dominant cause of the observed warming since the mid-20th century" – from Pachauri and Meyer (2014).

189 *if we double the amount of greenhouse gases released, we double the amount of global warming.* For example, see figure SPM.10b and figure 2.3 of chapter 2 of IPCC, 2018, which shows a roughly linear relationship between the amount of greenhouse-gas emissions and the predicted warming. See also the earlier more detailed analysis in Myhre et al. (2013).

189 *which could trigger irreversible changes that increase the temperature yet further.* This is referenced throughout Pachauri and Meyer (2014) for example: "Without additional mitigation efforts beyond those in place today, and even with adaptation, warming by the end of the 21st century will lead to high to very high risk of severe, widespread and irreversible impacts globally (high confidence)."

190 *the global average temperature rise of 0.97°C since 1850 is very unevenly distributed across the Earth's surface.* For example, see figure 1.3 of M. R. Allen et al. (2018), which shows the temperature change across a map of the world.

190 *water warms up much more slowly than the land.* This property is described in physics by the "specific heat capacity", which is the energy required to raise the temperature of one gram by one °C. By definition of the calorie, it takes one calorie of energy to raise the temperature of one gram of water by one °C. The specific heat capacity of soil depends on the moisture level, and for dry soil is only one fifth that of water, depending on soil type (Bowers and Hanks, 1962). Additionally, water evaporates more as it warms up, which stabilises the warming. When continental soil is dry then evaporation can't help to keep the soil cool.

190 *Some patches of ocean have hardly warmed at all in the past century. On the other hand, some land on most continents has already warmed by more than 1.5°C. The greatest warming is happening at the Arctic, which has now warmed by nearly 3°C.* This is apparent in the top panel of figure 1.3 of M. R. Allen et al. (2018), in which some patches of sea have not increased in temperature (blue colour) and yet central Africa, Canada and Russia have warmed by over 1.5°C (darker red colour). Arctic warming is accelerating because of the melting ice. When sunlight is reflected straight back into the sky from the white ice, it can't cause warming. However, when the ice melts into water then some of the sunlight warms the water, which then leads to more melted ice...

190 *If greenhouse-gas emissions continue rising at their current rate, warming is expected to increase by more than 10 additional degrees in the Arctic.* See the right panel of figure 2.2a from Pachauri and Meyer (2014).

190 *If global average warming is limited to 2°C, then we expect the Arctic will be ice-free one summer in every decade. If the warming can be curbed to 1.5°C then this is only expected to happen once a century.* See Meredith and Sommerkorn (2019).

190   *Over the course of this century, some places like Scandinavia and parts of China are expected to have over 20% more rain each year – other areas like Spain and South Africa are expected to have over 20% less.* This is shown in figure 2.2b in Pachauri and Meyer (2014).

190   *For example the UK will probably have more rain in the winter, and less rain in the summer.* See chapter 11 of Solomon et al. (2007) e.g. their box 11-1 figure 2.

191   *the relatively fast warming of the North Pole is speculated to cause changes in air currents, which in turn cause longer periods of extreme weather (e.g. heatwaves), which spread across large areas of the Northern hemisphere including the United States and western Europe.* See Kornhuber et al. (2017) and Mann et al. (2018) and Petoukhov et al. (2013).

Appendix B Impacts of climate change on food

Most of this book looks at how changing our food consumption affects the climate. Here we look at things the other way round – how will climate change affect the future availability of food?

Given the vast array of food choices in the supermarket, it's hard to predict what might be on the shelves in one year's time, let alone in 2050. However, the range of ingredients used to make most of our calories is in fact surprisingly limited, and nearly half the world's calories come from just three crops: rice, wheat and maize. This makes the task of forecasting food supply slightly easier.

Every farmer and gardener knows that the quality and quantity of a crop depend on the temperature and rainfall. By looking back at historical harvests and comparing them with the weather in the respective year, we can estimate how crop yields vary with temperatures and rainfall levels.

It turns out that as a result of climate change some parts of the world will be able to produce *more* food – for example in a region that was previously slightly too cold for a particular type of plant. Parts of Canada, Scandinavia and Russia are predicted to produce more food in a warmer world. However, most continental and equatorial regions are expected to produce much less food under the projected climate change, particularly South America, Africa, India, southern China, the Philippines and Australia.

We need pollinators, such as bees, to be able to produce edible grains and fruits. Climate change affects the number and spread of these pollinators, which can reduce crop yield. In addition, the spread of crop pests and diseases are affected, which can reduce crop yield further. Increased levels of carbon dioxide can increase yields of some crops, but this is predicted to come at the cost of lower nutrition, particularly in key minerals iron and zinc.

Some parts of the sea are now producing more fish than before, as fish adapt to changing sea temperatures and currents. Overall though, the total supply of fish is expected to decrease, and the communities that have been dependent on fishing for centuries will be hardest hit. One way to counterbalance the declining fish stocks is to grow fish in farms, either in tanks or in cordoned-off parts of the sea (chapter 27). However, sea farms are particularly vulnerable to storms. Furthermore, both fish and land-animal farming depend on availability of feed, which is affected by the same falling yield issues that affect human food. The amount of food we can produce from farmed fish and land animals is also affected by the spread of pests and diseases, which is likely to be worsened by climate change.

Finally, toxins in food tend to build up faster at higher temperatures. For example, aflatoxins (produced by mould) are encouraged by drought during the growing season followed by rainfall during harvest and high temperatures during storage. Aflatoxins cause liver cancer and are associated with stunted growth in children, and in severe outbreaks can cause death.

The impact of food shortages

As chronicled in the Bible, in past millennia the harvested grain was stored for years in case of a drought, or series of droughts. Today, droughts are still a major problem for food production: over 80% of the cost of crop losses from extreme weather events is currently attributed to droughts.

However, thanks to widespread international trade in food we don't currently need to store grain for years. When a harvest fails in one region, we can just import food from somewhere else where the weather was more favourable. Much of the internationally traded food is produced in highly productive regions, often called "breadbaskets". It is therefore crucially important to understand how changes in air currents can affect multiple continents at once. (e.g. the Northern hemisphere, see appendix "Climate change"). If a weather system knocks out several of these breadbaskets in the same year, then global food availability is reduced.

Furthermore, access to food currently depends critically on an impressively interconnected web of trade, delivering ingredients just in time to supply factories and consumers. In the same way that a run on banks can cause a financial crisis even if there was no good reason for the initial run, so even an imagined lack of food could cause changes in international trade that can increase food prices. Increased food prices have been found to match up with outbreaks of civil unrest, for example they are thought to have contributed to the French Revolution and more recently there was an increase in food prices of 50% during a period of just over 1 year leading up to early 2008, which was associated with riots in 30 countries.

Notes

Page

194 *nearly half the world's calories come from just three crops: rice, wheat and maize.* See P. K. Thornton and Cramer (2012).

194 *However, most continental and equatorial regions are expected to produce much less food under the projected climate change, particularly South America, Africa, India, southern China, the Philippines and Australia.* For more details see Schleussner et al. (2016) and Searchinger et al. (2013).

194 *Increased levels of carbon dioxide can increase yields of some crops, but this is predicted to come at the cost of lower nutrition, particularly in key minerals iron and zinc.* See S. Myers et al. (2014), S. S. Myers et al. (2017), Zhu et al. (2018) and the discussion in box 6 of IPCC (2018).

195 *Aflatoxins cause liver cancer and are associated with stunted growth in children, and in severe outbreaks can cause death.* For more information see Kepple and Holleman (2018).

195 *over 80% of the cost of crop losses from extreme weather events is currently attributed to droughts.* From Kepple and Holleman (2018).

195 *Increased food prices have been found to match up with outbreaks of civil unrest,* See Lagi et al. (2011); Bellemare (2014) and C. S. Hendrix and Haggard (2015).

195 *for example they are thought to have contributed to the French Revolution* Tilly (1968).

195 *there was an increase in food prices of 50% during a period of just over 1 year leading up to early 2008, which was associated with riots in 30 countries.* Brinkman and C. Hendrix (2010).

Appendix C Food in the future

How much might food change in the future? We start by looking back at changes that happened already during the 20th century. Then we look ahead at the projected increase in population and wealth and consider how this affects greenhouse-gas emissions. Finally we speculate on improvements that could help reduce the impact of climate change on food.

The pace of innovation in food

Close your eyes and imagine it's the year 2040. What did you have for your last meal? What are you looking forward to tucking into later? What will people be eating in 2050?

In some ways it's hard to imagine things being any different. But look backwards instead of forwards and you see some big changes. Only 100 years ago the home refrigerator was a new invention, but these days the developed-world's lifestyle would be impossible without it. (Fig. C.1). And in the last 100 years the home freezer and refrigerated transportation has allowed the routine purchase and consumption of pre-prepared meals on a scale unimaginable by our grandparents.

Soft drinks (chapter 21) and packets of potato crisps (chapter 20) are available in most food outlets, yet both came to prominence only in the second half of the 20th century. Massive supermarkets and online shopping allow us to get our food in record time. Many of the changes have been enabled by new technology, which allows companies to better cater to our preferences.

Could the food retailers of the future do an even better job of delivering tasty satiety and convenience? At the moment it looks like other factors will become more important than personal preferences in determining what you're digesting in twenty years' time. Poor food choices will cause more health problems (chapter 34), and as a result countries may impose taxes on unhealthy food options – for example sugar taxes to

Fig. C.1: Fridges through the ages.
Upper: "Refrigerator", 400BC. (URL 106)
Middle: 1920s refrigerator. (URL 107)
Lower: Modern fridge interior. (URL 108)

tackle the obesity crisis (chapter 36). In addition, we will be dealing with the impacts of climate change on food production (appendix "Impacts of climate change on food"), at the same time as trying to reduce greenhouse-gas emissions from food.

A growing demand for food

The human population rose from about 2.5 billion people in 1950 up to over 6 billion in 2000, and continues to rise (Fig. C.2). However, this growth rate is slowing down, partly because people are choosing to have fewer children. Opinion is divided over whether the population will continue to rise until the end of the century, or whether it will peak before 2050 and then start to fall. The United Nations 2017 forecast predicts that the number of people is likely to grow to nearly 10 billion in 2050. These extra people will have to be fed.

The recommended daily allowance of calories depends on age and physical activity levels but (as dieters will know) it is around 2000 kCal for women and 2500 kCal for men. Do you notice people around you (or yourself) putting on a bit of extra weight as they get older? It turns out that as people earn more money, they also tend to eat more!

Economic forecasts predict rising incomes, which is good news as it takes many people out of poverty, but is not such good news for the majority of people's waistlines. Putting this together with the population forecasts predicts a more than 50% increase in demand for food between 2005 and 2050.

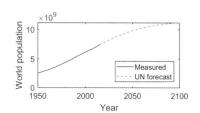

Fig. C.2: Population forecast showing the past rise in population (blue larger dots) and the United Nations forecast (red small dashes). Data from the UN via URL 109.

More meat, and more emissions

What sort of food will our future selves want to buy? As people get more money, they tend to eat more meat, as well as eating more food generally. A surprisingly tight correspondence has been found between the amount of meat people eat and their income:

- On an annual salary of around $10,000, people eat about 40 grams of meat a day, which corresponds to about 2 chicken breasts a week.

- This reaches 100 grams of meat a day as salaries approach $30,000.

- Worldwide, the amount of animal-based protein eaten per person has risen by over 50% since the 1970s.

The global trend for more meat is important for climate change because animal products contribute more to global warming than other types of food. Combined with the rising population, the rising demand for meat could almost double greenhouse-gas emissions from food.

Even ignoring other considerations of land and water availability, because of greenhouse-gas emissions alone we simply cannot scale up agriculture to satisfy consumer demand.

Mitigating the impacts of climate change on food

On top of all this, we will have to deal with the impacts of climate change on food (appendix "Impacts of climate change on food"). Research is ongoing into agriculture that is more resilient to the effects of climate change. Genetic engineering and accelerated traditional plant breeding can lead to varieties that cope better with higher temperatures, or are more resilient to extreme weather. Better crop protection and storage can also reduce food wasted along the supply chain, particularly in countries not already using the latest technology.

In addition, some currently less popular crops may become grown more widely. For example the black-eyed bean (often called the cow pea; see Fig. C.3) is particularly drought-tolerant and has been studied by NASA on space stations.

The effects of climate change are already being seen around the world, including an increased number of extreme weather events. Although sometimes tragic for the people involved, devastation gives us a chance to do better in future. We need to be ready to build back up the towns and food production systems in ways that are more resilient to climate change, and that actually help to reverse climate change (see chapter 37).

Notes

Page

197 *"Refrigerator", 400BC. (URL 106)* This ancient "Yakhchal" evaporation cooler was built in Iran in about 400BC. There is a large underground storage area, and ice that was brought from the local mountains in winter would have lasted all summer.

198 *The United Nations 2017 forecast predicts that the number of people is likely to grow to nearly 10 billion in 2050.* See United Nations (2019).

198 *It turns out that as people earn more money, they also tend to eat more!* Research shows that as the Gross Domestic Product (GDP) of a country increases so too does the daily number of calories consumed by each person (see the right panel of figure 2 in Tilman and Clark 2014).

198 *Economic forecasts predict rising incomes, which is good news as it takes many people out of poverty, but is not such good news for the majority of people's*

Fig. C.3: The black eyed bean (cow pea) might become more widely grown due to its weather resilience. (URL 110) (URL 111) (URL 112)

waistlines. See economic forecasts by the Food and Agriculture Organisation (Alexandratos and Bruinsma, 2012).

198   *more than 50% increase in demand for food between 2005 and 2050.* See Alexandratos and Bruinsma (2012).

198   *A surprisingly tight correspondence has been found between the amount of meat people eat and their income:* Shown in the left panel of figure 2 of Tilman and Clark (2014).

198   *Worldwide, the amount of animal-based protein eaten per person has risen by over 50% since the 1970s.* See Alexandratos and Bruinsma (2012) and figure 9 in Ranganathan et al. (2016).

199   *animal products contribute more to global warming than other types of food.* See figure 1 of Springmann et al., 2018.

199   *the rising demand for meat could almost double greenhouse-gas emissions from food.* Springmann et al. (2018) forecast a rise of about 87%.

199   *the black-eyed bean (often called the cow pea; see Fig. C.3) is particularly drought-tolerant* See P. Thornton, 2012 .

Bibliography

Web links

All hyphens in URLs, even those at the end of a line that look like a hyphen indicating continuation, are literal and are part of the URL.

(1). https://www.ipcc.ch/.

(2). https://ourworldindata.org/grapher/annual-ghg-emissions.

(3). https://www.gov.uk/government/statistics/ndns-results-from-years-5-and-6-combined.

(4). https://intake24.co.uk/.

(5). https://www.gov.uk/government/organisations/driver-and-vehicle-licensing-agency.

(6). https://www.iea.org/geco/emissions/.

(7). https://www.flickr.com/photos/sylvar/33774052742.

(8). https://en.wikipedia.org/wiki/File:Coffee_Bean.jpeg.

(9). https://www.maxpixel.net/Vegetables-Arable-Sugar-Beet-Agriculture-Turnip-3662944.

(10). https://pxhere.com/en/photo/1428395.

(11). https://www.tateandlyle.com/news/tate-lyle-reduces-its-footprint-carbon-trust.

(12). https://commons.wikimedia.org/wiki/File:Milk_-_olly_claxton.jpg.

(13). https://www.publicdomainpictures.net/en/view-image.php?image=627&picture=black-cow.

(14). https://www.goodfreephotos.com/vector-images/spotted-moocow-vector-clipart.png.php.

(15). https://commons.wikimedia.org/wiki/File:Abomasum_(PSF).png.

(16). https://www.oatly.com/uk/climate-footprint.

(17). http://www.bbc.com/future/story/20190806-how-vaccines-could-fix-our-problem-with-cow-emissions.

(18). https://www.perfectdayfoods.com/.

(19). https://www.flickr.com/photos/git/1497984118.

(20). http://maxpixel.freegreatpicture.com/Orphanage-Baking-Making-Bread-Africa-Tanzania-278480.

(21). https://www.pexels.com/photo/wheat-grains-closeup-photography-158603/.

(22). https://pixabay.com/en/roll-fresh-bread-rolls-baker-oven-983765.

(23). https://www.pexels.com/photo/bread-food-toast-breakfast-33309.

(24). http://www.dailymail.co.uk/sciencetech/article-2017338/The-perfect-piece-toast-Scientists-test-2-000-slices-216-seconds-optimum-time.html.

(25). https://pxhere.com/en/photo/760945.

(26). https://pixabay.com/photos/breakfast-egg-egg-boiled-egg-food-2209048.

(27). https://www.flickr.com/photos/usdagov/9733481041.

(28). https://commons.wikimedia.org/wiki/File:Curds_and_whey.jpg.

(29). https://pixabay.com/en/parma-parmesan-grinding-wheels-1075060/.

(30). https://www.theguardian.com/lifeandstyle/2018/apr/19/france-vegetarian-foods-no-meat-words.

(31). https://www.flickr.com/photos/sk8geek/4873400550.

(32). https://commons.wikimedia.org/wiki/File:Dr._Evans%27_How_to_keep_well;_(1917)_(14583500320).jpg.

(33). https://pixabay.com/en/piglets-farm-pig-livestock-pink-2736051/.

(34). http://www.geograph.org.uk/photo/1732631.

(35). https://pixnio.com/food-and-drink/burgers-and-sandwiches/lettuce-sandwich-breakfast-ham-lunch-food.

(36). https://pixabay.com/en/tomato-salad-shell-salad-cut-1288416/.

(37). https://www.maxpixel.net/Red-Organic-Plant-Tomatoes-Green-Vegetable-Tomato-2937255.

(38). https://apsgroup.uk.com/innovations.

(39). https://www.lettusgrow.com/.

(40). https: //www.flickr.com/photos/joshuaheller/3359701592.

(41). https://www.maxpixels.net/Harvest-Field-Agriculture-Potato-Landing-Plant-2168030.

(42). https://pxhere.com/en/photo/511640.

(43). https://commons.wikimedia.org/wiki/File: Potato_heart_mutation.jpg.

(44). https://www.maxpixel.net/Grain-Pods-Green-Soy-Agriculture-Food-Plants-941737.

(45). https://www.flickr.com/photos/wordridden/86406496.

(46). https://www.pexels.com/photo/apple-keyboard-breakfast-creamy-delicious-322339/.

(47). http://www.peakpx.com/602355/apple-orange-and-banana-fruit.

(48). https://pixabay.com/photos/apple-apple-tree-fruit-red-fresh-693971/.

(49). https://pixabay.com/photos/orange-tree-orange-grove-plantation-1117423/.

(50). https://www.pexels.com/photo/bowl-of-strawberry-fruits-2820144/.

(51). https://www.flickr.com/photos/jopoe/17784163712.

(52). https://www.maxpixel.net/Food-Bean-Cacao-Organic-Cocoa-Pod-Natural-2422040.

(53). https://pixabay.com/photos/cocoa-beans-cocoa-display-chocolate-373813/.

(54). ttps://pixabay.com/photos/almonds-tree-growing-branch-989529/.

(55). https://pixabay.com/photos/almonds-dried-almonds-food-nut-1326472/.

(56). https://pixabay.com/photos/nuts-peanut-roasted-cores-snack-1736520/.

(57). https://pixabay.com/photos/snack-snacking-potatoes-food-bowl-1555519/.

(58). https://pixabay.com/en/glass-straw-coke-sparkling-water-1055502/.

(59). https://pixabay.com/images/search/orange_juice/.

(60). https: //www.flickr.com/photos/gordonplant/5003941627.

(61). https://pixabay.com/fi/photos/black-forest-cake-leivonnaiset-shop-1382649/.

(62). https://nutritiondata.self.com/facts/cereal-grains-and-pasta/5798/2.

(63). https://www.flickr.com/photos/stone-soup/3157432397/in/photostream/.

(64). https://pixabay.com/photos/steak-meat-beef-eat-food-2272464/.

(65). https://bit.ly/2MqU5C2.

(66). https://www.nationalchickencouncil.org/about-the-industry/statistics/per-capita-consumption-of-poultry-and-livestock-1965-to-estimated-2012-in-pounds/.

(67). https://www.publicdomainpictures.net/en/view-image.php?image=105153&picture=bowl-of-rice.

(68). https://pixabay.com/en/in-rice-field-rice-2679153/.

(69). https://www.maxpixel.net/Field-In-Rice-Field-Seedlings-2293143.

(70). https://www.maxpixel.net/Rice-Rice-Field-Chiang-Mai-Thailand-Rice-Terrace-2306224.

(71). https://www.publicdomainpictures.net/en/view-image.php?image=24219&picture=fish-and-chips.

(72). https://www.telegraph.co.uk/news/2016/12/01/fishand-chip-shops-urged-serve-standard-sized-portions/.

(73). https://pixabay.com/photos/norway-salmon-farming-norwegian-sea-1183114/.

(74). https://pixabay.com/photos/carrots-vegetables-vitamins-food-4095322/.

(75). https://www.flickr.com/photos/adactio/5442139400.

(76). https://www.needpix.com/photo/1029572/glass-of-wine-wine-relaxation-wine-glass-drink-red-wine-alcohol-celebration-anniversary.

(77). https://www.publicdomainpictures.net/en/view-image.php?image=211069&picture=cold-beer.

(78). https://www.nutrition.org.uk/nutritionscience/nutrients-food-and-ingredients/dietary-fibre.html.

(79). https://wri-indonesia.org/en/resources/charts-graphs/share-total-food-available-lost-or-wasted.

(80). https://pixabay.com/fi/photos/tomaatin-outo-hauska-vihannekset-4432398/.

(81). https://www.flickr.com/photos/brettf/196682698.

(82). https://pixabay.com/fi/photos/kukkakaali-vihannes-
    tuoreet-849643/.

(83). https://commons.wikimedia.org/wiki/File:
    Your_food_is_the_best_-_Don%27t_waste_it_-_NARA_-
    _513725.jpg.

(84). http://www.wrap.org.uk/food-date-
    labelling?utm_source=PR&utm_medium=media-
    wrap&utm_campaign=date-labelling.

(85). https://www.lovefoodhatewaste.com/what-to-do.

(86). https://www.fda.gov/food/consumers/tips-reduce-
    food-waste.

(87). https://www.nhs.uk/conditions/vitamins-and-
    minerals/vitamin-d/.

(88). https://www.nhs.uk/live-well/eat-well/red-meat-and-
    the-risk-of-bowel-cancer/.

(89). https:
    //www.nutrition.org.uk/healthyliving/basics/fibre.html.

(90). https://www.gov.uk/government/publications/health-
    matters-obesity-and-the-food-environment/health-
    matters-obesity-and-the-food-environment--2.

(91). https://pixabay.com/photos/food-insect-nutrition-eat-
    protein-3348724/.

(92). https://www.flickr.com/photos/invvigren/6967490206.

(93). https://www.entocycle.com/insects.

(94). https:
    //www.theguardian.com/environment/2018/oct/10/we-
    label-fridges-to-show-their-environmental-impact-why-
    not-food.

(95). https://www.campaignlive.co.uk/article/pepsico-
    explains-measured-carbon-footprint-walkers-
    crisps/941668.

(96). https://www.carbontrust.com/home/.

(97). https://www.gov.uk/government/news/soft-drinks-
    industry-levy-comes-into-effect.

(98). https://climateseries.com/lectures/34-joseph-poore-
    climatechange-food-impact.

(99). https://www.climateandlandusealliance.org/scientists-
    statement/.

(100). https://models.pbl.nl/image/index.php/Welcome_
    to_IMAGE_3.0_Documentation.

(101). https://tim.blog/2007/10/25/weapons-of-mass-distractions-and-the-art-of-letting-bad-things-happen/.

(102). http://climatekids.nasa.gov/greenhouse-effect/.

(103). https://commons.wikimedia.org/wiki/File: Carbon_Dioxide_400kyr.png.

(104). https://www.climate-lab-book.ac.uk/2018/2018-visualisation-update/#more-5614.

(105). https://nsidc.org/arcticseaicenews/sea-ice-tools/.

(106). https://commons.wikimedia.org/wiki/File: Yakhchal_of_Yazd_province.jpg.

(107). https://commons.wikimedia.org/wiki/File: Kitchen_refrigerator_-_Haas-Lilienthal_House_-_San_Francisco,_CA_-_DSC05023.JPG.

(108). https://commons.wikimedia.org/wiki/File: LG_refrigerator_interior.jpg.

(109). https://ourworldindata.org/future-population-growth.

(110). https://www.flickr.com/photos/iita-media-library/7064543759.

(111). https://www.flickr.com/photos/iita-media-library/6918466632.

(112). https://www.flickr.com/photos/wwworks/11758940374.

(113). https://pixabay.com/fi/photos/pizza-ravintola-italian-ruoka-4425695/.

(114). https://www.pexels.com/photo/apple-apple-pie-close-up-cream-2767935/.

(115). https://www.needpix.com/photo/1075325/chocolate-mousse-aquafaba-vegan-chickpea-sweet-gourmandine-dessert-home-made-without-eggs.

(116). https://www.quorn.co.uk/files/content/Carbon_Footprint_Results_UK.pdf.

References

Aalde, H. et al. (2006). "Chapter 4: Forest Land". *2006 IPCC Guidelines for National Greenhouse Gas Inventories – Volume 4: Agriculture, Forestry and Other Land Use*, 1. https://www.ipcc-nggip.iges.or.jp/public/2006gl/pdf/4_Volume4/V4_04_Ch4_Forest_Land.pdf.

AHDB (2017). "Pig Pocketbook".
   https://pork.ahdb.org.uk/media/273703/pig-
   pocketbook-2017.pdf.

AHDB (2018a). "Pig Pocketbook".
   https://pork.ahdb.org.uk/media/275385/pig-
   pocketbook-2018.pdf.

AHDB (2018b). "Poultry Pocketbook", 1.
   https://pork.ahdb.org.uk/media/275384/poultry-
   pocketbook-2018.pdf.

Alexandratos, N. and Bruinsma, J. (2012). *World Agriculture
   Towards 2030/2050: The 2012 Revision*. FAO.
   http://www.fao.org/3/a-ap106e.pdf.

Allen, M. R. et al. (2018). *Global warming of 1.5°C. An IPCC
   Special Report on the impacts of global warming of 1.5°C above
   pre-industrial levels and related global greenhouse gas emission
   pathways, in the context of strengthening the global response to
   the threat of climate change, sustainable development, and efforts
   to eradicate poverty*. Ed. by V. Masson-Delmotte et al.
   Intergovernmental Panel on Climate Change.
   https://www.ipcc.ch/sr15/.

Allen, P. et al. (2019). *Zero Carbon Britain: Rising to the Climate
   Emergency*. Centre for Alternative Technology.
   https://www.cat.org.uk/info-resources/zero-carbon-
   britain/research-reports/zero-carbon-britain-rising-to-
   the-climate-emergency/.

Allwood, J. and Cullen, J. (2015). *Sustainable Materials -
   Without the Hot Air: Making Buildings, Vehicles and Products
   Efficiently and with Less New Material*. UIT Cambridge.

Almeida, J. et al. (2018). *Reusable coffee cups life cycle assessment
   and benchmark*. A report for Keepcup. DOI:
   10.13140/RG.2.2.35083.13607.

Amienyo, D. and Azapagic, A. (2016). "Life cycle
   environmental impacts and costs of beer production and
   consumption in the UK". *Int J Life Cycle Assess* 21.4, 492.
   DOI: 10.1007/s11367-016-1028-6.

Amienyo, D. et al. (2013). "Life cycle environmental impacts
   of carbonated soft drinks". *Int J Life Cycle Assess* 18.1, 77.
   DOI: 10.1007/s11367-012-0459-y.

Aranda, A. et al. (2005). "Economic and environmental
   analysis of the wine bottle production in Spain by means of

life cycle assessment". *International Journal of Agricultural Resources, Governance and Ecology* 4, 178. DOI: 10.1504/IJARGE.2005.007199.

Arnold, S. and Yang, Z. (2005). *UK Landfill Methane Emissions Evaluation and Appraisal of Waste Policies and Projections to 2050*. Tech. rep. http://randd.defra.gov.uk/Document.aspx?Document=GA01083_3432_FRP.pdf.

Audsley and Williamson (2010). "FCRN WWF How Low Can We Go?", 1. http://www.fcrn.org.uk/fcrn/publications/how-low-can-we-go.

Azapagic, A. et al. (2016). "The global warming potential of production and consumption of Kenyan tea". *Journal of Cleaner Production* 112, 4031. DOI: 10.1016/j.jclepro.2015.07.029.

Bajželj, B. et al. (2013). "Designing Climate Change Mitigation Plans That Add Up". *Environ. Sci. Technol.* 47.14, 8062. DOI: 10.1021/es400399h.

Bartzas, G. et al. (2017). "Comparative life cycle assessment of pistachio, almond and apple production". *Information Processing in Agriculture* 4.3, 188. DOI: https://doi.org/10.1016/j.inpa.2017.04.001.

Beauchemin, K. A. et al. (2010). "Life cycle assessment of greenhouse gas emissions from beef production in western Canada: A case study". *Agricultural Systems* 103.6, 371. DOI: 10.1016/j.agsy.2010.03.008.

Beddington, J. (2011). *Foresight. The Future of Food and Farming (2011) Final Project Report. The Government Office for Science, London*. Tech. rep. https://www.gov.uk/government/publications/future-of-food-and-farming.

Bellemare, M. F. (2014). "Rising Food Prices, Food Price Volatility, and Social Unrest". *American Journal of Agricultural Economics* 97.1, 1. DOI: 10.1093/ajae/aau038.

Berners-Lee, M. (2010). *How Bad are Bananas?: The Carbon Footprint of Everything*. Green Profile.

Berners-Lee, M. (2019). *There Is No Planet B: A Handbook for the Make or Break Years*. Green Profile.

Blake, L. (2014). *People, Plate and Planet. The impact of dietary choices on health, greenhouse gas emissions and land use. Part of* the Zero Carbon Britain project by Centre for Alternative Technology. https://www.cat.org.uk/app/uploads/dlm_uploads/2018/11/People-Plate-and-Planet.pdf.

Boustead (2005). *Eco-profiles of the European Plastics Industry Polyethylene Terephthalate (PET) (Amorphous grade)*. Tech. rep. http://www.inference.org.uk/sustainable/LCA/elcd/external_docs/peta_311147fa-fabd-11da-974d-0800200c9a66.pdf.

Bowers, S. A. and Hanks, R. J. (1962). "Specific heat capacity of soils and minerals as determined with a radiation calorimeter". *Soil Science* 94.6, 392. https://journals.lww.com/soilsci/Fulltext/1962/12000/SPECIFIC_HEAT_CAPACITY_OF_SOILS_AND_MINERALS_AS.7.aspx.

Brinkman, H. and Hendrix, C. (2010). *Food Insecurity and Conflict: Applying the WDR Framework*. Tech. rep. http://web.worldbank.org/archive/website01306/web/food.html.

British Plastics Federation and PlasticsEurope (2017). *Written evidence to the UK Environmental Audit Committee*. Tech. rep. http://data.parliament.uk/WrittenEvidence/CommitteeEvidence.svc/EvidenceDocument/Environmental%20Audit/Packaging/written/49788.html.

Buchspies, B. et al. (2011). *Life Cycle Assessment of High-Sea Fish and Salmon Aquaculture*. ESU-services Ltd., 1. esu-services.ch/fileadmin/download/buchspies-2011-LCA-fish.pdf.

Cain, M. et al. (2019). "Improved calculation of warming-equivalent emissions for short-lived climate pollutants". *npj Climate and Atmospheric Science* 2. DOI: 10.1038/s41612-019-0086-4.

CarbonClear (2012). "Disposable Cups vs. Reusable Cups", 1. https://carbon-clear.com/files/cup_assessment.pdf.

"CCaLC PVC Manual (V2.0)" (2011), 1. http://www.ccalc.org.uk/downloads/Manual_CCaLC_PVC_V2.0.pdf.

Chaouali, N. et al. (2013). "Potential Toxic Levels of Cyanide in Almonds (Prunus amygdalus), Apricot Kernels (Prunus armeniaca), and Almond Syrup". *ISRN Toxicology* 2013, 610648. DOI: 10.1155/2013/610648.

Cichorowski, G. et al. (2015). "Scenario analysis of life cycle greenhouse gas emissions of Darjeeling tea". *Int J Life Cycle Assess* 20, 426. DOI: 10.1007/s11367-014-0840-0.

Clarke, M. and Tilman, D. (2017). "Comparative analysis of environmental impacts of agricultural production systems, agricultural input efficiency, and food choice". *Environmental Research Letters* 12.064016, 1. DOI: 10.1088.

Clune, S. et al. (2017). "Systematic review of greenhouse gas emissions for different fresh food categories". *Journal of Cleaner Production* 140.Part 2, 766. DOI: 10.1016/j.jclepro.2016.04.082.

Defra (2012). "Green Food Project Curry Sub Group Report", 1. https://assets.publishing.service.gov.uk/government/uploads/system/uploads/attachment_data/file/69571/pb13798-greenfoodproject-currysubgroup.pdf.

Defra (2018). "Policy paper: Carrier bags: why there's a charge". https://www.gov.uk/government/publications/single-use-plastic-carrier-bags-why-were-introducing-the-charge/carrier-bags-why-theres-a-5p-charge.

Defra (2019). *United Kingdom Slaughter Statistics – October 2019.* Tech. rep. https://assets.publishing.service.gov.uk/government/uploads/system/uploads/attachment_data/file/830920/slaughter-statsnotice-12sep19.pdf.

Djekic, I. et al. (2014). "Environmental life-cycle assessment of various dairy products". *Journal of Cleaner Production* 68, 64. DOI: https://doi.org/10.1016/j.jclepro.2013.12.054.

Dong, H. et al. (2017). "Chapter 10: Emissions from Livestock and Manure Management". *2006 IPCC Guidelines for National Greenhouse Gas Inventories – Volume 4: Agriculture, Forestry and Other Land Use*, 1. https://www.ipcc-nggip.iges.or.jp/public/2006gl/pdf/4_Volume4/V4_10_Ch10_Livestock.pdf.

Doublet, G. and Jungbluth, N. (2010). *Life cycle assessment of drinking Darjeeling tea.* Tech. rep. esu-services.ch/fileadmin/download/doublet-2010-LCA-Darjeeling-tea-1.0.pdf.

Dummer, J. (2012). "Sodium Reduction in Canadian Food Products: With the Health Check Program". *Canadian Journal of Dietetic Practice and Research* 73.1. PMID: 22397960, e227. DOI: 10.3148/73.1.2012.e227.

Durlinger, B. et al. (2017). *Agri-footprint 3.0 Part 2: Description of the data.* Tech. rep. http://www.agri-footprint.com/wp-content/uploads/2017/07/Agri-Footprint-3.0-Part-2-Description-of-data-31-05-2017.pdf.

Dwivedi, P. et al. (2012). "Global warming impact of Florida's Not-From-Concentrate (NFC) orange juice". *Agricultural Systems* 108.C, 104. DOI: 10.1016/j.agsy.2012.01.006.

Edenhofer, O. et al. (2014). "Change 2014: Mitigation of Climate Change". *Working Group III Contribution to the Fifth Assessment Report of the Intergovernmental Panel on Climate Change.* https://www.ipcc.ch/report/ar5/wg3.

Eriksson, E. et al. (2010). *Carbon Footprint of Cartons in Europe.* Tech. rep. https://www.ivl.se/download/18.343dc99d14e8bb0f58b75c7/1445517446481/B1924.pdf.

Espinoza-Orias, N. et al. (2011). "The carbon footprint of bread". *Int J Life Cycle Assess* 16, 351. DOI: https://doi.org/10.1007/s11367-011-0271-0.

Evershed, R. and Temple, N. (2016). *Sorting the Beef from the Bull: The Science of Food Fraud Forensics.* Bloomsbury Sigma. https://www.bloomsbury.com/uk/sorting-the-beef-from-the-bull-9781472911339/.

Ferriss, T. (2011). *The 4-Hour Work Week: Escape the 9-5, Live Anywhere and Join the New Rich.* Vermilion.

Finnegan, W. et al. (2018). "Assessing the environmental impact of the dairy processing industry in the Republic of Ireland". *Journal of Dairy Research* 85.3, 396. DOI: 10.1016/j.jclepro.2015.08.025.

Frankowska, A. (2019). "Environmental impacts on the food-energy-water nexus in the UK food sector". Ph.D. thesis. University of Manchester.

Frankowska, A. et al. (2019a). "Environmental impacts of vegetables consumption in the UK". *Science of the Total Environment* 682, 80. DOI: https://doi.org/10.1016/j.scitotenv.2019.04.424.

Frankowska, A. et al. (2019b). "Life cycle environmental impacts of fruits consumption in the UK". *Journal of*

Environmental Management 248. DOI: https://doi.org/10.1016/j.jenvman.2019.06.012.

Frischknecht, R. and Jungbluth, N. (2007). "Overview and Methodology ". *ecoinvent*, 1. https://www.ecoinvent.org/files/200712_frischknecht_jungbluth_overview_methodology_ecoinvent2.pdf.

Fullana, P. et al. (2005). *Analisis del ciclo de vida del vino de crianza D.O.C. Rioja. Direccion General de Calidad Ambiental, Consejería de Turismo, Medio Ambiente y Política Territorial del Gobierno de La Rioja.* Tech. rep. https://www.interempresas.net/Vitivinicola/Articulos/102783-Analisis-de-ciclo-de-vida-del-vino-de-La-Rioja.html.

Garfi, M. et al. (2016). "Life cycle assessment of drinking water: Comparing conventional water treatment, reverse osmosis and mineral water in glass and plastic bottles". *Journal of Cleaner Production* 137, 997. DOI: https://doi.org/10.1016/j.jclepro.2016.07.218.

Garnett, T. (2007). *The alcohol we drink and its contribution to the UK's greenhouse gas emissions: a discussion paper.* Tech. rep. https://www.fcrn.org.uk/sites/default/files/ALCOHOL%20final%20version%20TG%20feb%202007.pdf.

Gates, S. (2017). *Insects: An Edible Field Guide.* Ebury Press.

Gerber, P. J. et al. (2013). "Tackling climate change through livestock – A global assessment of emissions and mitigation opportunities", 1. http://www.fao.org/docrep/018/i3437e/i3437e.pdf.

GLEAM Global Livestock Environmental Assessment Model (2017). Tech. rep. http://www.fao.org/fileadmin/user_upload/gleam/docs/GLEAM_2.0_Model_description.pdf.

Goucher, L. et al. (2017). "The environmental impact of fertilizer embodied in a wheat-to-bread supply chain". *Nature Plants* 3.3, 1. DOI: 10.1038/nplants.2017.12.

Greenhouse Gas Impacts of Food Retailing: Report for Defra (2008). Brunel University. http://sciencesearch.defra.gov.uk/Default.aspx?Menu=Menu&Module=More&Location=None&Completed=0&ProjectID=15805.

Grossi, G. et al. (2018). "Livestock and climate change: impact of livestock on climate and mitigation strategies". *Animal Frontiers* 9.1, 69. DOI: 10.1093/af/vfy034.

Hales, C. et al. (2017). *Prevalence of Obesity Among Adults and Youth: United States, 2015–2016*. Tech. rep. https://www.cdc.gov/nchs/data/databriefs/db288.pdf.

Haque, M. N. (2018). "Dietary manipulation: a sustainable way to mitigate methane emissions from ruminants". *Journal of Animal Science and Technology* 60, 15. DOI: https://doi.org/10.1186/s40781-018-0175-7.

Harst, E. van der and Potting, J. (2013). "A critical comparison of ten disposable cup LCAs". *Environmental Impact Assessment Review* 43.C, 86. DOI: 10.1016/j.eiar.2013.06.006.

Harwatt, H. and Hayek, M. (2019). *Eating Away at Climate Change with Negative Emissions*. Tech. rep. https://animal.law.harvard.edu/publications/eating-away-at-climate-change-with-negative-emissions-harwatt-hayek/.

Hemmings, P. (2016). "National Diet and Nutrition Survey Years 5 and 6", 1. https://www.gov.uk/government/statistics/ndns-results-from-years-5-and-6-combined.

Hendrix, C. S. and Haggard, S. (2015). "Global food prices, regime type, and urban unrest in the developing world". *Journal of Peace Research* 52.2, 143. DOI: 10.1177/0022343314561599.

Hristov, A. N. et al. (2015). "An inhibitor persistently decreased enteric methane emission from dairy cows with no negative effect on milk production". *Proceedings of the National Academy of Sciences* 112.34, 10663. DOI: 10.1073/pnas.1504124112.

Humbert, S. et al. (2009). "Life cycle assessment of spray dried soluble coffee and comparison with alternatives (drip filter and capsule espresso)". *Journal of Cleaner Production* 17.15, 1351. DOI: 10.1016/j.jclepro.2009.04.011.

IPCC (2014). "IPCC AR5 WGIII Chapter 8 Transport ", 1. https://www.ipcc.ch/pdf/assessment-report/ar5/wg3/ipcc_wg3_ar5_chapter8.pdf.

IPCC (2018). *IPCC Special Report: Global Warming of 1.5°C*, 1. http://www.ipcc.ch/report/sr15/.

Iriarte, A. et al. (2014). "Carbon footprint of premium quality export bananas: Case study in Ecuador, the world's largest exporter". *Science of the Total Environment* 472.C, 1082. DOI: 10.1016/j.scitotenv.2013.11.072.

Jeswani, H. K. et al. (2015). "Environmental sustainability issues in the food–energy–water nexus: Breakfast cereals and snacks". *Sustainable Production and Consumption* 2. Sustainability issues in the food–energy–water nexus, 17. DOI: https://doi.org/10.1016/j.spc.2015.08.001.

Jørgensen, H. et al. (2013). "Models to quantify excretion of dry matter, nitrogen, phosphorus and carbon in growing pigs fed regional diets". *J Anim Sci Biotechnol.* 4, 42. DOI: 10.1186/2049-1891-4-42.

Kepple, A. and Holleman, C. (2018). *The State of Food Security and Nutrition in the World: Building Climate Resilience for Food Security and Nutrition.* Food and Agriculture Organisation of the United Nations (FAO), IFAD, UNICEF, WFP and WHO, 1. http://www.fao.org/3/I9553EN/i9553en.pdf.

Khoshnevisan, B. and Rafiee, S. (2013). "Life cycle assessment of garlic production; a case study of Hamedan province, Iran". https://www.researchgate.net/publication/257138059_Life_cycle_assessment_of_garlic_production_a_case_study_of_Hamedan_province_Iran.

Kissel, D. and Harris, G. (n.d.). *Fertilizer Recommendations by Crops, Categorized.* Tech. rep. http://aesl.ces.uga.edu/publications/soil/CropSheets.pdf.

Klenk, I. et al. (2012). "The Product Carbon Footprint of EU Beet Sugar". *Sugar Industry Journal* 137, 1. https://pdfs.semanticscholar.org/8118/2a435edd44d2277e44f3e58b7265d87b686d.pdf.

Konstantas, A. et al. (2018). "Environmental impacts of chocolate production and consumption in the UK". *Food Research International* 106, 1012. DOI: 10.1016/j.foodres.2018.02.042.

Kool, A. et al. (2009). "Carbon footprints of conventional and organic pork", 1. https://www.researchgate.net/publication/41104476_Carbon_footprints_of_conventional_and_organic_pork_assessments_of_typical_production_systems_in_the_Netherlands_Denmark_England_and_GermanyCarbon_footprints_of_conventional_and_organic_pork_assessment.

Kornhuber, K. et al. (2017). "Summertime planetary wave resonance in the Northern and Southern Hemispheres." *Journal of Climate* 30, 6133. DOI: 10.1175/JCLI-D-16-0703.1.

Kriegler, E. et al. (2018). "Short term policies to keep the door open for Paris climate goals". *Environmental Research Letters* 13.7, 074022. DOI: 10.1088/1748-9326/aac4f1.

Lagi, M. et al. (2011). "The Food Crises and Political Instability in North Africa and the Middle East". *SSRN*. DOI: 10.2139/ssrn.1910031.

Larkin, A. et al. (2012). *What's Cooking: Adaptation and Mitigation in the UK Food System*. UK: University of Manchester, Sustainable Consumption Institute. https://www.research.manchester.ac.uk/portal/en/publications/whats-cooking-adaptation--mitigation-in-the-uk-food-system(8efa62f2-4681-4974-a52e-c4a8e25d86bd)/export.html#export.

Larkin, A. et al. (2018). "What if negative emission technologies fail at scale? Implications of the Paris Agreement for big emitting nations". *Climate Policy* 18.6, 690. DOI: 10.1080/14693062.2017.1346498.

Lasco, R. D. et al. (2006). "Chapter 4: Cropland". *2006 IPCC Guidelines for National Greenhouse Gas Inventories – Volume 4: Agriculture, Forestry and Other Land Use*, 1. https://www.ipcc-nggip.iges.or.jp/public/2006gl/pdf/4_Volume4/V4_05_Ch5_Cropland.pdf.

Ledgard, S. F. et al. (2011). "Carbon footprinting of New Zealand lamb from the perspective of an exporting nation". *Animal Frontiers* 1.1, 40. DOI: 10.2527/af.2011-0010.

Leinonen, I. and Kyriazakis, I. (2016). "How can we improve the environmental sustainability of poultry production?" *Proceedings of the Nutrition Society* 75.03, 265. DOI: 10.1017/S0029665116000094.

Leinonen, I. et al. (2011a). "Predicting the environmental impacts of chicken systems in the United Kingdom through a life cycle assessment: Broiler production systems". *Poultry Science* 91.1, 8. DOI: 10.3382/ps.2011-01634.

Leinonen, I. et al. (2011b). "Predicting the environmental impacts of chicken systems in the United Kingdom through a life cycle assessment: Egg production systems". *Poultry Science* 91.1, 26. DOI: 10.3382/ps.2011-01635.

Leinonen, I. et al. (2013). "The potential to reduce environmental impacts of poultry". *Agricultural Systems*, 1. https://dspace.lib.cranfield.ac.uk/bitstream/handle/

1826/8099/Comparing_the_environmental_impacts_of_alternative_protein%20crops-2013.pdf?sequence=1&isAllowed=y.

Li, Y. et al. (2016). "Plant Density Effect on Grain Number and Weight of Two Winter Wheat Cultivars at Different Spikelet and Grain Positions." *PLoS ONE* 11, 5. DOI: https://doi.org/10.1371/journal.pone.0155351.

Macdiarmid, J. I. et al. (2012). "Sustainable diets for the future: can we contribute to reducing greenhouse gas emissions by eating a healthy diet?" *The American Journal of Clinical Nutrition* 96.3, 632. DOI: 10.3945/ajcn.112.038729.

MacKay, D. (2009). *Sustainable Energy - without the hot air*. UIT Cambridge.

MacLeod, M. et al. (2013). *Greenhouse gas emissions from pig and chicken supply chains – A global life cycle assessment*. Food and Agriculture Organization of the United Nations (FAO). http://www.fao.org/3/i3460e/i3460e00.htm.

Malhi, Y. et al. (2004). "Increasing biomass in Amazonian forest plots". *Phil. Trans. R. Soc. Lond. B* 359, 1143. DOI: http://doi.org/10.1098/rstb.2003.1422.

Mann, M. E. et al. (2018). "Projected changes in persistent extreme summer weather events: The role of quasi-resonant amplification." *Science Advances* 4.10. DOI: 10.1126/sciadv.aat3272.

Martin, S. et al. (2018). *Case Study: Ceramic cup vs. Paper cup*. Tech. rep. http://www.openlca.org/wp-content/uploads/2018/09/comparative_assessment_openLCA_coffee_mugs.pdf.

McCarty, J. A. et al. (2014). "Lifecycle assessment of greenhouse gas emissions associated with production and consumption of Peanut Butter in the US". *Transactions of the ASABE* 57(6), 1741. DOI: 10.13031/trans.57.10703.

Meredith, M. and Sommerkorn, M. (2019). *IPCC The Ocean and Cryosphere in a Changing Climate – Chapter 3: Polar Regions*, 1. https://report.ipcc.ch/srocc/pdf/SROCC_FinalDraft_Chapter3.pdf.

Miah, J. H. et al. (2018). "Environmental management of confectionery products: Life cycle impacts and improvement strategies". *Journal of Cleaner Production* 177, 732. DOI: 10.1016/j.jclepro.2017.12.073.

Milà i Canals, L. et al. (2006). "Evaluation of the environmental impacts of apple production using Life Cycle Assessment (LCA): Case study in New Zealand". *Agriculture, Ecosystems & Environment* 114.2-4, 226. DOI: 10.1016/j.agee.2005.10.023.

Moudrý jr., J. et al. (2015). "Greenhouse gases emissions from selected crops growing within organic farming". *Acta fytotechnica et zootechnica* 18, 56. DOI: 10.15414/afz.2015.18.si.56-58.

Myers, S. S. et al. (2017). "Climate Change and Global Food Systems: Potential Impacts on Food Security and Undernutrition." *Annual Review of Public Health* 38.1, 259. DOI: doi:10.1146/annurev-publhealth-031816-044356..

Myers, S. et al. (2014). "Increasing CO2 threatens human nutrition". *Nature* 510.7503, 139. DOI: 10.1038/nature13179.

Myhre, G. et al. (2013). "Anthropogenic and Natural Radiative Forcing". *Climate Change 2013 – The Physical Science Basis: Working Group I Contribution to the Fifth Assessment Report of the Intergovernmental Panel on Climate Change*. Cambridge University Press, Cambridge, United Kingdom and New York, NY, USA, 659. DOI: 10.1017/CBO9781107415324.018.

Nadathur, S. et al. (2016). *Sustainable Protein Sources*. Elsevier Inc.

NCD Risk Factor Collaboration (NCD-RisC) (2016). "Trends in adult body-mass index in 200 countries from 1975 to 2014: a pooled analysis of 1698 population-based measurement studies with 19.2 million participants". *The Lancet* 387, 1377. DOI: 10.1016/S0140-6736(16)30054-X.

Nemecek, T. et al. (2012). "Estimation of the variability in global warming potential of worldwide crop production using a modular extrapolation approach". *Journal of Cleaner Production* 31, 106. DOI: https://doi.org/10.1016/j.jclepro.2012.03.005.

Nilsson, K. et al. (2010). "Comparative life cycle assessment of margarine and butter consumed in the UK, Germany and France". *Int J Life Cycle Assess* 15, 916. DOI: 10.1007/s11367-010-0220-3.

Nilsson, K. et al. (2011). "The environmental impact of the consumption of sweets, crisps and soft drinks", 1.

https://www.fcrn.org.uk/sites/default/files/sweets-crisps-drinks.pdf.

Noya, I. et al. (2016). "Carbon and Water footprint of pork supply chain in Catalonia: from feed to final products". *Journal of Environmental Management* 171, 133. DOI: 10.1016/j.jenvman.2016.01.039.

Ntiamoah, A. and Afrane, G. (2009). "Life Cycle Assessment of Chocolate Produced in Ghana". *Appropriate Technologies for Environmental Protection in the Developing World*, 35. DOI: https://doi.org/10.1007/978-1-4020-9139-1_5.

O'Brien, D. et al. (2014). "An appraisal of carbon footprint of milk from commercial grass-based dairy farms in Ireland according to a certified life cycle assessment methodology". *Int J Life Cycle Assess* 19.8, 1469. DOI: 10.1007/s11367-014-0755-9.

Oonincx, D. G. A. B. et al. (2011). "An Exploration on Greenhouse Gas and Ammonia Production by Insect Species Suitable for Animal or Human Consumption". *PLoS ONE* 5.12, 1. DOI: 10.1371/journal.pone.0014445.

Pachauri, R. K. and Meyer, L. A. (2014). *Climate Change 2014: Synthesis Report. Contribution of Working Groups I, II and III to the Fifth Assessment Report of the Intergovernmental Panel on Climate Change*. Geneva, Switzerland: IPCC. https://www.ipcc.ch/site/assets/uploads/2018/05/SYR_AR5_FINAL_full_wcover.pdf.

Pan, Y. et al. (2011). "A Large and Persistent Carbon Sink in the World's Forests". *Science* 333.6045, 988. DOI: 10.1126/science.1201609.

Payen, S. et al. (2015). "LCA of local and imported tomato: an energy and water trade-off". *Journal of Cleaner Production* 87.C, 139. DOI: 10.1016/j.jclepro.2014.10.007.

Petoukhov, V. et al. (2013). "Quasiresonant amplification of planetary waves and recent Northern Hemisphere weather extremes." *Proc. Natl. Acad. Sci. U.S.A.* 110.14, 5336. DOI: 10.1073/pnas.1222000110.

Ponsioen, T. C. and Blonk, T. J. (2012). "Calculating land use change in carbon footprints of agricultural products as an impact of current land use". *Journal of Cleaner Production* 28.C, 120. DOI: 10.1016/j.jclepro.2011.10.014.

Ponsioen, T. and Blonk, H. (2011). *Case studies for more insight into the methodology and composition of carbon footprints of table potatoes and chips*. Tech. rep. http://www.blonkconsultants.nl/wp-content/uploads/2016/06/Carbon-footprints-of-table-potatoes-and-chips-July-2011.pdf.

Poore, J. and Nemecek, T. (2018). "Reducing food's environmental impacts through producers and consumers". *Science*, 987. http://science.sciencemag.org/content/sci/360/6392/987.full.pdf.

Quested, T. and Luzecka, P. (2014). *Household food and drink waste: A people focus*. Tech. rep. http://www.wrap.org.uk/sites/files/wrap/People-focused%20report%20v6_5%20full.pdf.

Ranganathan, J. et al. (2016). *Shifting Diets for a sustainable Food Future. Working Paper, Installment 11 of Creating a Sustainable Food Future*. Washington DC: World Resources Institute, 1. http://www.worldresourcesreport.org.

Rayner, J. (2013). *A Greedy Man in a Hungry World: How (almost) everything you thought you knew about food is wrong*. William Collins.

Reay, D. (2019). *Climate-Smart Food*. Mitchell Beazley.

Recanati, F. et al. (2018). "From beans to bar: A life cycle assessment towards sustainable chocolate supply chain". *Science of the Total Environment* 613-614.C, 1013. DOI: 10.1016/j.scitotenv.2017.09.187.

Recchia, L. et al. (2019). "Environmental Sustainability of Pasta Production Chains: An Integrated Approach for Comparing Local and Global Chains". *Resources* 8, 56. DOI: 10.3390/resources8010056.

Reynolds, C. J. et al. (2019). "Healthy and sustainable diets that meet greenhouse gas emission reduction targets and are affordable for different income groups in the UK". *Public Health Nutrition* 22, 1503. DOI: 10.1017/S1368980018003774.

Roese, G. and Taylor, G. (2006). *Basic pig husbandry — the boar. Primefact 69*. Tech. rep. https://www.dpi.nsw.gov.au/__data/assets/pdf_file/0003/56127/Basic_pig_husbandry_-_the_boar_-_Primefact_69-final.pdf.

Rogelj, J. et al. (2019). "Estimating and tracking the remaining carbon budget for stringent climate targets". *Nature* 571, 335. DOI: 10.1038/s41586-019-1368-z.

Rose, C. et al. (2015). "The Characterization of Feces and Urine: A Review of the Literature to Inform Advanced Treatment Technology". *Crit Rev Environ Sci Technol.* 45, 1827. DOI: 10.1080/10643389.2014.1000761.

Ruiter, H. de et al. (2017). "Total global agricultural land footprint associated with UK food supply 1986–2011". *Global Environmental Change* 43, 72. http://www.sciencedirect.com/science/article/pii/S0959378017301176.

Scarborough, P. et al. (2015). "Reds are more important than greens: how UK supermarket shoppers use the different information on a traffic light nutrition label in a choice experiment." *Int J Behav Nutr Phys Act* 12, 151. DOI: 10.1186/s12966-015-0319-9.

Schleussner, C.-F. et al. (2016). "Differential climate impacts for policy-relevant limits to global warming: the case of 1.5 °C and 2 °C". *Earth Syst. Dynam.* 7, 327. https://doi.org/10.5194/esd-7-327-2016.

Schreiber, W. (2018). *Food in a warming world: The changing foods on the British plate.* WWF, 1. https://www.wwf.org.uk/sites/default/files/2018-03/Food_in_a_warming_world_report.PDF.

Seabra, J. E. A. et al. (2011). "Life cycle assessment of Brazilian sugarcane products: GHG emissions and energy use". *Biofuels, Bioproducts and Biorefining* 5.5, 519. DOI: 10.1002/bbb.289.

Searchinger, T. et al. (2013). *Creating a Sustainable Food Future: Interim Findings – A menu of solutions to sustainably feed more than 9 billion people by 2050.* Tech. rep. https://www.wri.org/publication/creating-sustainable-food-future-interim-findings.

Sheane, R. et al. (2011). *Identifying opportunities to reduce the carbon footprint associated with the Scottish dairy supply chain – Main report. Edinburgh: Scottish Government.* Tech. rep. https://www2.gov.scot/Resource/Doc/342351/0113918.pdf.

Siegrist, M. et al. (2018). "Perceived naturalness and evoked disgust influence acceptance of cultured meat". *Meat Science* 139, 213. DOI: 10.1016/j.meatsci.2018.02.007.

Solomon, S. et al. (2007). *Contribution of Working Group I to the Fourth Assessment Report of the Intergovernmental Panel on Climate Change*. Tech. rep. https://www.ipcc.ch/report/ar4/wg1/.

Springmann, M., Godfray, H. C. J., et al. (2016). "Analysis and valuation of the health and climate change cobenefits of dietary change". *Proceedings of the National Academy of Sciences* 113.15, 4146. DOI: 10.1073/pnas.1523119113.

Springmann, M., Mason-D'Croz, D., et al. (2016). "Mitigation potential and global health impacts from emissions pricing of food commodities". *Nature Climate Change* 7.1, 69. DOI: 10.1038/nclimate3155.

Springmann, M. et al. (2018). "Options for keeping the food system within environmental limits". *Nature* 562, 519. DOI: https://doi.org/10.1038/s41586-018-0594-0.

Stafford, N. (2012). "Denmark cancels 'fat tax' and shelves 'sugar tax' because of threat of job losses". *BMJ* 345. DOI: 10.1136/bmj.e7889.

Su, J. et al. (2015). "Expression of barley SUSIBA2 transcription factor yields high-starch low-methane rice". *Nature* 523, 602. DOI: 10.1038/nature14673.

Suarez, F. et al. (1997). "Insights into human colonic physiology obtained from the study of flatus composition". *American Journal of Physiology-Gastrointestinal and Liver Physiology* 272.5, G1028. DOI: 10.1152/ajpgi.1997.272.5.G1028.

Svanes, E. et al. (2011). "Environmental assessment of cod (*Gadus morhua*) from autoline fisheries". *Int J Life Cycle Assess* 16.7, 611. DOI: 10.1007/s11367-011-0298-2.

"Tesco Product Carbon Footprint Summary" (2012, accessed 2018), 1. https://www.tescoplc.com/assets/files/cms/Tesco_Product_Carbon_Footprints_Summary(1).pdf.

"The greenhouse gas footprint of Booths" (2012), 1. https://www.booths.co.uk/wp-content/themes/booths/images/Booths%20GHG%20Report%202012%20Final.pdf.

Thornton, P. (2012). *Recalibrating Food Production in the Developing World: Global Warming Will Change More Than Just the Climate*. CGIAR (formerly Consultative Group for International Agricultural Research) Research Program on Climate Change, Agriculture and Food Security (CCFAS) –

Policy Brief no. 6.
https://cgspace.cgiar.org/handle/10568/24696.

Thornton, P. K. and Cramer, L. (2012). "Impacts of climate change on the agricultural and aquatic systems and natural resources within the CGIAR's mandate". *CGIAR Working Paper*, 1. https://cgspace.cgiar.org/bitstream/handle/10568/21226/ccafs-wp-23-cc_impacts_CGIAR.pdf?sequence=7&isAllowed=y.

Tilly, C. (1968). "The Crowd in History. A Study of Popular Disturbances in France and England, 1730–1848. By George Rudé (New York: John Wiley & Sons, 1964. 281 pp. \$5.95 cloth; \$2.95 paper)". *Journal of Social History* 1.3, 296. DOI: 10.1353/jsh/1.3.296.

Tilman, D. and Clark, M. (2014). "Global diets link environmental sustainability and human health". *Nature* 515.7528, 518. DOI: 10.1038/nature13959.

Tuomisto, H. and Mattos, M. (2010). "Life cycle assessment of cultured meat production". *7th International Conference on Life Cycle Assessment in the Agri-Food Sector*, 1. https://www.researchgate.net/publication/215666764_Life_cycle_assessment_of_cultured_meat_production.

UK Committee on Climate Change (2018). "Reducing UK emissions – 2018 Progress Report to Parliament". https://www.theccc.org.uk/publication/reducing-uk-emissions-2018-progress-report-to-parliament/.

UK Government Department for Business, Energy & Industrial Strategy (DEFRA) (2016). "Greenhouse gas reporting: conversion factors". https://www.gov.uk/government/publications/greenhouse-gas-reporting-conversion-factors-2016.

UK Government Department for Business, Energy & Industrial Strategy (DEFRA) (2018). "Greenhouse gas reporting: conversion factors". https://www.gov.uk/government/publications/greenhouse-gas-reporting-conversion-factors-2018.

UK Government Department for Business, Energy & Industrial Strategy (DEFRA) (2019). "Greenhouse gas reporting: conversion factors". https://www.gov.uk/government/publications/greenhouse-gas-reporting-conversion-factors-2019.

United Nations (2019). *World Population Prospects 2019*. Tech. rep. https://population.un.org/wpp/Publications/Files/WPP2019_DataBooklet.pdf.

Vergé, X. P. C. et al. (2013). "Carbon footprint of Canadian dairy products: Calculations and issues". *Journal of Dairy Science* 96.9, 6091. DOI: 10.3168/jds.2013-6563.

Waste Resources Action Plan (WRAP) UK (2019a). *Courtauld 2025 Review - 2017/18*. Tech. rep. http://www.wrap.org.uk/content/courtauld-2025-review-201718.

Waste Resources Action Plan (WRAP) UK (2019b). *Food surplus and waste in the UK – key facts*. Tech. rep. http://www.wrap.org.uk/sites/files/wrap/Food%20Surplus%20and%20Waste%20in%20the%20UK%20Key%20Facts%20%2822%207%2019%29_0.pdf.

Wellesley, L. and Froggatt, A. (2015). *Changing Climate, Changing Diets: Pathways to Lower Meat Consumption*. Tech. rep. https://www.chathamhouse.org/publication/changing-climate-changing-diets.

Willett, W. e. a. (2019). "Food in the Anthropocene: the EAT–Lancet Commission on healthy diets from sustainable food systems". *The Lancet* 393, 447. DOI: 10.1016/S0140-6736(18)31788-4.

Williams, A. G. et al. (2006). *Determining the environmental burdens and resource use in the production of agricultural and horticultural commodities – IS0205. Report for Defra*. Cranfield University, Silsoe Research Institute, 1. http://randd.defra.gov.uk/Default.aspx?Module=More&Location=None&ProjectID=11442.

Winther, U. et al. (2009). *Carbon footprint and energy use of Norwegian seafood products*. SINTEF Fisheries and Aquaculture, 1. https://www.sintef.no/globalassets/upload/fiskeri_og_havbruk/fiskeriteknologi/filer-fra-erik-skontorp-hognes/carbon-footprint-and-energy-use-of-norwegian-seafood-products---final-report---04_12_09.pdf.

Wong, J. (2019). *10-a-Day the Easy Way: Fuss-free Recipes & Simple Science to Transform your Health*. Mitchell Beazley.

Zhang, B. et al. (2016). "Chilling-induced tomato flavor loss is associated with altered volatile synthesis and transient changes in DNA methylation". *Proceedings of the National Academy of Sciences.* DOI: 10.1073/pnas.1613910113.

Zhu, C. et al. (2018). "Carbon dioxide (CO2) levels this century will alter the protein, micronutrients, and vitamin content of rice grains with potential health consequences for the poorest rice-dependent countries". *Science Advances* 4.5. DOI: 10.1126/sciadv.aaq1012.

Ziegler, F. et al. (2012). "The Carbon Footprint of Norwegian Seafood Products on the Global Seafood Market". *Journal of Industrial Ecology* 17 (1), 103. DOI: 10.1111/j.1530-9290.2012.00485.x.

Index

The index does not include entries for the endnotes of each chapter. If you need to search the endnotes, we recommend using the ebook edition, which is available at no cost from all the usual suppliers.

Acknowledgements

I am very grateful to the team at UIT Cambridge / Green Books and especially my editor, Niall Mansfield, for lots of patience, excellent suggestions and for deeply understanding the subject and style of what I was trying to write. I am indebted to Althea Wilkinson for tireless work and encouragement, particularly on the endnotes and references – this book would have had many fewer references without you. I am extremely grateful to Angelina Frankowska for many hours of invaluable discussions about the emissions numbers and references, and to Christian Reynolds and Ximena Schmidt, for loads of fun and thought-provoking conversations and ideas that influenced this book.

I am very grateful to Joseph Poore for answering numerous questions about his dataset. Huge thanks to Hannah Ritchie for making Fig. 1.1 and providing the data to make Fig. 3 of appendix "Climate change". Thank you to Christian Holler for writing and helping me get set up using the latex files on which this book is based. Thanks to Ben Dare for fixing many LaTeX issues and references. Thanks to Ant Holloway for the sleeve photo of the author.

I am especially grateful for detailed comments from Jeff Forshaw, Bojana Bajzelj, James Hand, Aled Jones, Ed Pope, Rick Bruintjes, Adam Amara, Pete Smith, John Bridle, Nicola Terry, Ro Randall, Tom Heap, Tim Williams, Alison Fletcher, Andrew Markwick, Eileen Jensen, Oliver Jensen, Katherine Denby, Isobel Atkin, and Tom Quested.

I am also grateful for helpful discussions with Claire Abbott, Jade Ajagun-Brauns, Ursula Arens, Ali Birkett, Myles Allen, Tim Benton, Renata Bertazzi Levy, David Bodanis, Benjamin Bodirsky, Ian Boyd, David Brightman, John Crawford, Neil Chalmers, Joanne Cook, Sue Davies, Jane Dennet-Thorpe, Bob Doherty, Helen Downie, David Drewry, Maia Elliott, Jack Elvin-Poole, Lisa Emberson, Joe Fennell, Helen Ferrier, Les Firbank, Jeff Fordham, Emma Foster, Lucy Foster, Emma

Garnett, Tara Garnett, Rosie Green, Bruce Grieve, Howard Griffiths, Joanna Groves, Jason Halford, Rachael Hand, Duncan Harding, Jennie Hargreaves, Francesca Harris, Flora Hetherington, Leah Holmes, Hugh Hunt, Matt Holl, Claire Hoolohan, Julian Huppert, John Ingram, Tim Jervis, Lisa Johnson, Tilly Johnson, Anthony Jones, Alana Kluczkovski, Laura Knowlson, Elmar Kriegler, Ilias Kyriazakis, Tim Lang, India Langley, Carys Lavin, Alice Larkin, Henry Leveson-Gower, Melissa Lord, Mark Lynas, Jennie Macdiarmid, Andrew Markwick, Rachel Marshall, Wayne Martindale, Niall MacCrann, Carly McLachlan, John Mclaughlin, Geoff McBride, Lauryn McLaughlin, Dale Mellor, Mark Miodownik, Hugh Mortimer, Jo Mylan, Emma Nichols, Ian Noble, Victor Okafor, Katie Percival, Martyn Poliakoff, Caroline Pung, Mark Reed, Martin Rees, Maria Sanchez Poncela, Andrea Scalco, Ruth Slater, Elta Smith, Bjoern Soergel, Luke Spadavecchia, Laurence Stamford, James Stockdale, Sara Summerton, Savvas Tassou, Jacqueline Tereza da Silva, Sara Turnbull, Pippa Tyrell, Peter Wooton-Beard, Lucy Yates and Joe Zuntz.

Thanks to the University of Manchester for supporting me while writing this book, and for paying to enable the book to be available for free online. I have also been supported in this work by funding from N8 Agrifood, STFC, the University of Manchester and a University of Manchester Wellcome Trust Manchester Institutional Strategic Support Fund award [204796/Z/16/Z].

I am also grateful to the Greenhouse Gas and Dietary choices Open-source Toolkit (GGDOT) team and the Take a Bite out of Climate Change (takeabitecc) team, and all the anonymous people who asked pertinent questions in my talks and at GGDOT and takeabitecc events. Thanks also to all my colleagues for their patience when I kept disappearing to work on this book.

Most of all, huge thanks to my family Keith, Scott, Jasmine, Mum and Dad for all your encouragement, support and interest, and for many excellent ideas and questions which changed how I wrote the book.

Also published by UIT Cambridge in the *without the hot air* series

Drugs without the hot air
Making sense of legal and illegal drugs
David Nutt • 9780857844941
This second edition of David Nutt's brilliant and straightforward book explores the science of legal and illegal drugs, how they work, why people take them and the effects drugs have.

Sustainable Materials without the hot air
Making buildings, vehicles and products efficiently and with less new material
Julian Allwood, Jonathan Cullen • 9781906860301
This richly-informed book evaluates all the options and explains how we can greatly reduce the amount of material demanded and used in manufacturing.

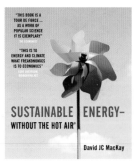

Sustainable Energy without the hot air
David JC MacKay • 9780954452933
The best-selling book on understanding sustainable energy and how we can make energy plans that add up.

Foreign language titles published by UIT based on *Sustainable Energy without the hot air*

Erneuerbare Energien - ohne heisse luft
Christian Holler, Joachim Gaukel
9781906860882

Energía Sostenible - sin malos humos
Javier Pascual et al.
9781912934188 (EPUB)